Judaism— Revelation of Moses Or Religion of Men?

By Philip Neal

York Publishing Company
Post Office Box 1038
Hollister, California 95024-1038

Unless otherwise noted,
all Scriptures used in
this book are quoted from
*The Holy Bible In Its
Original Order—A Faithful
Version With Commentary*
ISBN 978-0-9675479-9-2

About the Cover

The background Hebrew text

זכרו תורת משה

is from the opening of Malachi 4:4, which reads
"Remember the Torah of Moses"

ISBN 978-0-9819787-3-4
Copyright 2010
York Publishing Company
Post Office Box 1038
Hollister, California 95024-1038

Table of Contents

Foreword ……………………………………………….. *i*

Introduction ……………………………………………….. *iv*

Chapter One   Religion in First-Century Palestine ………………… 1

Chapter Two   The Early Seeds of Judaism ……….…………….. 24

Chapter Three   Hellenization and the Rise of the Pharisees ………. 35

Chapter Four   Pharisaism Gives Birth to Judaism …………………. 50

Chapter Five   Do We Really Need a *Second* Torah? …………… 56

Chapter Six   The *Futility* of the Jews' Oral Law ……………….. 70

Chapter Seven   The Deceptiveness of Judaism ……….…..……….. 81

Chapter Eight   Redemption and Restoration:

The Jews' Role in the Age to Come …..………… 114

Chapter Notes ………………………………………….. 132

Appendix One   The Development of the Talmud …………………. 150

Appendix Two   The Jewish Code of Law ………………………..… 151

Appendix Three   Who and What is a Jew? …………………………. 183

Appendix Four   The Apostle Paul's Perspective on Judaic

"Works of Law" ………………………………… 187

Appendix Five   Kabbalah—Judaism's Dark Side ………………… 242

Appendix Six   The Judeo-Christian Myth …………………….. 247

Bibliography ……………………………………………….. 252

Foreword

The Jewish community openly promotes Rabbinical Judaism as "the Old Testament religion of Moses." Overwhelmingly, Christians believe this premise to be accurate. Jews, it is assumed, are for the most part just like Christians—except they don't accept Jesus as the Messiah. As well, biblical scholars and theologians have taken for granted that Christianity itself is a direct, first-century *outgrowth* of Judaism. The popular view is that Jesus was a revolutionary Jewish rabbi who practiced the laws and traditions of Judaism, yet managed to sharply challenge the status quo.

In terms of religious *practice*, Judaism is centered on its collection of "oral traditions" known as the Talmud. The typical Christian understanding of the Talmud is that its precepts are detailed expositions on the Scriptures, and that its numerous highly-specific traditions are designed to protect the Jew from violating the written Torah or Law of God.

But are these and similar assumptions accurate? Is Judaism really the embodiment of the religion God gave to ancient Israel through Moses and the prophets? Is Christianity really an offshoot of Judaism? Did Jesus observe the traditions and customs of first-century Jewish religion? Does the Talmud really reflect the spirit and intent of the Scriptures?

Most Christians know little or nothing about Judaism, and appear quite oblivious of the centuries-old antagonism that still festers between the two religions. The constant conflict that took place between the first-century progenitors of Judaism (the Pharisees) and Jesus and His followers is found throughout the New Testament. But how could Jesus have found such *fault* with the very religion that was supposedly representative of the Old Testament? Noting this paradox, many Christians have wrongly concluded that Jesus must have been against Moses and the Old Testament.

Indeed, Judaism's bold claim to be the "natural descendant" of the religion of Moses has had a profound impact on how Christianity has interpreted the New Testament. But what if the Jews' claim is *false*? Would not such a faulty premise cause Christians to terribly misunderstand the New Testament? Is it possible that a flawed understanding of Rabbinical Judaism—one that fails to comprehend how the religion really developed and what it really teaches—will lead to a flawed understanding of Christianity and its message of salvation?

While most authors neglect to ask (let alone answer) such questions concerning the Jewish religion, Philip Neal's book, *Judaism—Revelation of Moses or Religion of Men?*, challenges Christians to explore the possibility that Judaism is *not at all* what it purports to be. This book broaches a key subject Christians everywhere need to understand: **Is Judaism legitimately the religion of Moses as set forth in the Old Testament, or is it merely a religion of men?**

In answering this question—to demonstrate *exactly* what Judaism entails—Philip Neal has drawn from a variety of scholarly works, including Judaism's own cherished writings: the Mishnah, the Talmud, the "Code of Jewish Law," and sundry classic rabbinic works. Yet, while similar books are more of a diatribe against Jews, Neal's book is straightforward, fair and balanced—and only seeks to reveal what Judaism actually teaches. As the reader will see, Neal has uniquely accomplished this by allowing the Jewish rabbis' themselves—*using their words*—to express the facts about their own religion: its pagan origin; how it has openly denied the Scriptures; its bias against non-Jews; how it has vilified Christianity.

As Neal demonstrates, Judaism is based on *secret* laws, traditions and scriptural interpretations that God allegedly "whispered into Moses' ear" at Mt. Sinai. The rabbis maintain that Moses was forbidden to make a written record of these esoteric instructions. Rather, the teachings were to be passed on *orally*, generation by generation, to only the most scholarly and pious Jewish leaders. However, centuries later, these "revelations" were written down, and exist today in the form of the Talmud. Importantly, these "oral traditions" form the very core, the foundation of Judaism—even to the exclusion of the Scriptures! As Neal brings out, rabbis consider these secret, oral laws and traditions to be *superior* to the written Law that God originally gave to the nation of Israel by the hand of Moses. Most do not realize that when rabbis speak of the "Torah of Moses," they are *including* their "oral traditions" along with the written Law (the Pentateuch) of Moses. But in actual *practice*, observant Jews revere and exalt the Talmud, and all but ignore the Scriptures.

How, then, can Judaism possibly be the true "religion of Moses"?

In researching the thousands of Talmudic laws and regulations, Neal has come to realize that Judaism is a religious system designed to *legislate morality* for its adherents. The daily life of the observant Jew is burdened with an exhaustive code of legal minutia that covers virtually every thought, situation or activity. As Neal brings out, such authoritarian oppression not only makes a mockery of true religion, it actually destroys the Jew's ability to "think for himself" in the development of genuine moral character.

As alluded to above, Christianity's poor understanding of Judaism has caused considerable confusion—especially when studying the apostle Paul's complex writings concerning law-keeping and grace. In certain key passages dealing with "law" and "works of law," it is widely assumed that Paul's intention is to condemn or abolish the laws and commandments of God. Rather, as Neal's book shows, Paul was, in those instances, explicitly rejecting the Jews' traditional "laws" and condemning the idea of attaining "righteousness" through Pharisaic "works of law." In fact, many of Paul's teachings on grace, works and law-keeping deal with Judaic traditions rather than God's Law as found in the Old Testament. This insufficiency in understanding Judaism—coupled with inaccurate translations of critical sections of Paul's epistles—has especially affected the Protestant view of "law and grace." Consequently, many Christians are mistakenly taught that Jesus and Paul abolished the laws and commandments of God through grace—yet nothing could be further from the truth!

As this book shows, Jesus upheld the written Law of God as found in the Old Testament—fully emphasizing its *spiritual intent*—while at the same time rejecting the traditional laws and practices of first century Jewish religion.

Without question, Neal's eye-opening book, *Judaism—Revelation of Moses or Religion of Men?*, is a must-read for every Christian who desires to fully understand the message of the New Testament, as well as the entire Bible.

Fred R. Coulter
June 2010

Introduction

"There is one who accuses you, even Moses."

What often puzzles the novice reader of the New Testament gospel accounts is the open conflict that repeatedly took place between Jesus and the Jewish religious leaders of the day. How could it be that Christ found such fault with their teachings—"beware of the doctrine of the Pharisees and Sadducees"—while at the same time acknowledging that the scribes and Pharisees occupied "Moses' seat"? This apparent dichotomy has led many Christians to assume that the scribes, Pharisees and Sadducees were in fact the first-century guardians of the revelation given to Moses at Sinai, and that Jesus opposed the religionists at every turn because He came to "nullify" the Mosaic Law and replace it with *grace*.

Clearly, such a position places Jesus sharply at odds with Moses. But was Jesus really in conflict with *Moses*—or did He have a particular axe to grind with those Jewish religionists who only made a *pretense* of following Moses? The fact is, most Christians naively believe that the Jewish leaders of Jesus' day were the legitimate representatives of the "religion" of the Old Testament—a belief *not* supported by history or Scripture!

Fully upholding Moses and the written Torah, Christ stated: "Do not think that I have come to abolish the Law or the Prophets; I did not come to abolish, but to fulfill" (Matt. 5:17). In one of His many encounters with the scribes and Pharisees, Jesus indicated that *they* were the ones in conflict with Moses, actually guilty of misappropriating the prophet's name: "There is one who accuses you, even Moses…. And if you do not believe his writings, how shall you believe My words?" (John 5:45-47). Showing that they only made a *pretense* of following Moses, Jesus reproved them, saying, "Did not Moses give you the Law, and [yet] not one of you is [genuinely] practicing the Law?" (John 7:19). Moreover, on several occasions Christ upbraided the Pharisees for "teaching for doctrine the commandments of men." He said, "Full well do you reject the commandment of God, so that you may observe your own *tradition*" (Mark 7:7-9; also Matt. 15:3).

Is it possible that first-century *Pharisaism*—which, as this book will show, is universally acknowledged by Jewish scholars as having been the prototype of Rabbinical Judaism—did not at all reflect the heart and spirit of the Old Testament? Could it be that the *true* "religion" God revealed first through Abraham and then codified through Moses—which is actually a *way of life* defined by God's laws and commandments—had over centuries been buried by sages under a mountain of Jewish tradition? And if Pharisaism was not reflective of the teachings of Moses and the Scriptures, then *how* did such a religion arise in Judah? How and when did the Jews lose sight of the simple Hebraic *way of life* defined by the Old Testament?

That such fundamental differences existed between the teachings of Jesus and what the apostle Paul would later call the "Jews' religion" (Gal. 1:13-14) begs the question: Was first-century Jewish religion a *corruption* of the ancient way of life God had given to the children of Israel through Moses? And what of modern-day Judaism—is it not simply a *continuation* of that same religious system of the Jews' *own* devising?

In a rather telling comment, historian Paul Johnson writes that there "have been four great formative periods in Jewish history: under Abraham, under Moses, during and shortly after the Exile, and after the destruction of the Second Temple. The first two [under Abraham, then Moses,] **produced the religion of Yahweh**"—that is, the true *way of life* defined by God's laws and commandments—"the second two **developed and refined it into Judaism** itself" (*A History of the Jews*, pp. 83-84; emphasis added). Johnson admits here that Judaism dates from the time *just after* the Babylonian Exile, and *differs* from what he calls the original "religion of Yahweh" formed under Abraham and Moses. Typical of scholars, however, Johnson suggests that Judaism is an *improvement* over the way of life given through the written Torah—as if God's Law needed to be "developed and refined." As this book will show, this is precisely the carnal mindset that anciently led to the development of Judaism's *centerpiece*—the so-called "oral law."

With a similar perspective, American rabbinical scholar Stephen S. Wise has stated, "The [Jews'] return from Babylon … [marked] the end of Hebrew-ism and the beginning of Judaism" (*The Other End of the World*, Roger Rusk, p. 182). Ernest L. Martin, widely recognized for his scholarly research on Judaism, writes: "History shows—and the Jews themselves admit—that their religion had drifted far away from the simple doctrines of Scripture, commonly called the 'Old Testament.' The Jews had **modified God's law** and even **instituted laws and commandments of their own** which were, in many instances, diametrically opposite of the precepts of Moses" (*Is Judaism the Religion of Moses?*, p. 1; emphasis added).

Again, did Jesus really have a problem with Moses and the Law, or was He simply dealing straightforwardly with the hypocritical religionists of His day? To paraphrase Matthew 16:12, Christ might just as well have warned His disciples to "beware of the *religion* of the Pharisees and Sadducees," identifying the precursor to Judaism for what it really was—a deeply flawed humanly-devised *religious system*. As this book will show, this Jewish system of religion evolved over centuries, based on a so-called "oral law" allegedly given to Moses along with the written Torah. Over time, this "oral law"—which Jesus called "traditions of men"—grew into a vast code of detailed rules and regulations. Ultimately, the "oral law" was published as the *Babylonian Talmud*—the undisputed authority for Judaism.

In *Exploring the World of the Jew*, John Phillips writes that while Jewish life had for centuries revolved around the written Torah, by the first century AD the Law had been "buried beneath vast accumulations of tradition and encrusted with enormous deposits of human interpretation. **The Torah itself has been largely superseded in Judaism by the Talmud**. The five books of the Torah can be written out in 350 pages. The Talmud takes up 523 *books* printed in 22 volumes" (p. 55; emphasis added).

Phillips adds: "The Torah is clear and concise, part of the inspired Word of God. The Talmud is wordy, rambling, argumentative, inconsistent, sometimes witty, sometimes boring, sometimes brilliant, sometimes inane. The laws of the Talmud constitute **cold concrete poured over Jewish life and hardened by time into a rigid prison for the soul**.... [For the Jew] the chief instrument of ... blindness to biblical truth has been the Talmud" (pp. 55 and 57; emphasis added).

Michael Hoffman has spent decades researching the Jews' religion. He concludes that "everything about Orthodox Judaism is either a distortion or a falsification of the Old Testament because it is based on ... traditions that *void* the Old Testament..." (*Judaism Discovered*, p. 145). Jesus Himself noted that the Jews' orally-derived traditions had a *nullifying* effect on the Scriptures (Mark 7:13). Arguing that Judaism only *poses* as the "religion" of Moses, Hoffman adds: "Talmudic texts can be minefields of deception and pits of derangement and bogus reasoning as befits those who would **replace the Bible with their own authority**. **Most of the laws of the religion of Judaism have no biblical warrant; they contradict and nullify the Word of God**" (p. 146; emphasis added). Indeed, Judaism's predecessors had to *violate* the Scriptures in order to reject Jesus—for the Scriptures testified of Him as the Messiah (John 5:39).

As this book will demonstrate, it was precisely because of the Jews' *denial* of the Scriptures as the exclusive revelation of God that the religion of Judaism developed. The prophet Hosea had already warned of those who would reject true knowledge (Hosea 4:6), and the apostle Paul appropriately described Pharisaic Jews as those who possessed a zeal for God, but one that was not based on true knowledge (Rom. 10:2).

Ultimately, it was the Jews' rejection of Jesus that sealed their fate. With a hardness of heart that had long been prophesied, they would remain shackled to a humanly-contrived, burdensome "code of law"—a works-based pseudo-righteousness (Rom. 9:31-33). Paul, however, makes it clear that the Jews' *unbelief* will one day be resolved. He states that "God did not repudiate His people whom He foreknew" (Rom. 11:2). He goes on to reveal that a "partial hardening of the heart has happened to Israel" and that, in time, "all Israel shall be saved" (verses 25-26).

Emphatically, Judaism is the product of carnal thinking, developed by those who, as we will see, completely missed the *spirit* and *intent* of the written Torah. Without question, the idea that Judaism is the consummation of the "religion" of the Old Testament makes a mockery of Scripture and turns truth upside down. It's time we understood—and *righted* the truth.

About This Book

There are many books on Judaism—most of which fall into one of *three categories*. First, there are those written by rabbis and Jewish scholars designed to "educate" the non-Jewish public. They enthusiastically portray Judaism as a wonderful religion, always connecting it to the Old Testament. The inexperienced reader is led to believe that Judaism is indeed the legitimate continuation of the "religion" of Moses and the prophets. The fact that the Talmud is held as *superior* to the Scriptures is hidden or understated.

Second, there are numerous books on Judaism written by well-intended Christian authors. Unfortunately, these books typically whitewash the entire subject, leaving the reader to erroneously conclude that Judaism is in fact based on the Old Testament—and that Judaism is, of all things, the *precursor* to Christianity. Touting the virtues of the mythical "Judeo-Christian brotherhood," the key flaws and aberrations of Judaism are overlooked. After all, from their perspective, if Jews would only accept Jesus, they would be almost … Christian.

Third, there are a few books (also written by "Christians") that deal unnecessarily harsh with Judaism. While they are not anti-Semitic, they do tend to be unbalanced and condemning. We are to judge righteous judgment (John 7:24), but in a spirit of kindness and mercy. Such books typically dredge up as much "dirty laundry" on the Jews as possible, but fail to offer significant hope for the future of the Jewish people. And none of the books written even from a Christian perspective succeed at getting to the *root* of the problem with Judaism—which is intensely spiritual in nature.

This book is different. It pulls no punches, but it is fair. The historic origins of the religion are examined along with key examples of its modern-day application. How and why did Judaism develop? What were the major influences? What fundamental ideas and circumstances led to the origin and advancement of the so-called "oral law"—and the Jews' subsequent abandonment of the Scriptures as the sole authority in human affairs? How does the practice of Judaism differ from the *way of life* presented in Scripture—and what spiritual harm, if any, is done to those who attempt to live by the Talmudic "code of law"? Importantly, this book examines Judaism from a spiritual perspective, dealing with the foundational *causes* of the religion. Moreover, this book holds out *hope*, showing that the Jews will yet fulfill their God-ordained role in the age to come.

Chapter One carefully examines the religion's Pharisaic underpinnings as revealed in the New Testament; to be sure, Jesus' many encounters with the Pharisees provide authoritative insight into the nature of Judaism. Chapters Two through Four trace the origin and development of the religion from its earliest "seed stage" in Babylon and post-exilic Judea through the Hellenistic and Maccabean periods and on into the latter part of first-century Palestine.

Chapters Five and Six deal with the spiritual aspects of the Jews' "oral law," focusing on how such a "code of law" is actually a cheap, failed substitute for a spirit-led conscience. Chapter Seven reveals the darker side of Judaism, dealing fairly with prominent issues such as idolatry, hypocrisy and racism. Chapter Eight examines the issue of the Jews' spiritual *unbelief*, and how that unbelief will be reversed in the future as the Jewish people fulfill a key role in God's plan of salvation.

As would be expected, this book leans heavily on the research of numerous scholars, many of which are Jewish. In fact, the author has endeavored to allow the Jews' *own* sages and rabbis—through various Jewish writings and dozens of quotations from the Talmud itself—to reveal the truth about Judaism and *convict themselves*. More importantly, the author has widely utilized the Bible. A key point emphasized throughout this book is that, by the rabbis' own admission, *Judaism is Pharisaism*. Thus, as noted above, the New Testament accounts dealing with the Pharisees are vital to our understanding of the heart and spirit of the religion.

Ultimately, this book was written for Christians—with the intention of answering one overarching question:

Is Judaism the "religion" of the Old Testament as mediated by Moses and the prophets—*or*, is it merely a false religion of men?

It is surprising how many Christians (even Sabbatarian Christians) do not understand the true nature of Judaism. This is partly because of "Judeo-Christian" propaganda, which would have us believe that Jews and Christians are spiritually "first cousins." Indeed, the overwhelming majority of Christians naively believe that Judaism is only a "step away" from their own faith—that if Jews would only accept Jesus as the Messiah, they would essentially be "Christian." But as this book will show, Judaism—as taught and promoted by Talmudic rabbis—is as far removed from real Christianity as east is from west.

Our society has been conditioned to avoid even the appearance of anti-Semitism. One unfortunate result is that Judaism is rarely held to close examination, let alone criticized. Often, when books such as this are published, Jewish apologists are quick to respond with anti-Semitic charges. Someone gets labeled a Jew-hater, and memories of the Holocaust are invoked. But such an attitude begs the question, "Does Rabbinical Judaism *hide* behind the cloak of anti-Semitism—using it to repel scrutiny?"

Emphatically, the purpose and thrust of this book is *not* anti-Semitic. In *every* religion of men—which would include nominal Christianity, Islam, various Eastern religions such as Buddhism and Hinduism, and, certainly, Judaism—there are those of the *laity* who are, for the most part, unwitting victims of false teachings. Clearly, they are to be held responsible for their own carelessness, naivety and failure to, as Paul admonished, "prove all things." But those held most accountable are the teachers, priests, pastors, scholars, gurus—and rabbis. They too are often deceived; but significant numbers of them are highly culpable in their biased handling of the truth. In Judaism, the rabbinate has shown itself to be particularly plagued by hypocrisy and gross negligence when it comes to the use of the Scriptures—the very Scriptures the Jews were entrusted by God to preserve (Rom. 3:2)!

To be sure, the *rabbis*—the heirs of the Pharisees—are the focus of this book, not the Jewish laity. In fact, the average Orthodox Jew does not fully realize what the rabbis believe or what the Talmud actually teaches.

Interestingly, more and more Orthodox Jews are coming to see the truth about their religion. For example, Avi ben Mordechai, who practiced Talmudic Judaism for most of his life, ultimately came to see the absurdity of the "oral law." In his commentary on the book of Galatians, he writes, "I realized that the [rabbis'] *halacha* [laws] had no end in sight; that it was nothing short of a deep, black hole and an endless system of legal minutiae. It was always tiring for me to try to keep up with all the daily demands [of Talmudic law]" (*Galatians—A Torah-Based Commentary in First-Century Hebraic Context*, p. 48). Mordechai's statement is reminiscent of what Paul wrote concerning his experience as a Pharisee, that he had once lived according to the *strictest* sect of the Jews' religion (Acts 26:5; the Greek word means *rigorous* and *exacting*—hence Jesus' reference in Matthew 23:4 to Pharisaic "burdens").

Throughout this book, the author has set the word *religion* in quote marks when referring to the "religion" of the Old Testament. The reason is that *religion* is a term laden with baggage. The simple meaning of the word has become tainted by ritualism and ceremony, by hierarchies and corporate organizations, and by dogmatism and politics. Similar terms—such as faith, belief, worship, creed, etc.—function poorly as well. Thus, it is incumbent upon the reader to understand that the *true* "religion" of Moses as presented in the Old Testament is a righteous *way of life* based on God's laws, commandments, statutes and judgments. At its core, it is profoundly *spiritual*, because it is based on eternal, spiritual principles.

Indeed, the "religion" based on the teachings of Moses and the Old Testament is the *true* precursor to Christianity—and is in no way reflected in the Jewish religion known as Judaism.

Religion in First-Century Palestine

*"The people worship Me in vain,
teaching for doctrine the traditions of men."*

If we are to understand Judaism and evaluate its claim to represent the "religion of the Old Testament"—the *way of life* God gave through Moses—then we must understand its historical context. While the seeds of Judaism were sown long before Jesus' time—even as far back as the Jews' exile in Babylon—it is in first-century Palestine that we get the clearest picture of the movement's *Pharisaic* roots. As will be emphasized throughout this book, Judaism—by the admission of the Jews' own scholars and rabbis—*is Pharisaism*. As we will see, the New Testament, though dismissed by Jews, provides a highly credible perspective on Judaism-in-the-making, allowing us to see right into the very *heart* of the religion.

If Judaism is anything, it is a religion of *contradiction*. An interesting similarity exists between Judaism and mainstream Christianity that best illustrates the point. As a religious *system*, Christianity appropriates the *name* of Christ while frequently contradicting what Jesus actually taught. This can be seen, for example, in the Orthodox observance of Sunday, while Jesus Himself kept and upheld the seventh-day Sabbath. Nominal Christianity insists that commandment-keeping is annulled under the New Covenant, whereas Christ unambiguously affirmed the Law (Matt. 5:17-19). Likewise, as will be shown, Judaism *claims* to follow the written Torah[1] as delivered through Moses, yet broadly contradicts the spirit and intent (and frequently the letter) of the Law through man-made traditions.

The Jews' religion of Jesus' day was similar to today's Christianity in another important aspect: it was anything *but* unified. Numerous sects and divisions dotted the religious landscape of first-century Judea—all claiming to originate with Moses, and each having its own set of beliefs.

Readers of the New Testament will likely be familiar with the major sects of first-century religion in Palestine: the scribes, Pharisees and Sadducees. Other groups included the Zealots, Herodians and Essenes—with many more minor offshoots. Before taking a look at each of the major players, we should first understand two key points. First, it is incorrect to view Judaism as the *sum total* of ancient Jewish religion. Rather, only the faction known as *Pharisaism* can be rightly labeled as Judaism. As will be brought out in detail, Judaism traces its origin directly to the dominant sect of the *Pharisees*. "**The Jewish religion as it is today traces its descent, without**

a break, **through all the centuries**, **from the Pharisees** [with their scribal leaders]. Their leading ideas and methods found expression in a [mass of] literature of enormous extent, of which a very great deal is still in existence [as the Talmud]" (*Universal Jewish Encyclopedia*, "Pharisees," p. 474; emphasis added).

Second, the average Jew of Christ's day was simply *not* interested in religion. In fact, it can be demonstrated that *less than five percent* of the total Jewish population in Palestine was directly associated with any of the major religious groups. Ernest Martin writes that "the overwhelming majority in Palestine had no direct membership in [the] religious denominations of Judaism [that is, first-century religion in general] and in most cases were not particularly religious at all" (*Is Judaism the Religion of Moses?*, p. 3). Like Christian "churchgoers" today, first-century Jews involved themselves in "religion" only occasionally—such as during the festival seasons of Passover, Firstfruits and Tabernacles. While many Jews occasionally attended Sabbath services at a local synagogue, the vast majority of Jews in no way considered themselves to be "members" of *any* religious group.

In *Essential Judaism*, George Robinson writes that the religious sects of that day "represented a small minority of the population of the Jewish world, probably no more than five percent in total…" (p. 320). He continues: "The Pharisees were the largest of the … [religious] formations; [Jewish historian] Josephus puts their number at 6000, although contemporary scholars believe that figure to be inflated" (p. 321). The second largest group at that time was the Essenes (not mentioned in the New Testament) who, according to Josephus, numbered at around 4000 (*Antiquities of the Jews*, XVIII, i, 5).

The Sadducees were a "small elite group whose numbers included the High Priest" (Robinson, p. 321). Martin puts their number at less than 3000. The remaining minor groups—such as the Zealots, Herodians, etc.—had comparably few in number. Most historians estimate that the total Jewish population of Palestine in Jesus' day was approximately three million. Thus, *less than five percent* of the Jews of Palestine actually belonged to the top religious sects, indicating a clear lack of interest in religion.

It is also worth noting that, relative to the Jewish population, there were *few* synagogues in Palestine. For example, Martin writes that, based on historical data, there was only *one* synagogue in Capernaum. Located in the area of Galilee, Capernaum was a significant city in New Testament times with a considerable Jewish population. Judging from archeological remains, the Capernaum synagogue—one of the larger ones in Palestine—could seat no more than 500. Martin contends that this ratio of few synagogues to large numbers of Jews is typical throughout Palestine, and is proof that relatively few Jews actually attended synagogue services (pp. 5-6).

Those Jews who did attend the synagogues on occasion—mostly from among the *am ha-aretz*, or the "Common People of the Land"—did so to hear the Scriptures read. But this does not mean that they endorsed or followed the teachings of any particular group. For example, the leaders of the synagogues were, for the most part, Pharisees. But the average attending Jew had no desire to practice the sect's strict, disciplinary regulations—and neither were they compelled to do so. Martin writes: "The Common People who did attend the synagogue services ... were not required to hold to the teachings of the Pharisees. The Pharisees exercised little real authority over the religious life of the people." He adds that there was "little exercise of any central religious authority" during Christ's day, and that it was "only over the lives of the 'pious' that the Pharisees saddled [their] harsh religion" of strict rules (p. 5).

While many were drawn to the piety of the Pharisees and generally held the scribes in high regard, there was, however, little desire to emulate either group. Thus, many "dabbled" in religion to one degree or another, but *few* actually associated themselves with any particular sect. Still, overall, the Pharisees had the tacit support of the people.

The Pharisees—Progenitors of Judaism

In terms of *influence*, the most important sects of first-century religion were the Pharisees and Sadducees—the Pharisees being the most prominent. As we will see, much of the Pharisees' influence was due in no small part to their close association with the *scribes*—that mystical clique of scholars held in the highest esteem by the people. The Essenes were second in *numbers* to the Pharisees, but exercised little influence. Robinson notes that the Essenes were a "monastic group ... [who rejected both the Sadducees and the Pharisees] as corrupt, and sought refuge from the daily world by withdrawing from society" (p. 321). Living mostly in the Dead Sea area, members of this antisocial sect were *ascetics*, and, as a group, are not mentioned in the New Testament. The apostle Paul denounces asceticism as a lifestyle in Colossians 2:21-23.

The Pharisees, who had the support of the Common People and controlled the synagogues, were fierce rivals of the Sadducees, who controlled the Temple. The key tenet of the Pharisees—and one that caused considerable controversy—was their insistence on following a so-called "oral law." Robinson writes that the Pharisees were the "foremost exponents of the idea of the Oral Torah, which would [by about 500 AD] become the Talmud,[2] as an *adjunct* to the Written Torah." Through their oral law, the Pharisees "brought the [ritual] purity laws, [which] previously applied only to the priestly caste, into the Jewish home ... [and established] boundaries of behavior, setting themselves apart from the general Jewish population in areas as diverse as food, dress, commerce, marriage and worship" (pp. 320-321).

According to Joachim Jeremias, the Pharisees "formed *closed communities*" (called a *haburot*) organized under the leadership of a scribe who served as an authority on the Scriptures. He writes that the Pharisees were not simply "men living according to the religious precepts laid down by Pharisaic scribes ... they were *members of religious associations...*" (*Jerusalem in the Time of Jesus*, p. 247). The influence of the Pharisees was not limited to the *haburot*, however, but reached into the greater community through the synagogue, which the scribes and Pharisees controlled.

Martin asserts that the Pharisees are best described as a religious fraternity or association, bound together in communal living to perform certain religious customs and traditions. "It is important to note that the Pharisees were merely an association of men who had bound themselves together to keep the Levitical laws of purity.... [But] they had not bound themselves to accept any [particular] creed or set of doctrines" (p. 10). In fact, it comes as a surprise to many that there was considerable *diversity* among the various Pharisaic communities when it came to doctrine. William Smith, author of *Smith's Bible Dictionary*, writes, "In the time of Christ [the Pharisees] were divided doctrinally into several schools, among which those of [rivals] Hillel and Shammai were the most noted" (p. 508, "Pharisees"). Hillel and Shammai were both scribes, or "doctors of the law," with the Shammai school being rigidly conservative and the Hillel school being more yielding or liberal. (Whenever we see Jesus interacting *positively* with Pharisees—such as with Nicodemus—it most likely involves those from the Hillel school.) Apparently, there was considerable latitude when it came to what Pharisees could believe or teach—as long as they abided by the commonly-held Pharisaical code of laws and traditions.

Martin adds that "no creed existed in the synagogues ruled by the Pharisees. [Thus] almost every opinion was tolerated..." (p. 11). This lack of unity was a primary reason the scribes and Pharisees were *unable* to teach with power and authority—a flaw duly noted by those Jews who attended the synagogue. "And they [the Jews] were astonished at His [Jesus'] doctrine; for He was teaching them as one having authority, and not as the scribes [teach]" (Mark 1:22).[3]

The Pharisees first came into prominence in the second century BC following the Maccabean struggle against Syrian oppression. The sect owes its "origin to the *Hasidim* of Maccabean times," writes Jeremias (p. 259). The Hasidim were the *pious* of the Common People who were rigidly opposed to the sweeping changes taking place in the Jewish nation under the influences of Hellenism. "It is from this time we first hear of the *Perushim* or Pharisees, 'those who separated themselves,' a religious party which repudiated the royal religious establishment, with its high priest [and] Sadducean aristocrats ... and placed religious observance before Jewish nationalism" (Paul Johnson, *A History of the Jews*, p. 108). Jewish historian Solomon Grayzel suggests that *Perushim* comes from a Hebrew root word meaning "to separate"—referring to the sect's desire to have as little as possible to do with Greeks or Jews who had adopted Hellenistic customs (*A History of the Jews*, pp. 76-77).

In his *Jewish New Testament Commentary*, David Stern adds that "those whose main concern was not the [Temple] sacrifices but the [written]

Torah were called *Hasidim*…. The successors to the *Hasidim* were known as *P'rushim*, which means 'separated ones,' because they separated themselves from worldly ways and worldly people. The *P'rushim* not only took the *Tanakh*[4] to be God's word to man, but also **considered the accumulated tradition handed down over centuries by the sages and teachers** [scribes] **to be God's word as well—the Oral Torah**—so that a system for living developed which touched on every aspect of life" (p. 18; "Matt. 3:7"; emphasis added).

The Pharisees' connection to the Common People was central to their success. According to Robinson, the Pharisees were the only group with a "popular base" (*Essential Judaism*, p. 321), and Josephus notes that the "Sadducees [those primarily of the priesthood] [were] able to persuade none but the rich, and [had] not the populace obsequious to them, but the Pharisees [had] the multitude on their side" (*Antiquities of the Jews*, XIII, x, 6). Jeremias writes that "the Pharisees were the people's party; they represented the Common People as opposed to the aristocracy on both religious and social matters. Their much-respected piety and their social leanings toward suppressing differences of class gained them the people's support and assured them, step by step, of victory" (p. 266).

Here, Jeremias refers to the Pharisees' *religious* victory over the aristocratic Sadducean party—a triumph enjoyed for much of the first half of the first century AD, but complete only after the destruction of the Temple. The political arena, however, was another matter. Jeremias notes that "the Pharisees' influence on *politics* and the administration of justice in Palestine before 66 AD [the start of the first Jewish revolt against Rome] must not be exaggerated. Their only real importance during this time was in the realm of *religion*, and here they, not the Sadducees, were supreme" (p. 263).

The Scribes—Venerated Leaders of the Pharisees

Frequently in the New Testament we see the *scribes* mentioned along with the Pharisees, almost as if the two were inseparable. The reason is that the scribes, by the first century AD, formed a considerable *subset* of the Pharisees. Robinson writes: "The Pharisees included in their ranks many of the scribes, the men who [from post-exilic times] copied the proceedings of the Sanhedrin and the religious courts" (p. 321). Martin notes that many scribes "adhered to the Pharisaical rules of piety and, in fact, represented a particular group within the Pharisees. They were the scholarly Pharisees—sometimes called 'doctors of the law' [see Luke 5:17, etc.]" (*Is Judaism the Religion of Moses?*, p. 25).

It was during the Babylonian Exile, according to Johnson, when the Jews, bereft of their Temple, "turned to their writings—their laws, and the records of their past. From this time we hear more of the scribes. Hitherto, they had simply been secretaries … writing down the words of the great. Now they [were becoming] an important caste, **setting down in writing** [in a rough, preliminary form] **oral traditions** [in addition to] copying the precious scrolls brought from the ruined Temple…" (p. 82; emphasis added). This statement offers considerable insight not only into the origins of the "doctors of the law," but also into the beginnings of the oral law. As we will see in following chapters, the seeds of *both* were sown in the period of the Exile—only to be nourished throughout post-exilic times and brought to fruition during the inter-testament period. By the second century BC, the scribes—who because of their Levitical heritage once operated in close association with the priesthood—had moved well beyond their ancient role as copyists to become the *primary teachers* of the Pentateuch. As a distinctly "religious" party made up of highly-educated individuals devoted to copying, guarding and interpreting the Scriptures, the scribes found themselves in *conflict* with a Hellenistic priesthood, and thus resorted to an alliance with the People of the Land. Eventually, the overwhelming majority of scribes became aligned with the Pharisees, successors of the Hasidim.

Indicating their strong historical connection, Grayzel says that the "party of the scribes … became known as the Pharisee party" (p. 76). This, however, is not entirely correct. As a unique sect, the scribes long predate the Pharisees; yet, as we will see, the scribes' rise to power was codependent on the dominance achieved by the Pharisees. Indeed, in terms of mindset, doctrine and practice, *most* scribes were virtually indistinguishable from the Pharisees. Jeremias admits that the composition of the Pharisaic community was "clouded in obscurity," and that the Pharisees "were so closely linked with the scribes that it is difficult to separate them … [particularly] since the scribes' rise to power marked the rise of the Pharisees also" (pp. 246, 252). Critical of scholarship that fails to make a distinction between scribes and Pharisees, Jeremias adds that the problem is amplified by the way Matthew and Luke in particular often lump the two groups together (p. 246, footnote 1; see, for example, Matt. 5:20; 12:38; 15:1; 23:2-29; Mark 2:16; 7:1, 5; and Luke 5:21, 30; 6:7; 11:44, 53; 15:2).

Jeremias notes an important distinction in how Jesus *reacted* to the Pharisees as opposed to the scribes. To be sure, Christ pulled no punches—but He was careful not to confuse their behavior, addressing specific faults as they applied to each group. For example, Jesus reproached the Pharisees primarily for (a) emphasizing their traditional laws of purity while *hypocritically* remaining impure inwardly (Luke 11:39-40), and (b) for emphasizing tithe-paying while *hypocritically* failing to exercise righteous judgment and the love of God (verse 42). Jeremias contends that these reproaches have "nothing to do with a theological education [i.e., a specific creed]; [rather] they are leveled at men who [ostensibly] led their lives according to the demands of the religious laws of the Pharisaic scribes [but in reality failed to do so]" (pp. 253-254).

In contrast, Jesus reproached the scribes for (a) imposing strict religious laws on others while neglecting to keep those same laws themselves (Luke 11:46); (b) being quick to condemn to death those sent by God (verses 47-51); (c) withholding vital knowledge from the people while making no use of it themselves (verse 52); and (d) excessive pride and vanity—demonstrated by their pious dress, love for public salutations, demand for the chief seats (particularly in the synagogues), and tendency to make long public prayers for show (Luke 20:46-47; Mark 12:38-40). While many of these same faults definitely apply as well to the Pharisees (e.g., Luke 11:43), these reproaches are, according to Jeremias, largely a reflection of the "scribal education" of such "teachers of the law" (*Jerusalem in the Time of Jesus*, p. 253).

While the majority of scribes clearly belonged to the party of the Pharisees, not *all* "teachers of the law" were Pharisees. Jeremias adds that we "must not underestimate the number of teachers [scribes] who did *not* belong to a Pharisaic *haburot* [community]" (p. 256). Some scribes, he says, could actually be found among the Sadducees, and a number of priests were scribes. While only a minority in the *haburot*, the scribes were nonetheless the "leading faction among the Pharisees. The *laity* who joined the Pharisaic communities and undertook to observe the Pharisaic laws on tithes and purity were far more numerous…" (pp. 257-258).

Jeremias also brings out the *synergetic* relationship that existed between the Pharisees and the scribes—an association particularly vital to the Pharisees (so important, in fact, that one wonders how they could function effectively without the scribes' scholarly leadership.) Recalling the sect's roots among the Hasidim, he writes that the Pharisaic community was "mostly composed of petty commoners, men of the people with no scribal education" (p. 259)—yet they lived "according to the **religious precepts laid down by Pharisaic scribes**" (p. 247, emphasis added). As models of piety, the party of the Pharisees represented "the ideal life **which the scribes, [those] men of divine and secret knowledge, had set before them**" (p. 267). According to Jeremias, "the leaders and influential members of Pharisaic communities were *scribes*" (p. 254), and the "Pharisaic communities **especially gave their scribes unconditional obedience**, and Pharisaic scribes were [among all first-century scribes] by far the most numerous" (p. 243, emphasis added).

This much is clear: As self-appointed guardians of Scripture and its proper observance, the Pharisees were *quite dependent* on the scholarly leadership of the scribes—who, in turn, benefited from their association with the Pharisees due to the sect's "popular base." There is every indication that the scribes played a pivotal role in the development of Pharisaic thought—which gradually morphed into Judaism. As we will later examine, the scribes and Pharisees largely share a similar evolution—both slowly arose to positions of influence near the same time, and both were usurpers of authority; more importantly, together they gradually created a theology that revolved around a so-called "oral Torah."

Central to the relationship between the scribes and the Pharisees is the fact that they both *despised* the Sadducees. This attitude can be traced back to the inter-testament period when both the scribes and the Hasidim (progenitors of the Pharisees) had nothing but contempt for a materialistic priesthood thoroughly corrupted by the Hellenistic movement of the second and third centuries BC.

Sadducees—Guardians of the Temple

If the Pharisees were "the separatists," then the Sadducees, as John Phillips suggests, were "the moralists" (*Exploring the World of the Jew*, p. 37). By "moralist," Phillips refers to the sect's strict adherence to the *written* Torah. In contrast to the Pharisees, he writes that the Sadducees "were never a large party numerically, but they made up for that in other ways. They were, for the most part, wealthy, aristocratic and influential. [Because of their elitist, Hellenistic past, they] were the materialists, the secularists of the day…. They opposed the *Mishnah* [codified oral law] and had no use for the cumbersome oral tradition so dear to the Pharisees. They interpreted the Law literally and severely" (p. 36). Jeremias adds that the "Sadducees formed a tightly closed group, with an elaborate tradition of theology and doctrine; they kept strictly to the exact text of Scripture…" (p. 232).

"Sadducee" is based on the Hebrew *Zadok*, a righteous priest during King David's time (I Kings 1:32); many take the term to mean "Sons of Zadok." According to Jeremias, the Sadducean party was made up of "chief priests [including the High Priest] and elders, the priestly and the lay nobility" (p. 230), and were in charge of the rites in the Temple in Jerusalem. Robinson adds that the sect "believed in the Written Torah and *only* the Written Torah and … in the primacy of the hereditary [Aaronic] priestly caste" (*Essential Judaism*, p. 321).

In spite of their loyalty to the Scriptures, the Sadducees were not without faults. They denied the scriptural reality of a resurrection for the dead as well as the existence of an angelic realm (Acts 23:8)—and Christ *included them* with the Pharisees in warning His disciples of the "leaven [doctrine] of the Pharisees and Sadducees" (Matt. 16:1-12).

The Sadducean party's adversarial position on the "oral law" created enormous tension between themselves and the Pharisees. Jeremias writes that the Sadducees "held strictly to the literal interpretation of the Torah … and thus found themselves in direct opposition to the Pharisees and their oral [law] which declared that the rules for purity for priests were binding on the pious laity too" (p. 231). He adds: "The conflict … dominated the profound religious revolution of [what would become] Judaism between the Maccabean wars and the destruction of Jerusalem" in 70 AD (p. 266). Robinson adds that in first-century Palestine the "lines within the Jewish community became sharply drawn around this issue" (p. 320).

Though still powerful and influential (at least in political circles), the Sadducees gradually lost more and more authority to the Pharisees. Jeremias writes that "a large number of important posts hitherto held by [Sadducean] priests and laymen of high rank, had, in the first century AD passed entirely, or predominantly, into the hands of [Pharisaic] scribes" (p. 237). Ultimately, the Jewish uprising against Rome in 66 AD and the subsequent destruction of the Temple "marked the [complete] decline of the lay nobility and of Sadducean influence, which had grown from the union of the priestly and the lay nobility. The **new and powerful ruling class of the [Pharisaic] scribes** had [already long] overtaken the ancient class of priestly and lay nobility, founded on the privileges of birth" (p. 232; emphasis added).

Nowhere was this more obvious than in the Sanhedrin, the supreme judicial assembly of post-exilic Jewish religion. The Sanhedrin "grew out of the union of … non-priestly heads of families, representatives of the 'secular nobility,' with the priestly aristocracy" (Jeremias, p. 223). Consisting of seventy-one members, the Sanhedrin of Jesus' day "fell into three groups: the chief priests who, in the person of the High Priest, held the presidency, the [Pharisaic] scribes, and the elders [the non-priestly nobility]" (p. 222). The priests and elders of the Sanhedrin were virtually all members of the Sadducean party, while the Pharisaic party in the Sanhedrin was "composed entirely of scribes" (p. 236).

The Pharisees did not always have a voice in the Sanhedrin. Made up originally of only the aristocracy—that is, the chief priests and nobility—the Sanhedrin admitted Pharisees for the first time under the rule of Queen Alexandra (76-67 BC), who held Pharisaic views (Jeremias, p. 223). "The decline of [the Sadducees'] power dates from the time of Alexandra; under her the Pharisees gained a foothold in the Sanhedrin, and the mass of the people rallied more and more to them…. [By the early part of the first century AD] the Pharisees, relying on their large number of supporters among the people, saw their power in the Sanhedrin becoming stronger and stronger" (p. 232). Jeremias adds that while the Sadducees controlled the Sanhedrin by a narrow margin, the growing influence of the Pharisees ultimately made itself felt, and those "high priests with Sadducean sympathies had to accustom themselves to withholding their views in council, and [were eventually compelled to submit] to carrying out [certain of] the Temple rites according to Pharisaic traditions" (p. 159).

In their fall from favor with the Common People, the Hellenized Sadducean priesthood abrogated their God-ordained responsibility to teach the Scriptures. By Jesus' day, the Pharisees, with their scribal leadership, had *usurped* much of that role and occupied "the seat of Moses"—leaving the Sadducees with only the administration of the Temple and its rituals. According to Phillips, the Sadducees compounded the problem in that they "denied the existence of angels, the truth of the resurrection, the immortality of the soul, and a future life" (*Exploring the World of the Jew*, p. 36). These doctrines were quite unpopular, so the Sadducees had *few* followers from among the Common People.

The priesthood's original position, however, is clear from Scripture. In matters of controversy, the children of Israel were to come to the *priest* and the judge in Jerusalem. "If a matter is too hard for you [the local judge] in judgment … being matters of strife [controversy] within your gates, then you shall arise and go up to the place [Jerusalem] which the LORD your God shall choose. And **you shall come to the priests**, [of the] the Levites, and to the judge that shall be in those days, and ask. And they shall declare to you the sentence of judgment" (Deut. 17:8-9).

Just before his death, Moses prophetically blessed each of the tribes of Israel. Of Levi—*and thus referring to the priesthood*—he said: "[Levi shall] **teach** Jacob Your judgments, and [**teach**] Israel Your Law. Let them [the priests] put incense before You, and whole burnt sacrifice on Your altar" (Deut. 33:10). In the time of Ezra and Nehemiah (a critical period which we will cover in detail later), "the Levites [under the direction of Ezra the priest] caused the people to understand the Law…. And they read distinctly from the Book of the Law of God. And they expounded the meaning and caused them to understand the reading" (Neh. 8:7-8). Apparently, this was the first time scribes—*non-priestly Levites*—had been used to officially teach the Torah. As we will later explore, this move may have inadvertently encouraged the scribes to eventually *usurp* the priesthood's God-ordained role as teachers of the Scriptures.

Clearly, it was God's intention that the *priesthood* was to teach the Law to His people. The prophet Malachi is unmistakable when he says that "the priest's lips should keep knowledge, and the people should seek the Law at his mouth; for he is the messenger of the LORD of hosts" (Mal. 2:7).

How, then, did the Sadducean priests of Jesus' day—who *should* have been teaching the Torah—*forfeit* that responsibility to the scribes and Pharisees? During the period of Syrian rule over Judah—a most difficult time in Jewish history which we will cover in detail in a later chapter—the priesthood had become corrupt and unfaithful in their duties. Instead of teaching the people God's laws and commandments, the priesthood had become chief proponents of Hellenism (Greek ways of life).

Ernest Martin writes: "Following the Maccabean victory [over the Syrians] there were many priests who were ready and willing to resume their ancient, God-given role as teachers and expounders of the Law. But there were also the lay teachers who … had made a notable contribution to the Maccabean cause at a time when many priests were outright Hellenists…" ("Between The Testaments," from *Tomorrow's World*, p. 23). These "lay teachers"—scribes and Hasidic laymen—organized themselves into what became the Pharisees and **rejected the sole authority of the priesthood to teach God's laws**. "With the passage of time … these [scribal] Pharisaic lay teachers succeeded in convincing the people that they were right and that the priests were wrong" (p. 42).

Religiously speaking, very few Jews were Sadducees. According to Martin, the sect's "materialistic concept of Scripture and the fact that they were mainly priests … rich and [politically] influential" made them unpopular with the Common People. Overall, they were "rigidly exclusive and insignificant in numbers" (*Is Judaism the Religion of Moses?*, p. 13).

The "Oral Torah"—Defining Element of Pharisaic Judaism

The concept of a so-called oral Torah surreptitiously given to Moses is at the very heart of Judaism—and, as we have seen, was at the center of the rivalry between the Pharisees and Sadducees. According to Grayzel, the idea of an oral law may have originated with the question of *how* to interpret the written Torah, particularly in an environment of rapid social and cultural change. He explains: "Essentially, the two parties differed on how to apply [religion] to the new problems of their [Hellenistic] age, and how to [best] interpret the [written] Torah, which was the basic authority of Jewish life" (*A History of the Jews*, p. 78). The problem was not the *validity* of Scripture—for both parties held it in the highest esteem. The problem was one of *interpretation*. Grayzel continues: "The Sadducees were in favor of a *strict interpretation* of the Torah … [and taught that the Jews were] to abide by every word written in the Torah, no less and no more…. The Pharisees [with their scribal leaders] were for a *liberal interpretation* for the Torah … [and] wanted to extend [its] principles to every possible phase of life." Grayzel takes the position that, in one sense, "the Pharisees made [what would become] Judaism much easier [i.e., *liberalized*] by regarding biblical laws as principles. This **enabled them to amend many practices to conform more closely to the changing needs of national life**" (p. 78; emphasis added).

The idea of "extending the *principles* of the Law to every area of life" is obviously biblical. In fact, Jesus came, at least in part, for that very purpose—for He did "not come to abolish [the Law], but to fulfill [the Law]" by showing *how* it could be applied in principle. It should be evident to even the novice Bible student that throughout Matthew five Christ *adds* to the written Torah a new *spiritual* dimension, sometimes referred to as the *spirit* of the Law (much more will be said about this in Chapter Six). What the scribes and Pharisees attempted to do was perhaps commendable, but there was just one problem: They lacked what Scripture calls a *heart*—"Oh, that there were such a heart in them that they would fear Me and keep all My commandments always" (Deut. 5:29). This "heart"—a mind yielded to and led by the Spirit of God—would have enabled them to see beyond the "letter of the law" and to discern the *spirit* and *intent* of the law as well. As we will later see, without having the spirit of the living God to guide them, these ancient "teachers of the law" not only *misinterpreted* the Law, they went on to *add to* the Scriptures via their alleged oral traditions.

Notice this telling comment by Jewish historian Moses Shulvass: "Unlike the Sadducees, the Pharisees opposed a rigid interpretation of the Pentateuch Law. To them, the Holy Writ was a 'living [i.e., *flexible*] Torah,' valid for all times and never in conflict with the time. By using the God-given **power of reason** and **special methods of interpretation**, various Pentateuch laws could be **reinterpreted** and **modified** to harmonize with the advanced ideas of each generation" (*A History of the Jewish People*,

Vol. I, p. 94; emphasis added). What "God-given *power of reason*"? What "special *methods* of interpretation"? Can God's laws really be "modified"? Again, the scribes and Pharisees *did not have the "heart"* to understand and apply the Scriptures the way God intended—but, indeed, "there is a way which seems right to a man, but the end thereof is the way of death" (Prov. 14:12).

Inspired by their long-cherished *traditions*, the scribal leaders of the Pharisees ultimately sought to "improve" upon God's laws by rationalizing that there in fact existed an "oral Torah" given to somehow complement the written Torah. Grayzel writes: "If they could find little support for their proposed laws in the Written Torah, they argued that there was also an Oral Torah, or teaching, **a set of traditions which had been handed down to them by the scribes of former days**, who in turn must have received them by tradition from their predecessors, [going] all the way back to Moses" (p. 78; emphasis added).

As quoted earlier, David Stern, in his *Jewish New Testament Commentary*, agrees: "The *P'rushim* not only took the *Tanakh* to be God's word to man, but also **considered the accumulated tradition handed down over centuries by the sages and [scribal] teachers to be God's word as well—** the Oral *Torah*—so that a system for living developed which touched on every aspect of life" (p. 18; "Matt. 3:7"; emphasis added). Johnson adds this: "The practice of the Oral Law made it possible for the [written] Mosaic code **to be adapted** to changing conditions" in Jewish life (*A History of the Jews*, p. 106; emphasis added).

In order to employ the so-called "oral law" in an effort to "amend" or "adapt" the Mosaic code, one would have to first presume that the "oral law" was *equal to* if not *superior to* the Law itself. As we will see, this is the very premise that made it possible for the "oral Torah" to eventually take precedence over the very Law of God. Rooted in *disbelief*, the Jews simply did not accept the absolute *exclusive* nature of the Scriptures. In this regard, Phillips writes: "The Pharisees were devoted to the oral law of the great rabbis [scribes], which later would be inscribed as the Mishnah (an early form of the Talmud). They were convinced that the Mishnah held the key to all the hidden depths of the [written] Torah, as well as having the answer to all the needs and problems of mankind. Their lofty aspirations **degenerated eventually into** *dogmatism*…. It was perhaps inevitable that **in time they would come to regard the oral tradition of the rabbis [scribes] as of equal authority with the written Law of Moses**…" (*Exploring the World of the Jew*, p. 36; emphasis added).

Of course, the Sadducean temple priests—insisting that the written Torah was forever unchangeable—were adamantly opposed to the idea that any such alleged "oral teaching could subject the Law to a **process of creative development**" (Johnson, p. 106; emphasis added).

This "process of creative development" is well described by Solomon Landman in his book, *Story Without End—An Informal History of the*

Jewish People. He writes that certain teachings had "come into Jewish life as a result of the interpretations of the [written] Torah that the learned schoolmasters [scribes] and elders of the community had made from time to time. For the Holy Scriptures had been written centuries before and did not deal specifically with every new situation Jews had to face.... By applying the spirit of the [written] Torah"—*but without the Spirit of God to guide them*—"[these self-proclaimed teachers] arrived at new regulations to cover the specific situation. These decisions [came to be] called the Oral Law, and were studied in the schools along with the Torah, the Written Law, thus becoming part of the **religious tradition** of the Jews. Most people accepted them as **extensions of the Torah**.... The makers of the Oral Law felt it their duty to build a '**fence around the Torah**,' to make rules that would keep the religion pure and the people holy" (p. 74; emphasis added).

Such traditions were "minute and vexatious extensions of the Law" and "had long been gradually accumulating" (*Smith's Bible Dictionary*, p. 508; "Pharisees"). Smith adds: "While it was the aim of Jesus to call men to the Law of God itself as the supreme guide of life, the Pharisees, upon the pretense of maintaining [the Pentateuch] intact, multiplied minute precepts and distinctions to such an extent that **the whole life of the [pious] Jew was hemmed in and burdened on every side by instructions so numerous and trifling that the [written] Law was almost if not wholly lost sight of**" (p. 508; emphasis added).

As a "fence around the Law," the oral law was, in theory, intended to prevent one from transgressing against the Pentateuch. However, by "fencing in" the written Torah with minute regulations, one is also relieved of the responsibility of *spiritual discernment*—of applying the spiritual intent of the Law to various situations. Again, applying the "principles" of the Law requires the guidance of God's Spirit, which was not generally available under the terms of the Old Covenant. Thus, as we will cover in detail later, the "oral law"—as a massive, complex code designed to regulate human conduct—is in a very real sense a humanly-devised *substitute* for a sound conscience led by the Spirit of God.

Judaism, of course, has never been able to substantiate the existence of an "oral Torah." The whole idea is based on tradition. Robinson writes that the sages of old "believed that there had been [an] oral interpretation of [the] Torah, almost from the moment Moses came down from Mt. Sinai with the tablets in his hands. After all, was it not said [by the sages] that God had given the Oral Law to Moses on Sinai as well as the [written] Torah ... [and] that the Almighty had **whispered it into his ear**?" (*Essential Judaism*, p. 313).

The Scriptures, however, are not silent on the matter. As we will see in Chapter Five, numerous biblical passages prove that such an oral law could never have come from God via Moses. For example, just before the children of Israel were to pass over the Jordan into the Promised Land, Moses recopied the Law (Deut. 31:9). Note that in verse 24, Moses "**completed** writing the words" of the laws of God in a book, and that "they were **finished**." The Law was *complete*. This same "finished" law would be used "as a witness" against Israel in her sins (verse 26)—thus, it was the *only* law God would (or *could*) use in judging His people. The existence of *any other law* would have *undermined* God's righteous judgment and *nullified* the entire written Torah!

Long before the development of the "oral Torah," the prophet Isaiah warned Israel to *look only* to "the Law [Torah] and to the testimony [of the prophets]! If they [who teach—such as the rabbis—] do not speak **according to this** [written] **Word**, it is because there is no light in them" (Isa. 8:20). This passage leaves no wiggle-room for proponents of an oral law—for it unequivocally declares that there is *one* and only *one* standard, the *written* Word of God.

We should, as well, not overlook the obvious fact that long after the death of Moses, the Jews' so-called oral law was *subject to centuries of revision and expansion*. So much for God "whispering into Moses' ear."

"Serpents, brood of vipers!"

We can learn much about first-century religion in Judea by simply studying Jesus' interaction with the Jewish religious leaders of the day. In fact, the gospels contain numerous accounts of various "conflicts" between Christ and the scribes, Pharisees, and, to a somewhat lesser extent, the Sadducees. Moreover, the substance of these conflicts provides vital insight into the "hearts and minds" of the Jewish leaders.

It seems that Jesus had considerably more negative encounters with the scribes and Pharisees (who, as we have seen, were largely inseparable) than He did with the Sadducees. There may be several reasons for this. First, as has been shown, the party of the Pharisees had a *great deal* more influence over the Common People than did the Sadducees. Thus they posed the greater danger, **particularly in leading people away from true Torah observance and toward humanly-devised traditions**. Also, the Pharisees were quite aggressive in proselytizing—"for you [Pharisees] travel the sea and the land to make [even] one proselyte" (Matt. 23:15). Perhaps the biggest reason, however, was that the scribes and Pharisees sat "in Moses' seat" (Matt. 23:2)—a position acquired surreptitiously, yet one that carried the serious responsibility of *judging* the people (see below).

Specifically, Jesus upbraided the Sadducees for their disbelief of the resurrection—candidly stating, "You do err, not knowing the Scriptures, nor the power of God" (Matt. 22:29). The matter proved to be a persistent sore spot for the Sadducees, for which they continued to persecute the apostles (Acts 4:1-3). The "chief priests" who plotted to kill Jesus (Matt. 26:3-4) were no doubt Sadducees (see Acts 5:17). Thus, while the Sadducean party is not mentioned by name in this regard, its leaders were obviously co-conspirators with the Pharisees in Jesus' death. Both parties feared that

Christ's growing popularity and influence would somehow lead to Roman intervention and a subsequent loss of their political status (John 11:47-48).

In one of the rare moments when the two rival parties were willing to lay aside their differences long enough to unite in action, the Pharisees and Sadducees came to where John was baptizing. More than just curious, they were no doubt planning a confrontation—and were particularly concerned about John's message of a coming "kingdom." John, however, took the first shot, calling them a "brood of vipers" (Matt. 3:7)—an expression Jesus Himself later used of the religionists. Right in the presence of the crowds gathered for baptism, John exposed the hypocrisy of the Jewish leaders, challenging them to bring forth "fruits worthy of repentance" (verse 8). John warned them: "And do not think to say within yourselves, 'We have Abraham for our father' "—i.e., don't assume that being of Abraham's seed guarantees a right relationship with God or entrance into the Kingdom of God. Emphasizing that there is no substitute for genuine repentance and obedience to the Pentateuch, he adds, "For I tell you that God is able from these stones to raise up children to Abraham"—a not-so-subtle warning that those who fail to measure up can be *replaced*. Indeed, "already the axe is striking at the roots of the trees [the corrupt religious leadership]; therefore every tree that is not producing good fruit is [to be] cut down and thrown into the fire" (verses 9-10). Jesus would later proclaim a similar warning, saying "every plant that My heavenly Father has not planted shall be rooted up" (Matt. 15:13; see below).

The message was not lost on the Pharisees and Sadducees, who no doubt winced under the sting of John's powerful indictment.

"Woe to you, scribes and Pharisees, hypocrites!"

In His numerous encounters with the scribes and Pharisees, Christ primarily focused on their *vanity* and *spirit of hypocrisy*—though certainly not ignoring their false teachings. It should be noted that Jesus' criticism of these religionists dealt mainly with their hypocritical *practices*, as opposed to content. When Christ did criticize the *content* of their message, it was not their handling of the Scriptures that He called into question—it was their "traditions of men" which they held to be *equal* to the Law of Moses. Such traditions often had the effect of nullifying the Word of God.

Comparing them to "whited sepulchers" which outwardly appear beautiful but inside were full of "all uncleanness," He bluntly told them that they too "outwardly appear to men to be righteous," but were actually "**full of hypocrisy and lawlessness**" (Matt. 23:27-28). When once dining with a Pharisee, Jesus declined to participate in the Pharisees' pre-meal "hand-washing" ritual. Noting their concern, He used the opportunity to emphasize their hypocrisy: "Now, you Pharisees [are quick to] cleanse the outside of the cup and the dish, but inside you are full of greediness and wickedness" (Luke 11:39). On another occasion He likewise broached the subject:

"Woe to you, scribes and Pharisees, hypocrites! For you cleanse the outside of the cup and the dish, but within you are full of extortion and excess. Blind Pharisees! First cleanse the inside of the cup and the dish, so that the outside may also become clean" (Matt. 23:25-26).

Calling attention to their selfishness and obsession with the physical, Jesus upbraided the scribes and Pharisees for having *neglected* "justice and the love of God" (Luke 11:42). Their overall concern with the external led naturally to a *neglect* of the "weightier" matters of the Law—those that dealt with the *spirit*. On another occasion He similarly warned them: "Woe to you, scribes and Pharisees, hypocrites! For you pay tithes of mint and anise and cumin, but you have **abandoned the more important matters of the Law—judgment, and mercy and faith**. These you were obligated to do, and not to leave the others undone" (Matt. 23:23). Jesus then summed up the religious leaders' hypocrisy by stating that they would go to extremes to avoid swallowing a *gnat*—the smallest of creatures—but would willingly "swallow a camel" (verse 24).

Jesus continually exposed the scribes' and Pharisees' hypocrisy in the way they adhered in many cases to the *letter* of the Law while conveniently ignoring or misapplying the *spirit* of the Law. A good example is found in Luke 14:1-6, where Jesus is again eating a meal with scribes and Pharisees—this time on the Sabbath. Knowing they were watching His every move, Jesus drew their attention to a man among them who had an affliction known as *dropsy*. "Is it lawful to heal on the Sabbath?" he asked. The religionists kept silent. Jesus proceeded to heal the man and send him on his way. He then asked, "Who among you shall have an ass or an ox fall into a pit, and will not immediately pull it out on the Sabbath day?" Again, they were silent, unable to reply—because they were trapped by their own hypocrisy. They knew full well that to rescue an "ox in the ditch" was good and right even on the Sabbath—something they would not hesitate to do. Would not the *spirit* of the Law then permit doing *good* on the Sabbath for someone suffering from a disease? Of course, the answer was obvious—but the scribes and Pharisees were bound by their oral *traditions* which included countless Sabbath "prohibitions." (Similar accounts are found in Matthew 12:9-13 and Luke 13:10-17.)

The religious leaders of Jesus' day had what Paul calls a "form of godliness" (II Tim. 3:5)—one that is based on the physical, on outward appearances, on presentation—yet devoid of any true spiritual depth. William Smith writes that "the Pharisees sought mainly to attract the attention and to excite the admiration of men…. Indeed the whole spirit of their religion was summed up, not in confession of sin and in humility, but in proud self-righteousness…" (*Smith's Bible Dictionary*, p. 508; "Pharisees"). He adds that "true piety consisted not in forms, but in substance, not in outward observances, but in an inward spirit. The whole system of Pharisaic piety led to exactly [the] opposite…" (p. 508).

In particular, Jesus took the scribes to task for their pretentiousness. "Beware of the scribes, who take pleasure in walking around in [long] robes, and in [conspicuous] salutations in the marketplaces, and in [having] the chief seats in the synagogues and the chief places in the feasts" (Mark 12:38 -39). Matthew includes the Pharisees, adding this: "And they do all their works to be seen by men. They make broad their phylacteries and enlarge the borders of their garments…. And they love … to be called by men, 'Rabbi, Rabbi' " (Matt. 23:5, 7). Phylacteries and tassels (borders) were worn by many men according to the instructions in Exodus 13 and Numbers 15. Christ was simply pointing out that these religionists had flamboyantly embellished these symbols in order to impress others.

In addition to making "long prayers" for *show*, Jesus also indicts them for "devouring the houses of widows" (Mark 12:40). Since these self-proclaimed religious leaders were dependent on financial contributions from their patrons, widows in particular were vulnerable to abuse and exploitation. "These," He added, "shall receive the greater condemnation."

Teaching "Traditions of Men"

Most notable of these "blind leaders of the blind" was their adherence to "traditions of men"—which were based on the Jews' so-called oral law. Jesus was asked, "Why do Your disciples transgress the tradition of the elders? For they do not wash their hands when they eat bread" (Matt. 15:2). This, of course, had nothing to do with good hygiene—or the official rituals held at the Temple—but referred to *traditional ritual* hand washings. The scribes and Pharisees were apparently puzzled and concerned that Jesus had neglected to teach such traditions to His disciples. As He often did, Christ answered their question with a question of His own. Turning the tables on them, He asked: **Why do you also transgress the commandment of God for the sake of your tradition?** For God commanded, saying, 'Honor your father and your mother'; and, 'The one who speaks evil of [his] father or mother, let him die the death.' But you say, 'Whoever shall say to [his] father or mother, "Whatever benefit you might [have expected to] receive from me is being given [instead] as a gift to the temple," he [then] is not at all obligated to honor his father or his mother [in caring for their needs]' " (verses 3-5). In this passage we begin to see how the scribes and Pharisees had "made void the commandment of God for the sake of [their] tradition" (verse six). Caring for elderly parents—and not treating them with contempt—is all part of the Fifth Commandment. However, according to this Jewish "tradition," one could simply *dedicate to God* whatever portion of his money or goods that *should have been used* to support his parents. This became a means of circumventing the clear responsibility of children toward their parents. Jesus continued: "Hypocrites! Isaiah has prophesied well concerning you, saying, 'This people draw near to Me [God] with their mouths, and with their lips they honor Me; but their hearts are far away from Me. But they worship Me in vain, **teaching for doctrine the commandments [traditions] of men**' " (verses 7-9).

In a parallel account, Mark says that in "leaving the commandment of God, you [scribes and Pharisees] hold fast the tradition of men…. Full well do **you reject the commandment of God, so that you may observe your own tradition**" (Mark 7:8-9). These religious leaders were guilty of "nullifying the authority of the Word of God" by their traditions (verse 13), which, as Jesus pointedly brings out, had been "passed down." In other words, the scribes and Pharisees had received their traditions from previous generations as part of the transmission of the so-called "oral Torah."

It is no wonder then that Charles Pfeiffer, in his *Old Testament History*, writes: "To the Pharisee [of Christ's day] ... **tradition was not simply a commentary upon the Law, but was ultimately raised to the level of Scripture itself**" (p. 596; emphasis added). Thus we can begin to understand why Jesus said, "There is one who accuses you, even Moses.... And if **you do not believe his writings**, how shall you believe My words?" (John 5:45-47)—and, "Did not Moses give you the Law, and [yet] **not one of you is [genuinely] practicing the Law**?" (John 7:19).

"Every plant which My Father has not planted"

Of considerable concern for the Jewish religious establishment was Jesus' growing popularity among the Common People and, in particular, His message about a coming "kingdom." Fearing Roman intervention in the matter, the Jewish leadership—both Pharisaic and Sadducean—stood to lose their status quo. Thus the scribes and Pharisees (and at times the Sadducees) opposed Christ at every turn, often plotting how they might "entangle Him" with His own words (Matt. 22:15) or catch Him breaking one of their "regulations" so they could level an "accusation against Him" (Luke 6:7)—and ultimately have Him "legally" put to death. More than once Jesus provoked the scribes and Pharisees into taking up stones, only to narrowly escape through the crowd (John 8:59; 10:31; 11:8).

Perhaps at no time did Christ raise the ire of the scribes and Pharisees more than when He questioned their fidelity to Abraham. Jesus said, "I know that you are Abraham's seed; but you are seeking to kill Me, because My words do not enter into your minds [that is, Jesus' words were unfathomable because of their unbelief]. I speak the things that I have seen from My Father, and you **do the things that you have seen from your father**" (John 8:37-38). Bristling, they replied, "Our father is Abraham!" Christ then said, "If you were [spiritually] Abraham's children, you would do the works of Abraham. But now you seek to kill Me, a man who has spoken the truth to you.... [Rather] you are doing the [evil] works of your [spiritual] father" (verses 39-41). As the Pharisees began to seethe with anger, Jesus cut right to the heart of their problem: "**You are of your father the devil**, and the lusts of your father you desire to practice" (verse 44). The encounter ended with their failed attempt at stoning Him (verse 59).

Later that same day Jesus healed a blind man. Afterwards, He said: "For judgment I have come into this world so that those who do not see might see, and [that] **those who see might become blind**" (John 9:39).

Picking up on Jesus' insinuation, some of the Pharisees who were listening mockingly asked, "Are we also blind?" Jesus said to them, "If you were [truly] blind, you would not have sin. But now you say, 'We see.' Therefore, **your sin remains**" (verses 40-41).

Clearly, the scribes and Pharisees were spiritually blind (Matt. 15:14). But because they claimed to "see"—to *understand* exactly what they were doing as occupants of "Moses' seat"—Christ held them fully accountable. They *rejected* the truth when it was presented first by John the Baptist—"But the Pharisees and the doctors of the Law had **set aside [rejected] the counsel of God** concerning themselves..." (Luke 7:30). These religionists would be held accountable as well because of Jesus' works. Notice this powerful indictment from John 15:22: "If I had not come and spoken to them, they would not have had sin; but now they have **nothing to cover their sin**." Verse 24: "If I had not done among them the works that no other man has done, they would not have had sin; but now they have both **seen** [understood] and [yet] hated both Me and My Father."

The Sadducees, scribes and Pharisees all heard repentance preached by John, but *rejected* it; they witnessed Jesus' powerful works, but *denied* them. In their vanity and lust for prestige and power, the religious leaders of first-century Palestine had abrogated their responsibility—for indeed they had "shut up the kingdom of heaven before men" (Matt. 23:13). Not only had *they* become disqualified from a place in that kingdom, but they were also *hindering* "those who [were to be] entering" that kingdom—*the Jews*. Thus, the kingdom of God was "taken from" them and "given to a *nation* that produces the fruits" of that kingdom (Matt. 21:43). This "nation" refers to *converted* believers, those Paul identifies as *spiritual* Jews (Rom. 2:29).[5]

As indicated in Matthew 21:45, the chief priests (Sadducees) and the Pharisees knew Jesus was speaking about them. On another occasion, Christ made it clear to His disciples that "every plant" not planted by His Father would be "rooted up" (Matt. 15:13). Indeed, John the Baptist had previously warned the scribes and Pharisees that the axe was already "striking at the roots of the trees" (Matt. 3:10).

There is no question that the religious leaders of Jesus' day knew full well that they had been "weighed in the balance" and found lacking. They *rejected* the truth when it was shown to them—and even *rejected* the Messiah Himself. Thus, they would bear their sin.

"The scribes and Pharisees sit in Moses' seat"

No discussion of first-century Jewish religion would be complete without a careful look at Jesus' statement in Matthew 23 concerning the scribes' and Pharisees' occupation of "Moses' seat." Jesus makes the profound as well as paradoxical assertion that the scribes and Pharisees "sit in Moses' seat" (verse two). He then says to the Jews, as well as to His own followers, that they are to *observe* and *do* whatever the scribes and Pharisees command them (verse three). An enigmatic statement to say the least, given that the remainder of Matthew 23 is a scathing indictment of the scribes' and Pharisees' corruption, outlined in seven successive "woes" covering their hypocrisy, greed, vanity, hatred, etc., and culminating in Jesus' exclamation, "You serpents, you offspring of vipers, how shall you escape the judgment of Gehenna [fire]?" (verse 33).

A dichotomy seems to exist: Are we really to understand Jesus' words—"all that they tell you, observe and do"—literally? If so, what are we to make of Jesus' stinging renunciation of the scribes and Pharisees, not only here, but as seen in numerous other encounters? Was Jesus inconsistent in His teachings—was He telling His followers to *obey* the dictates of the Jewish leadership in one breath while instructing them to *reject* their religious traditions in another?

Some view "Moses' seat" as a *seat of judgment* from which religious rulings were handed down. A religious "supreme court"—called the *Great Beth Din*—existed alongside the Sanhedrin in first-century Palestine (the Sanhedrin had by then become almost entirely *civil* in function). According to Ernest Martin, the Sanhedrin was "represented [by] both Sadducees and Pharisees, but the Great Beth Din was composed *only* of the scribes ... and Pharisees—the most eminent of religious leaders..." (*Is Judaism the Religion of Moses?*, p. 93).

Martin says the first *Beth Din* was formed under Moses when his father-in-law Jethro advised him to assign God-fearing men to assist in judging the children of Israel (Ex. 18). Only the most difficult cases were to be brought to Moses (verse 22). Thus, the "seat of Moses" was established to handle disputes in accordance with the precepts of God's Law (p. 94).

Moses later ordained that the same "seat of judgment" be perpetuated in Israel as the nation began to settle into the Promised Land. "If a matter is too hard for you [locally] in judgment, between blood and blood, between plea and plea, and between stroke and stroke, being matters of strife within your gates, then you shall arise and go up to the place [Jerusalem] which the LORD your God shall choose. And you shall come to the priests, the Levites, **and to the judge that shall be in those days**, and ask. And they shall declare to you the sentence of judgment. And **you shall do according to the sentence which they declare to you** from that place which the LORD shall choose. And **you shall be careful to do according to all that they tell you**. According to the sentence of the law which they shall teach you and **according to the judgment which they shall tell you**, **you shall do**. You shall not turn aside from the sentence which they shall show you, to the right hand or the left" (Deut. 17:8-11).

Notice the striking similarity between Moses' command and Jesus' instructions—"whatsoever they bid you [to] observe, that observe and do" (*KJV*). Christ appears to be paraphrasing Deuteronomy 17 in acknowledging the authority of the *Great Beth Din*. Thus, Jesus was actually saying that whatever judgments the scribes and Pharisees were handing down in their official capacity from the *Beth Din* ("Moses' seat"), those decisions must be followed. But, as Martin brings out, such judgments and decisions applied to the Jews as a whole—and were entirely *separate* from the frivolous and often contradictory traditions promoted by the scribes and Pharisees to their own followers. "There was a difference between the ordinary, independent teachings of the Pharisees which varied from time to time … and the commands which came *from Moses' Seat*. The commands *from Moses' Seat* did not entail matters of opinion among differing Pharisees, but rather they involved decisions of community importance which affected the whole of the Jewish nation…. Christ is not telling His disciples to obey the ordinary [tradition-based] teachings of the Pharisees, but He *is* commanding them *to obey every command* that came from Moses' Seat" (p. 92). For Jesus to do otherwise would have contradicted Moses.

Obviously, any time there is a conflict between *what God says* in His Word and what *any man says*—regardless of his position or level of authority—*God* is to be obeyed. For example, Peter and John were commanded by the Jewish leaders to abstain from preaching Christ in the area of Jerusalem—and were ultimately brought before a *council* (Acts 5:27-28). The Greek word here for *council* is not specific, and could refer to the Sanhedrin or the *Beth Din*. Note that Peter responds not by denying *their* authority, but by upholding God's *higher* authority. "We are obligated to obey God rather than men" (verse 29).

Other scholars contend that the "seat of Moses" was in first-century Judea representative of *authority* to *teach* the Scriptures. In fact, a literal *seat* existed in the major synagogues designated as "Moses' seat"—reserved for the elite scribal Pharisees. In his *Jewish New Testament Commentary*, David Stern writes, "The particular place in the synagogue where the leaders used to sit was known metaphorically as the seat of Moses or as the throne of [the] Torah, symbolizing the succession of teachers of [the] Torah down through the ages" (page 67; "Matt. 23:2"). But could the corrupt scribes and Pharisees really be credible teachers of the Torah?

A proper understanding of Matthew 23:2-3 reveals that there is no contradiction at all. In fact, Jesus' puzzling statement creates an important *contrast* between authority to judge *according to the Law* on the one hand, and the scribes' and Pharisees' *man-made traditions* on the other.

Christ did not address whether the scribes and Pharisees *rightly belonged* in Moses' seat—only stating that they indeed occupied it. As will be covered fully in upcoming chapters, the scribes and Pharisees surreptitiously presumed the role of teachers of the Scriptures when that responsibility was abrogated by the priesthood.[6] But regardless of *how* they came to occupy "Moses' seat," Jesus clearly affirmed their position—but *not* their example. He said, continuing: "But do not do according to their works; for they say and do not" (verse three). What Jesus was saying is simply this: The scribes and Pharisees occupy the judgment seat of Moses; insofar as they hand down judgments or teachings based on the written Torah, abide by those edicts and teachings. *But* do not follow their example—for as hypocrites they say one thing, and do another. He then refers broadly to their legal minutia of oral traditions—an altogether too difficult and unnecessary burden which they required of their patrons, yet, in their hypocrisy, failed to perform themselves (verse four).

Thus, Christ was actually *contrasting* the Mosaic Torah against the so-called oral law of the scribes and Pharisees—validating the Law of God while once again citing the Jewish leaders on their "traditions of men." This contrast served to set the stage for Jesus' subsequent seven "woes" against the scribes and Pharisees.

Again, it must be pointed out that Jesus' criticism of these religionists dealt primarily with their hypocritical *practice*—as opposed to their handling of the written Torah. Their real problem was their "traditions of men," which they held to be equal to Scripture and which often contradicted the laws of God, making them of no effect (Mark 7:13). The scribes' and Pharisees' preference for their traditions over the Scriptures frequently led to their failure to obey even the letter of the Law. This is why Jesus warned them, "Do not think that I will accuse you to the Father. **There is one who [already] accuses you**, **even Moses** [whom they claimed to follow].... Did not Moses give you the Law, and [yet] **not one of you is [genuinely] practicing the Law**?" (John 5:45; 7:19).

At no time did Jesus question the scribes' and Pharisees' authority as occupants of Moses' seat—and He never condemned anyone for *being* a Pharisee. But He did challenge their self-righteous piety that lacked the appropriate corresponding works. Thus, Jesus cautioned His followers to shun the scribes' and Pharisees' self-righteous and hypocritical practices. In fact, Jesus elsewhere warned that "unless your righteousness shall exceed the righteousness of the scribes and Pharisees"—who were held in high regard by the Common People—"there is no way that you shall enter into the kingdom of heaven" (Matt. 5:20). Christ's message was clear: True righteousness must be based on the heart, the inward *spirit*, and must spring from a genuine desire to obey God's laws fully, in both their letter and intent.

Viewed as a whole, Matthew 23 may be seen as a sort of lament, where Jesus grieves over the fact that the Jewish leadership had utterly failed in representing the *true* "religion" of Moses to the people—even to the point of rejecting their long-anticipated Messiah. Indeed, it is at the end of this strongly-worded chapter that we see Christ's love and compassion for His people. Using *Jerusalem* as representative of the Jewish leadership, He says, "Jerusalem, Jerusalem, you who kill the prophets and stone those who have been sent to you, how often would I have gathered your children together, even as a hen gathers her brood under her wings, **but you refused!** Behold, your house is [now] left to you [spiritually and physically] desolate" (verses 37-38). On another occasion Christ *wept* over Jerusalem, saying, "If you had known, even you, at least **in this your day [of opportunity and judgment]**, **the things [that would have made] for your peace**; but now they are **hidden from your eyes** [because of your unbelief]. For the days shall come upon you [in 69-70 AD] that your enemies shall cast a rampart about you, and shall enclose you around and keep you in on every side, and shall level you to the ground, and your children within you; and they shall not leave in you a stone upon a stone, **because you did not know the season of your visitation**" (Luke 19:41-44).

In the interest of fairness, it must be noted that some first-century Jewish leaders were *genuinely* seeking God. A certain *scribe*, for example, came to Jesus privately and said, in all sincerity, "Master, I will follow You wherever You may go" (Matt. 8:19). John the Baptist's father, Zacharias, a *priest*, and his mother, Elizabeth, were both "righteous before God, walking blamelessly in all the commandments and ordinances of the Lord" (Luke 1:5 -6). And, of course, Joseph "of Arimathea"—an "esteemed member" of the Sanhedrin (Mark 15:43)—who petitioned Pilate that he might take and bury Jesus' body. A secret "disciple of Jesus" (John 19:38), Joseph was a "good and righteous" (Luke 23:50) leader "waiting for the kingdom of God" (Mark 15:43). As a member of the Sanhedrin, Joseph no doubt voiced his concern that the long-anticipated Messiah had appeared—only to be ignored and ostracized. It is also certain that he attempted to defended Jesus as He was being falsely accused and condemned by the corrupt council.

Nicodemus—a Pharisee and probably a scribe—came to inquire of Jesus under the cover of night. Later, Nicodemus defended Christ (John 7:50-51) and assisted with His burial (John 19:39). And then there was "a man in Jerusalem whose name was Simeon; and this man was righteous and reverent, waiting for the [messianic] consolation of Israel; and the Holy Spirit was upon him" (Luke 2:25); and there was "Anna, a prophetess" who served God "day and night with fastings and supplications" (verses 36-37).

Roughly two decades after Jesus' death and resurrection, there were "**those who believed** [in Christ], **who were of the sect of the Pharisees**" (Acts 15:5). The apostle Paul, of course, boldly used his status as a Pharisee as a means of self-defense when standing before the Sanhedrin (Acts 23:6)—though it is certain he no longer continued in many of the sects' practices after his conversion.

These—and there were no doubt more—were the rare *exceptions*.

By the middle of the first century AD, *Pharisaism*—which would become Judaism—was a rapidly developing system of religion. One, *final* stage in its development remained—the period following the destruction of the Temple, which would result in the establishment of *rabbinic* Judaism and the compilation of the oral traditions as the *Mishnah*.

But already, in Jesus' day, "the synagogues and the chief outward forms of [what would soon become] Judaism were in [the] hands" of the scribes and Pharisees (Phillips, *Exploring the World of the Jew*, p. 37). As occupants of "Moses' seat," the scribes and Pharisees were the power behind mainstream Jewish religion. The question is, *How did they get there?*

CHAPTER TWO

The Early Seeds of Judaism

"When they knew God, they glorified Him not as God ... but became vain in their reasoning, and their foolish hearts were darkened. Professing themselves to be wise, they became fools."

The "Jews' religion" of first-century Palestine was the byproduct of centuries of change and upheaval. From the Babylonian Exile to the reforms of Ezra and Nehemiah—and from the Maccabean wars to the iron grip of Roman occupation—cultural, political and religious forces collided to shape the convoluted religion which would ultimately become known as *Judaism*. Benchmarks in that long and complex process include the augmented role of *scribes* after the close of the "age of the prophets,"[1] which led to the development of so-called *oral traditions*; the influence of Hellenism, which prompted the emergence of the *Hasidim*, progenitors of the sect of the Pharisees; the rise of *rabbinical* Judaism as a result of the fall of Jerusalem in 70 AD; and, finally, the writing of the *Mishnah* around 200 AD and the completion of the *Talmud* in 500 AD.

Yet, the term Judaism is often *misapplied*. It is typically assumed to be the "religion" of the Old Testament—or at least the "religion" of post-exilic Judea under Ezra and Nehemiah; the term is also frequently used to generalize the various religious movements of first century Palestine. But as has been premised, Judaism is *in no way* representative of the "religion" of Moses or the prophets. Neither is Judaism representative of the restorative period of Ezra and Nehemiah (though the stage *was* set at that time for the rise of the scribes to prominence)—nor is it a conglomerate of the various Jewish religions or creeds of Jesus' day. Rather, as will be demonstrated throughout this book, Judaism is a religious system which developed through the teachings of the Pharisees (with their scribal leaders) primarily in response to the Hellenization of Judea in the second and third centuries BC. (Even the term "Judeo-Christian" is quite misleading, as genuine Christianity is in no way congruent with Judaism; see Appendix Six.)

It is important to reiterate here that Judaism is *Pharisaic* in origin and reflects the specific ideology, doctrine and practice of that cult alone. The following quote from *The Jewish Encyclopedia* is telling: "[With] the destruction of the Temple [in 70 AD] the Sadducees disappeared altogether, leaving the regulation of all Jewish [religious] affairs in the hand of the Pharisees. Henceforth, Jewish [religious] life was regulated by the teachings of the Pharisees; the whole history of Judaism [developed] from the Pharisaic point of view, and a new aspect was given to the Sanhedrin of the past. A new chain of tradition supplanted the older, priestly tradition. **Pharisaism shaped the character of Judaism and the life and thought of the Jew for all the future**" (1905 edition, "Pharisees"; emphasis added).

When did Pharisaism *become* Judaism? Certainly, Pharisaism was alive and well by Jesus' time. However, the Pharisees obtained dominance only *after* the destruction of the Temple and the dismantling of the priesthood by the Romans. As will be brought out in a later chapter, 70 AD was a critical turning point in the development of Judaism, leading to the establishment of trained *rabbis* and academies at which to study the growing Mishnah—all of which gave significant impetus to the further development of the Pharisaic religion.

Thus, it seems that Judaism—as an organized and well-defined religious system—appeared as early as the *latter part* of the first century. Some scholars, however, contend that the Pharisees' religion could rightly be called Judaism only with the completion of the *Mishnah*. Michael Hoffman, for example, refers to the time frame (around 200 AD) in which "the corrupt and reprobate **oral occult tradition** of the [scribal and Pharisaic] elders was [finally] committed to writing and compiled as the Mishnah, comprising the first portion of the Talmud. At that juncture," he says, "the religion of Judaism was born" (*Judaism Discovered*, p. 140; emphasis added). [2]

To say the Jews' so-called oral law was pivotal to the development of Judaism is an understatement—for their oral tradition is the very heart and soul of the religion. In fact, while it took centuries for Judaism to firmly implant itself in Palestine, it all started with one, simple—yet incredibly Machiavellian—idea: a secondary *oral law* to "explain" the written Torah. Thus, as we examine the historical and religious development of Judaism, our focus must be to understand the *origin* and *character* of the one thing that stands between Moses and Judaism—the Jews' *oral tradition*.

The Babylonian Captivity

In the year 586 BC, Judah, the smaller of the two Hebrew kingdoms, came to its end. The prophet Jeremiah had repeatedly warned the Jews of the inevitability of captivity as punishment for their proclivity toward idolatry. Some 130 years earlier, the northern kingdom headed by the tribe of Ephraim had been defeated and taken into captivity by the Assyrians. They were never to return—scattered among nations, becoming the so-called "lost ten tribes" of Israel. In fact, Babylonians were brought in by the king of Assyria to occupy the land vacated by Israel (II Kings 17:6, 23-24). And now Judah—its nobles, its priests, the *am ha-aretz*, all but a remnant of the poorest—faced exile in Babylon.

As a matter of historical background, it is important to understand that the Jews of ancient Judea were comprised primarily of the tribes of Judah and Benjamin, and included the Levites (II Chron. 11:12-14). Yet they are collectively referred to throughout Scripture as the "Jews" (II Kings 18:26, 28; Ezra 4:12; Jer. 40:11-12; etc.). Thus, *Jews* represent but a small segment of the original 12 tribes of the nation of Israel. Tremendous confusion has resulted from the claim by Jews today that *they* are *Israel*. This claim is patently *false*; Jews still represent only a *tiny fraction* of what was once the biblical nation of Israel. Jesus, in fact, sent His Jewish disciples to preach the gospel to the "lost sheep of the house of Israel" (Matt. 10:6). (For more on the identity of Jews, ancient and modern, see Appendix Three.)

It was during the exilic period that the first seeds of Judaism were sown. It is precisely for this reason that J. D. Douglas writes, "Judaism is the religion of the Jews, in contrast to that of the Old Testament.... Judaism should be regarded as **beginning with the Babylonian exile**" (*New Bible Dictionary*, "Judaism"; emphasis added). What Douglas means is that the Babylonian captivity provided fertile ground for the origin of *new ideas* that would, in time, prove foundational in the development of Judaism. Paul Johnson makes the interesting observation that the Exile's "*creative force was overwhelming*" (*A History of the Jews*, p. 83). George Robinson writes that the Exile "impelled the leaders of the Jewish people to *reshape* their religious practice" (*Essential Judaism*, p. 296). In other words, the Jews were compelled by their new circumstances to *reinvent* their religion.

According to John Phillips, without their Temple and an organized priesthood, the Jews in exile "began to *experiment* with Judaism itself" (*Exploring the World of the Jew*, p. 31.) Judaism, of course, did not yet exist; here, Phillips erroneously uses "Judaism" to refer to the "religion" of Moses and the prophets. He adds, "They substituted the synagogue for the Temple, prayers for the Levitical rituals [and] **scribes for the priests**.... The destruction of the Jerusalem Temple by Nebuchadnezzar (586 BC) diluted the authority of the Aaronic priesthood to the point that **a new elite class arose and** [over time] **took their place, the rabbis**" (pp. 31, 58; emphasis added). Phillips' use of *rabbi* simply means *teacher*, referring to the scribes; the term *rabbi* was not generally used until much later. He continues: "During the captivity in Babylon, those **new teachers assumed the custodianship** of divine truth. In the process of time they evolved a [fundamental] principle: At Sinai, God had handed Moses *two* sets of laws: the *written* Law, inscribed on the tablets of stone, and the *oral* law, which, so they said, gave specific elaboration on the [written] Torah" (p. 58; emphasis added).

This all-important transition in the role of the scribes occurred slowly, imperceptibly—and certainly continued into the post-exilic period and the time of Maccabean rule. But Phillips' point is that *even in Babylon* the scribes were already beginning to expand their role, positioning themselves as authorities on the Scriptures. And while the idea of an adjunct oral law did not actually originate *in Babylon*, it did ultimately arise as a direct result of the scribes' new role as "custodians of the truth." Referring to those who worked alongside the prophets (Jeremiah, Ezekiel and Daniel) during exile, Solomon Grayzel likewise writes that "**another type of leader arose during this period**—*the scribe*. The scribe was a man whose chief interest lay in the preservation of the old [sacred] literature of the Hebrews. He collected the writings ... [and] made them available for the Babylonian exiles to read" (*A History of the Jews*, p. 18; emphasis added).

On this point it is prudent to repeat a statement by Johnson, quoted earlier. In exile, he writes, the Jews "turned to their writings—their laws, and the records of their past. **From this time we hear more of the scribes**. Hitherto, they had simply been secretaries, like Baruch, writing down the words of the great. **Now they became an important caste**, **setting down in writing** [in rough, preliminary form] **oral traditions** [in addition to] copying precious scrolls brought from the ruined Temple..." (p. 82; emphasis added).

Early scribes served kings as *secretaries*, such as Shaphan under Josiah (II Kings 22:3); other scribes took dictation, such as Baruch, who recorded what Jeremiah spoke (Jer. 36:32). They appear to be educated—able to read and write well. With their Levitical heritage and close association with both the priesthood and the prophets, the scribes from the exilic period began moving beyond their ancient position, gradually taking on a scholarly role—studying and, ultimately, *teaching* the Scriptures.

Prominent modern-day rabbis agree that Judaism traces its roots to the exilic period. In the 1934 Soncino edition of *The Babylonian Talmud*, the renown Rabbi J. H. Hertz[3] writes in the foreword: "The beginnings of Talmudic literature date back to the time of the Babylonian Exile ... [which was] a momentous period in the history of [the Jews]. During that exile, Israel [actually, **Judah**] **found itself**. [The Jews] not only **rediscovered the** [written] **Torah and made it the rule of life**, **but under its influence new religious institutions, such as the synagogue**, i.e., **congregational worship without a priest or ritual**, **came into existence**..." (p. 13; emphasis added).

Hertz's comment that the Jews' "rediscovered the Torah" suggests a "religious revival" of sorts. But now the *synagogue* (out of necessity) had become the center of worship; the *scribes* were fast becoming the premier teachers of the Law; and, most significant of all, the Word of God for the first time began to be *explored* and *interpreted* by non-priestly Levitical scribes—contrary to the explicit instructions of the Scriptures. Again, the prophet Malachi is unmistakable when he says that "the priest's lips should keep knowledge, and the people should seek the Law at his mouth; for he is the messenger of the LORD of hosts" (Mal. 2:7).

Despite the Jews' good intentions, the Babylonian Exile spawned an era of religious experimentation and free thinking. No wonder Hertz adds that even as early as the period of the Exile, Babylon was an "*autonomous* Jewish center" in the development of Judaism (p. 21). Ultimately, as we see following the restoration period under Ezra and Nehemiah, it was only a matter of time before the *scribes*—the grassroots leaders of Jewish religious revival—established their preeminence and began to imagine a so-called "oral Torah."

The Reformation of Ezra and Nehemiah

The Babylonian Empire passed into history in 539 BC, and the Medo-Persian Empire took its place. Cyrus the Persian had new ideas about how to govern the vast empire he had won from Babylon. Instead of forcing his subjects to become a cultural homogeny, he allowed each vassal state to retain a significant measure of independence. This meant the Jews would be afforded an opportunity to return to Palestine and restore their land and rebuild their Temple. Indeed, the Jews' exile in Babylon ended after 70 years, just as Jeremiah had foretold.

It must be realized, however, that the majority of Jews did *not* return to Palestine. Robinson writes that roughly 50,000 Jews—about ten percent of those exiled—returned to the Promised Land under the leadership of Joshua and Zerubbabel (*Essential Judaism*, p. 296). Most remained in the Mesopotamian area, and under the benevolent rule of Cyrus became land owners, built homes, schools and synagogues, started businesses—with many becoming wealthy and influential. Even with *later migrations* back to Judea, the overwhelming majority of Jews remained in the area. In fact, as late as the first century AD there were more Jews *still* in Babylon than in Palestine. This is why Peter—the apostle to the "circumcision" (Gal. 2:7)—spent considerable time in Babylon, preaching to the Jews of the Diaspora.

Under Joshua and Zerubbabel the Temple was rebuilt and dedicated in 515 BC. Fifty-eight years later, in 457 BC, Ezra the scribe led a second group of Jews to Judea. In addition to being a scribe *skilled* in the Law of God (Ezra 7:6), Ezra was a priest of the Aaronic line (verses 11-12, 21). The historian Josephus writes that Ezra was the "principal priest" of the Jews in Babylon (*Antiquities of the Jews*, XI, 5,1). Ezra had diligently "prepared his heart to seek the Law of the LORD, and to do it, and to teach [God's] statutes and ordinances" to the Jews (Ezra 7:10). Twelve years later, Nehemiah, an official of the Persian government, relocated to Palestine to assist Ezra.

Both Ezra and Nehemiah were on a mission—to restore the right worship of God and rebuild Jerusalem (its walls in particular). Ernest Martin writes that Ezra and Nehemiah—with the help of Malachi, the last of the prophets before John the Baptist—were "largely successful in bringing the people an awareness of God's true religion" ("Between The Testaments," from *Tomorrow's World*, Sept. 1971, p. 20). Once the wall of Jerusalem was rebuilt, attention was given to instructing the Jews in the ways of God. Ezra and Nehemiah instituted the practice of reading the Scriptures aloud to the people, interpreting the difficult passages. We read in Nehemiah that Ezra, assisted by certain Levites, "caused the people to understand the Law" as they "read distinctly from the Book of the Law" and "expounded the meaning" (Neh. 8:7-8). This passage suggests that *non-priestly* Levitical scribes were used—perhaps following a precedent set during exile—to expound the Scriptures to the people. Grayzel writes that "**the scribes**, Ezra's pupils and colleagues, **undertook to spread the knowledge of the** [written] **Torah** and of the prophetic literature" (*A History of the Jews*, p. 31; emphasis added). No doubt many of these scribes were, like Ezra, *also* priests. Apparently, however, Levitical scribes who were *not* of the Aaronic line had begun to be used to teach the Scriptures—a trend that would ultimately challenge the authority of the priesthood.

One of the difficulties of this time was that the average Jew could no longer speak Hebrew (the language of the Scriptures). Aramaic had replaced Hebrew as the language of culture and commerce. Of this, Charles Pfeiffer writes, "During the Exile there arose a change in the linguistic habits of the Jews. Aramaic, the language of diplomacy in the Persian Empire, became the vernacular of the Jews—both those who returned to Palestine and those who remained in the eastern provinces of the empire. Jews who spoke only Aramaic would not be able to understand the Hebrew Scriptures without an interpreter. The custom arose of reading the Hebrew bible in the synagogue service, after which an explanation would be given in the vernacular Aramaic" (*Old Testament History*, p. 494). This of course made the Common People *highly dependent* on the scholarly scribes for interpretation. Hinting at the significance of the situation, Pfeiffer adds: "This oral explanation in time became a discourse, **interpreting and applying the biblical message**. Generations later **these explanations**, or '*targums*,' **were themselves written down**…" (p. 494; emphasis added). Similar explanations and interpretations would eventually form the earliest *midrashim*—scribal commentaries on the Scriptures (*midrash* means to *comment* or *expound*; see Appendix One.) And remember, the scribes were not only experts on the Mosaic Law, they were skilled at preserving the spoken word in writing.

A pivotal accomplishment under the leadership of Ezra and Nehemiah was the formation of the *Great Assembly* (or Great Synagogue), a 120-member body of priests organized to guide the Jews in religious matters. As a religious "supreme court," the Great Assembly was, according to Martin, "the center of authority in regard to education … and teaching the people the Law of Moses" (*Is Judaism the Religion of Moses?*, p. 22). Martin brings out that the Assembly was—at least from the beginning—composed of *only* priests, with the High Priest as its head. However, the priests utilized "regular Levites … [who] did much of the actual teaching…. In effect, **the Levites represented the professional class among the people**" (p. 32; emphasis added). This "professional class" was made up of none other than scholarly *scribes* who, perhaps unintentionally, were already beginning to assume the coveted role of teachers of the Scriptures.

In his *Jewish New Testament Commentary*, David Stern writes that in post-exilic Judah "the earliest students, developers and upholders of the [written] Torah seem to have been of the hereditary priestly caste—Ezra himself was both a *cohen* [priest] and a *sofer* [scribe]. But later, as the *cohanim* were drawn back into caring for the sacrificial system as it developed during the Second Temple period, **a lay movement which supported the [written] Torah and favored its adaptation to the needs of the people arose and began to challenge the authority of the *cohanim***" (p. 18;

"Matt. 3:7"; emphasis added). This "lay movement"—Martin's "professional class" of Levitical scribes—would team up generations later with the Pharisees in the development of Judaism.

For now, the scribes were content to work under the leadership of the priests of the Great Assembly in expounding the Scriptures in a mostly straightforward fashion. However, once Ezra and Nehemiah passed from the scene, the scribes' push for preeminence would accelerate.

Rise of the *Sopherim*

The passing of Ezra and Nehemiah brought an *end* to what might be considered an "era of discipline"—a period marked by the circumspect use of the Scriptures. Moreover, with the passing of the prophet Malachi, the "age of the prophets" also ended. As we will see, a subsequent *change* in the leadership of the Jews would occur—subtly, imperceptibly.

Of this time, Grayzel writes that it was "as though a curtain fell upon Judea and hid from sight all that went on within the tiny land. In fact, during the century between 450 and 350 BC [or, most likely, about 430 to 330 BC], the entire ancient East seems to have fallen asleep" (p. 33). It was a century of relative peace and quiet, but one of gradual change. During this entire period the Jews were allowed complete freedom by the Persians to practice their own customs, traditions and religion as they saw fit. Grayzel adds that while records from that time are few, "**important changes were taking place** which make that century one of the most fruitful in Jewish history. These **changes were practically all intellectual and religious**, **therefore slow**, **outwardly invisible and un-dramatic**" (p. 33; emphasis added). And most importantly, key changes were taking place in the Great Assembly—both in its composition and in its thinking.

As brought out earlier, the Great Assembly was originally composed of only priests (or priestly scribes). Over time, however, this would change. The hereditary, Aaronic requirement for membership in the Great Assembly gradually became unimportant; rather, what became important was the level of scholarly *knowledge* possessed by the scribe. *Knowledge*, as we will see, equaled power and prestige.

Because of the growing emphasis on the role of *scribes*—as opposed to the role of the priesthood—the Great Assembly was typically referred to as *the Sopherim* (the plural of *sopher*, sometimes *sofer*), though the term is also used collectively of scribes in general. Originally, the *sopher* or scribe was much like a secretary—he recorded information, kept the royal archives and made copies of books. *Sopher*, in ancient Hebrew, meant to *count* or to *relate* a thing. Under Ezra, the *sopherim* were responsible for copying the scrolls of the Scriptures; as a safeguard against corruption, they *counted* every letter of each line. This *counting* is no doubt how the term *sopher* came to refer to the scribes. In a broader sense, however, scribes were looked upon with a certain awe. They were educated and could read and write; they were considered an elite group occupied with books and the interpretation of books. Ultimately, *scribe* became synonymous with *wise one* (see I Chron. 27:32).

According to Phillips, after the passing of Ezra and Nehemiah "**a new breed of interpreters**, the *sopherim*, or scribes, **emerged and took over the interpretation of Scripture**" (*Exploring the World of the Jew*, p. 34; emphasis added). Joachim Jeremias refers to the same period: "Together with the old ruling class composed of the hereditary nobility of priests ... **there grew up in the last centuries BC a new upper class**, **that of the scribes**" (*Jerusalem in the Time of Jesus*, p. 233; emphasis added). Over time, the Great Assembly moved from simply interpreting Scripture to creating laws and ordinances of their own. Robinson writes that during this time the Great Assembly "**offered oral rulings** on the [written] Torah and its precepts" (*Essential Judaism*, p. 312). These "oral rulings" were the beginnings of what would become the oral law. Notice what Hertz writes in his foreword to *The Babylonian Talmud*: "At the reestablishment of the Jewish Commonwealth, Ezra the *sofer*, or scribe ... formally proclaimed the [written] Torah the civil and religious law of the new commonwealth.... His successors, called after him *soferim* (scribes), otherwise known as the 'Men of the Great Assembly,' continued his work. [Over time] **their teachings and ordinances** received the sanction of popular practice, and came to be looked upon as *halachah*, literally 'the trodden path,' the clear **religious guidance** to the Israelite [Jew] in the way he should go" (p. 14). [4]

Phillips continues, adding that the scribes' "commentaries **gradually assumed semi-inspired status** and eventually [over a period of several decades] **practically replaced the Word of God altogether**. Those [very early] commentaries [however] were the **first tender shoots of the *Midrash*** [oral expositions on the Scriptures]. **In time**, **that exegetical growth flourished into the vast**, **tangled jungle of the Talmud**..." (p. 34; emphasis added). Phillips concludes that it was "in the *Midrash*"—those early *oral commentaries* on the written Torah—"that the *seeds* of the Talmud were sown" (p. 58).

Grayzel informs us that scribal "writers and teachers molded the destiny of the Jews.... The entire **transformation in the life of the Jews** from this time on [the period following Ezra and Nehemiah] was the result of **teaching and interpretation. The scribes encouraged knowledge** ... they created literature; **they formulated laws**. They **derived from the sacred books those ideas** which were to guide their own people and, in time, inspire others" (p. 37; emphasis added). He adds that "whereas in the days of [Ezra and] Nehemiah the influence of the scribes was slight, **a century later their ideas had become tremendously influential.... [Their] discussions [concerning Scripture] became embodied in traditional interpretations of the Bible** which, under the name of [the] **Oral Law**, guided the Jews of later ages" (p. 38; emphasis added). In reality, the scribes' traditional interpretations, commentaries and discussions on the Scriptures became the very foundation of the "oral law."

According to the *Cyclopedia of Biblical, Theological and Ecclesiastical Literature*, the sopherim were to perform the following functions: make copies of the Scriptures; prevent the corruption of Scripture (through their systematic counting of letters); read and interpret the Law to the people; set up schools for the study of the Scriptures; and, establish "**prohibitory laws**" to protect the written Torah from being violated (vol. 9, p. 466). What were these "prohibitory laws"? Simon the Just—a noted head of the Great Assembly near the close of this period, just before Greek culture was introduced to Judea—is thus quoted in the above volume: "Our fathers have taught us three things: to be cautious in judging, to train many scholars and **to set a fence about the Law**" (p. 468; emphasis added). Solomon Landman concurs, writing that "the makers of the Oral Law felt it their duty **to build a 'fence around the** [written] **Torah,' to make rules that would keep the religion pure and the people holy**…" (*Story Without End*, p. 74; emphasis added). [5]

Undoubtedly, this so-called "prohibitory fence" about the Torah—as well-meaning as it may have been—was central to the development of the oral law. The scribes' "teachings and ordinances," "oral rulings," "prohibitory laws" ("fences"), and *midrashim* all point to one thing—their new-found role as guardians of Scripture and expositors of religious *tradition*. Over time the scribes would become a distinct class of educated "doctors of the law"—covering not only the Scriptures, but the entire field of Jewish civil and religious law. The seeds of the Talmud had been sown: What began innocently enough as various interpretations, comments and rulings would eventually *take on an esoteric nature*, evolving into a complex legal code that would in time eclipse even the Scriptures.

Esoteric Knowledge as Power

The *reverence* given the sopherim was extraordinary. By the time of the beginning of Hellenistic influence—about a century after Ezra and Nehemiah—not only were the scribes virtually on an equal footing with the priesthood, they were deemed worthy of honor typically shown only to the prophets. Grayzel writes: "As in government the high priest replaced the king, so **in religious life the scribes took the place of the prophets**. More prophets were not needed because the Jews now had books in which were written down the ideas of the great prophets of the past…. The scribes, who were the teachers, read these books before an assembled multitude and interpreted what Moses and his successors demanded of the Jewish people" (*A History of the Jews*, p. 36; emphasis added).

Without question, the key to the scribes' esteemed position was their knowledge—*esoteric* knowledge to be exact. Such knowledge was regarded as more important than even the hereditary (Aaronic) standard followed by the priesthood. Jeremias discusses this at length: "When we look for the origin of these scribes, a varied picture emerges," he begins. "Among the scribes of Jerusalem ... we find men who were not of pure Israelite descent" (*Jerusalem in the Time of Jesus*, p. 233). In fact, it seems that various scribes "had pagan blood in their veins." And while such scribes "played a prominent role, it was not as a result of their origin [lineage]"—as many were of an "obscure birth" (p. 235).

Rather, according to Jeremias, "**it was knowledge alone which gave their power to the scribes**. Anyone [of any lineage] who wished to join the company of scribes by ordination had [only] to pursue a regular course of study for several years" (p. 235; emphasis added). Typically, at the age of 40 the trainee became a "member with full rights, an ordained scholar.... [And] only ordained teachers transmitted and created the **traditions derived from the** [written] **Torah** which ... were **regarded as equal to and indeed above the Torah**" (p. 236; emphasis added).

The growing influence and power of the scribes was apparent in everyday Jewish life. "When a community was faced with a choice between a layman and a scribe for ... the office of elder to a community, or ruler of the synagogue, or of judge, [the people] invariably **preferred the scribe**. This means that a large number of important posts hitherto held by priests and laymen of high rank had, [by] the first century AD, passed entirely, or predominantly, into the hands of the scribes." Again, *knowledge* was the key. "The deciding factor was not that the scribes were the guardians of tradition in the domain of religious legislation, and because of this could occupy key positions in society, but rather the fact, far too little recognized, that **they were the guardians of secret knowledge**, **of an esoteric tradition**" (Jeremias, p. 237; emphasis added).

Jeremias notes that the scribes' mysterious knowledge "had as its object ... the deepest secrets of the divine being" and was thus *not* to "be divulged to unauthorized people." Indeed, "the whole of the oral tradition, particularly the *halakah* [religious ordinances], was an esoteric doctrine to the extent that, although taught in places of instruction and in synagogues, it could not be propagated by the written word since it was the secret of God..." (pp. 237, 241). Similarly, Robinson brings out that the sopherim declined to put the oral traditions into writing because they knew such laws would *compete* with the Scriptures (which they did anyway). They also saw the oral law as "subject to future change, a malleable thing." Moreover, "to write it down would be to freeze it, to institutionalize it" (*Essential Judaism*, p. 313). Undoubtedly, the scribes also realized that to put such knowledge into writing and make it widely available would deprive it of its esoteric nature and subsequently dilute their authority and prestige. They, above all, understood that it was *secret knowledge* which gave them power.

Jeremias continues: "It is only when we have realized the esoteric character of the teachings of the scribes ... concerning the whole of the oral tradition, even with respect to the text of the Old Testament, that we shall be able to understand the social position of the scribes. From a social point of view **they were, as possessors of divine esoteric knowledge, the**

immediate heirs and successors of the prophets" (p. 241; emphasis added). By way of support, Jeremias quotes the *Palestinian Talmud*: " 'The prophet and the scribe, to whom shall we liken them? To two messengers of one and the same king.'… (j. Ber. i.7, 3b.56)" (p. 242). According to Jeremias, the context in which this Talmudic quote appears attempts to position the authority of the scribe *above* that of the prophet (p. 242, footnote 27).

In describing the lofty role of the scribes, Jeremias adds, "It may be that a [particular] scribe is of very doubtful origin, even of non-Israelite [origin], but that [fact] does not affect his prestige in the slightest…. Like the prophets, **the scribes are servants of God along with the clergy** [priests]; like the prophets, **they gather round themselves pupils to whom they pass on their doctrine**; like the prophets, **they are authorized in their office**, not by proving their [hereditary] origin like the priests were, but **solely by their knowledge of the divine will** which they announce by their teaching, their judgments and their preaching" (p. 242; emphasis added).

What scholars generally refer to as the "age of the prophets" passed with Malachi. Apparently, God would simply leave the Jews to their own devices until the introduction of the New Covenant by John the Baptist, the next prophet in line. Meanwhile, as Jeremias notes, "**the scribes were venerated, like the prophets of old, with unbounded respect and reverential awe**, as bearers and teachers of sacred esoteric knowledge; **their words had sovereign authority**" (p. 243; emphasis added). As we will see, it was the scribes' knowledge and scholarly authority that captured the imagination of the *Hasidim*—those pious, "People of the Land" who courageously fought against the corrupting influence of Hellenism. Ultimately, the *Hasidim* would become the Pharisees—led, empowered and motivated by the venerated scribes with their mystical knowledge.

CHAPTER THREE

Hellenization and
The Rise of the Pharisees

*"As I am their witness, the Jews have a zeal for God,
but not according to right knowledge."*

As subjects of the Persian empire, the Jews enjoyed relative peace and quiet—and complete freedom of religious practice. This, however, was about to change. In 332 BC—just over a hundred years from the time of Ezra and Nehemiah—Alexander the Great acquired Palestine. While he was quite tolerant of the Jews' religion, Alexander was committed to the creation of a world united by Greek language and culture—*Hellenism*.[1] As history records, Alexander himself posed little threat to Judea; his successors, however, would aggressively promote his Hellenistic policy. As we will see, it was the *corrupting influence* of Hellenism on the Aaronic priesthood that led to their loss of favor among the People of the Land and the subsequent rise of the *Hasidim*, the progenitors of the Pharisees. With the aid of their scribal cohorts, the outcome would ultimately be Judaism.

Already centuries old and rife with paganism, the underlying philosophy behind Hellenism was *freedom of the individual*—that every man had the "right to think for himself." Ernest Martin writes that "this philosophy—freedom of thought or individualism—which is seemingly altruistic in principle, resulted in myriads of confusing and contradictory beliefs among the Greeks in every phase of life. Every man was allowed his own ideas about the sciences, the arts, laws, and about religion. So varied were the opinions among the Greek scholars in the various fields of study that individuals took pride in contending with one another over who could present the greatest 'wisdom' and 'knowledge' on any particular subject" (*Is Judaism the Religion of Moses?*, p. 37).

The *pervasive influence* of Hellenism on Jewish culture and religion must not be underestimated. Within a generation of Alexander's conquest of Palestine, the entire ancient East throbbed with new life—new ideas, new names for old gods, new methods of administration, a new language, and new markets for trade—all of which led to the awakening of the East from the quiet lethargy of easygoing Persian rule. Importantly, Solomon Grayzel notes that Hellenism—as compared to the effects of exile in Babylon—was "more persistent and more subtle in its efforts to lure the Jews from their [Scripture based] way of life" (*A History of the Jews*, pp. 41-42). Martin brings out that the Jews found it impossible to escape the omnipresence of

Hellenistic thought. And Greek quickly became the language of commerce and social intercourse, making it necessary to acquire fluency in Greek (p. 77). In *Story Without End*, Solomon Landman writes that the Jews were "*charmed* by the customs and manners, by the very spirit of the Greeks" (p. 73). But as we will see, nowhere was this effect more pronounced than, ironically, among the leaders of the Jews—the chief priests.

Alexander's rule was short lived. No sooner had he been put to rest than his generals began to contend for control of the empire. A long and complicated series of wars followed between the dynasties formed by two particularly important generals, Ptolemy and Seleucus—with Palestine often caught in the middle. Judea first passed under the rule of the Ptolemies of Egypt; later, the Seleucids of Syria would control Palestine. Both Greek kingdoms were strict proponents of Hellenism.

One of the key changes of this period—probably under the rule of the Ptolemies—was the dismantling of the Great Assembly. Of this, Martin writes: "Within a score of years after the coming of the Greeks, the Great Assembly disappears from history as an organized body having religious control over the Jewish people. It is not known how the Greeks dismissed this authoritative religious body from its official capacity as teachers of the Law, but it is obvious that the authority of the Great Assembly was eroded and the Greek leaders forbade them to teach" ("Between The Testaments," from *Tomorrow's World*, p. 21).

Without the guidance of the Great Assembly, many Jews began to adopt Greek customs. Almost everything the Greeks brought to the Jews was antagonistic to the laws of God; the rule of Scripture was rapidly being replaced by Hellenistic ideas. Martin adds that the *Sopherim* were divested of all authority: "So thorough was the dissolution of the *Sopherim* **as a corporate body** [i.e., the Great Assembly] that we hear nothing more of any of its members outside of Simon the Just, the High Priest who died in 270 BC" (p. 44; emphasis added). But the highly-respected "doctors of the law" had by no means become extinct. As we will see, they continued quietly, exerting their influence wherever possible; in generations to come, they would find a new venue from which to teach their lofty doctrines—the *Pharisees*.

According to Martin, the period of Ptolemaic rule—roughly 100 years in duration—was an era of religious disarray during which Hellenism made its greatest inroads. Quoting the historian Jacob Lauterbach, Martin writes: "There prevailed a state of religious anarchy, wherein the practical life of the people was ... [no longer] controlled by the law of the fathers as interpreted by the religious authorities, nor were the activities of the teachers [scribes] carried on in an official way by an authoritative body. This chaotic state of affairs lasted for a period of about eighty years.... [During this time] many new practices [were] gradually adopted by the people" (pp. 45-46; from *Rabbinic Essays*, pp. 200, 206).[2] During this period of Ptolemaic rule, Greek ideas, customs and morality were rapidly absorbed by the Jews. According to

Martin, "what had been started by Alexander the Great was **brought to its greatest degree of perfection among the Jews during this one-hundred-year period**…. [The] Jews during this period of Egyptian control, by the sheer force of environment and circumstance, **surrendered themselves to Hellenistic ideas and ways of life**" (*Is Judaism the Religion of Moses?*, p. 39; emphasis added).

The Scribes Discover Greek Logic

Without question, Hellenization had a dramatic impact on the Jews *as a whole*, leaving no area of life untouched. However, the effects of Greek culture on the Jews' religion were most significant—in three specific areas. First, as amazing as it sounds, the priesthood's response to Hellenism was *outright acceptance*—and, as we will see, not without considerable consequences. Second, Hellenization led to the rise of a *new* religious element—the *Hasidim*, a grassroots movement of pious Jews who stood for the "old time" religion of Moses and the prophets.

Third, in the case of the scribes, the effects of Greek culture were *subtle*, yet equally profound. Though no longer functioning as an organized body (such as through the Great Assembly) the *sopherim* continued to be held in high regard. They continued in their study of the Scriptures, passing on their esoteric knowledge to eager students. For the most part, the scribes resisted the liberal ideas of Hellenism, finding them contrary to Scripture. But then, there was Greek *logic*—utterly irresistible to the scholarly mind of the scribe. Of this time, John Phillips writes that while many Jews, such as those of the Aaronic priesthood, "became outright Hellenists and openly embraced the liberal ideas of the day," the Jewish scholars "added new ideas to their approach to biblical truth. They **replaced the old and approved allegorical approach with a new, exciting logical approach**." It would not be long, he adds, "before a **lush new tangle of exegetical undergrowth** began to emerge to add to the already spreading" oral tradition (*Exploring the World of the Jew*, pp. 34-35; emphasis added).

Further tracing the development of the oral law to the time of Greek influence, Phillips makes this telling statement: "It was in the [oral commentaries of the] *Midrash*"—which first appeared following the time of Ezra—"that the seeds of [what would become] the Talmud were sown. In the conquests of Alexander the Great and the subsequent Hellenizing of the world, the Jews faced a tremendous survival challenge…. The naive and artless interpretations of the [written] Torah, offered by the *Midrash*, would no longer suffice in an age of intellectual vigor [*liberal thinking*]. The rabbis [scribes] **began to add Greek reasoning to biblical revelation. The result was the *Mishnah*, the work of a new set of Jewish scholars** known as the *Tannas*" (pp. 58-59; emphasis added; see Appendix One). *Mishnah* means "teachings." It is derived from the Hebrew root *shanah*, which originally meant "to repeat"—as in orally passing on a teaching. Composing a major portion of the Talmud, *Mishnah*—as "the oral doctrine from the earliest Midrash of the Sopherim"—is used generally to "designate the law which was transmitted orally" (*The Jewish Encyclopedia*, "Mishnah"). *Tannas* is Aramaic and, not surprisingly, means "repeaters."

Continuing Phillips' quote: "Instead of the allegories and homilies of the Midrash, the Tannas employed logic and reasoning borrowed from the Greeks…. Like the Midrash, [the Mishnah that developed] was a somewhat jumbled exposition of truth, and, like the Midrash, it kept on **diluting the Word of God with liberal quantities of fallible human opinion**" (p. 59; emphasis added). "The *artless* commentaries of the Midrash"—the simple, oral exegesis of Scripture—"were [during the time of Ptolemaic rule of Judah] seen by the Jews as inadequate in an age of Greek enlightenment. Adding Greek logic to their hermeneutics, the rabbis [scribes] **overhauled their views and developed the Mishnah**" (p. 63; emphasis added). [3]

By "artless," Phillips suggests that the scribes' *midrashim* were, as yet, *uncontrived*. They were genuine attempts to explain the Scriptures. But the idea of a so-called "oral law" was *most* contrived. In fact, with religious constraints cast off, *new ideas* found fertile ground among these Jewish scholars. Thus, while *outwardly* supporting the Scriptures and resisting Hellenization, the scribes could *justify virtually any doctrine* by making the claim that it was part of an esoteric oral tradition—hidden all along in the depths of the written Torah.

Rise of the "Pious Ones"

The rise of the *Hasidim* is of particular importance in the development of Judaism. As has already been mentioned, the Hasidim were, in fact, the immediate forerunners of the *Pharisees*. As a grassroots movement of *pious* Jews, their emergence must be understood primarily as a response to the wholesale acceptance of Greek culture by the Aaronic priesthood. The Hasidim were unalterably opposed to the corrupting effects of Hellenism; and, as we will see, it was precisely the indiscriminate adoption of Hellenistic ideals by the priesthood that propelled the Hasidim to the forefront—to "stand in the gap," as it were. [4]

Thus, to understand the role of the Hasidim in Jewish religion, we must first examine the lamentable response of the priesthood to the lure of Hellenism. On this point, Paul Johnson rhetorically asks, "How were the Jews to react to this cultural invasion, which was *opportunity*, *temptation* and *threat* all in one?" (*A History of the Jews*, p. 98). Ironically, those best equipped to resist the temptation of Hellenism proved the most vulnerable. Instead of realizing the humble, *servant nature* of their God-given role, the priesthood clearly identified itself with the nobility, the upper class, the elite of Judah, who were also strongly attracted to Hellenistic culture. Johnson continues: "Many of the better-educated Jews found Greek culture profoundly attractive…. [Many found themselves] torn between new, foreign ideas and inherited piety. It was a destabilizing force spiritually and, above all, it was a secularizing, materialistic force…. In Palestine, as in other Greek conquests, **it was the upper classes, the rich, the senior priests, who were most tempted**…" (p. 99; emphasis added). Similarly, Grayzel writes that Greek culture had its greatest effect on "the upper classes—the nobility, that is, **the chief families among the priests** who lived in Jerusalem…" (*A History of the Jews*, p. 49; emphasis added).

Describing the courageous position of the Hasidim, Landman writes: "[It was with a] mounting sense of horror that the pious elders watched the process of [the] Hellenization of the Jews…. The Pious Ones, or *Hasidim* as they came to be called, wanted the Jews to differentiate themselves sharply from the Greeks and from the Hellenized Jews as well…. The Hasidim were not simply fanatics or killjoys; they were objecting to the watering-down of Jewish life and faith, **particularly because it was the aristocratic priests … who had become** [the most] **Hellenized**" (*Story Without End*, pp. 75-76; emphasis added). Johnson likewise portrays the Hasidim: "Between the isolationists [those who would ultimately form such antisocial fringe groups as the Essenes] on the one hand and the Hellenizers [the wealthy nobility and the priesthood] on the other was a **broad group of pious Jews in the tradition of Josiah, Ezekiel and Ezra**. Many of them did not object to Greek rule in principle, any more than they had objected to the Persians…. They were quite willing to pay the conqueror's taxes provided they were **left to practice their religion in peace**" (p. 100; emphasis added).

In 198 BC, the Seleucid kingdom of Syria forced the Egyptians to give up Palestine. Like the Ptolemies, the Seleucids were of Greek origin and equally Hellenistic in culture and outlook. At the onset, conditions in Judea remained unchanged. In fact, the Seleucid ruler, Antiochus III (the "Great"), was favorably inclined toward the Jews. Conditions changed rapidly, however, with the coming of Antiochus IV (*Epiphanes*) in 175 BC. As we will see, the corruption of the Aaronic priesthood reached its apex during the rule of this iniquitous Seleucid ruler.

Shortly after he ascended the throne, a group of Hellenizing Jewish leaders approached Antiochus with a clever plan to speed up the process of Hellenization. This "reform party" paid Antiochus a large sum of money to remove the current High Priest, Onias III, and appoint his Hellenized brother, Jason, to the coveted office. They had hoped Jason would help promote Hellenistic ideals. By this time the priesthood was well Hellenized, which brought with it a callous disregard for the sanctity of the office. As Martin notes, "the position of High Priest had dwindled to more of an aristocratic political honor. There was little regard paid to the Law of God by these High Priests. Most of them were outright Hellenists" (*Is Judaism the Religion of Moses?*, p. 40).

Of this time of political intrigue, Johnson writes that "any possibility of Greeks and Jews living together in reasonable comfort was destroyed by the rise of **a Jewish reform party who wanted to force the**

pace of Hellenization. This reform movement ... was strongest among the ruling class of Judah [the priesthood], already half-Hellenized themselves, who wanted to drag the little temple-state into the modern age. Their motives were primarily secular and economic" (p. 100; emphasis added). He adds that "the Jewish reform movement found an enthusiastic but dangerous ally in the new Seleucid monarch, Antiochus Epiphanes. He was anxious to speed up the Hellenization of his dominion as a matter of general policy.... He backed the reformers entirely and replaced the orthodox High Priest Onias III with Jason..." (p. 102). As we will see, the damage done by these "reformers" was incalculable: not only would it soon lead to violent rage by Antiochus against the Jews' religion, it would virtually destroy any remaining confidence the people may have had in the already-corrupt priesthood.

According to Grayzel, the Common People—from which came the *Hasidim*—were outraged. "It was the first time since the Jews returned from the Babylonian Exile that a non-Jewish government had interfered in the succession to the high priesthood, treating the sacred office as if it were nothing more that an ordinary governorship.... [The Jewish] Hellenizers had full control of Judea's government.... [The resurgence of] Hellenized life brought with it a looseness in religious observance, as well as a characteristically Greek looseness of morals" (p. 55). Grayzel adds that "the Common People watched these events with growing horror. They ascribed them to the influence of Hellenism and to the **abandonment by the upper classes** [the priesthood] **of the principles of the** [written] **Torah** which the scribes had taught" (p. 56; emphasis added). As a reliable historical source, the extra-biblical book of II Maccabees informs us that under Jason's influence "the Hellenizing process reached such a pitch that **the priests ceased to show any interest in the services of the altar; scorning the Temple and neglecting the sacrifices**, they would hurry to take part in [Greek activities] .... They disdained all that their ancestors had esteemed, and **set the highest value on Hellenic honors**" (II Macc. 4:13-15; emphasis added).

The rapidly escalating pace of Hellenism and the corresponding corruption of the priesthood ultimately compelled the Hasidim to organize themselves in order to resist Antiochus and the Hellenizing Jews. But the Hasidim were peasants, farmers, artisans—the poor of the land. They were hardly in a position to fight against the Syrians. Moreover, the Hasidim (or anyone else for that matter) could never imagine Antiochus' next move—to entirely *outlaw* the Jews' religion!

Indeed, about three years later, in 171 BC, "Antiochus found it necessary to replace Jason as High Priest with the still more pro-Greek Menelaus [who was *not* of the Aaronic line]... (Johnson, *A History of the Jews*, p. 102). The reaction among the people was further outrage—with many taking sides and resorting to violence. "In 167 the [rapidly escalating] conflict came to a head with the publication of a decree [by Antiochus] which in effect abolished the Mosaic Law.... But both the Greeks and Menelaus himself overestimated his support. His [illicit] activities in the Temple provoked an uproar. The priests were divided. The scribes sided with his orthodox opponents. So did most pious Jews or *Hasidim*" (p. 103).

Antiochus' bold move—which ranged from forbidding circumcision and Sabbath observance to desecrating the Temple itself—did not go unmatched. The *Hasmoneans*—a staunch clan of Jews of priestly descent from an area northwest of Jerusalem—responded with a counteroffensive initiated by the aged Mattathias. Within a year the rebellion fell to his eldest son Judah, surnamed "the Maccabee." Under the banner of the *Maccabees* (as they were later called) the Jews managed to eventually drive the Syrians from Judea. After some three years of fighting, Jerusalem was finally cleansed of Syrians and Hellenizing Jews alike—and the Temple repaired and rededicated in 165 BC. Grayzel writes, "The High Priest Menelaus, the Hellenizing Jews, and the new pagan residents now fled from Jerusalem just as three years previously the pious Jews had fled before them" (*A History of the Jews*, p. 61).

It was a short-lived victory—as the Syrians quickly regrouped and besieged Jerusalem. However, distracted by an imminent threat to their capital, Antioch, the Syrians offered a truce—one that revoked Antiochus' decree against the Jews' religion, but offered no change in the leadership of Judea. Judah the Maccabee refused. As Grayzel notes, the Maccabees realized that "the [Syrian] treaty of peace would restore power to that very group of aristocratic [priestly] Jews who had begun the entire conflict" (p. 64). Judah's leadership, however, was overruled; naively, the Hasidim were intent on accepting the treaty. This, of course, proved disastrous, with the Syrians and Hellenizing Jews once again dominating every area of Jewish life; the old oligarchy was returned to power, including the appointing of non-priests to the office of High Priest. And, once again, Judah and his army came to the rescue—for the time being.

In fact, the Hasidim would find themselves beset again and again by the Syrians (and Hellenizing Jews) over a period of several more years. Sadly, as Grayzel notes, not only did the Maccabees' struggle end in "only partial victory for the Jewish people," it ended in "total defeat for its heroic leaders" (p. 69). Grayzel is here referring to the ill fate of the Hasmonean line. He writes that even in victory "the Jewish people were unable to maintain … the idealism that they had shown in the days of trouble [following Antiochus's decree]. The **later Hasmoneans** [beginning with John Hyrcanus, one of Mattathias' grandsons], **thirsting for power and glory**, **lost touch with [their] Jewishness**, so that their actions cast dark shadows upon the memory of their ancestors" (p. 69; emphasis added). By some estimates, however, the Hasmoneans' corruption actually began with Judah's successor, his brother Jonathan. After Judah's death in battle, Jonathan eventually succeeded in bringing an unsteady peace to the area—through diplomacy. But, unlike his brother, Jonathan used his position to acquire power and prestige. By tactful diplomacy—and by taking advantage of the bloody civil war occurring within the Syrian empire—Jonathan managed to become both

High Priest and governor of Judea. "It may be said," writes Grayzel, "that Jonathan turned the policy of the Hasmoneans from religious to secular…" (p. 71). As we will see, the corruption of the Hasmonean leadership would further the Hasidim's antagonism toward the aristocratic priesthood.

After Jonathan's murder, his brother, Simon, became High Priest and ruler. Already advanced in years, Simon was noted for his wisdom. He formed a second "Great Assembly"—but one quite different from Ezra's time. As Grayzel notes, "The aristocracy which had dominated previous assemblies [i.e., minor ruling councils] had in the meantime become identified with the Hellenizing Jews, so that, if they were represented at all, they were outvoted. The leaders of the Hasidic party [the Hasidim] were in the majority" (p. 72). This assembly—which would later develop into the *Sanhedrin* of Jesus' day—would not always be dominated by the Hasidim; at times the aristocratic priesthood (known later as the party of the Sadducees) would assume control.

Simon's death marked the end of a long and heroic struggle for religious freedom—from about 170 to 135 BC. Judea was now independent, and would remain so until the Romans began to interfere in 63 BC. It is, however, important to understand that the Maccabean wars were never really about religious freedom as much as they were about defending the Jews' right to self-rule. Martin writes, "**The majority of Jews had not been anxious to depart from their Hellenism. What they wanted primarily was their freedom from the foreign yoke**. The matter of religion was really [only] invoked to get the people united in one common cause—to drive the foreigner from Judea. There was no real desire among the multitudes to get back to the Law of God…. [Religion had] only become a major issue when Antiochus Epiphanes voiced his anti-religious decrees" (*Is Judaism the Religion of Moses?*, p. 42; emphasis added). As Martin suggests, once Jewish independence was firmly reestablished, most Jews went back to simply being Jews—rather *irreligious* Jews, in fact. Thus, the truly devout among the Hasidim were not only by this time relatively *few* in number, they were undergoing a radical transformation into the sect of the *Pharisees*—with an absolute devotion to the teachings of the scribes.

The next 70 or so years would be a period characterized by conflict, corruption and controversy—both political and religious. The effects of Hellenization on the upper class and the priesthood had become permanent; and now a new generation of Hasmoneans was in control, starting with Simon's son, John Hyrcanus. But unlike their predecessors, they were arrogant and hungry for power—and would quarrel even among themselves for control. More significant, however, was the ever widening rift between the Hasidim and the still-Hellenistic priesthood. In fact, what had evolved over numerous generations as a fundamentally moral conflict between the grassroots Hasidim and the elite priesthood was soon to erupt into virtual war between the Hasidic Pharisees and the aristocratic Sadducees.

The Perils of Internal Conflict

Of the time following Simon's death, Robinson writes, "At some point during the period in which the [later] Hasmonean dynasty ruled Palestine, three distinct groups emerged within the Jewish community"—the Pharisees, the Sadducees and the Essenes (*Essential Judaism*, p. 320). Some associate the reign of Hyrcanus (135-105 BC) with the appearance of the Pharisees. According to *The Jewish Encyclopedia*, for example, it was under the rule of Hyrcanus that the Pharisees appeared as a "powerful party opposing the Sadducean proclivities of [Hyrcanus] the king…. The Hasmonean dynasty, with its worldly ambitions and aspirations, met with little support from the Pharisees, whose aim was the maintenance of a religious spirit in accordance with their interpretation of the Law" ("Pharisees"). In his *Old Testament History*, Charles Pfeiffer notes that the ideals of the Hellenists "were perpetuated in the party of the Sadducees, [just] as the ideals of the Hasidim were perpetuated in the party of the Pharisees. These parties are first mentioned during the lifetime of Hyrcanus" (p. 580). Likewise, Grayzel informs us that "Hyrcanus's reign saw the emergence of two political parties"—the Pharisees and the Sadducees. "The party of the scribes [which, in fact, represented the Hasidim] … became known as the Pharisee party" (*A History of the Jews*, p. 76). Grayzel makes this statement because the scribes were by this time the scholarly leadership behind the Hasidic movement. *Pharisee* comes from a Hebrew root (*parus* or *parash*) which means "to separate"—indicating the sect's proclivity for *separating themselves* ritually and physically from Greeks or Hellenized Jews. Noting the Pharisees' aggrandizing claim to honor, Grayzel adds, "The Pharisees, spiritual descendants of the Hasidim, argued that their religion had saved the Jewish nation." The Sadducees, on the other hand, were "opponents of the Pharisees," and "remained in complete charge of the government" (p. 77).

The controversies of that day were on several fronts, but *two* were central to the development of Judaism. First, a dynastic struggle for the office of King-High Priest would soon erupt between Hyrcanus' offspring—particularly his grandsons, Hyrcanus II and Aristobulus II. The two would foolishly invite Roman intervention, resulting ultimately in Rome's occupation of Palestine. But it was the fierce rivalry between the Pharisees and the Sadducees that set the character of the day. The controversy was both political and moral: The Pharisees opposed the Hellenized Sadducean leadership on the grounds that they were unfit to lead the nation; moreover, the Pharisees considered the Sadducees to be utterly ignorant because of their rejection of the scribes' oral law. From the Sadducean perspective, the priests held that the Pharisees' oral law was both illicit and dangerous.

Landman writes that the upper classes and the aristocratic priesthood "organized themselves [for their own political gain] into the Sadducee party to back the political activities of the Hasmoneans…" (*Story Without End*, p. 82). He continues: "Because the Hasmoneans and their Sadducean backers busied themselves with political matters, the pious among the Jews began to feel that the commonwealth was [once again] becoming just another [Greek] state...." The Hasidim—for whom spiritual ideals were of paramount importance—"organized themselves in opposition to the Sadducees.... They formed themselves into a brotherhood, or fraternity, which became known as the Pharisees. Their watchword was strict observance of the laws of ritual and moral purity." While the Pharisees did not oppose the Temple or its services, they felt the priesthood had become compromised by their adoption of Hellenistic ideas—and, in particular, because they "disregarded the oral law" of the Hasidim's scribal leaders (p. 83).

Quoting Dr. Jacob Lauterbach, Martin explains the Pharisaic view: "Following the Maccabean victory there were many priests who were ready and willing to resume their ancient, God-given role as teachers and expounders of the Law. But there were also the lay teachers who [as the Hasidim] had ... made a notable contribution to the Maccabean cause at a time when many priests were outright Hellenists and supporters of Antiochus Epiphanes. Lauterbach says that the lay teachers 'refused to recognize the authority of the priests as a class, and, inasmuch as many of the priests had proven unfaithful guardians of the Law, they would not entrust to them the regulation of the religious life of the people' (Lauterbach, *Rabbinic Essays*, p. 209). It was these lay teachers who organized themselves into the party of the Pharisees" ("Between the Testaments," p. 23).

The Pharisees were not alone in their skepticism of the Sadducees. As Grayzel notes: "The Jews [as a whole] still looked upon the High Priest with awe because he was considered the head of the Temple, their most important religious institution. But the buying and selling of the office, the corruption and ignorance of some of the priests who occupied it, and the fact that they were supporters of Rome and under the thumb of the procurators, **made Jews look elsewhere for religious inspiration**" (p. 115). Echoing Grayzel, Martin adds, "During the period of religious anarchy [under Egyptian rule] ... a fundamental change took place in the attitudes of the priests. Many of the priests were outright Hellenists and steeped in the pagan philosophies of that culture. Not only that, many of them had sided with Antiochus Epiphanes against the Common People during the Maccabean Revolt. Such activities caused the Common People to be wary of the priests and their teaching" (*Is Judaism the Religion of Moses?*, p. 51). Again, most Jews were irreligious—but there was a general lack of trust for the Sadducean priesthood. Thus, the Pharisees began to find increasing support among the pious of the Common People.

At the heart of the controversy was the scribes' so-called oral law, having finally, after decades of fermentation, come to life as *the* central doctrine of the Pharisaic party. Of the Sadducean disdain for the oral law, Hertz writes: "The aristocratic and official element of the population—[which became] known as the Sadducees—unhesitatingly **declared every law that was not specifically written in the Torah to be a dangerous and reprehensible**

innovation. [However, the] opposition of the Sadducees only gave an additional impetus to the spread of the oral law by the scribes, later known as [rather, later associated with] the Pharisees" (*The Babylonian Talmud*, Foreword, p. 14; emphasis added). Referring to the "greater issues between the Pharisaic and Sadducean parties," *The Jewish Encyclopedia* brings out that "while the Sadducean priesthood prided itself upon its aristocracy of blood [Aaronic lineage], **the Pharisees created an aristocracy of learning** instead, declaring a bastard who is a student of the Law to be higher in rank than an ignorant high priest (Hor. 13a)...." Concerning the scholarly decisions of their scribal leaders—who consisted "originally of Aaronites, Levites and [even] common Israelites"—the Pharisees claimed that the scribes possessed a level of biblical authority that even "endowed them with the **power to abrogate the [Mosaic] Law at times** ... [going] so far as to say that he who transgressed their words deserved death (Ber. 4a)." In fact, the Pharisaic scribes' rulings were "claimed to be divine (R. H. 25a).... [Moreover, the Pharisees] took many burdens from the people by claiming for the sage, or scribe, the power of dissolving vows (Hag. i. 8; Tosef., i.)" ("Pharisees").

As long as Hyrcanus lived, the conflict between the Hasidic Pharisees and the Sadducean priesthood remained subdued. The rift, however, reached its climax during the days of his son, Alexander Jannaeus. Jannaeus showed extreme contempt for the Pharisees, even using foreign mercenaries to keep them in check. Soon enough, open civil war ensued. Procuring aid from the Syrians, the Pharisees briefly forced Jannaeus and his Sadducean sympathizers into hiding. In the end, however, the Pharisees suffered a massive defeat, with over 800 Pharisees crucified at Jannaeus' order.

Jannaeus was succeeded by his widow, Salome. Being a woman, she could not officiate as High Priest; thus, the office fell to her son, Hyrcanus II. His brother, Aristobulus II, assumed command of the military. Interestingly, Salome's brother, Simeon, was a leading Pharisee. According to Pfeiffer, this fact may have "disposed Salome Alexandra to seek peace between the opposing factions" (*Old Testament History*, p. 583). Up to this time, the *Sanhedrin*—which, as a ruling council, was a later development of the Great Assembly formed by Simon of the Maccabees—was composed entirely of Sadducean priests and wealthy aristocrats. Turning the tables, Grayzel writes that Salome "dismissed the Sadducees from their official positions and appointed Pharisees to their places in the Sanhedrin" (*A History of the Jews*, p. 82). Landman brings out that her son, Hyrcanus II, as High Priest, "appointed many Pharisees to the Sanhedrin which, up to that point, had been controlled by the Sadducees. The Pharisees were now in a position to influence both the religious and civil heads of the commonwealth" (*Story Without End*, p. 84-85). *The Jewish Encyclopedia* adds this: "Under Alexander Jannaeus (104-78) the conflict between the people, siding with the Pharisees, and the king [had become] bitter.... Under his widow, Salome Alexandra (78-69), the Pharisees, led by Simeon ben Shetah, came to power; they obtained seats in the Sanhedrin, and that time was afterward regarded as the golden age…" ("Pharisees").

Under Salome—and particularly with her brother as president of the Sanhedrin—the Pharisees made numerous contributions to Jewish life. Of note was the comprehensive system of education the Pharisees established throughout Judea. This education was, of course, primarily in the Scriptures—led by the esteemed scribes. As we will see, this triumph laid the foundation for what would become an expanded rabbinical system of education, which would prove critical to the popularity of the Pharisaic movement, the development of the Mishnah, and the birth of Judaism.

Near the end of Salome's mostly peaceful nine-year reign, the simmering conflict threatened to reignite. Pfeiffer explains: While the Pharisees were relishing their newfound recognition, "the Sadducees were resentful of the fact that they were deprived of power. To make matters worse, the Pharisees used their power to seek revenge for the massacre of their leaders by Alexander Jannaeus. Sadducean blood was spilt, and the makings of another civil war were in the air" (p. 583). Thus, following Salome's death, "the bloody vengeance … [the Pharisees] took upon the Sadducees led to a terrible reaction, and under [Salome's son] Aristobulus (69-63) the Sadducees regained their power" (*The Jewish Encyclopedia*, "Pharisees"). A bitter struggle ensued between Hyrcanus II and Aristobulus II, with the Pharisees pulling for Hyrcanus, the rightful heir of the Hasmonean dynasty.

The two brothers appealed to Pompey, Rome's general in Syria, in 63 BC to resolve their dispute over who would rule the Jews. According to Grayzel, the Pharisees—perhaps at the request of the Sanhedrin—also appealed to Pompey to remove both Hyrcanus and Aristobulus so that "Judea might go back to its ancient constitution whereby the High Priest ruled with the advice of a popular council" (p. 87). Pompey, however, sensed a prime opportunity for Rome and decided to annex Palestine. Hyrcanus II remained in office as a Roman figurehead; the Idumean Antipater—a political climber with Rome—ruled Palestine through his sons, Phasael and Herod. Grayzel describes the outcome for the rival parties: "Herod (from 37 BC) had not the slightest intention of letting the Jews rule themselves. He deprived the Sanhedrin of every vestige of political power. Neither the Pharisees nor the Sadducees any longer exercised political influence. Only their names continued to exist for the purpose of describing two groups which differed on religious matters" (p. 97).

With Judea now a vassal state of Rome, the last vestige of Jewish independence was removed. Stripped of its influence and authority, the Sanhedrin was largely impotent, and the office of High Priest would always be subject to the discretion of the Romans. (In fact, from 37 BC to the destruction of the Temple, 28 different men occupied the office of High Priest, which was originally to be held for life.) Moreover, the longstanding corruption of the priesthood had taken its toll. By Jesus' time, the Sadducees had regained much of their religious authority; but, as *The Jewish Encyclopedia* notes, "they no longer possessed their former power, as the people always sided with the Pharisees" ("Pharisees"). Indeed, while the Sadducees controlled the Sanhedrin by a narrow margin, the Pharisees' growing influence could not be ignored. According to Joachim Jeremias, high priests "with Sadducean sympathies had to accustom themselves to withholding their views in council, and [were compelled to submit] to carrying out [certain of] the Temple rites according to Pharisaic traditions" (*Jerusalem in the Time of Jesus*, p. 159). In the end, both the Pharisees and Sadducees were reduced by the Romans to mere religious sects.

The Synagogue as a Pharisaic Institution

A classic example of the Jews' extraordinary ability to adapt to adversity is seen in the development of the *synagogue*. During the period of the Exile, the Jews out of necessity met in small groups for fellowship, prayer and the reading of the Scriptures. Over time, such gatherings became more regular and more organized in nature. As Pfeiffer writes, "Out of this very real need [for fellowship, instruction and worship] the institution known as the synagogue gradually developed. The synagogue [quickly] became the community center for [exilic] Jewish life" (*Old Testament History*, p. 494). The synagogue continued to develop even after many of the Jews returned to Palestine and rebuilt the Temple. "After the return from captivity, when religious life was reorganized, especially under Ezra and his successors, **congregational worship**, consisting [of] prayer and the reading of sections from the [Scriptures], **developed side by side with the revival of the** ... **Temple** at Jerusalem, and thus led to the building of synagogues" (*The Jewish Encyclopedia*, "Synagogue"; emphasis added). For Jews who did not return to Judah—and subsequently became established throughout the Persian Empire, Egypt, and later, the Roman Empire—the synagogue continued as the center of Jewish religion. Thus, "from the generations of old [since Babylon], Moses has had in every city those who proclaim him in the synagogues, being read every Sabbath day" (Acts 15:21).

Granted, the synagogue developed out of a genuine need for religious stability. And it could well be argued that the very survival of the Jews of the Diaspora has depended on the synagogue. Yet, that system of worship—while certainly not wrong in and of itself—clearly did not represented God's original intent, which was the primacy of the Temple.[5] This point is important because it underscores the longstanding controversy between the Pharisees and Sadducees. The synagogue system actually developed in conjunction with the rise of the Pharisees, and came to be both *dominated* and *misused* under their authority. Moreover, as we will see, the scribes and Pharisees deliberately used the synagogue as a way of competing with the Sadducean priesthood—to draw Jews away from the Temple services.

As the Pharisees gained in popularity and influence during the Hasmonean period, the synagogue began to play an increasingly important role.

Paul Johnson writes, "In their battle against Greek education, [the Pharisaic] pious Jews began, from the end of the second century BC, to develop a national system of education. To the old scribal schools were gradually added a network of local schools where, in theory at least, all Jewish boys were taught the [written] Torah. This development was of great importance in the **spread and consolidation of the synagogue** [and] in the birth of Pharisaism as **a movement rooted in popular education**…" (*A History of the Jews*, p. 106; emphasis added). The Pharisees' emphasis on education is well documented. As quoted earlier, "while the Sadducean priesthood prided itself upon its [Aaronic] aristocracy of blood, **the Pharisees created an aristocracy of learning**…" (*The Jewish Encyclopedia*, "Pharisees").

The scribes and Pharisees accomplished this not only through their schools, but through the synagogues. As Landman writes, in time the Pharisees "**made the synagogue the dominant institution in Jewish life**, around which the entire life of the community revolved" (*Story Without End*, p. 85). In fact, according to Grayzel, the synagogue came to play such a critical role in Jewish life that it actually began to *replace* the Temple. He writes that shortly after the time of Ezra, "certain influences were already at work which eventually made the synagogue even more important than the Temple itself"—and that Jewish religion in the run-up to the first century AD was "undergoing a transformation which was making the Temple a secondary institution…" (*A History of the Jews*, pp. 118-119).

According to Grayzel, it was the Pharisees who influenced the Jews to believe that services at the synagogue were of *greater value* than rituals taking place at the Temple. While the "daily sacrifice" at the Temple was obviously conducted on behalf of every Jew, "those who recognized the leadership of the scribes and Pharisees were not satisfied with such indirect contact with God" (p. 119). The Pharisees believed that since God was everywhere, He could be worshipped both in and outside the Temple—and that He was not to be invoked by sacrifices alone. And remember, the Pharisees maintained their view that the still-Hellenized priesthood was corrupt and incompetent to represent God to the people. Thus, they advanced the synagogue as a place of worship, study and prayer—raising it to a place of central importance in the life of the people. The synagogue rivaled the Temple, clearly antagonizing the Sadducees.

By the first century AD, there were synagogues in every Jewish community. Jerusalem itself had several synagogues—there was even one inside the Temple complex! By that time, Grayzel writes, "the attitude of the Pharisees had triumphed…. [The] day was gone when [Jewish religion] depended upon priest and sacrifice, indeed, even upon the Temple itself" (p. 120). In fact, the Pharisees' clout was such that they were able to persuade the Jews to admit into the synagogue some of the non-sacrificial ceremonies of the Temple after it was destroyed. Their goal, writes Grayzel, was to "make the synagogue the heir to the Temple" (p. 196). Some of those ceremonies, having since been modified, form part of the synagogue rituals to this day. Indeed, as *Smith's Dictionary of the Bible* brings out, it is "hardly possible to overestimate the influence of the [synagogue] system" which tended to "diminish, and ultimately almost to destroy, the authority of the hereditary [Aaronic] priesthood" ("Synagogue"). Or, as Jeremias puts it, "the hereditary [Aaronic] Jewish aristocracy had to endure competition from an intellectual aristocracy [that of the scribes and Pharisees] and, after the destruction of Jerusalem, finally be overtaken [by their popularity and clout]" (p. 245).

Ideally, the scribes and Pharisees should have used the synagogues to teach the Scriptures *and* point the people to the Temple. But the rivalry between the Pharisees and the Sadducees was simply too deep. And now, the synagogue was poised to play an even greater role in the development of Judaism—for as Robinson writes, the synagogue would become *the* "central institution of Jewish worship life as a response to the tragedy of the destruction of the Temple [in 70 AD]…" (*Essential Judaism*, p. 311).

Pharisaism Gives Birth to Judaism

*"You reject the commandments of God all too well,
so that you may keep your own traditions."*

By Jesus' time, *Pharisaism*—what the apostle Paul once practiced and later called "the Jews' religion" (Gal. 1:13-14; *KJV*)—was poised to give birth to full-blown Judaism. All that was needed was one final catalyst, which, ironically, came in the form of the Roman destruction of Jerusalem and the Temple in 70 AD.

As touched on earlier, pinpointing exactly *when* Pharisaism "became Judaism" is largely a matter of opinion. Scholars unanimously agree, however, that the Pharisees made their greatest gains in influence only *after* the destruction of the Temple and the dismantling of the Sadducean priesthood. For example, quoting Jacob Neusner's *Rabbinic Judaism* (p. 31), Michael Hoffman writes that Judaism's "initial catalyst was neither the canonization of the Hebrew Bible nor [the Pharisees' studious] research of Scripture, but the demise of the Second Temple…" (*Judaism Discovered*, p. 215). From that time, Judaism developed entirely from the teachings of the Pharisees. As Joachim Jeremias notes, "the Sadducean role ended with the fall of Jerusalem, and the [religious] tradition [subsequently] handed down to us and fixed by the written word [in the form of the Mishnah] from the second century, **came exclusively from their enemies the Pharisees**" (*Jerusalem in the Time of Jesus*, p. 243; emphasis added). Indeed, as quoted earlier from *The Jewish Encyclopedia*, "Pharisaism shaped the character of Judaism and the life and thought of the Jew for all the future" ("Pharisees"). In a similar vein, George Robinson writes, "The importance of the Pharisees cannot be overemphasized. In the aftermath of the destruction of the Second Temple, it was only through the efforts of the rabbis, the heirs of the Pharisaic worldview, that Judaism [rather, Pharisaism, as Judaism had not yet fully coalesced] was able to survive at all" (*Essential Judaism*, p. 321).

In fact, it was precisely in the Jews' *struggle to survive* the events of 70 AD—and their subsequent defeat in 135 AD—that Judaism began to homogenize. Two developments were particularly important, both of which centered on *education*. First, the scribal role would give way to a new generation of highly organized teachers called *rabbis* (from a practical standpoint, scribe and rabbi are virtually synonymous). Derived from the Hebrew *rab* meaning *great*, rabbi means *great one* or *master*, but is typically used in the sense of *teacher*. While the term *rabbi* was widely used throughout New Testament times (John 1:38;

etc.), Robinson notes that the "rabbinical role" took on greater significance after 70 AD—that it was, in some fundamental way, a *new* role (p. 359; foot-note). Other scholars agree, writing that "the basic form of the rabbi devel-oped in the [post-biblical] Talmudic era, when learned teachers assembled to codify Judaism's ... oral laws" (wikipedia.org/wiki/Rabbi). [1]

Like the scribes of old, rabbis spent years in rigorous training. This new "rabbinic era" would be characterized by a network of academies in which to study the Scriptures as well as the growing body of oral laws. This naturally led to the *second* key development of the period: Rabbinical lead-ers would eventually conclude that the Pharisaic oral traditions had become largely unmanageable and should be codified, thus leading to the comple-tion of the Mishnah by the end of the second century—the point many scholars consider to be the true beginning of Judaism.

Post-Biblical Rabbinism

The rabbis from about 70 AD through the end of the second century understood that the Jews' survival depended not on war and physical strug-gle, but on a new approach—one in which their religion took center stage. Jews would no longer be concerned with the Temple or even national sover-eignty; instead, the Jewish people would establish their identity through the study of the Scriptures and the growing Mishnah. As a religion, Judaism would transcend all boundaries, enabling it to be practiced wherever Jews lived. And most importantly, because Jews would be living in what Solo-mon Grayzel calls "a land of the spirit," they would be virtually immune from Roman persecution (*A History of the Jews*, p. 192). From the rabbis' perspective, "*knowledge* was to give Judaism indestructible power" (p. 31).

Of this time, John Phillips writes, "As some of the more farsighted Jewish leaders saw it, **the only hope for national survival lay in produc-ing a counterculture**, **something distinctly Jewish**, something that would match, rival and outlast the culture[s] of the various Gentile countries in which the dismembered parts of the Jewish nation now lay buried.... For the centuries ahead, perhaps indefinitely, the Jews would have to survive without a land, a capital, a national government, or an army.... They [would need to] be able to adapt and change and yet remain the same" (*Exploring the World of the Jew*, pp. 42-43; emphasis added). Learning from their experience in Babylon, the scribes had long ago begun to *invent* a form of religion that would enable Jews to cope with the loss of homeland and Temple. As Phillips adds, "The basic concepts [of a new Jewish religion] had already been hammered out [by the Pharisaic scribes, as found] in the [traditions of the] Midrash and the Mishnah." The rabbis of the post-biblical period only needed to build on that religious system in order to make Judaism **the true home of every Jew** no matter where he lived, what language he spoke, or what cultural forces pressed upon him." In order for Judaism to succeed, its designers also knew that it had to be "**capable of being reshaped and adapted**" (p. 43; emphasis added). As we will see in the next chapter, *adaptability* is a key feature of the so-called oral law.

In his foreword to *The Babylonian Talmud*, Rabbi J. H. Hertz writes, "The delight of all those generations [following Ezra and Nehemiah] was in the Law of the Lord…. [Toward the end of the first century AD] academies arose for [the] **systematic cultivation of this New Learning, as well as for the assiduous gathering of the oral traditions current from times immemorial** concerning the proper observance of the commandments of the [written] Torah…" (p. 14). One of the foremost rabbis of the first century was Johanan ben Zakkai, who strategically secured Rome's permission to open a school in the coastal town of Jabneh (also known as Jamnia) following the destruction of Jerusalem. Of this center of Rabbinic Judaism, Hertz writes: "By his academy at Jabneh, [Zakkai] rescued [the Jews' religion] from the shipwreck of the Roman destruction that overwhelmed the Jewish nation in the year 70 AD. Jabneh became the rallying ground of Jewish learning and the center of Jewish spiritual life" (p. 15). In fact, while the synagogue was Judaism's link to the Common People, it was the rabbinical *academies* that gave Judaism its growth and prestige. Grayzel writes that the success of the Jabneh academy helped to "prove, more than any other single event in [Jewish] history, that Spirit is mightier than the Sword" (p. 195).

Under Zakkai and the new rabbinical leadership emanating from Jabneh, "knowledge was to identify a Jew. The [priestly] nobility of blood which had existed among the Jews before the destruction of the Jewish state was to be **replaced by a spiritual nobility of the mind and spirit**. This spiritual nobility, the most respected group among the Jews, especially in Palestine, came to be known as *rabbis*" (p. 197). (This *illusion* of "nobility of the mind and spirit" will be exposed for its massive hypocrisy in a later chapter.) According to Phillips, "Zakkai was convinced that the Jews needed the oral law for their survival. They needed the **Mishnah as a source of national identity** in the dark days ahead. Deprived of their Temple, the Mishnah would be their Temple" (p. 61; emphasis added). After also succeeding in reestablishing the Sanhedrin in Jabneh (albeit powerless and unrecognized by Rome), Zakkai set out to orchestrate the progress of the rapidly developing Mishnah. "Within ten years of the fall of Jerusalem, **rabbinic law had established itself firmly** at Jabneh" (p. 62; emphasis added).

Zakkai's work was continued by one of the most prominent rabbis of the period, Akiba ben Joseph. One of the key instigators of the Bar Kochba rebellion, Akiba was martyred in 132 AD and never saw the outcome of the failed revolt against Rome. Akiba is remembered most for his contributions to the development of the oral law. In fact, according to Hertz, Akiba was one of the "key architects" of the Mishnah. "**Akiba was the author of a collection of traditional laws out of which the Mishnah actually grew**…. His keen and penetrating intellect enabled him to find a biblical basis for every provision of the oral law" (p. 15; emphasis added).

Following the Jewish rebellion of 132-135 AD, the Jews' religion was again prohibited by Rome. Emperor Hadrian dismissed the Sanhedrin and closed the academies and synagogues; Sabbath observance and study of the Scriptures were forbidden on penalty of death; numerous rabbis were martyred. Decimating the population of Judea, a half million Jews died or were taken captive; thousands more fled to Babylon where there were still large Jewish communities. And no Jew was allowed to set foot in Jerusalem. However, according to Grayzel, "in time the Romans came to realize the uselessness of persecuting Judaism" (*A History of the Jews*, p. 185). By about 150 AD, Rome relaxed its prohibition against the Jews' religion. Rabbinical schools, synagogues and Jewish courts of law were soon reopened; a considerable number of Jews returned to Palestine—and, once again, the development of the Mishnah was top priority.

Judaism Finds Itself in the *Mishnah*

During the second century, the Mishnah continued to grow. With the passage of time, however, "the whole process of commentary and interpretation degenerated into foolish hair-splitting with each rabbi trying to outdo his fellows in wresting new absurdities from the Mishnah. Various schools of thought sprang up, each one claiming to have arrived at ultimate truth" (Phillips, *Exploring the World of the Jew*, p. 63). Enter Judah Hanasi, the great grandson of the illustrious Hillel. Grayzel writes that "few among the rabbis have left so deep an impression on Jewish life as Judah.... The Jews stood in great awe of him, and subsequent generations have spoken of him as 'Judah the Prince,' or 'Our Holy Teacher.'... His prestige as well as his authority were enhanced when Rome recognized him as hereditary head of the Jewish people, with the title of Patriarch" (p. 206).

As president of the Sanhedrin, Hanasi was determined to put an end to the confusion surrounding the oral law and personally took the Mishnah in hand. After sorting through the mass of material, he deleted ideas he considered nonsense and rearranged the remainder by subject matter. Grayzel describes Hanasi's codification of the oral traditions: "Judah the Prince undertook this work because such a [written] code was necessary in order to avoid [additional] confusion. There had been many teachers, and each one of them had left his interpretation as to what the duties of a Jew were to be under any set of circumstances. Anyone wanting to know the law or tradition on some matter might have to decide among a large number of opinions.... The great learning of Judah and his position as Patriarch combined to make the code arranged by him the final authority on any subject" (p. 207). Phillips adds that once Hanasi had codified the oral traditions, he "arbitrarily ... announced [that] the Mishnah [was] closed" (p. 64) With Hanasi's death, however, other prominent rabbis began *adding back* much of the content he had discarded—thus spoiling his hope of a closed Mishnah.

Additional reasons exist for the codification of the oral law into the Mishnah. Robinson notes that in the time dominated by Hanasi, "the sheer volume of oral rulings had become so unwieldy that the rabbis reluctantly assented to their recording" (*Essential Judaism*, p. 226). The rabbis' goal, adds Robinson, was to create "a written version of the [oral] law that would be impervious to the vagaries of oral transmission. [By then] the body of oral law had grown so great that no one could possibly recall all of it accurately. The [development] of the Mishnah eliminated that problem" (p. 323). Hertz likewise brings out the necessity of the rabbis moving on to a *codified* tradition: "The product of the feverish activity of the Pharisaic schools threatened to become too unwieldy to be retained by unassisted memory. For all [of] this teaching was oral, and was not [up to this point] to be written down" (p. 14).

As mentioned earlier, one of the goals of the rabbis was to create a religion which would transcend time, geography and culture. The codification of the oral law was a necessary component of this plan. The Jews' oral traditions had been accumulating for many generations; now they would take on a new role, that of uniting the scattered Jewish communities. Solomon Landman, for example, notes that it was precisely because of the desperate, scattered condition of the Jews that "scholars felt it necessary to take steps to preserve the Oral Law…" (*Story Without End*, p. 110). In his *Jewish New Testament Commentary*, David Stern writes that after two failed Jewish revolts, "the *P'rushim* [Pharisees] and their [rabbinical] successors were … free to **develop further their own received tradition** [oral law] and **make it the center of gravity for Jewish life everywhere**. Eventually [by about 200 AD], **due to the dispersion of the Jewish people … these oral materials were collected and written down [as] the *Mishnah*"** (p. 18; "Matt. 3:7"; emphasis added).

Robinson further explains the reasoning of the key architects of the Mishnah in the development of Judaism. "The writing of the Mishnah and of the Gemara [a portion of the Talmud, composed of commentary] were the rabbis' answer to the destruction of the Temple … [in which they would **create**] **a Judaism** based on guidelines and norms of behavior and practice that **enabled the Jews to survive an even longer exile than the Babylonian one**" (p. 311; emphasis added). He adds that after 70 AD "the rabbis would turn their attention to the codification of Jewish [oral] law, shifting the focus … from [the now defunct] Temple to the [oral] Torah, to **creating a Judaism whose invisible walls could not be breached**…. [As a] handbook of legal codes, [the Mishnah] **presented Judaism as a faith and practice not bound by the fleeting passage of historical time**" (pp. 323-324; emphasis added). According to Phillips, the rabbis were "creating a **cumbersome legal code** that would **effectively seal off Jews from all other peoples** and that, **by its uniform application**, **would bind the Diaspora together**" (p. 60; emphasis added).

During Hanasi's time, the rabbis of Palestine largely controlled the development of the Mishnah, carefully guarding their "copyright." After his death, however, several of his top colleagues moved to Parthia (where some two million Jews and other Israelites were residing) and opened academies of their own. As far as the development of Judaism was concerned, from that time "the center of interest ... moved away from Palestine to Babylon" (p. 64). In time, however, the Babylonian Jews found the Palestinian Mishnah awkward. Despite Hanasi's formal closing of the Mishnah, much had been added to the text; moreover, as Phillips notes, "it was obvious [to the Babylonian rabbis] that changes would have to be made. A new exegetical system was now developed [which became] known as *Gemara* (supplement)" (p. 64; see Appendix One). Thus, a new generation of rabbis arose (ironically known as "reasoners") and attempted to clarify and amplify the Mishnah. But the resultant Gemara was only a muddled rehash of the Mishnah—in Aramaic instead of Hebrew. And most significantly, whereas the Mishnah was, at least in theory, *based on the Scriptures*, **the Gemara was based on the Mishnah**. The rabbis who developed the Mishnah ostensibly regarded the Scriptures as the text from which they drew their "inspired" commentaries; the "reasoners," however, looked to the Mishnah as *their* "received text" and devised their new commentaries accordingly. What a convoluted scheme! It begs the question Jesus asked, "Can the blind lead the blind? Shall they not both fall into the ditch?" (see Luke 6:39).

Thus, after many generations of gestation, the Jews' so-called oral law—originally conceived by the esteemed *sopherim* and brought to fruition by the rabbis—had found a home in Pharisaic Judaism. Hoffman writes, "During this period [of the rabbis] the laws, doctrines and traditions of the [scribal] Pharisees processed from oral to written form as the Mishnah ... [and] became the *first written record* of the traditions of the Pharisees that formed the law of the **newly institutionalized religion of rabbinic Judaism**" (*Judaism Discovered*, p. 134; emphasis added). According to Hertz, what the rabbis had sought was "the full and inexhaustible revelation which God had made. The knowledge of the contents of that revelation, they held, was to be found in the first instance in the *written text* of the Pentateuch; but the [so-called "greater"] revelation, the [oral] Torah, was [to be found in] the *meaning* of that written text, [in] the Divine thought therein disclosed, as unfolded in ever greater richness of detail by successive generations of devoted [rabbis]" (Foreword to *The Babylonian Talmud*, p. 14).

But in the end, as Phillips notes, the Mishnah (and, subsequently, the Talmud) "had little to do with the [written] Torah. **The rabbis, while professing great reverence for the Mosaic Law, had buried [the Scriptures] beneath their oral traditions**" (*Exploring the World of the Jew*, p. 61). It was just as Jesus had said, "Well did Isaiah prophesy concerning you hypocrites, as it is written, 'This people honors Me with their lips, but their hearts are far away from Me. But in vain do they worship Me, teaching for doctrine the commandments [traditions] of men.' For leaving the commandment of God, you hold fast the tradition of men.... **Full well do you reject the commandment of God, so that you may observe your own tradition**" (Mark 7:6-9).

Do We Really Need a *Second* Torah?

"The Law of the LORD is complete, restoring the soul."

Without question, the *centerpiece* of Judaism is its "oral tradition," often called the "oral Torah." Rabbi Aaron Parry, Educational Director of the west coast branch of the international organization "Jews for Judaism," writes: "For Jews, belief in the oral tradition that is [compiled in] the Talmud is an essential cornerstone of [our] faith. This point, in fact, cannot be overstated" (*The Talmud*, p. 9). Moreover, it is a key tenet of Judaism that one cannot correctly understand or apply the principles of the written Torah without the interpretive help of the oral law. Parry defines the oral law as the "verbal explanation of the laws that God gave to Moses on Mt. Sinai" (p. 4). He asserts that "without the Talmud [the final written form of the oral traditions, completed about 500 AD], we [Jews] have no way of knowing how to interpret and apply the [written] laws of the Torah" (p. 4). "Jews believe that virtually **nothing of the Torah can be properly understood without the Talmud**…" (p. 9; emphasis added).

According to Parry, to command that no *work* be done on the Sabbath is insufficient—because, he says, the Law doesn't define "work." He argues that "only through an unwritten [oral] tradition are we able to know what constitutes the Torah's definition of work" (p. 5). Thus, Jews look to their oral traditions to tell them in the most specific manner possible what activities involve "work" on the Sabbath. As part of the oral law, there are literally *hundreds* of rules—ranging from the trivial to the absurd—designed to regulate Sabbath observance alone.[1] In fact, virtually every imaginable activity of daily life is covered by such oral traditions (see Appendix Two, where some of these laws are reproduced from Rabbi Solomon Ganzfried's *Code of Jewish Law*).

Avi ben Mordechai—who once actively followed the Talmudic code of law—writes that in Judaism "there is an inseparable bond between the written Law of [God] and the oral law of the rabbis" and that "neither can exist without the other." Moreover, from the perspective of the rabbis, **"it is impossible for life to be regulated only in accordance with the written code of Moses**, because, as the rabbis teach, the written code is vague and has no clarity or definition" (*Galatians: A Torah-Based Commentary in First-Century Hebraic Context*, p. 79; emphasis added). It is the *rabbis* who teach that the Scriptures are inherently insufficient. However, this idea is proven utterly false by Nehemiah 8:1-8, where Levitical scribes are shown to be quite successful at giving the "sense" of the Law and causing the people to "understand" the Torah readings—all without the help of an adjunct oral law.

This argument is at the heart of Judaism. *If* the Torah is inherently insufficient, then a supplementary set of oral instructions would make a welcome addition. But as we will see, the Law of God as presented in the Pentateuch is *quite sufficient on its own*—and this key premise of Judaism is in direct conflict with numerous clear passages of Scripture. One particular passage, for example, stands out: How can the Jew explain what David wrote in Psalm 19:7, that the "law [Torah] of the LORD is *perfect*" (*KJV*)? Here, the Hebrew word for "perfect" clearly means *complete*, full, whole, unblemished, lacking *nothing*. David adds, "The testimony of the LORD is *sure*"—meaning it is confirmed, established, verified. How can such a clear passage be reconciled with the Jewish idea of an adjunct "oral Torah"?

Connected to this assertion is the additional Jewish claim that *both* the written Torah and the oral Torah came into existence at the same time— that *both* were given to Moses at Sinai. According to Parry, the traditions were allegedly "transmitted orally from God to Moses, and from Moses to the generations that followed him" (p. 4). As mysterious knowledge "whispered in Moses' ear," the traditions were never intended to be written down, but passed on from sage to pupil across successive generations. They were the "secret knowledge" of the sages. Joachim Jeremias writes that "the whole of the oral tradition ... was an esoteric doctrine that ... could not be propagated by the written word since it was the 'secret of God,' and could only be transmitted orally from teacher to pupil..." (*Jerusalem in the Time of Jesus*, p. 241). Of course, once the cryptic traditions were *written down* in the form of the Talmud, they lost their esoteric character—making the idea of an oral tradition appear even more contrived.

Judaism's claim of a Sinai-based oral Torah is highly suspect. Was the so-called oral law actually given to Moses by *fiat*—whispered into his ear—or did it *evolve* over centuries as Jewish sages attempted to "explain" the written Torah? David Stern says the oral law is simply the "accumulated tradition handed down over centuries"? (*Jewish New Testament Commentary*, p. 18; "Matt. 3:7"). Note the key word, *accumulated*. Paul Johnson writes that the oral traditions subjected the written Torah to a "process of creative development" in which laws could be "adapted to changing conditions" (*A History of the Jews*, p. 106). Note the key phrase, *process of creative development*.

Ari Goldman writes that some non-Orthodox Jewish scholars admit that there is a "clear separation between the [written] Torah and its offspring, the Talmud and the oral traditions. These scholars trace how the [oral] **laws were added, updated, and even abrogated by rabbis over time**..." (*Being Jewish*, p. 259; emphasis added). He says that any approach that sees the Law and the oral traditions as inseparable "flies in the face of historical fact." Ultimately, Goldman considers the Talmud a book of "Jewish law, lore, custom and superstition" (p. 260). The 1905 edition of the

Jewish Encyclopedia takes a similar approach: "The Mishnah [a portion of the laws composing the Talmud] represents the culmination of a series of attempts to bring order to the vast **mass of traditions which had been transmitted orally for many centuries**…. The compilation of the Mishnah is not, however, the work of one man, or even of the scholars of one age, but rather **the result of a long process extending over a period of two centuries**" ("Mishnah"; emphasis added).

So much for God whispering into Moses' ear.

Even those rabbis who claim the oral traditions were delivered to Moses along with the written Law readily admit that the oral law *still* had to be *developed from* what was *implied* in the written Torah. In his rather straightforward book, *What Do Jews Believe?*, David S. Ariel writes that the Jewish sages believed "every word of the [written] Torah had some mysterious meaning that could be deciphered and **from which new laws could be discovered**" (p. 139; emphasis added). Thus, the so-called "oral traditions" were actually "discovered" by *deciphering* the written Torah. Ariel adds, "The [written] Torah, in [the rabbis'] view, was open to interpretation and amenable to uncovering new applications to life" (p. 141). Again, note the key phrase, *open to interpretation*. In fact, "the rabbis imply that the oral tradition—**the rabbinic system of interpretation of [the] Torah**—has as much legitimacy as the Torah itself" (p. 142; emphasis added). The Talmud itself states: "There is greater stringency in respect to the teachings of the Scribes than in respect to the [written] Torah … so that a biblical law may [if deemed necessary] be transgressed" (*BT Sanhedrin*, 88b).[2]

Ariel continues (perhaps unintentionally) to debunk the myth that God actually whispered the "oral Torah" into Moses' ear at Sinai—showing instead that the oral laws are nothing but humanly-devised traditions *supposedly* based on the written Torah. He writes: "According to the rabbinic tradition, the revelation of God at Sinai was not the *final* word. [With apologies to David, the Law is less than "perfect" after all.] **Revelation of God's teaching continues in the process of deliberation** throughout history by competent and learned Jews who meditate upon God's word and law. **This interpretive tradition invests the continuous unfolding of the divine revelation not in God but in the wisdom of the rabbis and the rabbinic tradition**" (p. 141; emphasis added). An astonishing statement to say the least. The Word of God is represented as *insufficient*; but any further "revelation" comes *not* from God, but from the interpretive *wisdom* of "competent and learned" rabbis! Continuing: "The basis for this [assertion] is the belief that everything that was, is and can be known from God was revealed at Sinai, but that **much of the content of the revelation was implicit**, rather than explicit, [hidden] within [the] Torah. **Jews can derive new insights, laws and interpretations after Sinai, all of which are implicit within the Torah text**…" (p. 141; emphasis added).

Ariel justifies this position by stating that the "commandments in the [written] Torah, reflecting a different society from the one in which the rabbis lived, often required **interpretation, refinement, elaboration,** and **change** in order to render them applicable to new situations. Every legal code generates an **evolving system of continuing legislation** and **legal authorities who can authorize the application of the original laws to new circumstances**. This [freewheeling interpretation of God's Law] is what the rabbis provided in the tradition of Oral Torah and in the institution of the rabbinate" (p. 142; emphasis added).

In the end, Ariel admits that while the oral traditions—what he calls a codified "system of Jewish behavior"—may have their origins in the written Torah, they are ultimately "the **product of Rabbinic Judaism**" (p. 161; emphasis added). At the same time, however, he claims that the idea of a *Torah-deciphered oral tradition* "gives divine sanction to the [entire] rabbinic system" (p. 139).

Divine sanction? On whose authority? What kind of credibility did these so-called "competent and learned" Jewish sages actually possess? Where in the entirety of Scripture is such a "rabbinic system" supported?

Rabbi Parry asks a similar question: "How do we know that the oral laws have not been corrupted over time? The Talmud ... is full of disagreements. Is this not proof that the information is inaccurate?" Unable to answer with authority, Parry *appeals to tradition*: "[Our] traditional Jewish practice ... holds that **the Talmud represents God's divine will and instruction. We trust in the power of the sages** of each generation, and their followers, to accurately transmit it" (*The Talmud*, pp. 9-10). This chain of transmission, by the way, purportedly includes some 120 generations of sages from Moses to the completion of the Talmud in about AD 500.

By the frank *admission* of the Jews' own scholars, Judaism is clearly a religion based on *blind* trust in men—certainly not in God. The so-called oral Torah is nothing more than an accumulation of *human ideas*—rabid commentary, eccentric musings of self-professed "wise sages" who simply could not (or would not) allow the Scriptures to speak for themselves. It is indeed as Michael Hoffman writes: "Where the sufficiency of Scripture is denied"—and it is grossly denied in Rabbinical Judaism—"the *fallacies* and [vain] *imaginings* of man come to the fore" (*Judaism Discovered*, p. 146). The so-called "oral Torah" is just that—a fallacious *imagination* of men.

The Jewish idea of "secret wisdom" privy only to a select rabbinate is totally unbiblical. Deuteronomy 29 says, "The secret things belong to the LORD our God"—*not* to an elite group of "competent and learned" sages—**"but the things which are revealed** [in the Scriptures] **belong to us and to our children forever"**—*why?*—**"so that we may do** [live by!] **all the words of this Law"** (verse 29). The knowledge of *how* to obey and please God is clearly revealed in the Scriptures—*fully and completely*. No secondary, *interpretive* "oral law" is needed.

God's Law Extant From Creation

The *spiritual principles* behind God's Law—such as love, mercy, outgoing concern, giving—have *always* existed, as they are integral aspects of God's own character. At creation, God ordained specific laws to govern His relationship with mankind—such as the seventh-day Sabbath (Gen. 2), which was later codified as the Fourth Commandment (Ex. 20). Though unstated, other laws of God are apparent from the creation of man. In instructing Adam and Eve, it is obvious that God intended for them to worship and obey Him above all—thus, the First Commandment was in effect from day one. God created other laws to govern human relationships. In murdering Abel, Cain was guilty of breaking the Sixth Commandment; he began, however, by *coveting* (prohibited by the Tenth Commandment) his brother's enviable relationship with God. (It is interesting to note that one cannot *covet* in a physical, letter-of-the-law manner. Coveting only occurs in the mind—thus, it is always *spiritual*.) Cain had been warned that *sin* desired to "have him," as it were (Gen. 4:7). Indeed, his *hatred* of Abel preceded his act of murder—which, as Jesus pointed out, meant that he was already guilty of breaking the spiritual *intent* of the Law (Matt. 5:22). According to the apostle Paul, "where no law is, there is no transgression"—no sin (Rom. 4:15). Thus, if Cain was *struggling against sin*, there must have been a law in force—for "sin is the transgression of the law" (I John 3:4; *KJV*).

There are numerous additional examples which can be used to demonstrate that God's laws were fully in force from the creation of man. Genesis six describes the corrupt, evil state to which mankind had degenerated in just a few generations. By what criteria or standard was man deemed evil and sentenced to destruction via the flood? Of that same generation, Noah was *righteous* before God (Gen. 7:1). Again, by what criteria was Noah judged as righteous? It is apparent that God's basic laws had to be fully in force in order for God to render such judgments—and such laws likely existed in some "codified" form even before Sinai.

In fact, long prior to Sinai, God said the patriarch Abraham "obeyed My voice and kept My charge, My commandments, My statutes, and My laws" (Gen. 26:5). We even see Abraham *tithing* to the priest Melchizedek in Genesis 14:20. Abraham's faithfulness was of course critical to not only God's plan to raise up the nation of Israel, but to the promise of the Messiah Himself. God's covenant promises to Abraham are *absolute* because of his faith and obedience. Is it any wonder, then, that Abraham is called the father of the faithful (Rom. 4:16; Gal. 3:7, 29); as such, Abraham's example of faithful obedience is central to the Christian calling (Heb. 11; James 2).

The point here is that God had established His Law as a *righteous way of life* long before the first Jew was born—long before the so-called oral law was ever imagined. This *same* precept-based *way of life* formed the basis of the all-important covenant promises given through Abraham—promises from which sprang the Old Covenant nation of Israel, and from which will yet come the New Covenant millennial reign of Christ. *Where* do we read in Scripture that Abraham—who figures so prominently in Judaism—ever second-guessed God's Law? Or that he felt God's precepts were in need of some kind of "higher interpretation" or "further development"? How was it possible for Abraham to please God—to become the "father of the faithful"—without the so-called oral law to guide him? The truth is, we read simply that Abraham "obeyed" the straightforward, clear-cut laws, commandments and statutes of God. How is it, then, that God's *way of life*—defined perfectly by His laws, commandments and precepts—is deemed in Judaism to be in sore need of an additional "oral" law?

The "Church in the Wilderness"

Because of its extensive code of traditions, Judaism deviates significantly from the pure *way of life* defined by the commandments, statutes and precepts of God as originally delivered to the children of Israel through Moses. While ostensibly an attempt to *interpret* the Torah—or perhaps build a hedge about the Law to prevent it from being broken—the oral law, in many cases, *obscures* the clear meaning of the Scriptures.

Jesus Himself warned that the Jews' traditions resulted in "nullifying the authority of the Word of God" (Mark 7:13)—rendering it "of none effect" (*KJV*). He said the Jews practiced *many* such traditions—all of which had been "passed down" (verse 13), showing again that such oral laws had *accumulated* over time, being passed from sage to pupil.

Because of the Jews' fixation with tradition, Judaism becomes the ultimate in self-deception wherein its adherents literally worship the true God *in vain* (Mark 7:7). Here, Mark quotes from Isaiah, who was already dealing with a similar condition in his time: "And the LORD said, '[This] people draws near Me with their mouth, and with their lips [they] honor Me [they *say* all the right things] but their worship of Me is made up of the **traditions of men learned by rote**, and their fear toward Me [and thus their lack of true obedience] is taught by the **commandments of men**' " (Isa. 29:13; also read Isaiah 58, an indictment against those who practice a *form* of religion without *substance*).

Thus, Judaism is a thorough, yet subtle, *corruption* of the pure *way of life* God had established through His Law under the Old Covenant. That Torah-centered *way of life* was intended to position the people of Israel as God's singular, premier nation—the *standard* after which all the nations of the world would ostensibly model themselves. "[This law] is your wisdom and your understanding in the sight of the peoples [of the nations] who will hear all these statutes, and say, 'Surely this great nation is a wise and understanding people.'… [For] what great nation is there that has such statutes and righteous judgments as are in all this law which I [Moses] set before you this day?" (Deut. 4:6-8). As a "kingdom of priests" (Ex. 19:6), Israel was to represent God and His way of life to the world. God's perfect Law, as *originally* given in codified form, was quite sufficient to not only govern the nation of Israel, but, ultimately, the entire world. In fact, the law that was given to the "church in the wilderness" (Acts 7:38) is the very law Jesus Christ and the glorified saints will administer in ruling all nations in the age to come—for "out of Zion shall go forth the Law" (Isa. 2:3). Israel, of course, never realized that grand potential, writing instead a long history of apostasy and rebellion. As we have seen, Israel's failure to carefully follow the Scriptures is what ultimately spurred the development of Judaism—a man-made religion of humanly-devised laws and traditions.

Leading up to the exodus, Moses was to present God to the children of Israel as "the God of Abraham, the God of Isaac, and the God of Jacob" (Ex. 3:15)—thus emphasizing not only the covenant promise of *deliverance* as detailed in Genesis 15:13-16, but the covenant promises of *nationhood*. As their journey to the Promised Land proceeded, the burgeoning nation soon found itself bound to the God of their fathers by their *own* contract—the Old Covenant—based on a codified form of the *same* laws, commandments and precepts that governed God's relationship with Abraham.

The nation of Israel was required by God to live a *way of life* that was *already well established*; indeed, the holy, righteous laws of God are decidedly *not* "Old Covenant"—nor are they "New Covenant." They are simply the *laws of God*—which, at their core, are based on profound, eternal spiritual principles. It is important to understand the *completeness* of the "Torah-based" *way of life* that God gave to the "church in the wilderness." Judaism, while claiming to be in full support of the written Torah, purports that the laws of God are insufficient, that one cannot live a godly life without additional, more detailed guidance (the oral law is *immensely* detailed). But the Scriptures reveal that the laws and commandments of God—as given to the children of Israel—are fully sufficient, complete and without need of *further development*.[3]

In Deuteronomy four, Moses reminded the children of Israel of the day they stood before God at Sinai, when God said, "Gather the people to Me, and **I will make them hear My words so that they may learn to fear Me** all the days that they shall live upon the earth, and [that] they may teach their children [to do likewise]" (verse 10). At that time, God "declared to [them] His covenant which He commanded [them] to perform, even the Ten Commandments" (verse 13). As shown by this passage, God's instructions to the people were given in a most *direct* fashion; in fact, there is not even the slightest hint that the people would have difficulty figuring out *how* to follow God's commandments—that they would need the "interpretive" help of a secondary, oral Torah. Moses concludes: "Therefore, know this day and fix it in your heart that the LORD is God in heaven above and on the earth beneath. There is none other. Therefore, **you shall keep His statutes and His commandments which I command you this day**, so that it may go well with you and with your children after you, and so that you may prolong your days upon the earth which the

LORD your God gives you forever" (verses 39-40). The children of Israel were to follow *only* what God had spoken *directly* and what was made *publicly known* through Moses. In a similar passage, God said: "Write **these words** for yourself, for **in accordance to these words** I have made a covenant with you and with Israel" (Ex. 34:27). Again, this passage—like so many others—*leaves no room* for an oral tradition originating with Moses and being passed down to subsequent generations.

In fact, God admonished the Israelites to *teach* their children, emphasizing that they were to be instructed in the *same* laws and precepts. "And the LORD commanded us to do all these statutes—to fear the LORD our God for our good always so that He might preserve us alive, as it is today. And **it shall be righteousness for us if we observe to do all these commandments** before the LORD our God as He has commanded us" (Deut. 6:24-25). To the Hebrews, *righteousness* was clear cut. It did not depend on mysterious traditions handed down from one generation to another; it did not require access to the "secret knowledge" of the sages. All that was required was that they faithfully and wholeheartedly observe God's laws and commandments.

As we've seen, God is a God of covenants. Scripture explicitly says that the Ten Commandments formed the "words of the [Old] covenant" (Ex. 34:28). And God warned Israel that He would *judge* the nation based on that agreement, even *avenging* their breaking of that covenant (Lev. 26:25). How could God *righteously judge* the nation of Israel on their obedience to a law that was, by design, impossible to follow without the added "insight" of a so-called oral law? Obviously, such a notion is quite absurd!

The Old Covenant was *written*—it was, so to speak, "on paper." Thus, it could be *enforced*. Even in Daniel chapter seven, we see that God will judge the coming end-time "beast" based on what will have been recorded in *writing*—as "books [of judgment] were opened" (verse 10). God can enforce and make judgments based on a written, contractual law; but an oral law that is not fixed in writing—that is continually evolving—*cannot be enforced*. Thus, even *if* such a law existed—which it does not, except in the minds of deceived Jews—it could never be binding.

We have already noted what Moses wrote in Deuteronomy 29 about the "secret things" of God—that they belong to God, and thus remain hidden. Conversely, the things God has revealed through His prophets (Moses being the foremost) were *put into writing* and *belong to the people*—openly and clearly, with nothing held back—that they might obey and please God. In a similar passage from Isaiah, God says, "I have not spoken in secret, in a dark [hidden] place of the earth. I did not say to the seed of Jacob, 'Seek me in vain.' I the LORD speak righteousness, I declare things that are right" (Isa. 45:19). It is most difficult to square this passage with Judaism—which teaches that God did in fact utter the oral law in *secret*, and that it is quite *vain* for one to attempt to follow the Pentateuch without the assistance of that oral law. In truth, however, God has been very straightforward with how He expects people to live.

Notice what Moses wrote concerning this *very subject*. After emphasizing that the people were to listen to the *voice of God* and to follow what was *written* (not passed down orally) in the Book of the Law, Moses said, "For this commandment"—the *way of life* defined by God's laws—"which I command you today **is not hidden from you**, **neither is it far off**. It is not in heaven that you should say, 'Who shall go up to heaven for us, and bring it to us, so that we may hear it and do it?' Neither is it beyond the sea that you should say, 'Who shall go over the sea for us to bring it to us, so that we may hear it and do it?' But **the word is very near you**, **in your mouth and in your heart**, **so that you may do it**" (Deut. 30:10-14). This passage clearly debunks the Jewish idea of the insufficiency of the Torah—for God's Law was not beyond Israel's understanding or ability to keep; it was no great, hidden mystery; it was not vague, complicated or half-baked. Rather, it was *near*, in their *mouth* and *heart*, indicating the *intimate connection* the people were to have with the Law. The phrase "in your mouth" means they were to become *conversant* with the Law—until, ideally, it was thoroughly incorporated into their hearts and minds (see Deuteronomy 6:6-9 on how the Israelites were to teach God's Law *daily* to their children so that it might be *in their hearts*). Thus, *familiarity* and *understanding* are implied. **No second**, **oral Torah was required**. All that was needed was a child-like *heart* willing to obey—which, as we will see, was the only thing "missing" under the Old Covenant.

Again, the "religion" of the "church in the wilderness" was a godly *way of life* expounded by the very laws and commandments of God. As such, it was *complete*; its principles could be applied to *any* real-life circumstance—*if* one had a *heart* to do so. Contrary to Jewish thought, the laws, commandments and precepts of God do not require "refinement"—nor do they need to be viewed through the lens of a so-called "oral law."

Shortly before Joshua was to take Israel into the promised land, Moses charged the people concerning *altering* God's laws, commandments and precepts: "You shall **not add to the word which I command you**; **neither shall you take away from it**, so that you may keep [only] the commandments of the LORD your God which I command you" (Deut. 4:2). Nothing was to be *added* or *taken away*—because the Law was *complete*. There was no need for improvement, refinement or fine-tuning via an adjunct oral law. Moses repeated the admonition: "Whatever I command you, be careful to observe it; you shall **not add to it nor take away from it**" (Deut. 12:32). Some Jews will argue that Moses is here *including* the oral law in what he "commanded Israel." But the oral law was by the Jews' own admission *secret* knowledge—it was not given to the people at large. Here, however, Moses is clearly speaking to the *entire* nation.

Orthodox Jews stubbornly argue that the Talmud does not *add to* the Scriptures, but is "along side of" them. In practice, however, the oral law does *add to* the Scriptures because the Talmud is unanimously acknowledged as the lens through which God's Word is viewed. In fact, it is widely acknowledged among Jewish scholars that the Scriptures have been largely superseded in Judaism by the Talmud. (As we will see in Chapter Seven, this "superiority of the Talmud" is a hallmark of Judaism's spirit of hypocrisy.) Jeremias writes: "Only ordained teachers [scribes] transmitted and created the tradition … [which] was regarded as **equal to and indeed above the Torah**" (*Jerusalem in the Time of Jesus*, p. 236; emphasis added). If *this* isn't "adding to" the Law, then what is?

God made a similar charge to Joshua after Moses' death. "Only be strong and very courageous so that you may **observe to do according to all the law which My servant Moses commanded you. Do not turn from it to the right hand or to the left**, so that you may prosper wherever you go. This **Book of the Law** [the *written* Law] shall not depart out of your mouth, but you shall meditate therein day and night, so that you may observe to do according to **all that is written in it**, for then you shall make your way prosperous, and then you shall have good success" (Joshua 1:7-8). Again, the command to follow God's Law *without variance*—without turning to the left or right—implies that the Law of God is *perfect* and has no need of enhancement or refinement. In other words, the Torah was in no way subject to "creative interpretation"—it was clear-cut and needed no "complementary" set of laws to make it work. Note the emphasis in this passage on what Moses had *written*. Israel was to follow the laws and commandments of God as they were written down. There is simply no allowance here at all for a second, *unwritten* law.

After much discussion and contemplation, Solomon, the "Preacher" of the book of Ecclesiastes, finally wrote, "Let us hear the conclusion of the whole matter [of living a happy, fulfilling life]: **Fear God, and keep His commandments. For this is the whole man**" (Eccl. 12:13). Oops. Didn't God realize that His laws and commandments were insufficient for such a lofty goal—that an additional "oral law" would be required if one was to truly achieve *wholeness* in his life? Such is the absurd thinking behind Judaism. Consider the statement made by the prophet Micah. "[God] has shown you, O man, what is good [through His Law]. And **what does the LORD require of you** but to do justice [as defined by His laws, commandments and precepts] and to love mercy and to walk humbly with your God?" (Micah 6:8). *If*, as scholars and rabbis such as Parry believe, the Law of God is inherently insufficient and somehow dysfunctional apart from the Jews' oral traditions, then passages such as these are *asking the impossible*.

Clearly, God's judgment on Israel was predicated on their adherence to His *written* Law: "I call heaven and earth to record this day against you that I have [through this *Book of the Law*] set before you life and death, blessing and cursing. Therefore, choose life, so that both you and your seed may live" (Deut. 30:19). Such judgment would have been patently unjust if a secondary, "secret" oral law was required in order to please God.

The prophet Jeremiah reiterates what was expected of the "church in the wilderness"—and what is expected of us today: "For I did not speak to your fathers, or command them in the day that I brought them out of the land of Egypt, concerning burnt offerings or sacrifices"—or, we might add, concerning any kind of *oral* tradition—"**but this [one] thing I commanded them**, saying, 'Obey My voice, and I will be your God, and you shall be My people; and **walk in all the ways that I have commanded you**, so that it may be well with you' " (Jer. 7:23). Again, the *way of life* God gave to the people of Israel was apparent—there was nothing hidden, secret or obscure. This passage shows what is uppermost in God's mind when it comes to His relationship with His people: obedience to *what He has said*—directly and through the prophets. There is absolutely *no allowance* in Scripture for a so-called oral Torah.

David's Outlook on God's Law

It is quite evident from the writings of David that the simple Torah-based *way of life* offered to the Hebrew people was complete, functional, understandable—and did not suffer from the lack of a so-called oral tradition. A "man after God's own heart" (see Acts 13:22), David exemplified the very heart and mind of God (in fact, one of the primary purposes of the book of Psalms is to give us a look into the mind of Christ).

David saw the Law of God for what it truly was: a *lamp* to his feet, a *light* to his path (Psa. 119:105). He sang, "O how love I Your law! It is my meditation all the day" (verse 97). David's outlook towards God's laws and commandments was nothing but positive, hopeful and certain; indeed, there is not even the slightest hint that he felt the Torah fell short in some way. When reading Psalms, particularly chapter 119, it quickly becomes unimaginable that David could ever say, "God's Law is great, but it's impossible to know how to apply it. I need another law to interpret the Torah—yes, a vastly detailed 'code of conduct.' After all, I don't want to use common sense or put any effort into understanding God's way."

But what David *did* say is profound: "**Your commandments make me wiser** than my enemies, for they are ever with me. **I have more understanding than all my teachers**, for Your testimonies are my meditation. I **understand more** than the ancients because I keep Your precepts. I have held back my feet from every evil way, so that I might keep Your word. I have not departed from Your ordinances, for You have taught me. How sweet are Your words to my taste! Yea, sweeter than honey to my mouth! **Through Your precepts I get understanding**; therefore I hate every false way" (Psa. 119:98-104).

David adds: "Your word I have hidden in my heart, so that I might not sin against you" (verse 11); "Your testimonies also are my delight and my counselors" (verse 24). Obviously, David both understood and highly benefited from God's laws and commandments—*without an oral law*.

"The entrance of Your words gives light; it gives understanding to the simple" (verse 130). Notice here that even the "simple"—those naive and immature—can learn and follow God's way as presented by the Torah. There is simply *no need* for a supplementary oral law!

Throughout Psalm 119 in particular, we see that David was *taught by God* as he prayerfully meditated on His word. For example, "Teach me, O LORD, the way of Your statutes, and I shall keep it unto the end. Give me understanding, and I shall keep Your law; yea, I shall observe it with all my heart…. Teach me good judgment and knowledge, for I have believed Your commandments" (verses 33-34, 66). God's laws, commandments and statutes are clear, but *effort is required* on our part to achieve a deeper understanding of God's way of life. The key is a submissive, willing heart and mind—something grossly lacking under the Old Covenant. As we will see, the problem for those caught up in Judaism is precisely that—the lack of a *right spirit* and approach to God's Word.

As noted earlier, David viewed the Law as perfect, complete— purified seven times like silver tried in a furnace (Psa. 12:6). He proclaimed, "I will never forget Your commandments, for **with them**"—*not* through man-made oral traditions—"**You have given me life**" (Psa. 119:93).

Did Jesus Uphold the "Oral Law"?

That Jesus Christ upheld the *written* Torah is well demonstrated in Matthew's gospel account: "Do not think that I have come to abolish the Law or the Prophets; I did not come to abolish, but to fulfill" (Matt. 5:17). Jesus "fulfilled" the Law initially by going on to *amplify* the laws of God by showing their spiritual application. In several passages Jesus says, *"You have heard it said"* or *"It has been said"*—each time referring to an Old Testament precept. In each case He adds, *"But I say to you"*—revealing a deeper, spiritual meaning to the Law that typically escaped the average Jew. In some cases, such as Matthew 5:43, Jesus was referring to the Pharisees' traditions. "You have *heard that it was said* [by the scribes and Pharisees], 'You shall love your neighbor and hate your enemy.' " Moses indeed taught that we are to love our neighbor (Lev. 19:18), but nowhere do the Scriptures say we are to hate our enemies. Rather, the corrupt religious leaders of the day taught Jews to hold Gentiles in contempt as enemies. As will be brought out in Chapter Seven, the Pharisees taught (as does Judaism today) that only a fellow Jew qualifies as a *neighbor*; in Judaism, non-Jews are actually considered to be subhuman.

Jesus further fulfilled the Law in the *perfect manner* in which He kept His father's laws and commandments. In fact, Jesus was the "Living Torah"—because he *personified* the very heart and spirit of the Law of God. This is no doubt what the apostle John had in mind when he wrote that the Law was "given through Moses, while grace and truth"—God's favor and ultimate means of salvation—"came through Jesus Christ" (John 1:17).[4]

It could be argued that the "Sermon on the Mount" of Matthew 5-7 was Jesus' premier discourse on how to live a godly way of life based on the

Law. Yet there was *not one word* spoken about a so-called oral law. Did Jesus miss a prime opportunity to support the "competent and learned" Jewish sages of the day? On the contrary—Jesus' focus was on the Law and the Prophets *alone* as given in the Scriptures. The fact that He said not one "jot or tittle" (the smallest of letters or accent marks) would pass from the Law proves that He was upholding the *written* Torah in its precise, original form—with *nothing* deleted or added to it.

When asked concerning the way to eternal life, Jesus said "if you desire to enter into life, keep the [written] commandments" (Matt. 19:17). In Luke we read of a similar account. "Now a certain doctor of the law [scribe] suddenly stood up, tempting Him, and saying, 'Master, what shall I do to inherit eternal life?' And He said to him, '**What is written in the Law? How do you read it?**' " Again, Jesus' reference is only to the *written* Law, not an oral law.

"Then [the scribe] answered and said, 'You shall love the Lord your God with all your heart, and with all your soul, and with all your strength, and with all your mind; and your neighbor as yourself.' And [Jesus] said to him, 'You have answered correctly. Do this, and you shall live' " (Luke 10:25-28). "Do *this*"—the laws and commandments as written in the Torah. Christ deliberately omitted any mention of the scribe's precious oral laws. Thus, not only did Jesus decline to endorse the Jews' traditions, He relegated them as *nonessential* in terms of salvation.

Concerning these same great commandments—love for God and love for neighbor—Jesus said, "On these two commandments hang all [the teachings of] the Law and the Prophets" (Matt. 22:40). In other words, the entire Torah—*and* the Prophets (and Writings) as they expand on the Law of God—can be summarized by the spiritual principles of love for God and neighbor. If the acclaimed "oral Torah" was so important, why did Christ not include it here? Do not the oral traditions of Judaism likewise reflect and support *love* toward God and neighbor? As will be brought out in Chapters Seven and Eight, Judaism's cherished traditions have *nothing* to do with genuine love for God or neighbor; rather, Talmudic Judaism is hypocritical, self-serving and creates only an *illusion* of righteousness.

As we have seen in Chapter One, Christ sharply upbraided the Jewish religious leaders of His day not only for their hypocrisy, but for their man-made traditions that resulted in "nullifying the authority of the Word of God" (Mark 7:13). Of course, Judaism rejects Jesus as the Messiah and discounts the entire New Testament—so His condemnation of their traditions falls on deaf ears. But for the Christian, it is significant that Jesus never once upheld the validity of the so-called "oral Torah"—thus demonstrating the exclusive nature of the Scriptures.

The Abrahamic Faith Once Delivered

Late in the 60s AD, the apostle Jude encouraged believers to "fight for the faith, which once for all time has been delivered to the saints" (Jude

3). When Jude refers to the "faith once delivered," he uses the term *faith* in the sense of a *way of life*. The Greek *pistis* refers not to mere *belief*, but to a conviction so profound that it leads the believer into a definite *way* of living.

For the early Church, that faith was established upon the teachings of Christ and the apostles—but it was built firmly on the *foundation* of the Old Testament Scriptures. In fact, the apostle Paul encouraged Timothy to "continue in the things that you did learn and were assured of, knowing from whom you have learned them; and [remember] that **from a child you have known the holy writings** [the texts that make up the Old Testament], which **are able to make you wise unto salvation through faith**, which is in Christ Jesus. **All** [such] **Scripture is God-breathed and is profitable for doctrine, for conviction, for correction, for instruction in righteousness**" (II Tim. 3:14-16). As the context shows, the "Scripture" to which Paul refers is what we now call the Old Testament (by this time, what would become the New Testament consisted of only a few early apostolic writings).

Thus, it can be said that the "faith once delivered" is the very *way of life* defined by the Law, Prophets and Writings. That first-century "way" (Acts 19:23) originated in the "Torah of faith"—as given to Israel and as expanded on by the life and teachings of Jesus the Christ.

Considering the undeniable connection of the Church to the Old Testament—and the fact that the Church was composed almost exclusively of Jews during its earliest years—why did Jesus' followers never recognize the validity of a so-called *oral* Torah? Did they not understand that the *written* Torah was, as the Jewish sages contend, *inherently insufficient*?

James says that there is but "one Lawgiver, Who has [the] power to save and to destroy" (James 4:12). Does the Lawgiver really need our help? Why is it the Jews have felt the need to remake, reinvent, or refine the Law of God? Why indeed should the Law of God even *need* refinement?

Have the Jews really somehow improved upon God's "perfect law of liberty" (James 1:25) by adding to it their elaborate code of traditions? Was the Hebraic *way of life* defined by the Torah somehow flawed, incomplete, deficient? As a nation, Israel repeatedly *fell far short* of adherence to God's Law. Does this point to a failure in some way of the Law *itself*—thus indicating a need to further "develop" the written Torah? Or—as we will see in the next chapter—does it not indicate a failure on the part of the children of Israel in their *application* of God's Law?

CHAPTER SIX

The *Futility* of the Jews' Oral Law

"O that there were such a heart in them that they would fear Me and keep all My commandments always."

Giving the early scribes the benefit of the doubt, *perhaps* the Jews' so-called "oral law" originated with good intentions. After all, to "build a fence" about the Torah to prevent it from being violated sounds good; to "amplify" the Law to make it easier to keep seems innocent enough. Hence, as Solomon Landman writes, it was through the Talmud that "the rabbis of old had tried to keep alive the principles of the ancient covenant [the written Torah] **by applying them to every activity of life**" (*Story Without End*, p. 114; emphasis added). To be sure, applying the *principles* of the Scriptures to "every activity of life" is exactly what God desires. But this is not what the Talmud does; rather, the Talmud attempts to *legislate* behavior in a comprehensive fashion. Is it really feasible to create a *code of law* that covers every conceivable circumstance a person might encounter? Apparently the rabbis thought so. The renowned British rabbi Joseph H. Hertz writes: "**Religion in the Talmud attempts to penetrate the whole of human life** with the sense of law and right. Nothing human is in its eyes mean or trivial; **everything is regulated and sanctified by religion** [the Talmud]. Religious precept and duty accompany man from his earliest years to the grave and beyond it. They [the precepts of the Talmud] **guide his desires and actions at every moment**" (Foreword to *The Babylonian Talmud*, Soncino Edition, pp. 25-26; emphasis added). While Hertz's statements may *sound like* the Talmud is merely a "guiding principle" in the life of the observant Jew, the opposite is true. In fact, the Talmud is a vast code of regulatory law that serves only to diminish human discernment in favor of rote obedience to rabbinic decrees. Conversely, the Scriptures teach that genuine morality stems from both the desire and the ability to *apply broad biblical principles* (such as the Ten Commandments) to any given situation. Or, put another way, God has accomplished with ten basic, living principles what the rabbis have failed to achieve with literally *thousands* of Talmudic precepts and regulations. (See Appendix Two, which features excerpts from Solomon Ganzfried's *Code of Jewish Law*.)

In *Exploring the World of the Jew*, John Phillips writes that, on account of the Talmud, the Torah has been "buried beneath vast accumulations of tradition and encrusted with enormous deposits of human interpretation. **The Torah itself has been largely superseded in Judaism by the Talmud**. The five books of the Torah can be written out in 350 *pages*. The Talmud takes up 523 *books* printed in 22 volumes" (p. 55; emphasis added).

He continues: "The Torah is clear and concise, part of the inspired Word of God. The Talmud is wordy, rambling, argumentative, inconsistent, sometimes witty, sometimes boring, sometimes brilliant, sometimes inane. The laws of the Talmud [which Christ called *grievous burdens*] constitute **cold concrete poured over Jewish life and hardened by time into a rigid prison for the soul**." Phillips concludes that, for Jews, "the chief instrument of … blindness to biblical truth has been the Talmud" (p. 57; emphasis added). As a former Talmud-observing Jew, Avi ben Mordechai similarly describes the oral law as "**a deep, black hole and an endless system of legal minutiae**" (*Galatians—A Torah-Based Commentary in First-Century Hebraic Context*, p. 48; emphasis added).[1]

Despite the massive legal code that today comprises the Talmud, the truth is that the oral law has *failed* to provide a protective "fence" about the Law. As we've seen, the Jews' oral traditions over time took on a life of their own. Going far beyond the alleged role of safeguarding the Torah, the Talmud has not only *supplanted* the Scriptures (a fact readily acknowledged in rabbinic Judaism), it has had a *nullifying* effect on the Law (Mark 7:13). But as we will see, the real failure of the so-called "oral Torah" is that it has inadvertently become a vain substitute for *conscience*. With the Talmud, Jews have little need for "moral sense"—everything, in theory, is laid out in black and white; under the oral law, discernment of right and wrong based on broad principles has been replaced by a vast code designed to regulate virtually every aspect of human conduct. How is it that Jewish sages failed to see what generations of experience have proven—that morality cannot be legislated? As the Scriptures themselves reveal, true morality—while clearly directed by basic laws—is only possible with the *right* "heart."

Obedience From the Heart

As has been shown, Judaism is a man-made religion predicated on a code of humanly-devised laws. The Jews, however, were not the first to try to *trump* God's laws with their own. In the Garden of Eden, Adam and Eve were given specific instructions—*laws*, in effect. In particular, they were commanded to *not* eat from the "tree of the knowledge of good and evil" (Gen. 2:17). This tree was symbolic, as it did not literally impart knowledge of any kind. Rather, taking of this forbidden tree represented one's willful intent to *define for himself* what was good and what was evil. The serpent misled Eve, "For God knows that in the day you eat of [this tree], then your eyes shall be opened, and **you shall be like God, deciding good and evil**" (Gen. 3:5). The actual meaning of the Hebrew text is that Adam and Eve would "come to know" good and evil through personal experience.

Thus, Adam and Eve chose to *discern for themselves*—using human reasoning and experimentation—what constituted good and evil. They would, in effect, create their own "code of law." While they may not have realized it at the time, their choice also meant rejecting God as sole law-giver; likewise, the Jews may not have realized that through their oral law they would—*in effect*—reject the Scriptures as the exclusive authority for human conduct. Nevertheless, learning to "discern" good and evil seemed like a good thing. We read in the New Testament about those who "through repeated practice have had their senses trained to *discern* between good and evil" (Hebrews 5:14). In fact, God *wanted* Adam and Eve to learn to discern between good and evil—but by living His way, with His laws as their guide. With the right heart and spirit, they would have learned to discern right from wrong by applying the broad principles of God's laws to every circumstance. No detailed code of conduct would be required—as long as they had the right "heart." Instead, they became a "law unto themselves."

According to the apostle Paul, a key facet of "human nature" is that people are universally *opposed* to law; we are by nature rebellious and resist being told how to live. Indeed, the "natural human mind"—the one we all inherited through Adam (Rom. 5:12), as opposed to the spiritually-directed mind of a genuine Christian—"is antagonistic toward God and is not willingly subject to the laws of God" (Rom. 8:7; author's paraphrase).

Thus, when it comes to law-keeping humans have a proclivity to look for *loopholes*—to find ways around laws they don't like. Ultimately, when laws are circumvented, additional laws must be passed to "close the loopholes." The volume of civil laws in society *increases* directly in response to law-breaking—not law-keeping—because of those who create loopholes for existing laws. But additional laws are not the answer, as they only further create a legalistic atmosphere. The answer is a matter of *heart*, of one's spirit and approach to law-keeping.

The Pharisees, for example, were experts at circumventing the clear instructions of Scripture. As brought out in Chapter One, Jesus indicted the scribes and Pharisees for creating loopholes around laws for the sake of convenience. "Full well do you reject the commandment of God, so that you may *observe your own tradition*. For Moses said, 'Honor your father and your mother.'... But you [teach], 'If a man shall say to his father or mother, "Whatever [financial] benefit you might [have expected to] receive from me is *corban*" (that is, set aside as a gift to God), he is [no longer] obligated to help his parents.' And you [thus] excuse him from doing anything [to help care] for his father or his mother, **nullifying the authority of the Word of God** by your tradition which you have passed down; and you practice many traditions such as this" (Mark 7:9-13). According to this Jewish "tradition," one could simply *dedicate to God* whatever portion of his money or goods that would normally have been used to support his parents—thus circumventing the clear responsibility of children toward their aging parents as part of the Fifth Commandment.

The Jewish leaders' preference for their own traditions led them into a works-oriented "righteousness" characterized by an obsession with physical rituals and letter-of-the-law observances. Even when they did obey the

Torah, it was at the expense of what Christ called the "weightier matters" of the Law—"judgment, and mercy and faith" (Matt. 23:23). Clearly, reliance on a humanly-devised "code of law" leaves little room for spiritual discernment, and tends to blind one to "justice and the love of God" (Luke 11:42).

Again, even the vast code of laws that makes up the Talmud cannot truly legislate morality for Jews. More laws only mean more loopholes. As long as a legalistic approach is taken—in which right and wrong is defined by a massive, ultra-specific code of conduct—law-keeping will only be mechanical, perfunctory. True morality, on the other hand, is a matter of the heart, of always seeking the best for others in a spirit of love and concern. This is why Paul wrote that *love fulfills the Law* (Rom. 13:10; also Gal. 5:14 and James 2:8). Such an approach does not require a detailed code of conduct; rather, it depends on understanding and appreciating the underlying intent and purpose of a fundamental set of laws—laws designed to broadly express love toward God and others—and applying those laws in a spirit of love to any circumstance that might arise. No such "code of law" can accomplish this.

Ultimately, God wants *obedience from the heart*—not from some set of laws performed by rote. Indeed, it has never been God's intent to legislate morality. Jesus demonstrated this when He stated that all which is written in the Law and the Prophets "hangs" on the two great commandments of *love toward God* and *love toward neighbor*. Those two broad principles are expanded by the Ten Commandments. Moreover, Christ clearly explained in Matthew (chapters five through seven) that there is an underlying *spiritual intent* to God's laws—an intent which is based, again, on love and outgoing concern for others.

Jesus *Intensified* the Law

Early in His ministry, Jesus made the unambiguous proclamation, "Do not think that I have come to abolish the Law or the Prophets; I did not come to abolish, *but to fulfill*. For truly I say to you, until the heaven and the earth shall pass away, one jot or one tittle shall in no way pass from the Law until everything has been fulfilled [brought to pass]" (Matt. 5:17-18). The primary meaning of "fulfill" in verse 17 is *to complete*. Does this imply that the Torah was *incomplete*—lacking something? Does Jesus' statement here support the rabbinical view that the Law was in need of some further development—or perhaps in need of a complementary set of laws?

As brought out in the previous chapter, the Law of God is *perfect* (Psalms 19:7; James 1:25). And, while it is clear that Jesus in no way diminished the Law, it is equally clear that He added no new laws to the Torah. How then did He *complete* the Law? In what is generally regarded as a messianic prophecy, the prophet Isaiah foretold that Christ would "*magnify the Law and make it glorious*" (Isa. 42:21). Most translations render the Hebrew *gadal* as to *magnify*, *exalt* or *make great*. But such renderings miss the point; the Torah was already held in the highest regard, already looked upon as *great*. In this key passage, *gadal* more accurately means to *increase* or *advance* something or someone. This is exactly what Jesus did—He increased, advanced or *intensified* the application of the Law by emphasizing its underlying spiritual intent and purpose. In fact, Christ brought obedience to a new level, making the Torah *more binding*.

Continuing in Matthew five, Jesus was quick to utilize the apposite example of the scribes and Pharisees, stating that "unless your righteousness shall exceed the righteousness of the scribes and Pharisees, there is no way that you shall enter into the kingdom of heaven" (verse 20). Having long abandoned the "weightier matters" of the Law, the Jewish religious leaders were obsessed with tradition and blinded by their own works-based "righteousness"—thus, they knew nothing of *genuine* righteousness based on heartfelt obedience to God. Christ was simply saying that entry into the Kingdom of God would require *obedience on a whole new level*—one that considered the deeper spiritual intent of the Law.

Jesus began His intensification of the Torah by demonstrating that behind the letter-of-the-law commandment "You shall not murder" was the deeper spiritual matter of being "angry with one's brother without cause" (verses 21-22). By implicating anger and hatred as the root cause of murder, Jesus was showing that there is a *spiritual component* to every law. Hatred leads to murder—thus, spiritually, in the mind, hatred *is* murder. Even if the physical act (or even the contemplation of the act) of murder never occurs, the commandment has already been violated through *hate*. Indeed, every physical act—good or evil—is preceded by a spiritual mindset or attitude. Thus, according to the *spiritual intent* of the Torah as magnified by Christ, hate *is* murder; looking on another person with lust *is* adultery; coveting *is* theft; etc. (It is interesting to note that the Tenth Commandment prohibiting *coveting* has no letter-of-the-law application. Granted, coveting may *lead to* the breaking of other commandments—such as with stealing—but coveting of itself is always spiritual, occurring only in the mind.)

As stated earlier, the Torah is based on love—"Love does not do any wrong to its neighbor; therefore, **love is the full expression of God's Law**" (Rom. 13:10). When a person has the right spirit or attitude—one of outgoing concern and love—he can apply the Law from the perspective of what is *best for others*. The spiritual intent of the Ten Commandments provides the necessary framework for discerning right and wrong in any circumstance a person might face. God's way is both profound and quite simple. Contrary to the approach of the Pharisees—which was to *legislate* Jewish life with a plethora of burdensome traditions and regulations—Jesus magnified the Law in such a way that it could be applied to any circumstance. In living by the spiritual intent of God's Law, one asks, "What is best in this particular circumstance for my neighbor?" However, a letter-of-the-law approach—particularly when the heart and mind are on the *self*—leads naturally to law-breaking and the creation of loopholes.

As noted at the beginning of this chapter, the Talmud, in theory, is an attempt to apply the principles of the Law to "every activity of life." But no such "code of law" could ever achieve such a lofty goal—and would only represent a vain attempt to legislate morality. The answer, as revealed by Jesus, is indeed to apply the principles of the Torah to "every activity of life"—*how?*—by considering and applying the *spiritual intent* of the Law in a spirit of outgoing love. When one's focus is on the intent of the Law—considering what is best for others in a spirit of love—loopholes no longer exist. No one is trying to get around the Law, and no one needs to reference a vast code of laws in order to regulate their conduct.

A practical example from the Scriptures best illustrates the point. Concerning the prohibition against work on the Sabbath, Talmudic pundits claim that the Torah is vague on what exactly constitutes *work*.[2] Granted, while passages dealing with Sabbath observance clearly show that "work" includes *more* than what we, today, would call "earning a living," there is no comprehensive list of what may or may not be done on the Sabbath. Clearly, such a list would be impossible, and would only be an attempt to legislate Sabbath-keeping. Thus, the Scriptures only include broad guidelines concerning resting on the Sabbath. The Talmud, however, includes hundreds of Sabbath prohibitions—most of which are absurd and asinine. In their foolish attempt to legislate Sabbath-keeping, the rabbis have covered everything from how far one may walk on the Sabbath (see Acts 1:12) to whether juice may be squeezed from a lemon![3] But is such a "Sabbath code" really necessary? When one understands the purpose of the Sabbath—that it was created as a gift for man, to be a delight, a joy, a time of spiritual rejuvenation—it becomes obvious that such "codes" actually make the Sabbath a burden.

When one is of the right spirit and attitude, he will willingly and gladly refrain from *anything* that interferes with keeping the Sabbath restful, exceptional and spiritually focused. Simple, mature *discernment* is all that is required. But to avoid making a glass of lemonade on the Sabbath because it requires "work" to squeeze a lemon? Such a fanatical approach reflects an inability to exercise common sense. Jesus encountered just such a mindset in dealing with the scribes and Pharisees, who accused Him of violating the Law by healing a woman on the Sabbath:

> "Now [Jesus] was teaching in one of the synagogues on one of the Sabbaths; and lo, there was a woman who had been afflicted with a spirit of infirmity for eighteen years, and she was bent over and unable to straighten herself up. And when He saw her, Jesus called her to Him and said to her, 'Woman, you have been loosed from your infirmity.' Then He laid His hands on her; and immediately she was made straight, and she glorified God. **But the [Pharisaic] ruler of the synagogue answered with indignation because Jesus had healed on the Sabbath**, and said to the people, 'There are

six days in which men are obligated to work; therefore, during those days come and be healed, **but not on the Sabbath day**.' Therefore, the Lord answered him and said, 'Hypocrite! Does not each one of you on the Sabbath loose his ox or his donkey from the manger and lead it away to drink? And is it not just as necessary for this woman, being a daughter of Abraham, whom Satan has bound, lo, eighteen years, to be loosed from this bond on the Sabbath day?' And after He said these things, all those who opposed Him were ashamed; and all the people rejoiced at all the glorious things that were being done by Him" (Luke 13:10-17; also see Mark 3:1-5).

The Pharisees failed to grasp the purpose or the spiritual intent of the Sabbath; in their fanaticism and misguided zeal (Rom. 10:2), even *doing good deeds* on the Sabbath was forbidden as "work." Similarly, when Jesus' disciples were passing through a field on the Sabbath and stopped to pick a modest portion of grain to eat (Matt. 12:1-2; Mark 2:23-24), the Pharisees were offended. The disciples' actions could hardly be construed as "harvesting" or "servile work"—both prohibited on the Sabbath by the Scriptures. But the Pharisees saw this as a violation of the Torah because their understanding of the Law was skewed by their devotion to tradition. Remember, to them, the Torah was too vague; it needed "fencing in" by a vastly more detailed code. Thus, according to their humanly-devised oral traditions, *any* plucking of grain on the Sabbath was a violation.[4]

Writing centuries later, Moses Maimonides, one of Judaism's most revered sages, verifies this particular Pharisaic perspective: "He that reaps [on the Sabbath] ever so little, is guilty [of violating the Torah] … and the plucking of ears of corn is a derivative of reaping" (*Mishneh Torah*, Hilchot Sabbat, c. 8. sect. 3 and 7.1).[5]

The scribes' and Pharisees' knee-jerking extremist mindset reflected not only their inability to exercise ordinary common sense, it also demonstrated their inability to exercise spiritual discernment as they labored under a system of legal minutiae. But proper obedience to God's Law requires a *right* spirit, heart and mindset—apart from which a person can only hope to mechanically follow some legalistic "code of law."

How the Talmud Leads to *Spiritual Apathy*

Clearly, the Jews' endeavor to magnifying or amplifying the Torah through their vast "code of law" is an effort to legislate moral behavior. Not only is this an untenable proposition, it is one fraught with adverse consequences. The fact is, any attempt to *legislate* morality leads paradoxically to the *destruction* of morality. (Here, morality may be defined as simply the ability to thoughtfully *discern* right from wrong, and then *choose* the right.)

When moral behavior is dictated by an extensive regulatory code, individual *discernment* becomes almost nonexistent; *judgment*—deciding between different courses of action—is rendered pointless; and, ultimately, *obedience* becomes mechanical. There is no reason to think, discern or ask, "What should I do?"—the "appropriate" course of action has been predetermined. Thus, the "code of law" becomes a cheap substitute for morality and conscience—which inevitably leads to spiritual *apathy*. True morality, on the other hand, requires that an individual think, discern and judge right from wrong based on *broad principles*—principles which focus more on underlying intent as opposed to specifics.

Perhaps this point can best be illustrated in how children are brought up. As parents, we want our children to grow up having *learned* to make sound decisions based on basic parental guidance. When they are young, children are naturally dependent on clear, specific parental "laws." But as they mature, they must learn to make discerning judgments based on broad principles—or they will be unable to think for themselves, always dependent on specific, letter-of-the-law "rules." Similarly, living by the "oral law" keeps the Jew in a state of *moral infancy*; as long as the Jew is dependent on the Talmud to guide his actions in "every activity of life," he will never develop genuine moral character, never have his "senses trained to *discern* between good and evil" (Hebrews 5:14).

What happens when there is no law or regulation that specifically addresses a particular question? For example, does the Bible forbid smoking? Not expressly. But one who genuinely seeks to please God will, in a spirit of discernment, realize that because smoking destroys health, it runs contrary to numerous biblical principles that uphold the value of human life. Does the Bible prohibit gambling? Again, not expressly by command. But it is not difficult to find biblical principles that apply—such as not exploiting others for "dishonest gain" (which would fall under the broader prohibition against *coveting*).

For the Orthodox Jew, however, such questions can be problematic. If a matter is not spelled out in the Jewish "Code of Law"—which attempts to address "every activity of life" according to Talmudic precepts (see Appendix Two)—Jews are taught to rely on the wisdom of their local rabbi, whose word, as we will later see, is *absolute*. This reliance on the Talmudic code—which in actual practice is referenced almost exclusively while the Scriptures are ignored—virtually destroys any chance the Jew might have of developing genuine moral discernment.

But by learning to apply the broad principles of the Law in a spirit of love toward God and love toward neighbor, one's conscience becomes *trained* to discern between good and evil—in any circumstance. Conversely, if one relies on a code of specific do's and don'ts, his or her "obedience" becomes mechanical, motivated by fear or compulsion—when it should be motivated by love and a genuine desire to obey God and serve the needs of others. We either "exercise" and develop our moral conscience or we allow it to wither. Thus, it becomes apparent that dependence on a code of law such as the Talmud actually *dulls the conscience* and leads ultimately to *spiritual apathy*.

The *Heart* of the Matter

A prominent factor in the history of ancient Israel was their failure to adhere to the laws and commandments of God. Again and again the nation would express its collective commitment to God's way, only to quickly relapse into former patterns of idolatrous disobedience. Just weeks after being miraculously delivered from slavery in the land of Egypt, the children of Israel zealously declared their allegiance to God at the foot of Mt. Sinai: "And you [Moses] speak to us all that the LORD our God shall speak to you, and **we will hear it, and do it**" (Deut. 5:27). Verse 28 shows that God was well pleased with their zeal. Knowing the hearts of men, however, God was also certain that the Israelites' enthusiasm would be short-lived—thus, He lamented, "Oh, how **I wish their hearts would stay like this always**, that they would fear Me and obey all My *mitzvot* [laws]; so that it would go well with them and their children forever" (verse 29; Stern's *Complete Jewish Bible*).

As noted by Moses, God had thus sized up the Israelites: "I have seen this people, and, behold, it is a stiff-necked people" (Deut. 9:13). Just prior to the nation entering the Promised Land, Moses admonished them, "You have seen all that the LORD did before your eyes in the land of Egypt to Pharaoh and to all his servants and to all his land. Your eyes have seen the great trials, the signs, and those great miracles. Yet the LORD has **not given you a heart to perceive, and eyes to see, and ears to hear**, [even] **unto this day**" (Deut. 29:2-4). The numerous miracles, signs and wonders proved insufficient to soften the hardness of their hearts; thus, God was *unable* to give them a heart and mind to perceive the true spiritual nature of His Law. To little avail, Moses had warned the Israelites to "lay up" God's words "in your hearts and in your souls" and to "circumcise the foreskin of your heart, and be no longer stiff-necked" (Deut. 11:18; 10:16).

As brought out earlier, God's *way of life* as defined by the laws and commandments of the Pentateuch was neither "hidden" nor "far off"; it could both be understood and lived if one had a *willing* heart. Indeed, Moses said "the word is very near you, in your mouth and in your heart, *so that you may do it*" (Deut. 30:11, 14). However, in his discourse concerning Israel's *unbelief*, the apostle Paul notes that the nation failed to obtain genuine righteousness (this subject is covered thoroughly in Chapter Eight). Paul shows that God had no choice but to harden the hearts of the children of Israel: "God gave them a spirit of slumber, eyes that are not able to see, and ears that are not able to hear" (Rom. 11:7-8). Concerning this "failure" of the Old Covenant, the apostle left no doubt that the *fault* was not with the Law, but *with the people* (Heb. 8:7-8).

While the Old Covenant required obedience only to the letter of the Law, the nation of Israel still failed to remain faithful in their relationship with God—and certainly never developed the *heart* to perceive the spirit of the Torah. Jesus' revelation concerning the *spiritual intent* of the Law underscores the fact that the Jews had little perception of the deeper spiritual issues of the Torah. Yet, Paul writes that the Law is *intensely spiritual* (Rom 7:14), being based, as we have seen, on the broad principle of love toward God and love toward neighbor. Paul's statement in Romans seven is not some fuzzy sentiment; rather, it demonstrates that the Law of God works first and foremost at the level of the mind and spirit—where the *conscience* either accuses or defends one's actions (see Rom. 2:15).

It was precisely this failure of the Jews *through unbelief* that led to the development of the so-called "oral Torah." Lacking "a heart to perceive, eyes to see and ears to hear" when it came to the true application of the written Torah, Jewish sages resorted to what *seemed right* in their own eyes— they attempted to legislate morality and establish their own works-based "righteousness" using a mass of humanly-devised traditions and laws. Thus Paul summarizes: "Brethren, the earnest desire of my heart and my supplication to God for Israel is for salvation. For I testify of them that [the Jews] have a zeal for God, but not according to [true] knowledge. For they, being ignorant of the [genuine] righteousness that comes from God, and seeking [through their traditions and codes of law] to **establish their own** [works-based] **righteousness**, have [in hardness of heart] not submitted [themselves] to the righteousness of God" (Rom. 10:1-3).

Similarly, Mordechai argues that the Pharisees' works-righteousness was a "**false system of justification**, [based on] a Pharisaic system of decrees and traditions." He adds that such an approach "produced a torah of **false 'righteousness'** replete with its many reforms [ostensibly] developed by using the Law of Moses as a source text. *Works of the law* **had become another torah** [the Pharisees' oral laws and traditions] added to the written Torah of Moses" (*Galatians*, p. 216; emphasis added).

A right *heart* would have led the Jews to an understanding of the spiritual intent of the Law, enabling them to exercise spiritual discernment and apply the principles of the written Torah in any circumstance. No supplementary oral law would ever have been needed. But owing to their unbelief and hardness of heart, the Jews have (perhaps unknowingly) allowed their rabbinical scholars to substitute the Talmud *in place of* a spiritual mindset. Thus the oral law becomes a cheap, *failed* replacement for a spirit-led conscience.

While it is readily acknowledged that the Holy Spirit was uniquely given to the *elect* of the church age as a "helper" (see John 14:26; 15:26; 16:7; etc.), it is a mistake to assume that Israel was spiritually helpless. God is *impartial* (Acts 10:34), and stands ready to help anyone whose heart is pure before him—"for the eyes of the LORD run to and fro in all the whole earth to show Himself strong on behalf of those whose heart [spirit, intent, attitude] is perfect toward Him" (II Chron. 16:9). The very fact that God compelled Israel to *choose* proves that they were not helpless and that they exercised significant control over their moral lives. "I call heaven and earth to record this day against you that I have set before you life and death, blessing and cursing. Therefore, *choose life* so that both you and your seed may live" (Deut. 30:19). Yet, as a people, the children of Israel were unwilling to seek God with their whole heart, with all their soul—thus they were never able to experience obedience on a spiritual level. In the end, a perfunctory letter-of-the-law obedience was all they could accomplish—and even that was haphazard at best.

Morality Requires *Personal Choice*

The Jews' approach—as well-intended as it may be—is based on flawed human reasoning. Indeed, "There is a way that seems right to men, but it only leads to death" (Prov. 16:25; author's paraphrase). It should be noted that *all* religions have gone down this same well-worn path of attempting to legislate morality in one way or another. Catholicism has its catechisms; in Islam, conduct is dictated in the Koran; the various Eastern religions have humanly-devised codes as well. Protestantism, on the other hand, teaches that the Law has been rendered obsolete by Jesus' sacrifice—replaced by an ethereal "goodness" in one's heart. But like Adam and Eve, adherents of such an approach become a "law unto themselves."

Judaism has essentially attempted to accomplish through the "oral law" what can only be achieved through a genuinely *spiritual* approach to the Law of God. Sadly, the Jews' dependence on the Talmud precludes the possibility of such an approach and ultimately even removes the element of *personal choice* from morality. Granted, the Talmud might, to some degree, create a "hedge" about the Law; but in so doing, such a code invariably impedes personal choice and discernment based on conscience. Ultimately, human beings are not moral robots; we cannot be programmed via a code of law to react morally to every conceivable circumstance in life.

But what *does* work—according to the wisdom and design of the Creator Himself—is moral freedom of choice in which the individual is held responsible for both discerning and choosing a moral path based on broad principles of law (such as the Ten Commandments) as opposed to some exhaustive regulatory code. Anything else ultimately destroys morality.

CHAPTER SEVEN

The Deceptiveness of Judaism

*"The heart of man is hopelessly deceitful;
who can even begin to understand it?"*

The Jewish notion of an "oral tradition" somehow passed on from God to Moses—which is *the* central plank of Judaism—stands exposed as a fraud. The utter impossibility of such an "oral law" proves that Judaism is most decidedly *not* the true "religion" of the Old Testament. Judaism, at best, reflects the seriously misguided efforts of men to please God; at worse, Judaism embodies that which is universally condemned in any religion—hypocrisy, idolatry and self-righteousness.

Judaism is by no means alone in this particular criticism, as nominal Christianity functions largely as a fair-weather, "Sunday-only" religion with little real-life influence on its followers. Protestantism is quite tainted by hypocrisy and self-righteousness, and Catholicism clearly demonstrates a proclivity for idolatrous forms of worship (particularity with its contra-biblical reverence for the virgin Mary and its virtual deification of its popes). Regardless of the belief system, wholesale idolatry, hypocrisy and self-righteousness are always signs of false religion.

In the case of Judaism, the rabbis' claim to follow the Scriptures while openly venerating and exalting the Talmud epitomizes the spirit of hypocrisy. Talmudists idolatrously exalt their rabbis and consider the word of their rabbis as supreme, even above Scripture. And, as we will see, Judaism is a religion of self-justification, wherein its adherents claim a form of "righteousness" based on ritual works. Judaism is also shockingly racist in nature, secretly teaching that non-Jews are "less than human."

Judaism—A Religion of Hypocrisy

As has been shown, Judaism *is* Pharisaism. Recall what Jesus had to say about the hypocrisy of the Pharisees and their scribal leaders: "Guard yourselves from the leaven of the Pharisees, which is hypocrisy" (Luke 12:1). Hypocrisy was their signature trait. In the book of Matthew, Jesus duly noted how the sect typically taught one thing, but practiced another. He warned, "But do not do according to their works, **for they say and do not**. For they bind heavy burdens and [those which are] hard to bear, and lay them on the shoulders of men; but they [themselves] will not move them with [even] one of their own fingers" (Matt. 23:3-4). Here, Jesus compares the Pharisees' *traditional regulations* to physical "burdens" one might bear on his shoulders; the idea is that the Pharisees were openly *severe* to others, but privately *indulgent* to themselves.

Jesus continued: "But woe to you, scribes and Pharisees, hypocrites! For you devour widows' houses, and as a pretext you offer prayers of great length. Because of this, you shall receive the greater judgment" (verse 13). The Pharisees financially abused widows and the needy while only *appearing* to be pious. "Woe to you, scribes and Pharisees, hypocrites! For you shut up the kingdom of heaven before men; for neither do you yourselves enter, nor do you allow those who are entering to enter. Woe to you, scribes and Pharisees, hypocrites! For you travel the sea and the land to make one proselyte, and when he has become one, you make him twofold more a son of Gehenna [destruction] than yourselves" (verses 14-15). It wasn't enough that the Pharisees themselves were living contrary to the ways of God's kingdom—their corrupting influence was hindering others from attaining genuine righteousness.

It is important to understand that the *spirit* of ancient Pharisaism is *alive and well* in modern Judaism. Rabbi Louis Finkelstein (1895-1991) was chosen in 1937 by the Jewish Communities of the World as one of the top rabbis best representing the "lamp of Judaism" to the world. His most recent post was head of the Jewish Theological Seminary of America. In the foreword to Volume I of his two-volume 1946 work *The Pharisees*, Finkelstein wrote: "Pharisaism became Talmudism, Talmudism became Medieval Rabbinism, and Medieval Rabbinism became Modern Rabbinism. But throughout these changes of name, inevitable adaptation of custom, and adjustment of law, **the spirit of the ancient Pharisee survives unaltered**. When a Jew [today] reads his prayer, he is reciting formula prepared by pre-Maccabean [scribal] scholars ... [and] when he studies the Talmud, he is actually repeating the arguments used in the Palestinian [rabbinical] academies" (*The Pharisees*, Vol. I, p. 21; emphasis added).

Finkelstein adds that not only have the "outer accoutrements of Pharisaism ... survived in [the modern Jews'] life," but "**the spirit of the doctrine** [of the Pharisees] **has remained quick and vital**." He writes that "ancient Pharisaism has wandered" from Palestine to almost the entire world, wherein "the disciples of the Pharisees have sought on the one hand to preserve the old, and on the other to create the new." He notes that various Jewish leaders—"spirits of diverse types, yet united in their common loyalty to the ancient teachings"—have over the centuries arisen to maintain "Pharisaism as a religious movement" (pp. 21-22; emphasis added).

Finkelstein points out two 19th-century rabbis—Isaac Spektor and Israel Salanter—as "equals of the greatest of the Pharisaic or Talmudic sages," whose "lives approached [those of] the ancient Pharisees..." (p. 22). (Later we'll see how Spektor was instrumental in the Jews' abrogation of the biblically-commanded land sabbatical.)

Although unintended, Finkelstein's emphatic linking of ancient Pharisaism to modern Judaism works as an indictment against the religion.

It is indeed the same spirit, the same doctrine, the same ritual traditions—and, above all, the same *hypocrisy*. As we will see, the hypocrisy of Judaism is most evident in the many *loopholes* designed to circumvent not only the Scriptures, but even the Jews' own oral laws. But perhaps the most glaring hypocrisy of all lies in how Judaism claims to be the religion of Moses, as based on the written Torah, while simultaneously venerating the Talmud as superior to the Scriptures.

The "Superiority" of the Talmud

We have already seen in previous chapters how Judaism reveres the Talmud above the Scriptures—quoting such scholars as John Phillips, who wrote that, on account of the Talmud, the Scriptures have been "buried beneath vast accumulations of tradition and encrusted with enormous deposits of human interpretation. The Torah itself has been largely **superseded in Judaism by the Talmud**.... [The development of the oral law] had little to do with the [written] Torah. The rabbis, **while professing great reverence for the Mosaic law, had buried [the Scriptures] beneath their oral traditions**" (*Exploring the World of the Jew*, pp. 55, 61; emphasis added). As noted earlier, the Talmud itself claims preeminence over the Scriptures: "There is greater stringency in respect to the teachings of the scribes than in respect to the [written] Torah" (*BT Sanhedrin*, 88b). "Some teachings were handed on orally, and some things were handed on in writing ... [but] we conclude that the ones that are handed on orally are more precious" (*BT Hagigah*, 1:7V).

This hypocritical approach to the Scriptures remains well intact in modern Judaism. Rabbi Aaron Parry, an Educational Director with the international organization "Jews for Judaism," writes that, for Orthodox Jews, "the Talmud represents God's divine will and instruction" (*The Talmud*, p. 10). In another of Finkelstein's works, *The Jews: Their History, Culture, and Religion* (1949), he notes the singular authority of the Talmud. "The Talmud derives its authority from the position held by the ancient academies. The teachers of those academies, both of Babylonia and of Palestine, were considered the rightful successors of the older Sanhedrin.... At the present time the Jewish people have no living central authority comparable in status to the ancient Sanhedrin or the later academies. Therefore, any decision regarding the Jewish religion [i.e., how to live one's life] **must be based on the Talmud**"—never mind the fact that Isaiah 8:20 says *Scripture* alone is the sole authority in human affairs—"as the final resume of the teaching of those authorities when they existed" (vol. 4, p. 1332; quoted in *The Jewish Religion—Its Influence Today* by Elizabeth Dilling, p. 1).

In *Judaism Discovered*, Michael Hoffman quotes Robert Goldenberg, Professor of Judaic Studies at the State University of New York: "In a paradox that determined the history of Judaism, the Talmud was Oral Torah in written form, and as such **it became the clearest statement the Jew**

could hear of God's very word…. The Talmud provided the means of determining how God wanted all Jews to live, in all places, at all times…. **The Talmud revealed God speaking to Israel**, **and so the Talmud became Israel's way to God**" (*Back to the Sources: Reading the Classic Jewish Texts*, pp. 166-167; Hoffman, p. 141; emphasis added).

Hoffman also notes that, according to the Talmud, there are *three levels* of study in Judaism. The **highest is to study the Talmud**, the second is the Mishnah, and the third (and lowest) is to study the Scriptures. Studying the Scriptures is, in the opinion of the sages, a matter of indifference to God; studying the Talmud is *meritorious* (*BT Baba Mezia*, 33a). Hoffman writes that "while Judaism pays elaborate lip-service to the Bible, the Bible is not a factor in the rise, formation, progress and emendations of rabbinic law … [**and serves only**] **as a prestigious cover and front for what are**, **in fact**, **entirely man-made enactments** [and] figments of rabbinic imagination… (pp. 132-133; emphasis added).

While this is denied among rabbis, the following rabbinic passage demonstrates the Jewish belief in the superiority of the oral law over the written Law of the Bible: "[The] difference between [the] written and oral regulations finds expression in the appraisal that 'The sages safeguarded their own enactments [oral laws] more than those of the [written] Torah' and in the hyperbolical statements concerning **the supreme authority of the expositions and decisions of the rabbis. The Almighty Himself is bound by them**" (*Pesiqta de-R. Kahana*, Para, ed. Mandelbaum, p. 73; quoted by Hoffman, p. 132). As this astonishing passage reveals, the rabbis consider their laws and rulings to be *superior* to those of the Scriptures—and that God Himself, as if conceding His inferior status, is bound by such rulings!

Scholars are anything but shy when it comes to admitting how *little* the Scriptures have actually influenced the development of Judaism. In the introduction to the 1988 Yale University English translation of the Mishnah (a key part of the Talmud), the editors write that the Mishnah is "remarkably indifferent to the Hebrew Scriptures." Indeed, "Scripture plays little role in the Mishnaic system. The Mishnah rarely cites a verse of Scripture, refers to Scripture as an entity, links its own ideas to those of Scripture, or lays claim to originate in what Scripture has said…. **[The] Mishnah stands in splendid isolation from Scripture**…. Since some of the named authorities in the chain of tradition appear throughout the materials of the Mishnah, the claim is that what these [sages] say comes to them from Sinai through the processes of *qabbalah* [the handing down of traditions]…. [Thus] **the Mishnah does not cite Scripture [because] it does not have to**" (*The Mishnah: A New Translation*, pp. 13; 35-36; quoted by Hoffman, pp. 288, 294; emphasis added). In other words, the Mishnah, and thus the Talmud, rests *totally* on the alleged authority of the sages, in "splendid isolation from Scripture"!

In spite of the pretentious claim that the Law as given by Moses is the foundation of the Jews' religion, Judaism clearly portrays the Talmud as "morally superior" to Scripture. Jewish author Herman Wouk writes, "The

Talmud is to this day the circulating heart's blood of the Jewish religion. Whatever laws, customs or ceremonies we observe—whether we are Orthodox, Conservative, Reform or merely spasmodic sentimentalists—we follow the Talmud. It is our common law" (*The Talmud: Heart's Blood of the Jewish Faith*, published serially in the *New York Herald-Tribune*, Nov. 1959 installment; quoted by Dilling, p. 2).

Karaite Jews represent a notable exception to this Jewish hypocrisy concerning the Scriptures. Scorning the Talmud and upholding Scripture as the supreme authority, the Jewish sect arose in Babylon in the 8th century AD. Reminiscent of the Pharisees' hatred toward the Sadducees (a sect, you will recall, which denied the validity of an oral tradition), Karaites are even today disdained as "idolatrous" by modern Pharisaic Judaism.

"Hedge" Around the Law or System of Loopholes?

Nowhere is Judaism's hypocrisy more evident than in the numerous rabbinic loopholes designed to circumvent not only the Scriptures, but, amazingly, many of the rabbis' own Talmudic laws. Hoffman writes that "hypocrisy and double standards are Judaism's stock in trade." American minds are conditioned by the mainstream media to "believe that Orthodox Judaism is a rigorously scrupulous, ultra-conservative Old Testament religion. They mistake the elaborate outer show of piety that historically was the hallmark of Pharisaic mentality for genuine biblical sanctity." However, he writes, when the religion is closely examined the "situation-ethics of Judaism's counterfeit Torah [the Talmud] are brought to light and the antibiblical consequences of making the Holy Scriptures subsidiary to rabbinic enactments are made manifest" (p. 677).

Hoffman contends that the Jews' so-called oral traditions are not really a protective "hedge around the Torah" at all, but serve as loopholes to get around the Law. He writes that the phrase "hedge around the law" is a "generic euphuism invoked to cover falsification and abrogation of the biblical text" (p. 172). The typical Christian understanding of the Jews' "oral law" is that such traditions are "detailed expositions of [biblical] Law ... in the form of innumerable and highly specific injunctions designed to build a hedge around the Torah and thus guard against any possible infringement of the Law by accident or ignorance" (*Zondervan Pictorial Bible Encyclopedia*, Vol. 4, p. 748). Hoffman, who scoffs at this view as an example of Christian naivety, asks, if the Pharisees and sages were so careful in guarding the Scriptures against any possible infringement, "how is it that they came to infringe on that very Word by denying that the Scriptures testify of Jesus Christ?" (p. 173).

The idea that Judaism's oral "hedge laws" originated as a pretext for a system designed to circumvent the Scriptures is overstated. As is often the case, the truth is somewhere in between. It is almost certain that the "oral traditions" of the Jewish sages were originally intended to protect the written Torah; but, human nature being what it is, the "oral law" has over the centuries morphed into a theological system replete with loopholes. Such loopholes are clearly designed to get around certain laws of Scripture as well as some of the Jews' own less convenient regulations. (One might wonder why such Talmudic regulations cannot simply be *repealed* rather than circumvented by additional rabbinic rulings. The Talmud, however, by its very design, does not allow for deletion; apparently, existing laws or rulings can only be clarified, commented on, expanded on, or contradicted by subsequent laws and rulings.)

Regardless of the original intent behind the Jews' oral "hedge laws," Judaism remains guilty of misusing Scripture in an attempt to justify their beloved traditions. The philologist John Selden (1584-1654) explains this process: "It is a most common thing among the Talmudists to seek for some support for their additional customs from some words of the Scriptures, and, as it were, try to hedge [their traditions] behind some biblical word, interpretation or analogy…. [Thus] the original words [of the Scriptures] are twisted and distorted with great boldness to give some seeming confirmation to their customs [irrespective] of the sense of the original" (Hoffman, pp. 173-174; quoted from John Owen's 1661 Latin *Theologoumena Pantodapa*, published under the title *Biblical Theology*, 1994, p. 577).

Indeed, when it comes to "situation ethics," the Talmud and rabbinic Judaism provide the modern Judaic with a system of clever, *yet hypocritical*, loopholes. For example, because Thanksgiving is considered Christian (and thus a form of idolatry), Jews are forbidden to celebrate the American holiday. But Jews are also taught not to refuse a free turkey—as long as they are careful to eat it on a *different* day. Similarly, Christmas gifts are *given* by many Jews in order to obtain favor; the gift is simply "renamed" and given a few days before the holiday (Hoffman, pp. 373-374).

Here are a few more examples:

Based on a flawed interpretation of Deuteronomy 7:2, rabbis teach that Gentiles are not to be shown favor. But a loophole exists to make it possible to give a gift to a Gentile—the gift is considered a *business bribe*.

Since charging interest on a loan violates the Torah (Lev. 25:36-37; etc.), Talmudic Jews have a loophole designed to allow them to charge interest on loans made to fellow Jews. The rabbinical provision *heter iska* simply classifies such loans as "investments" (Hoffman, p. 447).

Moses taught that anyone who committed adultery with his neighbor's wife should be put to death. The rabbis, however, get around this by defining "neighbor" as "a fellow *Jewish* neighbor" (*BT Sanhedrin*, 52b). This led to the rabbinic ruling that adultery with a Gentile's wife was not adultery at all (Hoffman, p. 330).

The rabbis also ruled that cursing one's parents—a violation of the Fifth Commandment—was not a sin unless the curse *included* the name of God (*BT Sanhedrin*, 66a).

Hoffman writes: "The Talmud itself admits that most of its endless rules and regulations have little scriptural basis and that the oral tradition of the Mishnah supersedes the written law of the Scriptures" (p. 287). For example, he notes the Mishnah's *Hagigah*, 1:8a: "The **absolution of vows** hovers in the air, for it has nothing [in the Scriptures] upon which to depend. The [numerous] **laws of the Sabbath**, festal offerings, and sacrilege—lo, they are like mountains hanging by a string, for they [the rabbis] have little Scripture for many laws" (p. 288; emphasis added). The question of the "absolution of vows" will be examined later; but first, an examination of Judaism's approach to the Sabbath will prove quite revealing.

Sabbath Anxieties

Even a casual reading of the Scriptures shows that the Sabbath was created by God *for man to enjoy* as a time of rest and rejuvenation, spiritual reflection and contemplation, and joyous fellowship. But for Orthodox Jews, the Sabbath is often an anxiety-ridden day filled with burdensome rabbinical regulations. In the Talmud, tractate *Shabbat* identifies thirty-nine categories of activity prohibited on the Sabbath by Jewish law. These categories are then expanded into a vast tangled web of nitpicky, trivial rules. With literally *hundreds* of regulations (many of which are quite complex) dictating how the Jew is to "properly" observe the Sabbath, the day is easily robbed of its meaning and becomes nothing more than a futile exercise in self-righteousness as the Talmud-observing Jew anxiously tries to avoid violating rabbinical regulations.

"In Judaism, the Talmudic burlesque of the Sabbath is not a God-given period of rest, but rather a rabbinic plague of mountains of bureaucratic rules and regulations governing everything from ovens to elevators to automobiles…. Fear and anxiety over whether the hundreds of trivial *Shabbat* rules are fulfilled or broken robs the Judaic of the rest that God intended for us to experience on a truly biblical Sabbath" (Hoffman, pp. 943, 947).

A Jew, for example, may fret if his shoestring breaks on the Sabbath. Since tying *knots* on the Sabbath is forbidden by the Talmud, how can he repair the break? (Tying one's shoelaces together is permitted, however, since the knot is *temporary*.) Installing a new shoestring is also prohibited, as it violates the law against "weaving"—and is also considered *melachah*, or "creative work." Similarly, if there is a need to tie up a garbage bag on the Sabbath, a *temporary* knot must be used—and the Jew must remember to come back after the Sabbath and retie the knot, making it permanent. While these are trivial, nonsensical matters, they represent genuine concerns in the minds of Talmudic Jews.

In *Teshuvah: A Guide for the Newly Observant Jew*, Rabbi Adin Steinsaltz writes that observing the Sabbath day means concerning oneself "completely with personal reflection and matters of the spirit, **free of struggle and tension**." Steinsaltz, however, admits that "the body of Shabbat prohibitions can appear to be **an endless maze of details**," adding that such "elaborations" are intended as a "hedge around the more fundamental prohibitions" and thus "prevent certain habitual activities from leading to Shabbat violations." He advises that Sabbath-keeping "**details need to be mastered**" and that one should avoid making "assumptions about what is permitted and what is not" (myjewishlearning.com; emphasis added).[1]

The Web site chabad.org—used to promote ultra-Orthodox Judaism throughout the world—notes this about Sabbath observance: "The **Shabbat laws are quite complex**, requiring careful study and [the help of] a qualified teacher. At first, it's often overwhelming and seems like an impossible number of restrictions. But spending *Shabbat* with others who are *Shabbat* observant will show you that eventually you, too, will become comfortable with the *Shabbat* laws" (emphasis added).[2]

A Sabbath observance "free of struggle and tension"—*really?*

As a *former* Talmud-observing Jew, Avi ben Mordechai has personally experienced the burden of Rabbinical Judaism. In his commentary on the book of Galatians, Mordechai writes, "[Eventually,] I realized that the [rabbis'] *halachah* [laws] had no end in sight; that it was **nothing short of a deep, black hole and an endless system of legal minutiae. It was always tiring for me to try to keep up with all the daily demands** [of Talmudic law]. I did not have a difficult time agreeing with Rebbe Nachman of Breslov (1772-1810) who once said that his daily religious obligations **felt like a crushing burden** (*The Empty Chair*, p. 40)" (*Galatians—A Torah-Based Commentary in First-Century Hebraic Context*, p. 48; emphasis added). Mordechai candidly adds that it has been his observation that those who choose to submit to Pharisaic Judaism with its vast code of laws will ultimately "end up in *denial* of the written Torah" (p. 371).

In Judaism, even the definitions of *work* and *rest* are anything but clear—leading to more Sabbath anxiety. Rabbi Aaron Parry writes that "*rest* can mean many things… The ambiguities of these meanings are what the Talmud addresses in the tractate *Shabbat*" (*The Talmud*, p. 61).

"The Bible doesn't prohibit work in the classic sense of the word. But it does prohibit *melachah*…. The distinction between work and *melachah* can be difficult to grasp…. *Melachah*, which means creative work in Hebrew, refers to **work that is creative** or that **exercises control or dominion over one's environment**" (p. 61; emphasis added). Thus, "on *Shabbat* we abstain from *creating* and not necessarily from *exertion*…. So, it's not an issue of stressful versus un-stressful—it's an issue of creative versus non-creative" (chabad.org).[3]

Exodus 20:10 commands us to "do no manner of *melachah*" on the Sabbath. Throughout the Old Testament, *melachah*—mostly translated *work* or *business*—means, simply, *work*; Hebrew Lexicons say *melachah* refers primarily to one's occupation. In Judaism, however, the prohibition against "creative work" stems from Genesis 2:3, where God rested from His work of creating. Steinsaltz explains: "The concept of *melachah* is understood both in the simple sense of 'work,' which is its plain meaning, and in the more complex sense that flows from the context in which it first appears, the story of the Sabbath of creation…. What is decisive is not the degree of effort involved, or whether the action receives monetary compensation, but rather whether [the action or work] **results in the appearance of something *new*** in the physical world. Thus, relatively **effortless activities like writing are forbidden**" (myjewishlearning.com; emphasis added). Obviously, an almost unlimited number of activities may be considered "creative." For the Talmudic Jew, the level of vigilance required to avoid *melachah* on the Sabbath leads to obsessive paranoia—not rest and peacefulness.

This clever manipulation of Scripture—a tactic commonly employed in Judaism—obscures the plain meanings of both *rest* and *work*. Thus, for observant Jews, the Sabbath becomes a day of senseless *burdens*—not unlike the ones Christ referred to in Matthew 23:4. For example, the rule against *melachah* regulates the proper use of a simple can opener. Rabbi Menachem Posner asks, "Is it permissible to use a can opener on Shabbat?" He replies, "There are different opinions regarding this matter. [Those] cans which will be needed on Shabbat should be opened prior to Shabbat—thus avoiding a **questionable situation** [Such uncertainty has to cause at least a little anxiety!]. The main concern is that opening the can *creates* a [new] useable receptacle. Such an act could conceivably [lead to] the formation of a utensil. The key therefore is to avoid *creating* a receptacle." Posner then gives this clever advice: "Many people will open the top of the can while puncturing its bottom. This prevents the container from becoming a useful receptacle" (chabad.org; emphasis added).[4]

Likewise, cooking is forbidden, not because it is *work* (see Ex. 16:23), but because it is *creative*; playing musical instruments—even for relaxation and to add to the joy of the Sabbath—are prohibited as *creative*. Driving a car is forbidden because it involves "the creative manipulation of physical resources" (*The Talmud*, p. 63); moreover, driving a car requires "kindling a fire" (via its internal combustion engine) and could well lead to a "carrying" violation. (These two key issues—"kindling a fire" and "carrying"—are central to the Talmudic Jew's rigid observance of the Sabbath and are discussed below.)

Again, such absurd regulations—and there are *hundreds* of them—rob the Sabbath of its intent and purpose. Clearly, the mindset behind such rabbinic teachings is precisely that of the ancient Pharisees: "Woe to you, scribes and Pharisees, hypocrites! For you [are very careful to] pay tithes of mint and anise and cummin, but you have abandoned the more important matters of the Law—judgment, and mercy and faith. These you were obligated to do, and not to leave the others undone. Blind guides, who [meticulously] filter out a gnat, but [willingly] swallow a camel!" (Matt. 23:23-24).

Similarly, Talmudic Jews knowingly allow certain liberties that are clearly contrary to Scripture (swallowing a camel), but go to extremes to "avoid even the tiniest gnat" by being fanatically obsessed with a multitude of trivial laws that accomplish nothing except to create a facade of piety. Such liberties violate the Scriptures either through misunderstanding and misapplication or through the deliberate circumvention of the Law through clever loopholes.

Sabbath Loopholes

Aside from how senseless it is that Judaism actually features a body of laws on such trivial subjects as "how to wash dishes" to how one should "use the toilet" on the Sabbath, it is the numerous rabbinic *loopholes* concerning Sabbath observance that stand out as evidence of the religion's Pharisaic hypocrisy. Like many rabbinical rulings, such loopholes not only circumvent the clear teachings of Scripture, they also provide clever ways for Jews to skirt their *own* Talmudic laws.

For example, the biblical prohibition against "kindling a fire" on the Sabbath—grossly misunderstood in Judaism—is not only taken to fanatical extremes by Talmudic Jews, it is also an area of Jewish ritual observation that is fraught with hypocrisy. Exodus 35:3 reads, "You shall kindle no fire throughout your living places upon the Sabbath day." Misunderstanding this passage, Orthodox Jews assume they are not to *start* a fire of any kind on the Sabbath—even to keep warm. Jews will argue that it is permissible to *have* a fire on the Sabbath, as long as it was started prior to the beginning of the Sabbath. (According to one authority, one could technically start the fire *outside* on the Sabbath and then bring the fire inside the house.) Interestingly, however, they overlook the fact that *maintaining* a fire throughout the day actually entails more "work" than the simple act of *kindling* a fire. Thus, it is illogical that *kindling* a fire would violate one's respite from work on the Sabbath, while maintaining a fire would not. Many Jewish authorities, however, argue that *feeding* a fireplace or stove with wood is also prohibited as the act contributes to further "combustion."

Are we really to understand this passage to mean that one is not to kindle a fire on the Sabbath in one's home—even in order to keep warm? The fact is, this prohibition refers primarily to kindling fires for the purpose of conducting one's livelihood in an agrarian society. Notice the context, which is set by verse two. "Six days shall work be done, but on the seventh day there shall be to you a holy day, a Sabbath of rest to the Lord. Whoever does work in it shall be put to death." There are many ways in which the Sabbath could be violated; yet, the prohibition against kindling fires is the *only* command in the entire passage concerning the Sabbath. *Why?*

When one reads the remainder of the chapter, which deals with the work of building the Tabernacle (and note the reference in verse 35 to "engravers," which is sometimes translated "smiths"), it becomes clear that the prohibition against kindling fires on the Sabbath was given not only in regard to routine work necessary in an agrarian society, but particularly in reference to fires utilized in the work of building and crafting implements for the Tabernacle. Again, the idea that on the Sabbath one can *have* a fire, but cannot *kindle* a fire, is ludicrous. Clearly, the intent of the passage in question is that one cannot have a *work fire* on the Sabbath—period.

Moreover, if Exodus 35:3 was dealing with building a fire in one's *home*, the Hebrew *bayith* would likely have been used. Rather, the term *mowshab* is used, which is generic for "dwelling place" and frequently carries the same weight as city, town or village. The sense of this passage is that, throughout all of their settlements, the Israelites were not to kindle work fires on the Sabbath—even when it came to building the Tabernacle. But starting a fire in the home, even on the Sabbath, was clearly permissible. Granted, one was to prepare ahead of time, before the Sabbath, by gathering wood (see Num. 15:32). But from that point on, kindling and maintaining a fire for heating food or bodily warmth required little effort.

Would Jesus—who is "Lord of the Sabbath" (Matt. 12:8)—hesitate to kindle a fire on the Sabbath to keep from being miserably cold? He thought nothing of stopping by a field of grain on the Sabbath to allow His disciples to satisfy their hunger (verse one). They weren't "harvesting" a crop—which would have been a violation of the Sabbath—they were simply getting a quick meal. The Pharisees, however, obsessed with their own contrived Sabbath regulations, accused them of violating the Sabbath.

Likewise, Talmud-thumping Jews today attempt to apply Exodus 35:3 via Pharisaic rules. Not only will they not kindle a fire on the Sabbath—though they have no problem having a non-Jew come over and start one for them!—they will also refuse to turn on a light, or a stove, or anything that generates heat or might be construed as a "fire"! In his *Guide for the Newly Observant Jew*, Rabbi Steinsaltz notes: "[It] is not permitted to kindle or handle fire on Shabbat, a fact that has always been of great practical significance [How, one wonders, has *not* having fire been practical?]. Not only is smoking prohibited, so is operating a vehicle or tool requiring internal combustion…. Warm foods are permitted on the Sabbath when their preparation does not require ignition [turning on the stove or oven] or changing the heat of the oven on the Sabbath itself….

"In our own time, Shabbat observance has been made easier by the introduction of automatic timing devices ('Shabbos clocks') to turn electrical appliances on and off, and thermostatically controlled heating elements for keeping food warm." But if Jews really believe it is wrong to kindle (or handle) a fire (or turn on a stove, or flip on a light) on the Sabbath, then why is it permissible to have an automatic timer do the work? Even if you set the timer before the Sabbath, *you* still caused the appliance to be turned on. Isn't this approach at least somewhat disingenuous? Naturally, Steinsaltz explains the "logic" behind the loophole: "These technological advances may be used because the **Shabbat prohibitions apply not to the processes themselves, but to the human performance of them**. Still, there are numerous *halakhic* restrictions [there's that anxiety again] involved in the use of such devices" (myjewishlearning.com; emphasis added). "Numerous restrictions" on the use of automatic timers? Even the loophole itself is complicated!

Again, one must revisit the rabbis' clever definition of work—or *melachah*. "[On] Shabbat we abstain from *creating* and not necessarily from *exertion*…. When we drive a car, for example, we are *creating* fire (in the internal combustion engine). When we turn on the light, we are *creating* an electrical circuit. And so on with all other Shabbat prohibitions. So, it's not an issue of stressful versus un-stressful—it's an issue of *creative* versus non *-creative*" (chabad.org).

On the ultra-Orthodox Web site chabad.org, Rabbi Eliezer Zalmanov is asked about having a non-Jew load wood for a fireplace on the Sabbath. "Our house is heated by a wood burning stove. Our winters are cold. To keep warm, we must load the stove several times a day…. However, we are faced with a dilemma on Shabbat—feed the fire or be cold, sometimes very cold. Can we ask a non-Jew to load the stove?" Zalmanov answers: "Though ordinarily **it is not permitted to ask a non-Jew to violate the Sabbath for us**, there are a few exceptions to this rule…. Now, while your situation—a wood burning stove—may be an anomaly in today's day and age, it was the norm before the twentieth century. As such, it is discussed in the *Code of Jewish Law*—which rules that one may ask a non-Jew to load the wood" (emphasis added; Zalmanov cites *Alter Rebbe's Shulchan Aruch*, or "Code of Jewish Law," *Orach Chaim 276:15*; see Appendix Two).[5]

The hypocrisy here is palpable. If it is wrong for a Jew to kindle a fire (or load a stove) on the Sabbath, then it should also be wrong for a non-Jew. Otherwise, in Zalmanov's own words, you are knowingly causing the non-Jew to "violate the Sabbath." However, as we will see later, this is really a moot point. Jews believe the Sabbath was made for *Jews*, not for Gentiles. Thus, to ask a non-Jew to "violate the Sabbath" is oxymoronic. Zalmanov's suggestion is misleading to say the least, and cleverly obscures the Jews' disdain for Gentiles.

Another set of patently hypocritical rabbinic loopholes involves what is known as a "Sabbath day's journey"—or, the distance one can "legally" travel on the Sabbath. First, it should be noted that no such restrictions are found in Scripture. While Acts 1:12 makes a passing reference to "a Sabbath day's journey," there is no proof that such a restriction was sanctioned or observed by Jesus or His disciples. Rather, the rule originated as a part of Jewish tradition. Albert Barnes notes that a Sabbath day's journey was "two thousand paces or cubits; or seven furlongs and a half—not quite one mile…. The distance of a lawful journey on the Sabbath was **not determined by the laws of Moses, but [by] the Jewish teachers [who] had fixed it at two thousand paces**. This measure was determined because it was a **tradition** that, in the camp of the Israelites when coming from Egypt, no part of the camp was more than two thousand paces from the tabernacle; and over this space, therefore, they were permitted to travel for worship" (*Barnes' Commentary*, "Acts 1:12"; emphasis added).

Ostensibly, the origin of this Jewish tradition is Exodus 16:29—"Do not let anyone *go out of his place* on the seventh day." However, as Barnes notes, the Jewish sages reasoned that the children of Israel were allowed to travel at least the distance to the tabernacle—some "two thousand paces or cubits" at the most. Thus, they concluded, a Sabbath day's journey would be set at 2000 paces.

This distance, however, eventually proved to be too limiting. Thus, subsequent rabbis looked for a loophole—or, at least, an amendment—to the tradition. "Over the centuries, the authorities within the rabbinical circles of Judaism found ways, from examining the miniscule details of the Law, to increase the distance that an Israelite may travel on the Sabbath day. In ancient times they [had] determined that one may travel on the Sabbath within the city boundaries [a distance of] 2000 cubits.... Then, after some time, the rabbis interpreted 'place' [in Exodus 16:29] to mean *city*, so that it would be acceptable to travel 2000 cubits *outside* the city limits on the Sabbath day."

But even this loophole was eventually found to be insufficient. "[The] Pharisees [later] *doubled* the distance that one might travel by yet another minute detail. They inserted a rule that if one placed food preparations at another location, then that [second location] figuratively became his abode [his *place*, per Exodus 16]...." Thus, the Jew was allowed to travel 2000 paces outside the city to his second "place"—then travel another 2000 paces from that "figurative abode"—making his actual "Sabbath journey" a total of up to 4000 paces. Yet, technically, he was never more than 2000 paces from his "place." Moreover, the rabbis later reasoned that since a person would need to return home, that same journey could be legally retraced, for a total of 8000 paces (*How Far Was a Sabbath Day's Journey?*, bible-history.com).[6]

Jesus, however, taught that the Sabbath was made *for* man, and not man for the Sabbath (Mark 2:27). As Lord of the Sabbath (verse 28), Jesus repeatedly reproved the Jewish religious authorities for misunderstanding the spirit of the Law and laying heavy Sabbath burdens upon the people. As we have seen, such Pharisaic burdens are alive and well today.

The Sabbath Prohibition Against "Carrying"

Another peculiar case in point is the rabbinic ruling against "carrying," one of the 39 categories of activities forbidden on the Sabbath. The original Talmudic ruling is based, once again, on Exodus 16:29, "let no man *go out of his place* on the seventh day," and Jeremiah 17:21-22, "*carry no burden* on the Sabbath day.... Nor carry out a burden from your houses* on the Sabbath day...." From these passages come the rabbinic prohibition against transferring an object—such as a pen or pencil, a woman's purse, a set of car keys, an umbrella, a sack lunch, or even one's small baby—*from* a private domain ("his place") *to* a public domain on the Sabbath day. However, in keeping with Jesus' statement concerning Pharisaic hypocrisy— "they say but they do not"—clever rabbinic loopholes exist in order to get around this absurd Sabbath regulation.

Again, this is a classic case of gross misunderstanding by Jewish sages. When Jeremiah used the term *burden*, was he really referring to simple items such as pen or pencil, one's purse, a book, an umbrella, etc.? Or, as the context shows, was he not referring to the transporting of *goods* for

the purpose of being sold on the Sabbath? Verses 21 and 24 mention bringing such burdens through the gates of Jerusalem. For what purpose? In a
similar passage, Nehemiah had to confront Jews and non-Jews alike who
persisted in bringing such "burdens" to Jerusalem on the Sabbath (Neh.
13:15-22). Here, the context is clearly about conducting the business of *buying and selling* on the Sabbath.

For those who understand the purpose of the Sabbath and have a
modicum of common sense, it is easy to see that carrying a purse, wallet,
basket of food, or a child on the Sabbath is no *burden* at all and certainly
does not constitute *work*. Recall the incident in John five where, after healing a man on the Sabbath, Jesus instructed him to take up his "bed" (more
like a sleeping bag or bedroll) and go his way. The scribes and Pharisees
were offended to say the least—as the man violated an early form of the
Jews' prohibition against "carrying." But by no means did the man violate
any biblical law or ordinance.

As brought out earlier, the key is understanding of the spirit of Law.
While there is no biblical sanction against "carrying" or transporting everyday objects on the Sabbath—in one's home or in public—it is obvious to
those who understand the spirit and intent of the Law that packing up one's
household and having a "moving day" on the Sabbath would be wrong, as
the entire day would be one of extensive work. But the idea that carrying
such mundane items such as one's purse or a pencil into the "public domain" violates the Sabbath is, to say the least, a ludicrous example of the
nitpicky, obsessive paranoia that has become an integral part of Judaic Sabbath-keeping.

From a moral standpoint, if you are going to boast of such Sabbath
regulations—as absurd as they are—then, by all means, *abide by them*. If
carrying everyday items into the "public domain" on the Sabbath is really
forbidden by the Law, then the stipulation *must* be obeyed. But apparently
Talmudic Jews are more interested in following their own humanly-devised
traditions than in obeying the Scriptures. In this case, the rabbis get around
the "carrying" prohibition through what is called an *eruv*—a make-believe
border that converts entire neighborhoods into giant "private domains."

Note the flagrant hypocrisy. "On *Shabbat*, all activities associated
with work are prohibited, and according to traditional Jewish law include
formal employment as well as traveling, spending money, and *carrying
items outside the home, in the public domain*. The prohibition against
'carrying' includes house keys, prayer books, canes or walkers, and even
children who cannot walk on their own. **Recognizing the difficulties this
rule imposes, the sages of the Talmud devised a way to allow for
'carrying' in public without breaking the rule**. Through this means,
called an *eruv*, communities are able to turn a large [public] area into one
that is considered, for Jewish [legal] purposes, a large private domain, into
which items may be carried" (Sharonne Cohen, *String Around the City*, my-
jewishlearning.com; emphasis added).[7]

The term *eruv* refers to "the act of mixing or combining and is short-hand for *eruv hazerot*—the mixing of [private and public] domains." Once a number of private and public properties have been integrated into a single, larger "private domain," individuals are then permitted to "carry" objects within the boundaries of the *eruv*. However, "having an *eruv* does not mean that a city or neighborhood is enclosed entirely by a literal wall. Rather, the *eruv* can be symbolically comprised of a series of pre-existing structures (walls, fences, electrical poles and wires) and structures created expressly for the *eruv*, often a wire mounted on poles. In practice, then, the *eruv* is a symbolic demarcation of the private sphere, one that communities come together to create" (Cohen).

Hoffman labels the tactic for what it is: "A *loophole* for nullifying these rules against carrying is found in the rabbinic concept of the *eruv* ... in which a symbolic ritual wire is strung around a city neighborhood, thereby creating the *eruv*.... [An *eruv* typically] encloses several blocks. The area within the *eruv* is then considered a private domain where carrying is permitted" (*Judaism Discovered*, p. 944).

In Steinsaltz's *Guide for the Newly Observant Jew* (myjewish-learning.com), we find another component to the *eruv*—a shared meal. He writes: "The two central practices connected with [an *eruv*] are the creation of a symbolic fence around a city (or any part of it) formed by an arrangement of posts and wire, and a symbolic communal meal shared by all those participating in the *eruv*." According to Steinsaltz, in some larger cities it is not practical to erect the necessary "boundaries." In such cases, however, the *eruv* can be formed through a shared meal—by which all participants in the *eruv* are considered to be living in a common, *private* dwelling. The rabbis with chabad.org add: "Everyone in the city (or area of the *eruv*) contributes food (or, as is usually done, one person in the city can supply the food for everyone) and this food is kept in one of the houses. This symbolizes that all the people who dwell within the *eruv* are now 'sharing' food, and are therefore one, big happy family living in one 'private' domain." [8]

Lorne Rozovsky of chabad.org writes that an *eruv* is "one of those traditions which has blossomed from a basic [biblical] principle into a **highly complicated legal matter**" (*What is an Eruv?*; emphasis added). [9]

Highly complicated? When the plain teachings of the Scriptures are clouded by vain, humanly-devised *traditions*—which are themselves subject to numerous revisions and deceptive loopholes—then, yes, religion *does* get complicated. But the *teachings of Moses* as set forth in the Old Testament are straightforward, honest, practical—and, above all, not subject to the revisionist whims of men. To borrow a phrase from the apostle Paul, Rabbinical Judaism has "changed the truth of God into a lie" (Rom. 1:25), and can *in no way* represent the God of the Scriptures.

The Land Sabbath Abrogated

The Old Testament explicitly states that "you shall sow your land six years, and shall gather in the fruits of it. But the seventh year you shall let it rest and lie still, so that the poor of your people may eat. And what they leave, the animals of the field shall eat. In the same way you shall deal with your vineyard and with your olive-grove" (Ex. 23:10-11; also Lev. 25:1-5). If Judaism's claim to be the embodiment of the "religion of Moses" was at all valid, one would suppose that Orthodox Jews who own agricultural land today would follow this injunction to allow the land to rest every seventh year. After all, violation of the land Sabbath was one of the key reasons for God punishing ancient Judah (Lev. 26:34, 43; II Chron. 36:20-21).

But such is not the case. In keeping with the hypocrisy of Pharisaic Judaism, a loophole has been created by rabbis that allows Jewish land to be temporarily "sold" to a non-Jew so that it might remain productive (and profitable) even on the *shmita*, or sabbatical year. In direct defiance of God's command, the land Sabbath has never been officially observed in the modern state of Israel. This particular nullification of God's Word by "greater than God" rabbis is called *Heter Mechirah* ("leniency of sale").

"According to the Talmud, observance of the sabbatical year is of high accord.... Nonetheless, rabbinic Judaism has developed *halakhic* (religious law) devices to be able to maintain a modern agricultural and commercial system while [ostensibly] giving heed to the biblical injunctions. Such devices represent examples of flexibility within the *halakhic* system" (wikipedia.org/wiki/Shmita). Numerous *shmita* rulings have appeared since the first century, all designed to get around the land Sabbath command.

In more modern times, according to Hoffman, a rabbinical ruling to *relax* the land Sabbath requirement was issued in 1888—and implemented in the sabbatical year of 1889—by Rabbi Shmuel Z. Klepfish of the rabbinic court of Poland. Klepfish, regarded as one of the outstanding Jewish legal authorities of his time, intended that the measure provide relief for the impoverished Jewish settlements of those days (*Judaism Discovered*, p. 913).

Soon afterwards, Rabbi Yitzchak (Isaac) E. Spektor engineered the *Heter Mechirah* loophole that nullifies the sabbatical year through its mock-sale of Jewish land to Gentiles. Hoffman includes this quote from the 1978 *Encyclopedia Judaica*: "On the question of agricultural labor in Eretz Israel, in a *shemittah* ('sabbatical') year, he [Spektor] favored its permission by the nominal sale of land to a non-Jew, a measure which is employed to the present day" (Vol. 15, pp. 259-260; Hoffman, p. 914-915). The online *Wikipedia* explains Spektor's approach: "In the late 19th century, in the early days of Zionism, Rabbi Yitzchak Elchanan Spektor came up with a *halakhic* means of allowing agriculture to continue during the *shmita* year. After ruling ... that the biblical prohibition consists of not cultivating the land owned by Jews ('*your* land,' Exodus 23:10), Rabbi Spektor devised a mechanism by which the land could be sold to a non-Jew for the duration of that year under a trust agreement. Under this plan, the land would belong to the non-Jew temporarily, and revert back to Jewish ownership when the year was over. When the land was sold under such an arrangement, Jews could continue to farm it. Rabbi Abraham Isaac Kook, the first Chief Rabbi of British Mandate Palestine, adopted this principle, which became known as the *Heter Mechirah*" (wikipedia.org/wiki/Shmita).

Hoffman adds that "all subsequent Israeli Chief Rabbis have continued to uphold the validity of the *Heter Mechirah*" (p. 915)—which means that since its inception the modern nation of Israel has *never* kept the land Sabbath as mandated by Scripture!

The "Absolution of Vows"

One of the more striking rabbinical loopholes is one that allows Jews to intentionally break vows—which Scripture forbids (Num. 30; etc.). The controversial rabbinic ritual—the *Kol Nidrei* rite of Yom Kippur—entails the nullification of all vows made in the *coming* year, thus allowing the Talmudist to conveniently break his word with impunity. Hoffman writes that this rite is portrayed in the media as a "noble plea for forgiveness and atonement for having broken promises in the *past*"—which would indeed be a commendable exercise (p. 966). But the loophole is specifically designed to give *advance* absolution for the upcoming year. "This advance stipulation is called *bitul tenai* and is the basis for a Judaic being absolved in advance of breaking promises that he will make in the future…" (Hoffman, p. 967).

Rabbinical Judaism makes no attempt to justify the doctrine of *Kol Nidrei* by the Scriptures; indeed, the Mishnah plainly admits that the rite has absolutely no biblical basis. "The absolution of vows hovers in the air, for it has nothing [in the Law] upon which to depend" (*BT Hagigah*, 1:8a). Even the highly respected Maimonides confirms that the rite is in no way scriptural: "[The absolution from oaths] has no basis whatsoever in the Written Torah" (*Mishneh Torah, Sefer Haflaah, Hilkhot Shevuot*, 6:2).[10]

Concerning the ritual, the Talmud says: "And he who desires that none of his vows made during the year shall be valid, let him stand at the beginning of the year [on Yom Kippur] and declare, 'Every vow which I make in the future will be null' " (*BT Nedarim*, 23a, 23b). The Mishnah adds: "He who desires that none of his vows made during the [upcoming] year shall be valid, let him stand at Rosh haShanah [the beginning of the year] and declare, 'Every vow which I may make in the future shall be cancelled,' provided that he remembers [the stipulation] at the time of [making] the vow" (*Mishnah Nedarim*, 3:1).

Note that the action taken to nullify vows is taken at the *beginning* of the year with regard to vows made in the *future*. The distinction is critical as it contradicts the popular perception of *Kol Nidrei*—that it is a humble rite of repentance and contrition. The hypocrisy of the *Kol Nidrei* rite adds to the pretentiousness of the whole Yom Kippur ceremony—an observance laden with hollow displays of penitence, piety, fasting and prayer.

In explaining the *Kol Nidrei* rite, Rabbi Louis Jacobs, a leader of Conservative Judaism in the United Kingdom, emphasized that a Jew's vows are valid "**only if the vow is uttered with** *full intent*. A person's declaration beforehand that all vows he will take in the year ahead are null and void means that **any vow he will make is held to be without sufficient intention and hence without binding power**" (myjewishlearning.com; emphasis added).[11]

Yet, as Hoffman notes, the rite is far from an ancient practice. "*Kol Nidrei* is an integral pillar of a proud, resurgent and assertive religion that continues to [self-righteously] announce to the world that it is the standard-bearer of justice and ethics" (p. 970).

Jesus simply taught, "But **let your word be good**, your 'Yes' be yes and your 'No' be no; for anything that is added to these is from the evil one" (Matt. 5:37; also James 5:12). The *Kol Nidrei* rite exposes Judaism to the disdain and indignation of honest men everywhere. Clearly, any religion that teaches men how to absolve themselves of commitments cannot be the religion of the God of the Old Testament.

The "Divine" Status of Rabbis

In a subtle but clearly cultish fashion, Judaism embodies the dogma of *control*—by which every observant Orthodox Jew is "enslaved down to the most minute and intimate particulars of his or her daily life…. The religion of Judaism, the religion of [the] Talmud … is an all-encompassing form of totalitarianism" (Hoffman, pp. 147, 819). This element of control is made possible only because of the exalted status given to rabbis. In fact, the status enjoyed by rabbis can only be described as *idolatrous*. As we will see, in the eyes of the Talmudic Jew, the rabbi is much more than simply a teacher, guide or mentor; the rabbi is a virtual "demigod," worthy of reverence, awe and adulation. While it is carefully understated, the Talmud clearly bestows its sages with a certain level of divinity. For example, the Talmud teaches that the commands of the rabbis are more important than the commands of the Scriptures: "My son, be more careful in [the observance of] the words of the scribes than in the words of the [written] Torah, for in the laws of the Torah there are positive and negative precepts; but, as to the laws of the scribes, **whoever transgresses any of the enactments of the scribes** [and, by extension, today's rabbis] **incurs the penalty of death**" (*BT Eruvin*, 21b). The Talmud also says that the decrees of rabbinic councils are not to be questioned, as such councils carry authority *equal* to that of Moses (*BT Rosh Hashanah*, 25a); moreover, the Talmud makes the fallacious claim that even the Scriptures teach that the rulings of the rabbis must be obeyed—and that those who obey the rabbis are holy, while those who disobey are wicked (*BT Yebamoth*, 20a).[12] With such blatant self exaltation, it is no wonder that writers like Hoffman argue that "**Judaism teaches the ultimate delusion, the supremacy of the rabbi above God**" (p. 304).

Avi ben Mordechai, who spent much of his life under the oppressive rule of Rabbinical Judaism, explains how the ancient sages blatantly trashed the context of Deuteronomy 30:12—seizing the single phrase, "it is not in heaven"—in an attempt to claim "sole authority on earth" and justify their lofty position. "*Lo bashmayim hi* ["It is not in heaven"] is a doctrine of Pharisaism evidenced from at least the days of Rabbi Eliezer [about 90 AD]. The rabbis teach that God assigned all His earthly jurisdiction over to them, supposedly telling them that they will be His voice to all Israel on earth, based on Deuteronomy 30:12. No voice of [God] is needed for guidance; the Pharisees and now the rabbis have removed that. They tell us (directly or indirectly) to have faith in them. This includes their *carte blanche* authority on earth to correct, repair, add to or take away from the written Word—on earth—all under the skirt of an oral law love affair. It is forbidden to annul what they pass down; [one may] only improve upon it…. Anyone who brings forth an opinion contrary to established oral tradition—even if he was known to be a holy prophet—is to be ignored" (*Galatians*, p. 412).

As Mordechai brings out, Judaism's most honored sage, Maimonides, wrote in his introduction to the Mishnah: "If there are 1,000 prophets, all of them of the stature of Elijah and Elisha, giving a certain interpretation, and 1,001 rabbis giving the opposite interpretation, you shall 'incline after the majority' and the law [ruling] is according to the 1,001 rabbis, not according to the 1,000 venerable prophets…. And so if a prophet testifies that the Holy One, Blessed be He, told him that the law [ruling] of a certain commandment is such and such … that prophet must be executed…. [For] it is written, 'it is not in heaven' (Deuteronomy 30:12). Thus, **God did not permit us to learn from the prophets**, **but only from the rabbis** who are men of logic and reason." Mordechai notes that this is not "some obscure teaching" of Judaism, but a "basic tenet of rabbinic doctrine." According to Rabbinical Judaism, the sages have the "**full prerogative to make laws in addition to or in spite of the written Word**, because they believe Scripture says, '*it is not in heaven*' " (p. 413; emphasis added). Indeed, according to the Talmud, the sages view their enactments as having the same (or greater) force and authority as the laws and commandments of the Scriptures (*BT Ketubot*, 84a).

Obviously, without the Talmud, the rabbi is nothing. In fact, it is the mastery of the Talmud that gives the rabbi his mystical authority. On the surface, the rabbi is a teacher of the "wisdom" contained in the Talmud; on a deeper, cultish level, the rabbi is seen as the *embodiment* of such wisdom. By no means is Judaism alone in this criticism; to one degree or another, every religion devised by men tends to deify its teachers. And the process always begins with the supposition that a religion's sages have access to *secret knowledge*. As you will recall, biblical scholar Joachim Jeremias noted that "it was knowledge alone which gave … power to the [ancient Jewish] scribes" (*Jerusalem in the Time of Jesus*, p. 235). "Only ordained teachers [scribes and, later, *rabbis*] transmitted and created the tradition derived from the [written] Torah which, according to Pharisaic teaching ... was regarded as equal to and indeed above the Torah. **Their decisions had the power to 'bind' or 'loose' for all time the Jews of the entire world**" (p. 236; emphasis added). Again, "the decisive reason for their dominant influence over the people ... [was] that **they were the guardians of a secret knowledge, of an esoteric tradition**" (p. 237; emphasis added).

Jeremias continues: "It is only when we have realized the esoteric character of the teaching of the scribes [rabbis] ... concerning the whole of the oral tradition, even with respect to the text of the Old Testament, that we shall be able to understand the social position of the scribes [rabbis]. From a social point of view they were, as **possessors of divine esoteric knowledge**, the **immediate heirs and successors of the prophets**.... We understand therefore that the scribes [rabbis] were **venerated**, like the prophets of old, with **unbounded respect** and **reverential awe**, as bearers and teachers of sacred esoteric knowledge; **their words had sovereign authority**" (pp. 241, 243; emphasis added). In fact, the Talmud actually states that the rabbis are *greater* in stature than even the prophets (*BT Baba Bathra*, 12a).

Concerning the rabbis and their absolute authority, "even if they tell you right is left or left is right, you must listen to them" (*Sifrei Deuteronomy*, 154-11 and the *Midrash Rabbah Exodus*, 47-1; quoted by Mordechai, p. 240). But God says in Isaiah 5:20-21, "Woe to those who call evil good and good evil; who put darkness for light and light for darkness; who put bitter for sweet and sweet for bitter! Woe unto them that are wise in their own eyes, and prudent in their own sight!"

It was only a matter of time before the rabbis began to see *themselves* as the "embodiment of their own teachings." Referring to Judaism's tendency to worship its own leaders, Hoffman writes that the rabbi is seen as the *Talmud incarnate*. "[The rabbi] actualizes this divine status through rote memorization and vain repetition of the Talmud and Talmudic interpretations ... in a manner similar to the import which Eastern religions attach to mantric incantations. The Talmud mantra is believed to give the rabbi supernatural power and his intrinsic divinity is made evident by this means. He himself **becomes an object of worship** ... because, **having achieved his full manifestation as the incarnate Torah** [both written and oral], **he himself becomes the main source of Judaic salvation and revelation**" (Hoffman, pp. 294-295; emphasis added).

Hoffman quotes Rabbi Jacob Neusner, one of the world's foremost authorities on Judaism, as claiming that "the Babylonian Talmud *represents God in the flesh*..." (*Rabbinic Judaism*, p. 62; Hoffman, p. 295). Later, paraphrasing Neusner, Hoffman says that in Judaism "the authority of the Mishnah is derived from the authority of the rabbi, because **whatever the rabbi declares to be from Sinai is from Sinai**, **because the rabbi *is* Sinai incarnate**" (p. 295; emphasis added).

The inevitable conclusion is that if the Talmud is God incarnate, and the rabbi fully embodies the Talmud—then, the rabbi is, at least on some level, *divine*. Hoffman again quotes Neusner: "[The] rabbis believe that the man [who is] truly made in the divine image is the rabbi; he embodies revelation—both oral and written—and all his actions constitute paradigms that are not merely correct, but holy and heavenly. Rabbis enjoy exceptional grace from heaven" (*Invitation to the Talmud—A Teaching Book*, p. 8; Hoffman, p. 514).

The rabbis' demigod status is easily seen in how their Talmudic students hold them in reverential awe. In what Hoffman calls the "Cult of the Guru," he says that in Judaism "the relationship between teacher (*rebbi*) and student (*talmid*) is one of slavish idolatry" wherein the rabbi is a "guru, whose image is engraved before [the student's] eyes" and "is adored by [the] awed and cowed follower" (p. 296). Quoting a March 16, 2007, article by Rabbi Elozar Kahanaw entitled "Between Rabbi and Talmud Student," Hoffman writes: "[The rabbi] often spoke to his *tamidim* [students] about the importance of establishing a bond of closeness between *rebbi* and *talmid*. In every matter, in every circumstance, it is necessary that the image of one's *rebbi* be engraved before one's eyes. In every question that arose and in every issue, [the Talmudic student is to always ask] 'What would my *rebbi* … say about this?' " (p. 296).

Talmudic students endeavor to imitate their guru-like rabbis in all things, being so infatuated with the "wisdom" of the rabbis that they think everything the rabbi says and does is divinely inspired. Just how wise *are* the rabbis? They are wise enough to be frightened of going to the bathroom, believing that devils reside in latrines. The Talmud teaches that, on coming from a toilet, a man must not have sexual intercourse without first walking half a mile, as the demon of the toilet will be with him for about that length of time. If he does not walk the half mile, any child conceived after going to the bathroom will be epileptic (*BT Gittin*, 70a). The rabbis *wisely* prescribe a hand-washing ritual to remove the demon.

Hoffman concludes that the attitude of the student toward the rabbi is one of "*extreme idolatry*. They [the students] adore them [the rabbis] as infallible, supernatural, prophet-like figures" (p. 297). For example, the late Grand Rabbi Menachem M. Schneerson of New York was lauded by fellow rabbi Ariel Sokolovsky as "Rebbe-Almighty" (Saul Sadka, "The Lubavitcher Rebbe as a god," *Haaretz*, Feb. 12, 2007). Sadka adds that Schneerson's followers would routinely chant, "Long live our Master, our Rebbe, King Messiah." Proclaiming their "dedication to the Rebbe above all else," they affirmed, "As far as we are concerned, **we can pray to the Rebbe and he can deal with God for us**. The Rebbe was not created; the Rebbe has always been around and always will be…. [You must] **start with God and work your way up to the Rebbe**" (quoted by Hoffman, pp. 298-299; emphasis added).

Hoffman says that Schneerson's followers viewed him as a demigod. "They are loath to state this explicitly, but they will assign him characteristics of God, pray to him and, when pressed, suggest that there is really no difference between him and God, except that Schneerson is higher." From Sadka's article, Hoffman adds: "Since the Rebbe was perfection personified, he is **greater than any man** that ever lived; ergo **he is godly—omnipotent, omniscient** and **unlimited**.... None [of his followers] have a problem with **praying to Schneerson** [or] **using his books for divination in place of the Bible**. Even amongst those viewed as moderates, 'the Rebbe' is often substituted for God in normal conversation.... Does this not **idolize Schneerson** in the literal sense? **We cannot connect to God directly—we need the Rebbe to take our prayers from here to there** and to help us in this world. We are told by our rabbis that **a great man is like God**, and the Rebbe [Schneerson] was the greatest man ever" (p. 300; emphasis added).

Rather than having faith in God and learning to think for themselves, **Talmudic students are taught to have absolute faith in their rabbi**. Hoffman quotes an article—"It is Mitzvah to Heed the Words of Our Sages"—published by the Ahavas Emes Institute in which such faith is emphasized. "**Having faith in [our] sages ... is a tenet of Judaism** and is no less obligatory than the laws pertaining to forbidden foods or the laws pertaining to money matters.... [Thus] **regarding all matters of faith** and mitzvah observance, **we must rely on the decisions of the sages instead of making our own**.... [The] **more trust a person has in our ... sages**, **the greater his chances for the salvation** he so yearns for" (Hoffman, p. 937; emphasis added).

Could the *idolatry* be any more evident? In Judaism, the rabbi *takes the place of God*, much like the priest assumes the mediatory role of Christ in Catholicism.

Rabbinical Power and Abuse

Like any cultish religion that deifies its leaders, fear and intimidation figure prominently in Judaism, running like an undercurrent in the relationship between rabbi and student. After all, "Judaism teaches that the rabbi's word *is* the word of God. The rabbis' enactments are *equal* to those of God" (Hoffman, p. 935). Naturally, then, the rabbi is someone to be feared. A good example of how rabbis subtly utilize intimidation can be seen in their approach to the Jews' day of fasting and mourning known as *Tisha B'Av*—the ninth day of the Jewish month of Av.

Historically, *Tisha B'Av* has been a day of suffering and catastrophe. Solomon's Temple was destroyed by the Babylonians on this day in 515 BC; likewise, the Second Temple, build by Herod, was destroyed by Roman armies on the ninth of Av, 70 AD. Numerous other calamities are held by the Jews to have occurred on this date. *Tisha b'Av*—which occurs in either July or August—is a time of mourning and contrition. Numerous regulations dictate how the devout Jew is to go about mourning—such as not wearing leather shoes, not bathing, going without food and water, not greeting friends or socializing, etc. Rabbis consider the day to be *specially cursed* by God (Hoffman, p. 932).

According to Hoffman, of the several catastrophes commemorated in Judaism on this date, "the one that occupies the center of attention is the destruction of the Second Temple by the Romans" (p. 932). He also notes that the rabbis *use* the calamity to *leverage obedience* and *reverence* from their followers. In conjunction with mourning the destruction of the Temple and the exile of Jews, rabbis are almost fanatical in reminding their disciples of *why* such destruction came upon the Jewish people in the first place. They ask, "What were the Jews' forefathers of the first century guilty of that resulted in the terrible destruction of the Temple?" Sidestepping the truth, however, rabbis quickly quote the Talmud: "[Jerusalem] was destroyed only because they [the Jewish laity] demeaned [the] *Talmidei Chachamim* [Talmud scholars]" (*BT Shabbat*, 119b).)

Why should we be surprised that rabbis would deflect the blame *away from* their Pharisaic ancestors—and, thus, away from *themselves*—and shift it onto the Jewish people? With disdain and contempt, they dismiss what the New Testament gives as *the* singular reason for the destruction of Jerusalem and the Temple—the rejection of Jesus as the Messiah by the Jewish leadership. "And when He came near and saw the city [Jerusalem], He wept over it, saying, 'If you had known, even you, at least in this your day [of judgment], the things [that would have made] for your peace; but now they are hidden from your eyes. For the days shall come upon you that your enemies shall cast a rampart about you, and shall enclose you around and keep you in on every side, and shall level you to the ground, and your children within you; and they shall not leave in you a stone upon a stone, **because you did not know the season of your visitation**" (Luke 19:41-44). Jerusalem is here personified by its corrupt leadership; Christ was actually addressing the Jewish religious leaders who reject Him. Likewise, He laments: "Jerusalem, Jerusalem, you who kill the prophets and stone those who have been sent to you, how often would I have gathered your children together, even as a hen gathers her brood under her wings, **but you refused**! Behold, your house is left to you desolate. For I say to you, you shall not see Me at all from this time forward, until you shall say, 'Blessed is He Who comes in the name of the Lord' " (Matt. 23:37-39).

The rabbis' stance on why Jerusalem and the Temple were destroyed gives them a formidable tool by which they are able to intimidate and control their followers—*fear*. As Hoffman writes, the rabbis "teach that the Second Temple was destroyed not due to the horrible corruption of their spiritual ... [predecessors], but because the Jews of the first century **failed to sufficiently idolize the Pharisees**.... Hence, the ninth of Av represents a ritualized reminder that **all those Judaics who seek the liberty to think freely according to conscience**, independent of the [Jewish] traditions of men, **bring ruin upon Judaism**" (p. 934; emphasis added).

But the rabbis take their diabolical heavy-handedness a step further.

If the Jewish laity of the first century could be held accountable for the destruction of Jerusalem and the Temple, could not similar lackadaisicalness be the cause of the Messiah delaying His appearing? Hoffman argues that "*Tisha b'Av* reinforces rabbinic mind control over the Judaic people. They are told that the Temple will not be rebuilt and the Messiah will not come unless they rededicate themselves in **total subservience to the tyrannical rule of the rabbis**, the heirs of the tyrannical religious rulers who crucified [the] Messiah" (p. 934; emphasis added).

As a former Talmudic Jew intimately familiar with Judaism, Avi ben Mordechai notes that "the Pharisaic system appeals to a man's base appetite for self-aggrandizement. It is a [religious] system that leads to a hierarchy of masters and slaves. In turn, this will lead to one who controls another, with the result that people will live in fear of their peers and spiritual taskmasters and not in fear of YHWH [God]" (*Galatians*, p. 371).

By creating and perpetuating the myth of the "Oral Torah"—with its vast wealth of mystical, esoteric knowledge—both the age-old scribe and the modern-day rabbi have mastered the art of manipulating and controlling their followers. The observant Jew simply has no idea of the *deception* into which he has fallen. On the surface (and certainly as portrayed in the mainstream media) the rabbi is admired as a prudent teacher, spiritual guide and skeptical philosopher—one who holds the answers to life's most perplexing problems. In reality, however, he does what all teachers, gurus and leaders of humanly-devised religions ultimately do: Assuming a sort of messianic character, he presumptuously positions himself between his followers and God, as if their salvation was dependent on *him*. In Judaism, the rabbi's god-like status makes such a position most palpable.

Rabbinical Self-Righteousness

An arrogant spirit of self-righteousness is readily apparent in Rabbinical Judaism—even to the point of racial nationalism. When the Talmud states, for example, that God wears phylacteries on which are inscribed *praises* for the Jewish people (*BT Berakhot*, 6a-b)—or that God asks rabbis for *rabbinical blessings* (*BT Berakhot*, 7a)—it becomes obvious that there is a disturbing tendency in the religion (and certainly in the rabbinate) toward self-worship. Indeed, with smug self-assurance, the sages have proclaimed that no rabbi can ever be condemned to hell (*BT Hagigah*, 27a).

Just how arrogant are the rabbis? In Daniel Boyarin's controversial book, *Border Lines: The Partition of Judeo-Christianity*, he describes what he calls the "complete rabbinic takeover of religious life and practice via the Oral Torah." Boyarin portrays the ancient development of the oral tradition as something of a *coup* against God, in which "**not even God**, not even the angels, **can compete with the rabbis and their [oral] Torah**. The [oral] Torah is no longer in heaven. It is on earth in the possession of the rabbinic institution" (p. 171; emphasis added). He adds that Rabbinical Judaism thus represents a "particular [form] of power/knowledge ... [that] **seeks to effect a transfer of authority and of control over discourse from heaven** ... to earth [through] the allegedly God-given authority of the majority of the rabbis." A necessary aspect of this "transfer of authority" has been the "**divine submission to rabbinic power**" in which "divine voices have nothing to say in the lives of Jews anymore. Only the rabbis, designed the sons of God, and their [oral] Torah serve that function. **Only the majority decision of the rabbis has power and authority, and only their knowledge is relevant**" (p. 172; emphasis added).

Could the rabbis' arrogance and conceit be any more obvious? Yet, God says, "I, the LORD your God, am a *jealous* God" and "My glory I will not give to another" (Ex. 20:5; Isa. 42:8). What a fearful position, indeed, to be found in *direct opposition* to the ever-living God of Scripture!

The self-righteous conceitedness replete within Judaism can also be seen in the rabbinic concept of Jewish "chosen-ness." Dr. Raphael Jospe, senior instructor and lecturer in Jewish Philosophy at the Open University of Israel in Jerusalem, has conducted extensive research on this topic. In his article, "The Concept of the Chosen People: An Interpretation," he suggests that, while various rabbinic scholars have differing approaches to this controversial subject, there is considerable consensus that "the Jews *chose* to be chosen" (myjewishlearing.com).[13]

Jospe presents two radically differing perspectives from medieval rabbinism, both of which "reverse the logic and chronology of election." In the first, it is theorized that the Jews possess a *divine biological faculty* enabling them to "communicate prophetically with God"—thus, "they, and *only* they, could receive the Torah [both written and oral] in divine revelation." This means that "one cannot argue that God chose Abraham and his progeny. Rather, because only Abraham, and subsequently the Jewish people, were already endowed with the biological capacity to receive divine communication, God could reveal the Torah to them. This is not to say that the Jews first chose God. It means that God could choose *only* them to receive the Torah because they alone had the prior capacity to receive it. The Jews did not choose God, but it was the Jews who made God's choice possible." Perhaps this helps to explain why the Talmud states that striking a Jew is, in God's eyes, an assault on the "Divine Presence" (*BT Sanhedrin*, 58b).

The second viewpoint—developed by the legendary 12th-century Jewish philosopher Moses Maimonides—is based on the alleged initiative of the Jews, or specifically, that of their ancestor Abraham. According to Jospe, Abraham "arrived at a rational understanding of God through speculation and reasoning." Rabbi Maimonides, he writes, described Abraham as "weaning himself from the prevailing idolatry [of his day] and contemplating the cosmos without the benefit of any teacher, until, at the age of forty, 'he attained the way of truth and apprehended the right line [of thought] by his correct reason ... and he [thus] knew that there is one God who governs the sphere and created everything, and that in all existence there is no God besides Him.' " Jospe concludes that, ultimately, the initiative was entirely Abraham's. "God did not choose Abraham; rather, Abraham *discovered* God" (myjewishlearing.com).

In a similar vein, Hoffman notes that there is a "huge chasm between Christian and rabbinic theology. The Christian believes himself to be absolutely worthless and irredeemable without Christ—a sinner sentenced to eternal death, were it not for ... the propitiatory sacrifice of Jesus.... In contrast, **Judaism is replete with racial conceit**. [As author Eli Soble wrote,] '**The Jewish people and God are wholly one**.... [The Jews'] redemption will take place because of the **merit of the Jewish people**' " (p. 303; quoting Eli Soble's "Our Rebbe is the Messiah," *The Jerusalem Post*, Jan. 30, 2008; emphasis added).[14]

As we will see in the next chapter, there is definite biblical validity to the idea of the Jews being a chosen people—chosen for a specific purpose in God's overall plan. But most decidedly, that does *not* mean that Judaism is in any way representative of the "religion" (way of life) God established through Moses and the prophets. The prevailing Judaic approach to the "chosen" status of the Jewish people is strikingly conceited. Rather than humbly seeing themselves as chosen for a special purpose—through no inherent merit of their own (see Ezekiel 16:1-14)—there is instead a haughty, even *racist*, elitism that characterizes itself in discrimination against non-Jews. In fact, according to Rabbinical Judaism, Deuteronomy 7:2 is considered a proof-text—taken completely out of context, of course—that Gentiles are to be shown absolutely no favor. After all, the Talmud itself teaches that non-Jews are actually *sub*human (*BT Kerithoth*, 6b; *Yebamoth*, 61a; *Baba Mezia*, 114b).

Rabbinical Racism

Elizabeth Dilling writes, "The Talmud's basic law [concerning race] is that only the Pharisee Jew ranks as a man, or a human being. All others rank as animals" (*The Jewish Religion: Its Influence Today*, p. 2). In each of the Talmudic passages referenced above, non-Jews are said to be "not of Adam"—i.e., *not human*. The 1905 *Jewish Encyclopedia* links this teaching to the Pharisees, who, grossly misapplying Ezekiel 34:31 ("and you My sheep ... are men"), held that "only Israelites were *men* ... [and] Gentiles they classed not as men but as barbarians" ("Gentiles").

"The basic Talmudic doctrine includes more than a super-race complex. It is an *only*-race concept. The non-Jew thus ranks as an animal, has no property rights and no legal rights under any code whatever" (Dilling, p. 16). According to the Talmud, Gentile children are animals (*BT Yebamoth*, 98a), and Gentile girls are in a state of filth from birth (*BT Abodah Zarah*, 36b). In general, non-Jews are inclined to bestiality, lewdness and murder; Eve, the Talmud claims, had sexual intercourse with the serpent, transmitting lust to Gentiles, from which Jews are exempt (*BT Abodah Zarah*, 22a).

The Talmud also instructs Jewish men to say the following prayer every day: "Thank you God for not making me a Gentile, a woman or a slave" (*BT Menahoth*, 43b-44a).[15]

Moses, however, taught *one law* for Israelite and foreigner alike (Ex. 12:49; Lev. 24:22). Over time, Jewish tradition made it unlawful for a Jew to associate in any way with a non-Jew (Acts 10:28)—a prejudice swiftly dealt with by the early church (Acts 10:34; Gal. 3:28; Col. 3:11). While the Talmud actually encourages hatred towards one's enemies (*BT Pesahim*, 113b), Jesus taught otherwise. "You have heard that it was said [by self-righteous scribes and Pharisees expounding their oral traditions], 'You shall love your *neighbor* and hate your enemy.' " As previously noted, the rabbis define *neighbor* as "a fellow *Jewish* neighbor" (*BT Sanhedrin*, 52b). Jesus continues: "But I say to you, love your enemies, bless those who curse you, do good to those who hate you, and pray for those who despitefully use you and persecute you" (Matt. 5:43-44).

In a perverse attempt to "explain" Rabbinical Judaism's bias against Gentiles, the *Jewish Encyclopedia* submits that Jews feared the "vile and vicious character of Gentiles" and that "discriminations against Gentiles, while strictly in accordance with the just law of reciprocity and retaliation, [had] for their object to civilize the heathen" ("Gentiles"). After all, the ancient sages had written that while the deeds of Jews are righteous, Gentiles are capable only of sin (*BT Baba Bathra*, 10b).

In his essay "The Non-Jew in Jewish Law," educator Jeffrey Spitzer writes that "Jewish law tries to separate Jews from Gentiles in order to prevent Jews from adopting idolatrous behaviors.... There are exceptions and loopholes, but the general force is to discourage interaction between Jews and non-Jews." Citing the ancient sages, Spitzer adds that various Talmudic rules assume that Gentiles are, at best, unreliable—and, at worst, malevolent and violent. For this reason, Gentiles are grouped together with dishonest butchers, gamblers, usurers and thieves (*Shulhan Arukh Hoshen Mishpat*, 34; myjewishlearning.com).[16]

It should come as no surprise, then, that it is forbidden in the Talmud for one to teach the Scriptures to Gentiles. The *Jewish Encyclopedia* says "the Talmud prohibited the teaching to a Gentile of the Torah.... R. Johanan [an ancient sage] says of one so teaching: 'Such a person deserves death.... It is like placing an obstacle before the blind' (*Sanhedrin*, 59a; *Hagigah*, 13a)." And, "Resh Lakish [another ancient sage] ... said, 'A Gentile observing the Sabbath deserves death' (*Sanhedrin*, 58b) ... inasmuch as 'the Sabbath is a sign between God and Israel alone' " ("Gentiles").

Importantly, Hoffman notes that such prejudice is far from limited to some narrow sect of Judaism, but overwhelmingly represents the rabbinic mindset within modern Orthodox Judaism. According to Hoffman, the American mainstream media frequently features stories about rabbis reaching out to non-Jews in a "spirit of brotherhood." He argues that such rhetoric is but part of a clever public relations campaign aimed at naive Gentiles.

"These [media] lies are laughable to those who were raised inside Orthodox Judaism…. If we look at the precepts by which Talmudic youth are raised, trained, formed and educated, we discover the reality of Judaism, aside from the hypocritical and fantastic image of benevolence that is projected on its behalf by media moguls" (*Judaism Discovered*, p. 463).

Hoffman contends that there is a "bigoted image of Gentiles" that Jewish youth "imbibe from Orthodox Judaism's religious elders." "In the eyes of the rabbis, the Gentile is eternally Esau"—persecuting the Jew (or Jacob, Esau's biblical rival). Hoffman writes that Jewish children are taught from earliest childhood that "friendship with Gentiles is temporary" and that "the Gentile can never be your friend." They are taught that the Gentile is "another Esau come to kill the Jews…. War with him is unavoidable and eternal. The first step in the war is our segregation" (p. 463).

In her book *The Hole in the Sheet*, Evelyn Kay writes of this Jewish preoccupation with Gentile persecution. "[The] essence of anti-Goyism [anti-Gentile] is passed to Jewish children with their mother's milk, and then nurtured, fed and watered carefully into a full-blown phobia throughout their lives…. Their attitudes are then perfectly formed. They know how to hate…. They [the rabbis] want [Jewish] children to hate the Goyim…. They want to deny the humanity that links all people…. Anti-Goyism is a foundation of the Orthodox and Hasidic [Judaic] philosophy and way of life" (pp. 112-115; quoted by Hoffman, p. 464).

The rabbinic bias toward all things non-Jewish extends as well to Christianity. Noting the underlying motive for their contempt, Spitzer writes that "most [rabbinic] authorities considered the Christian belief in the Trinity as idolatrous"—as it naturally contradicted Jewish monotheism. Hoffman concurs: "The rabbinic authorities teach that Christianity … constitutes idol worship and any place set aside for the worship of Jesus Christ [viewed as a second God] is a house of idol worship" (p. 379). He writes that "Maimonides ruled unequivocally that Christians are idol worshippers (*Hilchos Ma'achalos Asuros*, 11:7)" (p. 381).[17]

Rabbinical disdain for Christianity is well documented in the Talmud. For example, Christians and others who reject the Talmud will go to hell and be punished there for all generations (*BT Sanhedrin*, 90a); those who read the New Testament (considered non-canonical by the sages) will have no portion in the world to come (*BT Rosh Hashanah*, 17a); when the Messiah comes, He will destroy all Christians (*BT Sanhedrin*, 99a). There are *many* similar statements sprinkled throughout the Talmud, expressing condemnation for both Christians and Jesus.[18]

The central prayer of Judaism, the *Amidah* (recited three times each day), contains a section called the *Birkat HaMinim*, which pronounces a curse on Judaism's enemies. According to Hoffman, the section—when properly rendered from the Talmud—reads, "Let there be no hope for the wicked and for Christians" (p. 279, footnote 272).

According to the on-line encyclopedia Wikipedia, *Birkat HaMinim* "asks God to destroy those in heretical sects" (wikipedia.org/wiki/Amidah).

From a Judaic perspective, Christians are fundamentally heretical. Today, this particular portion of the *Amidah* is typically rendered, "Let there be no hope for *slanderers*, and let all *wickedness* perish in an instant...." The word for *slanderers*, however, was originally *minim*—and all credible scholars admit that *minim* refers to sectarians or heretics.

"The prayer has undergone since the days of Gamaliel many textual changes, as the variety of versions extant evidences.... [In] order to obviate hostile misconstructions, the text was modified.... Originally, the opening words were *La-zedim ula-minim* [using *minim*, those of heretical sects].... For *minim* was substituted the expression *all doers of iniquity*." The *Birkat HaMinim* is thought to be the brainchild of Gamaliel II, who invoked the prayer "against heretics, traitors, and traducers: the *minim* and the *posh'im*.... The latter were the free thinkers; the former, [were] the Judaeo-Christians" (jewishencyclopedia.com; "Shemoneh 'Esreh").[19]

According to Hebrew researcher John Parsons, the *Birkat HaMinim* was "instituted at the council of Yavneh sometime after the destruction of the Second Temple, and was composed in response to the Essenes and early messianic believers in Yeshua [Jesus].... [The] Talmud (*BT Berakhot*, 28b-29a) states that the original form of this blessing had the term *laminim*, which is rendered 'for the sectarians,' which was generally understood to be the Essenes and Messianic Jews of that time." Parsons adds that the malediction served as a litmus test against suspected followers of Christ. "A messianic Jew could faithfully recite the other eighteen blessings of the *Amidah*, but could hardly invoke a curse on followers of Yeshua [Jesus]. In this way, [Jews] not reciting the *Birkat HaMinim* were suspected of heresy and subject to ... excommunication" (hebrew4christians.com).[20]

In spite of the conciliatory revisions, the original Talmudic version of the *Birkat HaMinim* remains as a viable tenet of Rabbinical Judaism. We must recall the words of the preeminent Rabbi Louis Finkelstein: "Pharisaism became Talmudism, Talmudism became Medieval Rabbinism, and Medieval Rabbinism became Modern Rabbinism. But throughout these changes of name, inevitable adaptation of custom, and adjustment of law, **the spirit of the ancient Pharisee survives unaltered**.... [For indeed,] **the spirit of the doctrine** [of the Pharisees] **has remained quick and vital**" (*The Pharisees*, Vol. I, pp. 21-22; emphasis added).

Judaism's Pretentious Display of Piety

As we can see, on a truly spiritual level, nothing has changed since the first century when Jesus denounced the scribes and Pharisees as blind guides, hypocrites and "whitewashed tombs" who were more interested in the adulation of men than in being right with God. Many of the modern "trappings" associated with Judaism reveal the vanity behind the religion. For example, Orthodox Jews today continue the Pharisaic *tradition*—based on an overly-literal interpretation of Deuteronomy 11:18, etc.—of wearing phylacteries (or *tefillin*), tiny leather boxes containing passages from Scripture that are worn on or above the forehead and on the left arm next to the heart. The Mishnah requires all males thirteen and older to wear *tefillin* each day (*Shebu*, 3.8, 11). The boxes are held in place by special leather straps. Apparently, the Pharisees would *broaden* the leather straps in order to make them more prominent. "And **they do all their works to be seen by men**. They make **broad their phylacteries** and **enlarge the borders** [fringes or tassels] of their garments; and they love the [place of honor] at the suppers, and the chief seats in the synagogues, and the salutations in the market-places, and to be called by men, 'Rabbi, Rabbi' " (Matt. 23:5-7).[21]

If one intends to wear phylacteries (as misguided as that may be), it should be done out of a sincere desire to fulfill Scripture—not in a self-righteous attempt to draw attention to one's piety. Similarly, modern Jews attempt to follow the injunction in Numbers 15:38-39 by wearing fringes or knotted tassels (*tzitzit*) on their "prayer shawls," or *tallit*. (Apparently, the original command applies to one's *garment* in general, and is not restricted to the so-called "prayer shawl.") As noted in Matthew 23:5, the Pharisees would lengthen their *tzitzit* in a pretentious and prideful display which drew Jesus' condemnation. Even when not praying, Orthodox Jews often wear the *tallit* under their shirts, purposely displaying the knotted tassels at the waist.

The Jewish skull-cap worn on the back of the head—known today as a *kippah*—is based entirely on rabbinic tradition. Such caps are noted in the Talmud as a sign of a rabbi's *high status* (*BT Kiddushin*, 8a). In his book *Understanding Judaism*, Rabbi Benjamin Blech writes that the *kippah* is worn with the intention of making a "religious statement" and serves as a "visible way of identifying oneself as an observant Jew"—underscoring, once again, the modern-day Pharisaic mindset of conceit and vanity.

He adds that the *kippah* is also the Jew's way of "acknowledging that there is One above us" and signifies the Talmudist's "acceptance of a higher power" (p. 308). Interestingly, the apostle Paul wrote almost exactly the *opposite*—that covering one's head while praying brought shame to his Head. "But I want you to understand that the Head of every man is Christ, and the head of the woman is the man, and the Head of Christ is God. Every man who has a *covering on his head* when he is praying or prophesying puts his Head [Christ] to shame" (I Cor. 11:3-4).

Another accoutrement worn pretentiously by Jewish men is the long, braided *peyos* or "sidelocks." The practice is based on an erroneous understanding of Leviticus 19:27: "You shall not shave around the sides of your head, nor shall you disfigure [or *mar*] the edges [sides] of your beard" (*NKJV*). "The biblical injunction not to 'mar the edges of your beard' in the fashion of pagan worshipers was interpreted by the rabbis as a prohibition against shaving in general" (*The Encyclopedia of the Jewish Religion*, 1986, page 59; "Beard"). While the subject of wearing *beards* remains somewhat controversial, it is the common practice among conservative Judaics. However, the *peyos*—which has become a standard fixture among pious Talmudists—may be seen as an extreme answer to the prohibition. Much like the *kippah*, the wearing of "sidelocks" identifies one as an *observant* Jew. Ultra-conservative Hasidic Jews let their *peyos* grow particularly long.[22]

All of this self-righteous showiness fits with Hoffman's description of how Judaics celebrate their *Yom Kippur* holiday. He characterizes the event as an "extravaganza of Pharisaic displays of penitence and purification, [and] fasting and prayer, that allegedly give evidence of the supposed special relationship which Talmudist enjoy with God. Quite a gaudy show is made of the confessional…, the catalogue of sins which is meaningless as a form of self-accusation, since the Judaic recites the whole litany whether he is actually guilty of each transgression or not. Like so much of Judaism, Yom Kippur as practiced by the rabbis is an empty tradition signifying little more than self-justification through works-righteousness" (*Judaism Discovered*, p. 965). Moreover, the *Kol Nidrei* rite (discussed earlier) makes the whole Yom Kippur ceremony—with its pretentious displays of penitence and piety—an exercise in hypocritical self-righteousness.

Like their Pharisaic predecessors, modern rabbis love the adulation and applause of men. As Jesus said, everything they do is to be "seen of men" (Matt. 23:5). Like "whitewashed tombs" they *appear* beautiful on the outside—but, on the inside, they are wholly unclean (verse 27).

Jesus' timeless instructions in Matthew chapter six offer insight into the mindset of the Pharisaic rabbi: "Beware that you do not bestow your alms **in the sight of men in order to be seen by them**; otherwise you have no reward with your Father Who is in heaven. Therefore, when you give your alms, **do not sound the trumpet before you**, as the hypocrites do in the synagogues and in the streets, **so that they may have glory from men**. Truly I say to you, they have their reward. But when you give your alms, do not let your left hand know what your right hand is doing, so that your alms may be in secret; and your Father Who sees in secret shall Himself reward you openly. And when you pray, you shall not be as the hypocrites, **for they love to pray standing in the synagogues and on the corners of the streets, in order that they may be seen by men**. Truly I say to you, they have their reward…. And when you fast, **do not be as the hypocrites, dejected in countenance; for they disfigure their faces in order that they may appear to men to fast**. Truly I say to you, they have their reward. But when you fast, anoint your head and wash your face, so that you may not appear to men to fast, but to your Father Who is in secret; and your Father Who sees in secret shall reward you openly" (Matt. 6:1-5, 16-18).

Indeed, the venerated "trappings" of Orthodox Judaism—the lavish phylacteries, the exaggerated tassels, the ubiquitous skull-cap and the long "sidelocks"—represent nothing but a prideful display of self-righteousness. In contrast, God says "to this one I will look, to him who is of a poor and contrite spirit and who trembles at My Word" (Isa. 66:2)—*not* at the words of Jewish tradition. "Surely," as King David wrote, "every man at his best state is altogether vanity" (Psalm 39:5).

The Deceptiveness of Judaism

As this chapter has unequivocally demonstrated, Rabbinical Judaism is plagued by idolatry, hypocrisy and self-righteousness. There may indeed be a zeal for God, but it is a misplaced zeal that is "not according to [true] knowledge" (Rom. 10:2)—for it is wholly based upon a humanly-devised code of law that stands in sharp opposition to the written Word of God. As such, Judaism is a *deceptive* religion of men—and can in no way represent the true "religion" of God as delivered by Moses and the prophets of the Old Testament. As Mordechai notes, "We Jews are supposed to be a 'People of the Book'—the written Torah. Any other ideology, doctrine, teaching or philosophy that **sets itself up to compete with the written Law of Moses** is … nothing more than a [humanly-devised] religion…" (*Galatians*, p. 177; emphasis added). Indeed, *any* religion characterized by deceit, hypocrisy, self-righteousness and idolatry cannot be of the Holy One of Israel, and must of necessity be *false*.

As we have seen, Judaism's rabbis proudly claim to have perpetuated the *spirit* of the ancient Pharisees—the very ones Jesus reproved as deceitful vipers, blind guides and hypocrites; the very ones He said were *of* the devil, the father of lies (John 8:44). Judaism is a cultish religion in which its adherents—albeit unknowingly—both *worship* and *fear* their rabbinical leaders. Talmudists make no effort to hide their belief that the Talmud and the rabbi are all-important, while God and the Scriptures are secondary. In utter hypocrisy, Judaism has totally ignored a *central* passage of Scripture: "Look to the written Torah and to the testimony of the prophets! If anyone does not speak or teach according to this word alone, it is because there is no truth in them" (Isa. 8:20; author's paraphrase).

Where does this passage leave the Talmud?

The prophet further writes: "Hearken to Me [alone], you who know [true] *righteousness*, the people in whose *heart* is [written] My Law; do not fear the reproach of men, nor be afraid of their revilings" (Isa. 51:7). Does the observant Jew really "know righteousness"? Can the Talmudic Jew honestly say that God's *laws* and *commandments* are being written in his heart? Does not the Talmudist fear the rabbi more than God?

All humanly-devised religions are, at their core, *deceptive*. As the prophet Jeremiah explains, "the heart of man is hopelessly deceitful; who can even begin to understand it?" (Jer. 17:9; author's paraphrase). Indeed, as Hoffman has rightly observed, *Judaism is the ultimate in self-deception*, wherein a people *uniquely* called of God have scorned and rejected Him in favor of their own traditions and demigod rabbis. For Talmudists, perhaps the greatest deception is, as Hoffman has also noted, that Judaism is a religion of "self-justification through works-righteousness" (p. 965). As long as the observant Jew adheres to the vast code of ritualistic laws of the Talmud (and stays in favor with his rabbi), he is considered "righteous."

But this is merely the righteousness of the scribes and Pharisees—of which Jesus said, "unless your righteousness shall *exceed* the righteousness of the scribes and Pharisees, there is no way that you shall enter into the kingdom of heaven" (Matt. 5:20). What was Jesus saying? By any moral standard, the Pharisees were absolutely *un*righteous; but by their *own* standard, the oral law, they were quite "righteous." As brought out in the remainder of Matthew five (as well as in chapter six), Jesus was steering His listeners *away from* the ritual works-based pseudo-righteousness of the scribes and Pharisees, and was demonstrating the true righteousness that comes from keeping the laws and commandments of God with a pure heart according to their *spiritual intent*. Any so-called "righteousness" that is based on *works* of a humanly-devised code of law is only *self*-righteousness.

As we will see in the concluding chapter, Rabbinical Judaism, "being ignorant of the righteousness that comes from God," has attempted to "establish its own righteousness" through ritual works of law (paraphrased from Roman 10:3). But Judaism, like all false religions of men, is destined to fail—and ultimately be abolished. More importantly, the future of the Jew—once freed from the shackles of Judaism—could not be brighter!

CHAPTER EIGHT

Redemption and Restoration: The Jews' Role in the Age to Come

*"And in those days, men from all nations will
take hold of the garment of a Jew saying, 'Let us go with you,
for we have heard that God is with you.' "*

Near the end of His ministry, in what was no doubt one of Jesus' most impassioned moments, He lamented, "Jerusalem, Jerusalem"—using Jerusalem to personify the *Jewish leadership*, primarily the scribes and Pharisees, as they sat in "Moses' seat"—"you who kill the prophets and stone those who have been sent to you, how often would I have gathered your children, as a hen gathers her brood under her wings, **but you refused!** Behold, **your house is left to you desolate**. And truly I say to you, you shall not see Me at all until the time comes [at My return] that you say, 'Blessed is He Who comes in the name of the Lord' " (Luke 13:34-35).

The phrase "your house is left to you desolate" has a double meaning—one physical, the other spiritual. The obvious meaning is that the Jews' rejection of Jesus as the Messiah would by 70 AD lead to the destruction of their "house"—their Temple and religious institutions, their Sanhedrin, their way of life, and, of course, Jerusalem itself. Less obvious, however, is the spiritual connotation behind the word *desolate*. While the scribes and Pharisees could hardly disagree with Jesus' support of the Law and the Prophets, they would have nothing to do with His repudiation of their precious oral laws and traditions. Consequently, the Jewish leadership would remain shackled to what Michael Hoffman calls a religion of "self-justification through works-righteousness" (*Judaism Discovered*, p. 965). In their overt rejection of Jesus, they would never even begin to approach the godly righteousness that is based on heartfelt obedience to the Scriptures through faith in the Messiah. Indeed, adherents of the Pharisees' *religion of works* would remain spiritually *desolate*, barren of fruit worthy of the Kingdom of God.

"I will require it of him"

In a parable aimed right at the heart of the Jewish leadership, Jesus labeled the scribes, Pharisees and Sadducees as "evil husbandmen" who had *failed* to "render unto God the fruits of His own vineyard." The result would be that the "vineyard" would be "leased to other husbandmen who would bring forth those fruits" (paraphrased from Matt. 21:33-41). Those "other husbandmen" would be oriented around the prophetic "Stone that the build-ers rejected" (verse 42)—the rejected Christ. Jesus concluded, "Because of this"—because of their rejection of the Messiah and their refusal to follow the written Torah as opposed to their oral traditions—"I say to you, **the kingdom of God shall be taken from you**, and it shall be given to a nation that produces the fruits of it" (verse 43). That "nation"—which we will later examine in the context of Christianity's so-called "Replacement Theol-ogy"—is a *spiritual* nation, the *ekklesia* of God (see I Peter 2:4-10).[1]

Of course, "the [Sadducean] chief priests and the Pharisees knew that [Jesus] was speaking about them" (Matt. 21:45). They had in fact heard it before. In Matthew 23:14, for example, Jesus warned them, "Woe to you, scribes and Pharisees, hypocrites! For **you shut up the kingdom of heaven before men**; for neither do you yourselves enter, nor do you allow those who are entering to enter." After an intense encounter with the scribes and Pharisees concerning their "traditions of men" and how such traditions had a negating effect on the Scriptures, Jesus privately told His disciples, "Every plant that My heavenly Father has not planted shall be rooted up" (Matt. 15:13)—a not-so-subtle warning the Jewish leaders' days were numbered.

In fact, one of the reasons Jesus came was to *judge* the spiritual lead-ership of the Jewish nation. In John chapter nine, after healing a man who had been blind from birth, Jesus made a rather cryptic statement—intentionally within earshot of the Pharisees. "For judgment I have come into this world so that those who do not see might see, and those who see might become blind" (verse 39). Picking up on Jesus' insinuation, the Phari-sees mockingly asked, "Are we also blind?" Jesus answered, "If you were blind you would not have sin. But now you say, 'We see.' Therefore, **your sin remains**" (verses 40-41). As occupants of "Moses' seat," the scribes and Pharisees *knew* they were guilty of undermining the Word of God as they favored their traditions; moreover, they, along with the chief priests, *knew* that the time had come for the Messiah to appear. But, as we will see, the Jewish leaders were more concerned about maintaining the political and re-ligious status quo than seriously watching for the Messiah. The Pharisees might as well have proclaimed, "We see!"—for they knew *exactly* what they were doing. As such, the religious leadership of first-century Palestine re-ceived the greater condemnation—for to him who is given much, **much is required** (Luke 12:48). This is why Jesus warned the scribes and Pharisees that they were in danger of eternal damnation through *gehenna* fire (Matt. 23:14, 33)—they knew too much!

The prophet Daniel, while in exile with the Jews in Babylon, brought to light the actual era when the Messiah would appear. His prophecy of Daniel chapter nine—though subject to some debate and various methods of interpretation—clearly pointed to the early part of the first century AD. In *The Everlasting Tradition*, scholar Galen Peterson writes: "In the case of Daniel, the facts [of the prophecy] speak for themselves. And they speak of a Messiah who came exactly when He was promised to come" (p. 53). Still, the exact date was not known; but the Jewish leadership of that day *knew* the time was right for the Messiah to appear. Joseph of Arimathea, a member of the Sanhedrin, was a "good and upright man" who was "waiting for the kingdom of God" (Luke 23:50-51). As the Greek indicates, he was "looking expectantly" for the kingdom, thus the Messiah's appearance. How did he *know* to be looking? The entire Sanhedrin *knew* to be looking!

Another interesting prophecy—found in Genesis 49:10—alerted the Jewish leadership to the imminent appearance of the Messiah. The passage reads, "The scepter shall not depart from Judah, nor a lawgiver from between his feet, until Shiloh comes. And to Him shall be the obedience of the people." The term *Shiloh* means "the one to whom it belongs." The Greek Septuagint reads, "the one for whom it [the scepter] is reserved." Peterson notes that this passage was widely understood by Jewish sages to be a reference to the Messiah. "The rabbis [the Pharisaic scribes] had long agreed that Jacob's prophecy meant that the kingdom of Judah would retain its ability to govern itself until [the] Messiah came" (p. 64).[2]

But the Jewish leaders of early first-century Palestine had a problem. Herod Archelaus, the Roman ruler over the province of Judea, was corrupt and oppressive. Faced with the threat of a Jewish uprising, Rome removed Archelaus around 5 AD. While this was welcome news to the Sanhedrin, Archelaus' removal had unintended consequences—it meant the loss of the Jews' right to enforce their laws. Instead, such power—the power of life and death—was placed into the hands of Rome's new appointee, Coponius. To the Sanhedrin this was a devastating blow. In their eyes, according to Peterson, the *scepter* had been removed. "The removal of the scepter resulted in the loss of their ability to administer the Mosaic Law. Although they would be allowed to enforce excommunication and minor forms of punishment … they would no longer be able to try capital cases. The supreme punishment of execution was the true standard of power. And now it was gone" (p. 62).[3] While the precise application of the prophecy of Genesis 49:10 is uncertain, it is important to note that in the minds of the members of the Sanhedrin, the new circumstances "mandated that [the] Messiah be present" (p. 64).

Without a doubt, the Sanhedrin of Jesus' day knew full well that the time had come for the appearing of the Messiah. But, were they *really* looking? In what Peterson calls "the day the rabbis blinked," he writes that the Jewish religious leaders arrived at several fallacious conclusions. First, they assumed that *they*—being the most learned and esteemed religious body in all of Judea—would certainly recognize the Messiah if He were to appear. Second, it was apparent to *them*, based on *their* limited understanding of the Messiah, that He had in fact *not* appeared. Finally, with great consternation, the Jewish sages came to the conclusion that God had "revoked His prophecy and His obligation."[4] Thus, according to Peterson, "an atmosphere had been created that stifled messianic anticipation" (p. 65).[5] A few years later, when Jesus made His public debut, the scribes, Pharisees and Sadducees were consumed by turf battles and efforts to preserve the political status quo. Still, in the back of their minds, they were looking for the Messiah, as evidenced by John the Baptist's encounter with the Pharisees in John chapter one.[6] But would they recognize Him? Would they receive Him joyfully, with a genuine desire to follow Him? Moses had already warned what would happen to those who *refused* the Messiah. "The LORD your God will raise up unto you a Prophet from the midst of you, of your brethren, One like me. To Him you shall hearken" (Deut. 18:15). In verse 19, quoting God Himself, Moses adds that "whatever man will not hearken to My words which He [the Messiah] shall speak in My name, **I will require it of him**."

Jesus a "Stone of Stumbling" to the Jews

Why did the Jewish leaders of Jesus' day fail to recognize Him as the Messiah? Was it simply oversight—or does the answer have more to do with human lust for power and status? As we have seen, at virtually every turn, Jesus rankled the sensitivities of the Jewish religionists. Moreover, He left them without excuse as to who He was. Granted, Jesus shied away from outright *claiming* to be the Messiah; in fact, as a thorough study of the gospel accounts will show, Jesus only hinted indirectly at His true identity. But His works and teachings spoke volumes. In John chapter 15, Jesus warned His disciples about the certainty of being persecuted for His sake; concerning those who hated Him—the scribes, Pharisees and Sadducees—He said, "If I had not come and spoken to them [at which time He *convicted* them], they would not have had sin; **but now they have nothing to cover their sin**…. If I had not done among them the **works that no other man has done** [such as healing a man blind from birth], they would not have had sin; but now **they have both seen** [My works] and [still] hated both Me and My Father" (verses 22, 24). Again, Jesus left them *no excuse*. Even the pitiful man who had been healed by Jesus of his lifelong blindness gave a powerful testimony to the Jewish leaders. "This is truly an amazing thing, that you do not know where He has come from, yet He has opened my eyes. Now we know that God does not hear sinners. But if anyone is God-fearing and is doing His will, He hears him. From the beginning of the world it has never been heard of that anyone has opened the eyes of one who was born blind. If this man were not from God, He could do nothing" (John 9:30-33). Of course, the Pharisees responded in self-righteous conceit: "You were born wholly in sin, and you are teaching us?" (verse 34). With such arrogance, how could they ever recognize the Messiah?

Attempting to explain the Jewish perspective on the Messiah, Rabbi Hayim Donin writes: "The Messiah in Jewish thought … would be a person who would bring about the political and spiritual redemption of the people of Israel through the ingathering of the Jews to their ancestral home of Eretz Yisrael [the Land of Israel] and the restoration of Jerusalem to its spiritual glory" (*To Be A Jew—A Guide to Jewish Observance in Contemporary Life*, p. 14). This is similar to what Jesus' own disciples expected: "Lord, will

You restore the kingdom to Israel at this time?" (Acts 1:6). Rabbi Donin adds that "claimants to the messianic title arose at various times throughout Jewish history. The criterion by which each was judged was: Did he succeed in accomplishing what the Messiah was **supposed to accomplish**? By this criterion, clearly none qualified" (p. 15; emphasis added).

But what was the Messiah *supposed* to accomplish? Their expectations of physical and political restoration were certainly justified from Scripture. But the Jewish leaders never expected a Messiah who was planning to *die* for the sins of the nation (as well as the whole world). To them, the idea of a "suffering Messiah" was not only foreign, it was offensive. As *Barnes' Commentary* explains: "[To] the Jews, the doctrine that the Messiah was to be crucified gave great offence; it excited, irritated, and exasperated them; they could not endure the doctrine, and treated it with scorn…. It is well known that to the Jews no doctrine was more offensive than this, that the Messiah was to be put to death" (commentary on I Cor. 1:23). Moreover, that the Messiah should die by crucifixion was especially offensive, since, as they understood the Law, such a one was *accursed* of God (see Deut. 21:23).

Clearly, as was foretold by the prophet Isaiah, the Jewish leaders had "stumbled at the Stone of stumbling" (Rom. 9:33; more on this passage below). In this regard, the apostle Peter describes Jesus as "a Stone of stumbling and a Rock of offense" to the Jews—especially to those scribes and Pharisees who "stumble at the Word, being disobedient [to God's command to acknowledge and listen to the Messiah], **unto which unbelief they also were appointed**" (I Pet. 2:8).

The scribes, Pharisees and Sadducean priests all suffered from a *lack of belief*—rooted in their own pride and self-importance. Ultimately, preserving the status quo was more important than giving serious thought to the appearance of the Messiah. Why did the Jewish leaders *really* reject Jesus as the Messiah? *Political expediency*. After Jesus performed one of His most powerful miracles—raising Lazarus from the dead—the religionists were driven to their wit's end. "Then the chief priests and the Pharisees gathered a council [the Sanhedrin] and said, 'What shall we do? For this man does many miracles' " (John 11:47). Behind closed doors, they could not deny Jesus' miracles—but they could never acknowledge them *publicly*. To do so would be to admit that Jesus *could* be the Messiah, and would severely alter the tenor of their relationship with Him.[7] They reasoned: "If we allow Him to continue in this manner, all [Judea] will believe in Him, and [ultimately] the Romans will come and **take away from us both this place and the nation**" (verse 48). Thus, from that day forward "they took counsel together, so that they might kill Him" (verse 53).

The Jewish leaders understood the dangers of irritating the Romans. They rationalized that nationhood itself was at stake; however, they were also acutely aware of a more personal risk—their own political and religious positions of authority and prestige. The scribes and Pharisees stood to lose their superior position as religious leaders and occupants of "Moses' seat." The Sadducean priesthood stood to lose their political clout and aristocratic standing.[8]

As we have seen, the Jewish leaders only made a *pretense* of following Moses. Thus Jesus reproved them, saying, "Did not Moses give you the Law, and [yet] not one of you is [genuinely] practicing the Law?" (John 7:19). Jesus also said, "But **if you** [genuinely] **believed Moses** [concerning both the Law and the Messiah, instead of being consumed by tradition] you would have believed Me; for he wrote about Me. And **if you do not believe his writings**, **how shall you believe My words**?" (John 5:46-47).

Just as Jesus had foretold, the Jewish leadership did not know the season of their *visitation* (Luke 19:44). And now, their *unbelief* had exacted a price no Jew could ever have imagined. The Messiah had indeed come, only to be rejected and killed; and soon, Jerusalem and the Temple would face complete destruction at the hands of the Romans. But an even greater desolation loomed, one that for centuries would imprison Jews in absolute *spiritual darkness*—a pseudo-righteousness based on Judaism's Talmudic *works of law*.

The Judaic Snare of "Works-Righteousness"

In the book of Romans, the apostle Paul has much to say about *false* "forms" of righteousness—particularly the idea that one can become "righteous" through humanly-devised *works of law*. While there may be various applications to the apostle's teachings on this subject, it is obvious that his arguments apply quite well to the Pharisaic model. In fact, in many cases Paul *directly addresses* the problem of Pharisaic "works-righteousness."

Paul speaks of those who "suppress the *truth* in unrighteousness" (Rom. 1:18). Only those in a position of religious authority can *suppress* the truth in such a manner. This brings to mind Jesus' statement that the scribes and Pharisees—guardians of "Moses' seat"—had *nullified* the Scriptures through their traditions (Matt. 15:6; Mark 7:6). In a nutshell, the apostle has aptly described the Jewish leaders' spiritual plight: In unrighteousness, the scribes and Pharisees had rejected the Scriptures as the ultimate source of *truth*, choosing instead to follow their own traditions—which *they* believed equated to righteousness. Paul continues: "When they knew God [during the restoration period under Ezra and Nehemiah], they glorified Him not as God"—they lost their fear of God and their reliance on God, looking instead to their own human understanding—"neither were they thankful [for the infallible truth of the Scriptures], but they became vain in their own reasoning"—eventually imagining such ideas as their so-called "oral law"—"and their foolish hearts were [spiritually] darkened" (Rom. 1:21). Does this not accurately describe the Jewish religionists as we see them in Jesus' day—as well as what we see in Rabbinical Judaism today? Verse 22:

"While professing themselves to be *the wise ones*, they became fools." The ancient scribes were called *wise ones*, as are rabbis today.[9]

It is in this context—the Jews' failure to simply *believe* God and honor His word—that Judaism has foolishly set about to establish a *form of righteousness* through works of traditional laws. Paul squarely addresses the issue, contrasting the Jews' failure to achieve righteousness with the Gentiles' newfound favor with God. In Romans 9:30-33, he writes:

> "What then shall we say? That Gentiles, who had *not* been pursuing righteousness [as they had no prior knowledge of the Law], attained genuine righteousness, even the righteousness and justification which is *by faith*"—because they came to *believe* in Jesus as the Messiah and as the "Living Torah" of God, through whom they would learn to *obey the Law* according to its spiritual intent, and through whom they would have spiritual *redemption* from past sins. "But the *Jews* [Paul uses Israel, meaning the Jews],[10] though they [the Jewish leadership that held sway over the people] followed a 'law' which *they* believed would lead to righteousness, have never attained genuine righteousness. Why? Because they pursued a 'form of righteousness' and justification through Pharisaic *works of law* instead of through faith in Christ." Belief in Jesus as the Messiah would have led them away from their Judaic traditions and into genuine, heartfelt obedience to the Scriptures. "In fact, they were offended by that 'stumbling stone'—exactly as Isaiah foretold: 'Behold, I place in Zion a Stone of stumbling and a Rock of offense, but everyone who believes in Him shall not be ashamed on the day of judgment' " (author's paraphrase throughout Rom. 9-10).

David Stern writes that the Jews "missed the Messiah because they did not grasp that the first requirement of the [written] Torah is *faith*"—or *belief* (recall Jesus' statement to the Pharisees, "If you had *believed* Moses"). The truth is, one cannot please God without faith, which means *believing* God (Heb. 11:6). He adds that obedience to "the Torah of Moses requires faith and offers righteousness by faith, just like the New Covenant"—thus, "righteousness must be grounded in trusting God" (*Jewish New Testament Commentary*, pp. 392-393; "Rom. 9"). Stern defines faith simply as "trust in God," adding that the Jewish leaders trusted instead in their *own works* (p. 392). The Jews have had the right goal, but they have gone about it all wrong; they understood that the Law offers righteousness (Deut. 6:25; etc.), but they went astray in thinking that such righteousness could be achieved by adhering to the "additions" and "amendments" *which they made* to the Scriptures—their so-called "oral law." The apostle Paul continues, showing the exact nature of the Jewish leaders' misunderstanding.

"Brethren, my heart's desire and my prayer to God for the Jews is for their salvation. For **I bear them witness** that they have a zeal for God, but not in accordance with *correct* knowledge" (Rom. 10:1-2).

It is important to note here that Paul says he was a first-hand *witness* of the Jews' zeal for God—proving that it was *Pharisaic* zeal. As a former Pharisee (Acts 26:5; etc.), Paul had fully participated in that same misguided fanaticism. This verse is critical because it demonstrates that *Pharisaism* was at the root of the Jews' failure to achieve righteousness. As has been amply demonstrated throughout this book, Pharisaism is based on a highly-flawed premise: the existence of a so-called "oral law" that supersedes the written Torah of Moses. This approach has led the Jews to seek what Hoffman, again, has rightly called "self-justification through works-righteousness." Thus, at the heart of the Jews' failure to achieve right-eousness was (and is) their *disbelief* in the exclusivity of the Scriptures and their insistence on their oral traditions. Verse three:

"For not knowing about God's righteousness"—not under-standing that true righteousness comes through heartfelt obe-dience to the written Torah in a genuine spirit of belief and faith in God *and* His Messiah—"and seeking to **establish their *own* righteousness**" and self-justification through ad-herence to a humanly-devise *code of law*—"they did not *sub-ject* themselves to the righteousness of God."

Note the Jews' failure to *subject* or *submit* themselves to God's way of making one righteous. Recall Jesus' words to the Jewish leadership in Luke 13:34, "*but you refused!*" Indeed, any chance the Jews might have had of experiencing true righteousness was made impossible by their *rejection* of Jesus as the Messiah and their *refusal* to set aside their "oral traditions" in favor of the written Torah.

Paul then makes an enigmatic statement that has proven to be a huge stumbling-block for Protestantism. Verse four: "For **Christ is the end of the law** for righteousness to everyone who believes" (*NKJV*). Given the fact that throughout the New Testament both Jesus and Paul uphold the veracity of the Law,[11] it is impossible to assume (as does mainstream Christianity) that Christ was somehow the *termination* of the Law. What then could Paul mean by this statement?[12]

The *context* of this entire passage is that the Jews—through a lack of belief or faith in both God (and thus His word) and Jesus as the Messiah—have failed to submit themselves to God's formula for righteousness. Genu-ine righteousness and justification before God can only be attained through a Messiah-centered approach to obedience to the Law.

Accordingly, in Stern's view, the Jews failed to "grasp the central point of the [written] Torah." He adds: "Had [the Jews] seen that **trust in God—as opposed to self-effort**, **legalism and mechanical obedience to** [their own Pharisaic] **rules**—is the route to the righteousness which the Torah itself not only requires but offers, then they would [have seen] that the goal at which the Torah aims is **acknowledging and trusting in the Messiah**…. [Thus, they would have understood] that the righteousness which the Torah offers is offered through Him and only through Him" (p. 395; "Rom. 10:4"; emphasis added).

Stern further writes that "a person who has trust in God, which the Torah itself requires, will—precisely because he has this trust, which forms the basic ground of all obedience to the Torah—understand and respond to the Gospel by also trusting in God's Messiah Yeshua [as opposed to *stumbling* at that "Rock of offence"]…. Only by believing in Yeshua will [one] be able to [fully] obey the Torah" (p. 396).

Given the context of this passage—that the Jews failed to believe in God's way to righteousness through Christ, and that they were steeped in Pharisaic *works of law* as a way of self-justification—a paraphrased rendering of Romans 10:4-5 could include the following (to study this passage in greater detail, see Appendix Four):

> "But for those Jews who *believe* God and accept His Messiah, Jesus has brought an *end* to vain efforts to achieve 'righteousness' through humanly-devised *works of law*. For Moses indeed writes that the man who practices the righteousness which is based on the Torah *alone* shall find life by that righteousness." [13]

In other words, for those who genuinely *believe* God—which means following *His* formula for righteousness—justification and righteousness are achieved through Christ-centered obedience to the Torah of Moses, thus putting an *end* to futile attempts at self-justification through ritual works and human regulatory codes. On the other hand, Judaism's formula of adherence to a humanly-devised *code of law* founded upon a so-called "oral Torah" is a prescription for failure—ending only in delusional *self*-righteousness and spiritual oppression.

As a former practicing Orthodox Jew, Avi ben Mordechai—whose personal experience with Rabbinic Judaism was detailed in the previous chapter—has observed that those who choose to submit to Pharisaic Judaism will ultimately "end up in *denial* of the written Torah" (*Galatians*, p. 371). As we have seen, Judaism's oral law has been established only at the expense of the Scriptures. Mordechai brings out that not only are Judaism's traditional laws a clear violation of Deuteronomy 4:2 and 12:32—where we are commanded to neither *add to* nor *take away* from the Law—they also represent a clear lack of *belief* in God. On this all-important point, he contends that "when we allow for a new religious law [such as the "oral law"] to be enacted and legally annexed to [God's] existing Law, it is like saying to [God], '**we do not believe in You**' " (p. 244; emphasis added).

Mordechai has done extensive research into the apostle Paul's use of such phrases as "works of law"—particularly in the book of Galatians. Scholars have long recognized that the epistle primarily addresses the issue of "Judaizers" who wanted the Galatian believers to adopt Jewish customs, become circumcised, and even follow the traditions and laws of the Pharisees. Expressing dismay at how easily Judaizers had led them astray, Paul asks, "O foolish Galatians, *who* has bewitched you...?" (Gal. 3:1). According to Mordechai, the Gentile converts of Galatia were under considerable "internal pressure to submit to local Pharisaic decrees and traditions..." (p. 217). When properly approached within the overall *context* of the book of Galatians, the phrase *works of the law* "can be understood as a **false system of justification**, which was [based on] a **Pharisaic system of decrees and traditions**." He adds, "*Works of the law*, as it was understood in the first century, produced a torah of false 'righteousness' [the Talmudic code] replete with its many reforms [ostensibly] developed by using the Law of Moses as a source text. *Works of the law* had **become another torah** added to the written Torah of Moses" (p. 216; emphasis added).[14]

It was within this framework that Paul had prefaced his corrective epistle by stating that "a man is **not justified by works of law**." He adds that even "we [converted Jews] also have believed in Christ Jesus in order that we might be justified by the faith of Christ, and **not by works of law**; because **by works of law shall no flesh be justified**" (Gal. 2:16). He thus concludes, "I do not nullify the grace of God; for if righteousness [and thus *life*] is through [Pharisaic] **works of law**, then Christ died in vain" (verse 21). Mordechai puts it like this: "If the Pharisaic system of law and tradition was able to impart life (which only the written commandments can do), then the death of Yeshua was for nothing" (p. 227).

In a key passage generally misunderstood by mainstream Christians, Paul writes, "For as many as are **of the works of the law** are under the curse; for it is written, 'Cursed is everyone who does not continue in all things which are written in the Book of the Law, to do them' " (Gal. 3:10; *NKJV*). This verse is typically assumed to mean that the Law of God is a *curse*. But read the passage carefully: It quotes Deuteronomy 27:26, which says, "Cursed is he who does not confirm all the words of this Law to do them." The curse is on the one who *fails to obey* the written Torah—because obedience to God's way of life *brings life*. This is why Jesus told the rich young man, "if you desire to *enter into life*, keep the commandments" (Matt. 19:17).[15]

What then could Paul mean by the earlier phrase, "For as many as are of the *works of the law* are under the curse"? Again, given the irrefutable fact that throughout the New Testament Paul fully upholds the veracity of the Law, it is impossible to conclude that the laws and commandments of God are a curse. However, given the context of the book of Galatians as presented by Mordechai, it becomes obvious that Paul was referring to *works of Pharisaic laws*. As Mordechai discovered, those who choose to seek self-justification through Pharisaic Judaism—*works of law*—will ultimately "end up in *denial* of the written Torah." As Jesus said in principle, one cannot "serve two masters; for either he will hate the one and love the other, or he will hold to the one and despise the other" (Matt. 6:24). **The Scriptures and the Talmud are mutually exclusive**. The Scriptures claim absolute authority (Isa. 8:20; etc.) and leave no room for an "oral tradition," while the Talmud labors in vain to establish itself as authentic. In the end, those who attempt to attain righteousness by Pharisaic *works of law* (as do all practicing Orthodox Jews) are "under the curse." Why? Because they will be in *denial* of the written Torah—they will not be in a position to "confirm all the words of this Law to do them" (Deut. 27:26).[16]

Mordechai concludes that the "foundation of Paul's polemic was this: No amount of submission to the established traditions of men was (or is) able to justify (establish as righteous) one who wants to be joined to the 'saved' Torah community of Israel"—for "**submitting to the Pharisaic oral law … was to essentially nullify the teaching and work of [Jesus]**" (p. 218; emphasis added). Genuine righteousness is not obtainable by submitting to Pharisaic "works of law." The Scriptures tell us that righteousness is attainable only by faithfully walking according to the commandments of God. "And the LORD commanded us to do all these statutes—to fear the LORD our God for our good always so that He might preserve us alive, as it is today. And **it shall be righteousness for us** if we observe to do all these commandments before the LORD our God as He has commanded us" (Deut. 6:24-25). Clearly, Jesus' straightforward teaching from Matthew five is that we are to observe *only* the written commandments of Moses according to their *spiritual intent* with an interpretation that is based on *context*—that is, letting the Bible interpret the Bible.

Moreover, righteousness also entails being spiritually *justified* in the sight of God. Such justification—wherein one is found to be in *right standing* with God—cannot be achieved even through perfect obedience to the Law. Why? Because, as Paul brings out in Romans 3:23, "all have sinned, and come short of the glory of God." Current obedience cannot atone for past sin. Thus, for one to be justified of past sin—and be in a fully righteous state before God—those sins must be *removed* through the application of Christ's sacrifice, just as was foreshadowed by the Passover and various Temple rituals. Ultimately, salvation is a matter of being *justified of past sins*, and of living a life of *heartfelt obedience* to the Scriptures through the help of Christ. To paraphrase Mordechai, the Messiah is the "living Torah," and by His Spirit we are "led into Torah truth"—that is, we have the Law of God written in our hearts by God's Spirit (p. 221).

The *Temporary* Blindness of the Jews

From a Jewish perspective, one of the most contemptuous teachings of evangelical Christianity is the idea that God has *replaced* Israel (or the Jews) with the Church. In so-called "Replacement Theology," the Church is now the *new* Israel. To say the least, the doctrine seriously offends Jewish claims of exclusively being *the* chosen people of God. The teaching insists that, because of the Jews' rejection of Jesus as the Messiah and their disdain for the Gospel, God has *revoked* the covenants He made with the nation of Israel. As Peterson notes, Replacement Theology teaches that the Church has "replaced Israel in every way and that the scores of [covenant] promises regarding the messianic kingdom must be interpreted symbolically" (*The Everlasting Tradition*, p. 100).

At first glance, certain biblical passages would *seem* to support the doctrine. Through Moses, God had warned the children of Israel that He would "move them to jealousy with **those which are not a people**" and "provoke them to anger **with [an unlearned] nation**" (Deut. 32:21). Likewise, Isaiah recorded this prophetic warning from God: "I revealed Myself to **those who asked not for Me**; I am found by **those who did not seek Me**. I said, 'Behold Me, behold Me,' to **a nation not called by My name**. [Meanwhile,] I have spread out My hands all the day to a rebellious people [Israel] who walk in the way that is not good, even after their own thoughts; a people who without ceasing provoke Me to My face..." (Isa. 65:1-3). As we have seen, Jesus gave a similar warning to the Jewish leaders of His day: "Because of this [their rejection of Jesus as the Messiah], I say to you, the kingdom of God shall be taken from you, and it shall be **given to a nation that produces the fruits** of it" (Matt. 21:43). Peter brings out that the *elect*, the *ekklesia* of God, is that *nation*: "But you are a chosen stock, a royal priesthood, **a holy nation**, a people for a possession of God, that you might proclaim His excellent virtues [bring forth fruit worthy of the Kingdom of God], Who called you out of darkness into His marvelous light; who once **were not a people**, but **now are the people of God**; who had not received mercy, but now have received mercy" (I Pet. 2:9-10).

But does the Church, the elect, actually *replace* Israel in the plan of God? Unequivocally, *no*. The apostle Paul holds out great hope to Israel when he proclaims that "the gifts and the calling of God are *irrevocable*" (Rom. 11:29; *NKJV*). To be sure, Paul's treatise in Romans 10-11 leaves no room whatsoever for Replacement Theology. Israel's *original* destiny—its "gifts and calling"—will yet be fulfilled. But Paul also shows that the Jews have been *temporarily* blinded by their own unbelief, and that the *remedy* for such blindness, according to God's wisdom, is for them to be *provoked to jealously*.

Paul notes that the Jews—the scribes, Pharisees and priests—had not *believed* the Gospel message (Rom. 10:16). Then, addressing the opening of the Gospel to Gentiles, he puts the above-quoted prophetic passages into perspective:

"Were the Jews not forewarned? First, God had said through Moses, 'I will provoke you to jealousy through **those who are not a people**. I will anger you through **a people without understanding**.' Then Isaiah boldly predicted, 'I was found by **those who were not seeking Me**, and I was revealed to **those who were not inquiring after Me**.' But to the Jews, God has said, 'All day long I have stretched out My hands in an offer of mercy to a people who are disobedient and contrary' " (verses 19-21).

Note that for purposes of *contrast* with unbelieving Jews, Paul refers to the spiritual "people of God" as *Gentiles*—even though the calling of the *elect* (Rom. 11:7) began with Jews. Of course, as the Church grew it became predominantly non-Jewish. Moreover, from a New Covenant perspective, that "nation" is neither Jewish nor Gentile—for all are one spiritually (Rom. 10:12; Gal. 3:28). It is the fact that God has temporarily *favored Gentiles over Jews* that will ultimately provoke the Jews to jealousy (keep in mind the tremendous contempt Jews have for non-Jews).

Paul continues his key discourse in Romans chapter 11 (paraphrased and abridged):

"Now then I ask, 'Has God rejected His people?' May it never be! **God has *not* rejected His people** whom He foreknew. What then has happened? The righteousness the Jews have sought through their own *works of law* has never been realized. Instead, an *elect* has obtained genuine righteousness through God's favor, and the Jews have been *temporarily* left to their stubbornness—just as it was foretold: 'God has given them a spirit of slumber, eyes that are not able to see, and ears that are not able to hear,' even as it is to this day" (verses 1-2, 7-8; see Deut. 29:4; Isa. 29:10; Jer. 5:21; etc.)

As this passage clearly shows, the Jews, even in wholesale unbelief, have *not* been "replaced." Even the "elect" has not replaced the Jews. As we will see, both the *Jews* and the *elect* have distinct roles in the millennial age to come.

Again, the *favor* God has shown to *Gentiles* will be the *catalyst* for the Jews' repentance.

"Now, did the Jews stumble to the extent that their failure is permanent? May it never be! But in their failure, salvation has come to the Gentiles—*why?*—**to provoke the Jews to jealousy**! Moreover, if the Jews' stumbling means *spiritual* riches through the Gospel for the world—and if their condition of being *temporarily less favored* brings such riches to the Gentiles—then **how much greater riches will result from the Jews' full restoration?** For if their temporary rejection opens up spiritual reconciliation to the world (because the Gospel is now preached to all), what will happen when the Jews are fully reconciled to God and accepted? It will be like one raised from the dead!" (verses 11-12, 15).

The existing Jewish condition of *unbelief*—manifested in their ongoing rejection of Jesus as the Messiah and in their idolatrous obsession with Talmudic tradition—is not permanent. Clearly, as foreseen here by Paul, the Jews' condition will be *reversed*—once they are "provoked to jealousy" and repent. Then, as Paul also indicates, the Jews will become a *tremendous blessing to all mankind!* There is even the subtle suggestion in verse 15 that Israel's redemption and restoration in the messianic age will result in *life* itself. After all, Jesus did say that salvation is "of the Jews" (John 4:22).

Meanwhile, God is able to use the Jews' unbelief to further His plan of salvation. Using the analogy of an olive tree, Paul continues in Romans 11 showing that as some of the natural branches (Jews) were "broken off," others from a "wild tree" (Gentiles, or the elect) were "grafted in"—to then partake of the nourishment of the root (verse 17). The *root*—which "bears the branches" (verse 18)—refers to the covenant promises God made to Abraham (see Deut. 10:15). As verse 28 notes, "concerning the *election*, they [too] are beloved for the fathers' sakes." Indeed, God's covenantal commitment to Abraham, Isaac and Jacob was designed to ultimately include Gentiles. Thus, through *faith*, non-Jews can become co-heirs with Israel of the blessings of the New Covenant.[17] In the end, as long as the Jews "do not continue in unbelief," God will "graft them in again" (verse 23).

In Romans 11:25, Paul begins to hold out marvelous hope for the Jews (and for all of Israel).

"Brethren, I do not want you to be ignorant of this *previously hidden knowledge*, lest what has happened to the Jews cause you to become wise in your own conceits. So understand this: There has been a **partial hardening of the Jews' heart**—but only until the *elect* is fully prepared."

As we have seen, this hardening of the heart was foretold first by Moses in Deuteronomy 29:4, and later by the prophets Isaiah and Jeremiah. The final phrase of this verse—"until the fullness of the Gentiles be come in" (*KJV*)—is quite vague in most translations. Keep in mind that throughout this section of Romans, Paul is using *Gentile* synonymously with the *elect* (Rom. 11:5, 7, 28)—the Church of God (Col. 3:12; II John 1). Paul's heavy use of the term is intentional, for it is the realization that messianic salvation has been offered to *Gentiles* that will provoke the Jews to repentance. Clearly, the phrase does *not* mean that the composition of the Church would be entirely Gentile, for it obviously began with Jews; nor does it mean that the Church must grow until it encompasses *all* Gentiles, for the elect would always be a "little flock" (Luke 12:32). Rather, this phrase shows that the problem of Jewish unbelief **will be resolved at the return of Christ** when His bride—the Church—will have fully *made herself ready* (Rev. 19:7).

Redemption and Restoration In the Age to Come

In rejecting the Jews, to whom salvation had come *first* (Rom. 1:16), God opened the Gospel to non-Jews. The astonishing realization that God has indeed *passed over* the Jews and offered salvation through Jesus the Messiah *to Gentiles* will ultimately provoke the Jews both to anger and jealousy. That anger and jealousy, coupled with genuine *repentance*, will be the catalyst for Jewish salvation. Thus, Paul continues in Romans 11 with this hopeful proclamation:

> "And so **all Israel shall be saved**, according as it is written concerning the Messiah: 'Out of Zion shall come the Deliverer, and He shall turn away ungodliness from Jacob [Israel]. For this is My covenant, which I [God] will make with them when I have taken away their sins' " (verses 26-27). For, as noted earlier, the one-of-a-kind calling that God has given to the Jews (as well as to all of Israel) **"is in no way revoked"** (verse 29).

Romans 11:26-27 is taken from Isaiah 59:20-21. However, Paul does not quote the latter part of verse 21: " '[And in that day,] My spirit that is upon you [shall not depart], and **My words** [the Scriptures alone] **which I have put in your mouth, shall not depart out of your mouth**, nor out of the mouth of your seed, nor out of the mouth of your seed's seed,' says the LORD, 'from now on and forever.' " This is similar in tenor to God's promise of a new covenant with Israel in the millennial age:

> "Behold, the days are coming when I will make a new covenant with the house of Israel, and with the house of Judah [then rejoined as one]. Unlike the covenant I made with Israel when I brought them out of Egypt—which they continually broke, although I was like a husband to them—in this new covenant **I will write My Law in their hearts**. I will be their God, and they shall be My people. No one will admonish his neighbor to 'know the LORD'—for they will *all* know Me, from the least of them to the greatest. And I will forgive their iniquity, and I will remember their sins no more" (abridged and paraphrased from Jer. 31:31-34).[18]

In the age to come, Judaism will cease to exist—along with all other man-made religions. Only the *true* "religion" of the Old Testament will exist as amplified spiritually by Jesus and the apostles in the New Testament. For in those days, "people [from all nations] shall go and say, 'Come, and let us go up to the mountain [government headquarters] of the LORD, to the house of the God of Jacob [Israel, including the Jews]. And He will teach us of His ways, and we will walk in His paths.' For out of Zion shall go forth the Law, and the Word of the LORD from Jerusalem" (Isa. 2:3).

Even after having "disowned" Israel and the Jews for a time, God declares through Hosea that "the number of the children of Israel shall be as the sand of the sea, which cannot be measured nor numbered. And it shall be in the place where it was [once] said to them, '*You are not My people*,' there it shall [instead] be said to them, '*You are the sons of the living God*.' Then the children of Judah [the Jews] and the children of Israel shall be gathered together [as one nation], and shall set over themselves one head [a king of the Davidic line, possibly a reference to Jesus Himself] and they shall come up out of the land [of their end-time captivity]..." (Hosea 1:10-11).

Moreover, in the midst of soon-coming end-time calamity, Scripture shows that God will deliver the Jews from destruction and establish them again in the land of Palestine. "Behold, I will make Jerusalem a cup of trembling unto all the people all around, when they shall be in the siege both against Judah and against Jerusalem. And in that day I will make Jerusalem a burdensome stone for all people. All who burden themselves with it shall be cut in pieces, though all the nations of the earth be gathered together against it.... And it shall be in that day that I will seek to destroy all the nations that come against Jerusalem" (Zech. 12:2-3, 9). God says that He will "open [His] eyes upon the house of Judah" and that "Jerusalem shall be inhabited again"—for He will "save the tents of Judah *first*" (verses 4, 6-7).

Moreover, the New Testament foretells of the end-time repentance and conversion of the tribes of Israel—but note that the Jews (Judah) are listed *first* (Rev. 7:1-8).

The Jews' Ultimate Destiny

The idea of *destiny* is central to the religion of Judaism. However, as David Ariel notes, "the question of Jewish destiny remains unresolved, as the fundamental issues concerning the Jews' place in the world are under continual [rabbinic] revision." Thus, the rabbis are "constantly posing new approaches" to the Jews' "struggle with the issue of Jewish destiny and distinctiveness" (*What Do Jews Believe?*, p. 133).[19]

What do Jews today think about their own destiny, about their status as God's "chosen people"? It seems they have lost sight of their original purpose of being a *model* nation. Instead, looking *inwardly*, Judaism has focused on being "treasured" by God. Ariel notes that, as a consequence of Rabbinical Judaism, Jewish distinctiveness is today found in "personal spirituality" and the pursuit of Jewish survival. "There are many Jews today who have abandoned the idea of chosen-ness in favor of the idea that the Jewish people have a mutual responsibility to one another to insure [the Jews'] survival and the survival of the State of Israel as a safe haven for Jews throughout the world" (p. 132).

Ariel continues: "Although there have been various interpretations of the higher purpose of Jewish existence—whether it is the **belief in Judaism as a constant striving for the realization of an ideal** or the **belief that Judaism is a spiritual process**—Jews can all agree that *the search for such meaning* is at the very heart of the Jewish people" (p. 133; emphasis added). Note that Ariel inextricably links Jewish destiny with Judaism. It seems that a biblically-defined destiny that finds purpose and meaning for the people of Israel as a whole has given way to a self-seeking destiny centered on Judaic *religious practice*. The following statements—which could *easily* apply to Eastern religion as well as, to a lesser degree, nominal Christianity—are highly representative of Orthodox Judaism and hint strongly at the Jews' watered-down approach to their own destiny: "The Jewish view of human destiny begins with the belief that God created the first human being in His own image. Each individual is the earthly representation of God, and all people participate equally in this noble stature…. Everything has a purpose, and the purpose of human life is to refine the image of God within us…. The spiritual dimension of Judaism is the emphasis on strengthening the image of God, the divine spark … [which] is within each of us…. Jews believe that all of human life can be understood as the spiritual process of experiencing God within the world. To experience the divine within the world is to realize God's presence. Ultimately, to know yourself is to know God" (Ariel, pp. 50-51).

This popular view of Jewish destiny compromises the idea of the Jews being God's "chosen people," and effectively lumps the Jews in with the rest of humanity in its search for "spiritual enlightenment." But from a biblical perspective, it is a huge mistake to confuse the destiny of the people of Israel with the destiny of the rest of the world. God calls no other nation "My elect" (Isa. 45:4; 65:9, 22); to no other nation has God said, "But you, Israel, are My servant, Jacob whom I have chosen, the seed of Abraham, My friend, whom I have taken from the ends of the earth, and called you from its uttermost parts. And I said to you, 'You are My servant; I have chosen you, and have not cast you away' " (Isa. 41:8-9). What other nation has been called to *model God's way* to the world (Ex. 19:6)? What other nation has teachings and laws so profoundly wise that the nations of the world would seek after them (Deut. 4:6)?

Without question, in the age to come, the nation of Israel *will fulfill* their original God-ordained role as a *model* nation for the world. But they will do so under the *direct leadership* of the glorified saints, those "grafted" in as "spiritual Jews" because of the Jews' unbelief. As noted earlier, the Jews and the *elect* have distinct roles. As spirit-born immortal children of God, the saints will rule as kings and priests over the earth with Christ (Rev. 5:10; 20:6). Under their leadership, the Law will go forth from Jerusalem

(Isa. 2:3), and the knowledge of God's way of life will cover the earth like the seas (11:9). The twelve apostles will each rule over a tribe of Israel (Luke 22:30)—as the nation, in turn, fulfills its role as the premier "model" nation that all humanity will ultimately desire to follow.

In fact, the Jews' *ultimate destiny* is captured in a single, profound statement made by the prophet Zechariah concerning the millennial age: "In those days *ten men* out of all the nations will *take hold of the garment of a Jew*, saying, 'We will go with you, for **we have heard that God is with you**' " (Zech. 8:23; author's paraphrase). In the culture of Zechariah's day, taking hold of another's garment meant looking to that individual for guidance and protection. The *ten men* are representative of all nations—thus, the *entire world* will follow the then-righteous example of the nation of Israel.

Meanwhile, observant Jews continue to practice a "form of righteousness" as slaves to rabbinic codes of law. Following in the footsteps of their Pharisaic progenitors, they remain blinded by *unbelief*. In this age, Jews *as a whole* will never experience the genuine righteousness that comes from a true Scripture-based relationship with God through the mediatory role of Jesus as the Messiah. Indeed, Zechariah prophesied that the Jews would not recognize Jesus until He returns as the "Conquering Messiah" to rescue them in the "latter days." In utter repentance, they will also understand that He is the *same* Jesus their ancestors had killed. "And I will pour out a spirit of compassion and supplication on the Jews and on the inhabitants of Jerusalem, so that **when they see the One whom their own fathers had killed**, they will in repentance mourn for Him, as one mourns for an only child, and in bitterness weep over Him, as one weeps over a firstborn" (Zech. 12:10; author's paraphrase).[20]

As the *final* Old Testament prophet, Malachi looked past his own time and into the period of Jewish history that would ultimately set the stage for the development of *Judaism*. In so doing, he predicted a grave crisis in godly leadership in which the laws and commandments of God would be held in contempt. Then, looking toward the consummation of the age, he warns of the coming of a final, end-time "Elijah" whose mission will be to *turn the hearts* of the Jews back toward their fathers, Abraham, Isaac and Jacob—back to the *true* "religion" of the Old Testament (Mal. 4:5-6). In verse four, with a warning that seems particularly applicable to Jews caught up in Talmudic Judaism, the prophet appeals to his readers to "**remember the Torah of Moses**."

The Jews *will remember*. And in the age to come, Jesus' words in John 4:22 will never be more true—that *"salvation is of the Jews"*!

Chapter Notes

CHAPTER ONE

1. *Torah*, in Hebrew, literally means *teaching*, *direction* or *instruction*, but is most often translated *law*. In typical usage, the Torah (or the *Law*, as used by Jesus in Matthew 5:17) is the first five books of the Old Testament, also known as the Pentateuch (from the Latin *penta teukhos*, "five books").

Rarely, some use Torah to refer to the entire Old Testament, since as a whole it consists of "teachings." In the Bible, "*the law*" is used in a variety of ways and does not always refer to the Torah or Pentateuch in its entirety.

In Judaism, the so-called "oral Torah" (the Talmud) is made up *only* of humanly-devised traditional laws. Many rabbis create confusion by speaking of "the Torah" without differentiating between the *written* Torah of God and the *oral* traditions of Judaism. Still worse, rabbis frequently use "Torah" to refer collectively to both.

For the sake of clarity, any rabbinical reference to the "oral Torah" is so noted throughout this book by inserting, where necessary, the word "oral" in brackets—"[oral] Torah"—to distinguish it from the *written* or *Mosaic* Torah or Pentateuch.

2. Reduced to its simplest form, the *Talmud* consists of two parts:

1) The *Mishnah*, written in Hebrew, is the compilation of esoteric *traditions* and *teachings* devised and preserved orally by Jewish sages over centuries. As such, the Mishnah "represents the commitment to writing of the occult legends and lore of those [scribes] who had preserved secret knowledge" (Michael Hoffman, *Judaism Discovered*, p. 145). It was completed around 200 AD in Palestine.

2) The *Gemara*, written in Aramaic, is rabbinical *commentary* on the Mishnah. "All the opinions and decisions resulting from three hundred years of discussion" of the Mishnah were finally put into writing. "Completed in 500 AD, this monumental work [combined with the Mishnah] became known as the *Babylonian Talmud*" (Solomon Landman, *Story Without End*, p. 114). Still, the Talmud continued to evolve long afterward, with numerous portions being added (see Appendix One).

While the rabbis of Palestine controlled the development of the Mishnah, the rabbis of Babylon produced the Gemara. Because the Talmud was put into its "final" form under the authority of the Babylonian rabbis, it is called the *Babylonian Talmud* (designated as *BT* throughout this book). In Judaism, the *Jerusalem Talmud* is all but disregarded as inferior.

The Talmud is almost exclusively the domain of rabbis. Most Jews who practice Judaism simply follow the teachings of their local rabbi; some utilize references such as the *Code of Jewish Law* (see Appendix Two). Prior to the publication of the 1934-48 Soncino edition of *The Babylonian Talmud*, there was no usable English translation of the Talmud. "Humanly speaking, [the Talmud] has done more to shape ... the Jew than anything else in [their] long and remarkable history" (Hoffman, p. 56).

3. Obviously, Jesus spoke with authority because He was filled with the Holy Spirit and moved powerfully by the Father. That aside, Christ was able to teach with authority because He had a clear, unmistakable message. With absolute conviction and certainty, He said what He meant and meant what He said. In contrast, because of their intellectual vanity, the scribes and Pharisees tolerated a wide variety of opinions and ideas within their ranks; their wishy-washy approach made it impossible to speak with authority.

4. *Tanakh* is a Jewish term for the Old Testament.

5. As *converted* believers (Acts 3:19; Matt. 18:3) and *spiritual* Jews (Rom. 2:29), the Church (the *elect*) is being "built up as a spiritual house—a holy priesthood—to offer up spiritual sacrifices, acceptable to God through Jesus Christ" (I Pet. 2:5). As a "chosen stock," the Church is to become "a royal priesthood, **a holy nation**" at Jesus' return (verse nine)—destined to rule with Christ in the age to come.

6. Some translate Matthew 23:2 to read that the scribes and Pharisees had "seated themselves" in Moses' seat (*New American Standard Bible*, etc.), demonstrating the fact that the religionists had *usurped* the position.

CHAPTER TWO

1. The so-called "age of the prophets" ended with Malachi. The ensuing void—lasting some 400 years, until John the Baptist—left the Jews to their own devices, and, one might argue, permitted the development of Judaism.

2. The use of the term "Judaism" in modern translations of Galatians 1:13-14 is erroneous, giving the impression that *organized Judaism* was already extant in New Testament times. Galatians 1:13-14 is translated "the Jews' religion" in the *KJV*, etc., and is derived from a Greek word that simply means "to live as Jew." The "Jews' religion" as once practiced by Paul was Pharisaism, which evolved into full-fledged Judaism *after* the books of the New Testament were completed.

3. Dr. Joseph Herman Hertz was the Chief Rabbi of Great Britain until his death in 1946. Hertz wrote the foreword to the 1934 Soncino edition of *The Babylonian Talmud* (the first usable English translation of the Talmud).

4. *Halakhah* (or halacha, halachah) is a Jewish term used broadly for religious law—including biblical, Talmudic and rabbinic law, as well as various customs and traditions.

5. According to Avi ben Mordechai, a former Talmud-observing Jew, the rabbis justify their "fence around the [written] Torah" from Genesis 26:5, where it says Abraham "kept My [God's] charge." The rabbis say the phrase means "protected My protections"—indicating a need to *protect* the Law with a "fence." Mordechai notes that because the rabbis are **bent on seeing their oral tradition in everything**, they perform what is called biblical *eisegesis*"—which means that they "**read their predetermined views into texts** like [Genesis 26:5], teaching that Abraham made fences around [God's] commandments" (*Galatians—A Torah-Based Commentary in First-Century Hebraic Context*, p. 249; emphasis added). But Abraham simply did what the Hebrew says, he protected or guarded God's laws and commandments in a heartfelt desire to obey them.

CHAPTER THREE

1. *Hellenism* refers broadly to ancient Greek culture—covering everything from religion, philosophy and ideals to language, education, politics and the arts. The uninhibited pursuit of knowledge, logic and reason was its centerpiece. The spread of Hellenistic civilization was primarily the result of the conquests of Alexander the Great.

2. A Jewish scholar and historian, Dr. Jacob Z. Lauterbach (1873-1942) was a prolific writer; his *Rabbinic Essays* were published in 1989 by the Hebrew Union College Press, Cincinnati, Ohio.

3. Philo of Alexandria (20 BC to 50 AD), a Hellenistic Jewish writer and philosopher, is noted for his infusion of Greek logic into the growing Judaic religion. Philo utilized Greek logic as a way of "defending and justifying" the Jewish religion—as a way to harmonize Greek philosophy with Jewish exegesis (wikipedia.org/wiki/Philo). Through his writings, "Philo deduces formally from the Old Testament all those philosophical doctrines which he had in fact appropriated from Greek philosophers." Philo's goal, it appears, was to persuade his fellow Jews that Greek philosophy was neither hostile nor opposed to the teachings of the Jewish religion (earlyjewishwritings. com/philo.html).

4. From the Hebrew *hasid* ("pious"), *Hasidim* referred originally to Jewish "Puritans" of the Maccabean period; the term is also used of followers of "Hasidic Judaism," a Jewish movement which originated in Eastern Europe in the 18th century (see Appendix Five).

5. Some scholars see the synagogue system of worship as *contrary* to the centrality of Temple worship. For example, in his *Old Testament History*, Charles Pfeiffer explains: "Pre-exilic Judaism looked to the Jerusalem Temple as the focal point of its spiritual life. Worship at local shrines, or 'high places,' continued through much of Israelite history, but **the prophets**, and the kings who supported them, **abolished such worship** and **insisted on the primacy of the Temple**. In this way the unity of the God of Israel was emphasized, in contrast to the concept of local gods which was prevalent in the ancient world" (p. 541; emphasis added). Scripture backs up this assertion. For example, Deuteronomy restricts the worship of God to where He had *placed His name*—the Temple in Jerusalem (Deut. 12:5-7, 11). Likewise, there is a prohibition against offering sacrifices in any other place (verses 13 -14). At the dedication of Solomon's Temple, the children of Israel were directed to Jerusalem as the *one* place to which they were to seek—to bring their offerings, sacrifices and tithes. They were to pray toward the Temple; and, in times of trouble, they were to look to where God's name had been placed (I Kings 8:29-30, 33, 35, 38, 42-44, 48). Moreover, it was there in Jerusalem where the Temple stood that the people were to come to enquire of the judges and priests in matters of controversy (Deut. 17:8-13).

Still, Jesus and the apostles used the synagogues in order to proclaim the Gospel (Matt. 4:23; Acts 19:8; etc.). But notice Christ's own words: "But beware of men; for they will deliver you up to councils, and they will scourge you in **their** synagogues" (Matt. 10:17). Christ said the synagogues were *their* synagogues. Jesus also told the Pharisees that they had persecuted the prophets and wise men in "**your** synagogues" (Matt. 23:34).

CHAPTER FOUR

1. Contrast the Jews' use of the term *rabbi* with what Jesus taught: "[The scribes and Pharisees love] salutations in the marketplaces, and to be called by men, 'Rabbi, Rabbi.' But you are not to be called Rabbi; for one is your Master, the Christ, and all of you are brethren" (Matt. 23:7-8).

CHAPTER FIVE

1. The ancient rabbis developed 39 categories of "work" prohibited on the Sabbath—allegedly based on the written Torah:

> sowing, plowing, reaping, binding sheaves, threshing, winnowing, selecting, grinding, sifting, kneading, baking, shearing wool, washing wool, beating wool, dyeing wool, spinning, weaving, making two loops, weaving two threads, separating two threads, tying, untying, sewing two stitches, tearing, trapping, slaughtering, flaying, salting meat, curing hide, scraping hide, cutting hide up, writing two letters, erasing two letters, building (construction), tearing down (demolition), extinguishing a fire, kindling a fire, hitting with a hammer, and carrying (transporting an object from a private domain to a public domain).

Literally hundreds of oppressive Sabbath prohibitions are based on these 39 categories; moreover, there are hundreds of additional prohibitions not covered by these categories—such as the laws describing what may be handled or touched on the Sabbath; how far one may walk on the Sabbath; what may be eaten on the Sabbath; etc.

2. *BT* designates the *Babylonian Talmud*; *Sanhedrin*, in this case, designates the particular *tractate*; 88b is the folio number.

3. In the event that specific instruction or direction was needed apart from what was provided by the Scriptures, a method was established by which the children of Israel could enquire after God Himself. For example, Moses judged the people in various matters, even enquiring of God when necessary (Ex. 18:13-16). A similar approach was instituted once Israel settled into the Promised Land: "If a matter is too hard for you in judgment [too difficult or questionable to be handled locally] … being matters of strife within your gates, then you shall arise and go up to the place [Jerusalem] which the LORD your God shall choose. And you shall come to the **priests**, [of] the Levites, and to the **judge** that shall be in those days, **and ask**. And they shall declare to you the sentence of judgment" (Deut. 17:8-9).

While this passage does not specifically mention enquiring of God, the context makes it clear that God was *directing* the judgment. At times, *urim* was used to discern God's will in a matter. "And he [Joshua] shall stand before Eleazar the priest, who shall **ask for him according to the judgment of urim before the LORD**" (Num. 27:21). Scripture does not describe just how *urim* (and *thummim*) worked; nevertheless, God was able to communicate His will to the High Priest through these devices.

Prophets were also used to enquire of God (I Sam. 9:9; 28:6). But at no time did God sanction the use of a so-called "oral Torah" in order to establish His will in an uncertain matter.

4. Mainstream Christians typically misapply this passage to makes it appear that Moses was the giver of a harsh, unbending set of laws that condemn and kill—while Jesus substituted grace and truth *in place of* the Law. But nothing could be further from the truth. The *KJV* is misleading; the word "but" implies opposition, and should read "while." The Law is not opposed to grace, nor is grace opposed to the Law. Rather, the two work together. By *defining sin* (Rom. 7:7), the Law guides the believer in God's way of life; on the other hand, grace makes it possible for the believer to have forgiveness in the event the Law is transgressed (Rom. 3:23-25).

CHAPTER SIX

1. Mordechai's statement is reminiscent of what Paul wrote concerning his experience as a Pharisee—that he had lived according to the *strictest* sect of the Jews' religion (Acts 26:5; the Greek word means *rigorous* and *exacting*).

2. Complicating matters is the fact that the ancient rabbis have expanded the definition of *work* to include *creative* actions, or *melachah*, in which one *creates* or exercises control or dominion over one's environment. *Melachah* is discussed in detail in Chapter Seven; see www.chabad.org/library/article_cdo/aid/484231/jewish/What-constitutes-creation.htm.

3. The absurd prohibition against squeezing a lemon on the Sabbath is found in Solomon Ganzfried's *Code of Jewish Law*, p. 91; see Appendix Two.

4. *The Anchor Bible Dictionary* adds this interesting comment: "At times Jesus is interpreted to have abrogated or suspended the Sabbath commandment on the basis of the controversies brought about by Sabbath healings and other acts. Careful analysis of the respective passages does not seem to give credence to this interpretation. The action of plucking the ears of grain on the Sabbath by the disciples is particularly important in this matter. Jesus makes a foundational pronouncement at that time in a chiastically structured statement of antithetic parallelism: 'The Sabbath was made for man and not man for the Sabbath' (Mark 2:27). **The disciples' act of plucking the grain infringed against the rabbinic** *halakhah* [religious laws] of minute casuistry in which it was forbidden to reap, thresh, winnow and grind on the Sabbath (*Sabb.* 7.2). Here again, **rabbinic Sabbath** *halakhah* **is rejected**, as in other Sabbath conflicts. Jesus reforms the Sabbath and restores its rightful place as designed in creation, where the Sabbath is made for all mankind and not specifically for Israel, as claimed by normative Judaism (*cf Jub.* 2:19-20, see D.3). The subsequent logion, 'The Son of Man is Lord even of the Sabbath' (Mark 2:28; Matt. 12:8; Luke 6:5), indicates that **man-made Sabbath** *halakhah* **does not rule the Sabbath, but that the Son of Man as Lord determines the true meaning of the Sabbath**. The Sabbath activities of Jesus are neither hurtful provocations nor mere protests against rabbinic legal restrictions, but are part of Jesus' essential proclamation of the in-breaking of the Kingdom of God in which man is taught the original meaning of the Sabbath as the recurring weekly proleptic 'day of the Lord' in which God manifests his healing and saving rulership over man" (*The Anchor Bible Dictionary*, Vol. 5, pp. 854-855; emphasis added).

5. Regarded as one of Judaism's greatest scholars, Rabbi Moshe ben Maimon (1135-1204), or Moses Maimonides, is perhaps best known for his vast work, *Mishneh Torah*. Quote from (John) *Gill's Commentary* on Matthew 12:2; www.biblestudytools.com/commentaries/gills-exposition-of-the-bible/matthew-12-2.html.

CHAPTER SEVEN

1. Reprinted from Rabbi Adin Steinsaltz's *Teshuvah: A Guide for the Newly Observant Jew*; www.myjewishlearning.com/practices/Ritual/Shabbat_The_Sabbath/History/Rabbinic_I.shtml. Currently living in Jerusalem, Steinsaltz is the author of numerous works that bring traditional Torah scholarship and Hasidic thought to contemporary audiences.

2. From the site www.chabad.org/library/article_cdo/aid/95907/jewish/The-Shabbat-Laws.htm. As a division of the Chabad-Lubavitch Media Center, chabad.org operates under the auspices of the Lubavitch World Headquarters. Chabad-Lubavitch is a Hasidic/Kabbalist movement that began in the 1940s in Eastern Europe and Russia. The movement considers itself to be the most "dynamic force" in Jewish life today.

3. www.chabad.org/library/article_cdo/aid/484231/jewish/What-constitutes-creation.htm

4. www.chabad.org/library/article_cdo/aid/485596/jewish/Is-it-permitted-to-use-a-can-opener-on-Shabbat.htm

5. www.chabad.org/library/article_cdo/aid/960077/jewish/Heating-a-Home-on-Shabbat.htm

6. www.bible-history.com/backd2/sabbath.html

7. See www.myjewishlearning.com/practices/Ritual/Shabbat_The_Sabbath/In_the_Community/Eruv.shtml.

8. See www.chabad.org/library/article_cdo/aid/257752/jewish/Eruv-Shabbat Rest.htm.

9. www.chabad.org/library/article_cdo/aid/700456/jewish/What-is-an-Eruv.htm

10. Rabbi Moshe ben Maimon (1135-1204), or Moses Maimonides, is in Judaic circles regarded as *the* preeminent medieval Jewish philosopher and one of the greatest Torah scholars of the Middle Ages. Although many of his ideas were opposed by his contemporaries, Maimonides was embraced by later Jewish thinkers. Today, his views are considered a cornerstone of Jewish thought; his 14-volume *Mishneh Torah* is upheld as an authoritative codification of Talmudic law (wikipedia.org/wiki/Maimonides).

11. Jacobs adds that the evening service of Yom Kippur is actually named after the *Kol Nidrei* declaration, indicating the importance Judaism places on the ritual. A leading writer on Judaism and Masorti Rabbi, Dr. Louis Jacobs (1920-2006) was the first leader of Masorti Judaism (also known as Conservative Judaism) in the United Kingdom. Found at www.myjewish learning.com/holidays/Jewish_Holidays/Yom_Kippur/In_the_Community/Prayer_Services/Kol_Nidrei.shtml.

12. According to the Talmud, the first-century rabbinic schools of Hillel and Shammai are *both* correct. Even when their decrees differ, both are considered to be the words of God (*BT Erubin*, 13b).

13. See www.myjewishlearning.com/beliefs/Issues/Jews_and_NonJews/ Jewish_Chosenness/Traditional_Views/Covenant_and_Chosenness.shtml.

14. Soble's statement—"The Jewish people and God are wholly one"—is from the *Zohar* and is typical of Kabbalist philosophy; see Appendix Five.

15. Virtually all English versions of the Babylonian Talmud have been censored to a degree that renders them unreliable. The reason for such censorship is to "soften" passages that would otherwise appear to express hostility and disdain toward non-Jews. The exception is the Steinsaltz edition (1989, unfinished), which retains the original wording. When compared to the popular Soncino Talmud, published in London from 1934 through 1948, the censorship becomes apparent. For example, many passages of the Soncino edition render the Hebrew *goyim* (Gentiles or non-Jews) as simply "heathen" or "idolaters." The Steinsaltz edition uses the original Talmudic wording with no attempt to hide the meaning through cosmetic euphemisms (Hoffman, *Judaism Discovered*, p. 330, footnote 353).

    "The [unfinished] out-of-print Random House publication of *The Talmud: The Steinsaltz Edition* is widely regarded as the most accurate and least redacted of any English language edition and is sought after on that basis by scholars and collectors. Controversial Talmud passages previously obscured, omitted entirely or confined to footnotes in English translations like the Soncino Talmud, receive full exposition in the Steinsaltz Talmud" (wikipedia.org/wiki/Adin_Steinsaltz).

16. See at www.myjewishlearning.com/beliefs/Issues/Jews_and_NonJews/ Legal_Issues/Non-Jew_in_Jewish_Law.shtml. Jeffrey Spitzer is Chair of the Department of Talmud and Rabbinics at Gann Academy, Waltham, MA.

17. According to Hoffman, this passage is censored in many editions of Maimonides' work (p. 381).

18. Hoffman states that the majority of rabbinic authorities teach that Christianity is idol worship. On this point he references *Minchas Elazar*, 1:53-3; *Yechaveh Da'as*, 4:45; *Darchei Teshuvah*, 150:2; and *Tzitz Eliezer*, 14:91.

    Concerning Jesus Himself, the Talmud contains several disparaging references. For example, the Talmud claims that Christ and His disciples practiced sorcery and black magic, led Jews astray into idolatry, and were sponsored by foreign, Gentile powers for the purpose of subverting Jewish worship (*BT Sanhedrin*, 43a. This tractate states: "On Passover eve they hanged Jesus of Nazareth … because he practiced sorcery."). It is also held that Jesus was sexually immoral, worshipped statues of stone, and was cut off from the Jewish people because of wickedness (*BT Sanhedrin*, 107b; *Sotah*, 47a). *BT Shabbos*, 104b, claims that Jesus learned witchcraft in Egypt.

19. From the article "Shemoneh Esreh," at www.jewishencyclopedia.com/view.jsp?artid=612&letter=S. The *Amidah*, also known as *Shemoneh Esreh*, is a collection of 18 benedictions forming the second portion of the Jews' daily prayers (the *Shema* is the first portion).

20. www.hebrew4christians.com/Prayers/Daily_Prayers/Shemoneh_Esrei/Birkat_HaMinim/birkat_haminim.html

21. The basis for wearing phylacteries was derived from four biblical passages—Exodus 13:9, 16 and Deuteronomy 6:8 and 11:18. But, as is so often the case, the rabbis have misunderstood the spiritual intent behind the scriptural instruction. While the rabbis have arbitrarily chosen a few passages to place inside their *tefillin*, it should have been obvious that "these words which I command you this day" (Deut. 6:6)—referring to *all* the laws and commandments given in chapter five—could not possibly be "worn" on one's hand or forehead. Likewise, in Exodus 13, what was to be "bound upon their hands" as "frontlets between their eyes" was the *memory* of the events of the Feast of Unleavened Bread when God delivered Israel from Egypt (verses 3-8), and the *memory* of God redeeming the firstborn of both man and beast (verses 11-15).

Thus, upon close examination it becomes clear that the phrase "bind them for a sign upon your hands so that they may be as frontlets [*tefillin*] between your eyes" is a *figure of speech* and not a command.

The rabbinic commentator Samuel ben Meir ("Rashbam")—Rashi's grandson—was wise enough to realize the true meaning of this expression. Commenting on Exodus 13:9, Rashbam wrote: "*For a sign upon your hand.* According to its plain meaning ... 'It shall be remembered always **as if it had been written** upon your hand'—similar to 'he put me as a seal upon your heart' (Cant 8,6) [Song of Solomon 8:6]. *Between your eyes.* Like a piece of jewelry or gold chain which people put on the forehead for decoration" (karaite-korner.org/tefillin.shtml; emphasis added). Karaite Jews do not wear phylacteries.

Rashbam rightfully interprets the passage as a metaphor that teaches us to remember the written Torah always and treasure it like a piece of fine jewelry. Indeed, not everything in the Law is to be taken literally. A classic example of this is, "You shall circumcise the foreskin of your heart" (Deut. 10:16). Similar figures of speech are found in the Book of Proverbs: "My son, hear the instruction of your father and forsake not the law of your mother, for they shall be an ornament of grace to your head and chains around your neck" (1:8-9). "Do not let mercy and truth forsake you; bind them around your neck; write them upon the tablet of your heart" (3:3; also see 6:20-21 and 7:2-3).

In light of these verses from Proverbs, the real meaning of the *tefillin* passages becomes clear: We are to always remember the Law of God as if it were written out in plain sight on our hands; we are to treasure the Torah as a precious jewel one would proudly wear.

22. Leviticus 19:26-28 reads: "You shall not eat anything with the blood. You shall not observe times nor practice witchcraft. You shall not round the hair of your temples, nor [destroy or mar] the edge of your beard. You shall not make any cuttings in your flesh for the dead, nor tattoo any marks on you. I am the LORD." In typical rabbinic fashion, the sages have isolated one aspect of this passage—"You shall not round the hair of your temples, nor mar the edge of your beard." Talmudic tradition explains this to mean that a man may not shave his beard with a razor with a single blade, since the cutting action of the blade against the skin "mars" the beard.

However, as the context clearly indicates, God is not speaking here of "normal grooming practices," but of things associated with pagan rituals or necromancy. Note the references to eating food with blood, "observing times," practicing witchcraft, body laceration for the dead, and tattoos—all of which were prominent in paganism.

In fact, one of the pagan practices of the time was deforming (and plucking) the facial hair and cutting the skin as a part of *mourning for the dead*. It was also a custom of the heathen to cut or trim their beards and hair into special shapes in honor of a particular pagan deity. To "round the edge of your head" means to cut off the hair around the sides of the head, such as with the pagan "bowl cut" (*Unger's Bible Dictionary*, "Hair").

Remember, the Israelites had just come out of Egypt where they had been exposed to numerous pagan rites. This passage is not about grooming or hairstyles—it is a prohibition against pagan practices, the type of false worship the Bible forbids (Deut. 12:30-32).

CHAPTER EIGHT

1. The Greek *ekklesia* (a composite of "to call" and "out of") refers to the spiritual body of believers God has *called out of* the ways of the world (John 17:14-15) and into the Church Jesus built ("I will build My *ekklesia*," Matthew 16:18). The term is usually translated *church* or *assembly*, and is synonymous with the *elect* (although *elect* sometimes refers to physical Israel).

2. This view of the prophecy of Genesis 49:10 is complicated by the fact that, from all appearances, the *scepter* has on more than one occasion been "removed" from Judah. Did the Jews really govern themselves according to their own civil laws throughout their years of captivity in Babylon? Did not the Jews lose all rights of self-rule under the Syrian oppression of Antiochus Epiphanes? What about Emperor Hadrian's severe prohibitions against the Jews in 135 AD? Clearly, our understanding of Genesis 49:10 is incomplete.

At any rate, the Jewish leaders of early first-century Judea believed that the scepter *had departed* from Judea and that the event signaled the arrival of the Messiah.

3. Thus, the Jewish leaders were forced to appeal to Rome in order to have Jesus put to death (Matt. 27:1-2).

4. Peterson further describes the dismay of the Jewish leaders: "When the members of the Sanhedrin found themselves deprived of their right over life and death, a general consternation took possession of them; they covered their heads with ashes and their bodies with sackcloth, exclaiming, 'Woe unto us, for the scepter has departed from Judah and the Messiah has not come' " (p. 65; Peterson quotes this from M. Lemann's *Jesus Before the Sanhedrin*, p. 30).

5. According to Peterson, the decline in messianic anticipation among Jews was only just beginning. "A philosophy that … had begun [in the early first century] with the failure to recognize the timing of the Messiah's coming [gradually] developed into widespread doubt of the reality of the Messiah" (*The Everlasting Tradition*, p. 121). In spite of the fact that leading rabbis were well aware of Daniel's prophecies concerning the appearing of the Messiah, there was a consensus among rabbinic scholars that their religion should focus more on the Scriptures than on the coming of the Messiah. The outcome of their approach was easily predictable: "[The rabbis'] decision to no longer trust the precision of prophecy would send shockwaves that continue [even today] to echo throughout Judaism. A philosophy would soon begin [initially among *kabbalistic* rabbis] where Scripture would take on far more **allegorical rather than literal meaning**. Eventually, many [Jews] would view the Messiah as a **figure of speech** for an age of peace and harmony instead of [a literal] Prince of Peace" (p. 121; emphasis added).

About the time the Talmud was finalized and Rabbinical Judaism found its footing, the promise of a personal Messiah began to give way to the idea of a "messianic age of enlightenment." In one of several similar passages, the Talmud notes: "All of the predestined dates for redemption have passed [without the Messiah's appearance] and the matter [of salvation] **now depends only on repentance and good deeds**" (Rabbi Rabh, *BT Sanhedrin*, 97b). Salvation, once clearly linked to the Messiah, became the domain of rabbis and their study of the Talmud.

The Jews' *de-emphasis* of messianism would have far-reaching consequences. "[Mainstream] Christianity would later follow [the rabbis'] lead by *spiritualizing* a great many themes of the Bible, including the nation of Israel [and the reality of a messianic kingdom on earth]" (Peterson, p. 121). In turn, this would play into the hands of those who espoused "replacement theology," wherein the Jews are denied a literal role in the age to come. Today, *Reform Jews* in particular believe in a "messianic age" as opposed to a literal, "embodied Messiah."

6. In John one, it is obvious that the Jewish religious leaders thought John *might* be the Messiah, which he denied (verse 20). Verse 21 shows that they were also looking for an *Elijah*-figure and one they called "the Prophet." (Apparently, the religionists did not understand that "the Prophet" of Deuteronomy 18:15 was a reference to the Messiah.) It is interesting to contrast the cynical, self-preserving approach of the Jewish leaders with the open, positive and hopeful response of Jesus' earliest followers (verses 37-49).

7. The miracle of Lazarus being raised to life was incontestable, as the Jewish leaders had their own witnesses of the event (John 11:45-46). Yet, the religionists no doubt dismissed Jesus' miracles as sorcery, reminding themselves of the wonders performed by Pharaoh's magicians just prior to the Exodus. Surely they recalled Moses' warning about false prophets performing "wonders" in order to lead people astray (Deut. 13:1-3). Indeed, from their skewed perspective, Jesus was doing exactly that—leading the people away from the laws and traditions of the Pharisees.

8. The Greek of John 11:48 actually reads "*this place*." While most scholars take this as a reference to the Temple, J. W. McGarvey notes: "It is more likely that 'place' refers to their seats in the Sanhedrin, which they would be likely to lose if the influence of Jesus became, as they feared, the dominant power. They feared then that the Romans would, by removing them, take away the last vestige of [Jewish] civil and ecclesiastical authority..." (*McGarvey's Commentary*;" John 11:48").

9. We might ask the same question as did the prophet Jeremiah: "In their calamity, the 'wise' are ashamed and afraid—for they have *despised* the Word of God. What *wisdom* could they possibly possess?" (paraphrased from Jer. 8:9). As this book has amply demonstrated, Rabbinical Judaism holds the Scriptures in utter *contempt* through its unabashed preference for humanly-devised traditions. It is exactly as Hoffman has noted: "Everything about Orthodox Judaism is either a distortion or a falsification of the Old Testament because it is based on ... [human] traditions that void the Old Testament..." (*Judaism Discovered*, p. 145).

In Romans two, Paul warns Jews about judging Gentiles, noting the Jews' own proclivity for breaking God's laws and commandments. Here again, the application of the passage to Pharisaic hypocrisy and self-righteousness is most striking. "You who call yourself a Jew [Pharisee]—you who allegedly make your stand on the Law, and boast in God, and have knowledge of His will, and approve of the wonderful things revealed in the Law—you indeed boast of being a guide to the blind, a light for those in darkness, an instructor of the foolish, a teacher of babes, because you possess in the Scriptures the embodiment of knowledge and truth. You, who presume to teach others, **do you not first teach yourself**?… You who boast in the Law, are you **dishonoring God through your failure to practice the Law**? For **through you and your disobedience the name of God is blasphemed among Gentiles**" (paraphrased from Rom. 2:17-24).

10. Paul often uses the terms *Israel* and *Jew* interchangeably; insofar as the context of Romans 9-11 is concerned, it was the *Jewish* leadership that rejected Jesus as the Messiah and sought a "form of righteousness" through Pharisaic works. The so-called "lost tribes" of Israel—the "other sheep" of which Jesus spoke in John 10:16—were not involved, having long been scattered among various Gentile nations (see Appendix Three). Thus, the author uses *Jew* throughout these passages with the understanding that, in the age to come, *all of Israel* will have salvation and play a pivotal role in the millennial kingdom.

11. See Appendix Four for detailed evidence that both Jesus and Paul fully upheld the validity of the laws and commandments of God.

12. Avi ben Mordechai notes that one reason Paul's writings are difficult to understand is that he typically employed an established scholarly style of teaching based on the use of *ellipsis*—a sort of intellectual shorthand marked by missing words or phrases which required the reader to make interpretive assumptions (*Galatians*, p. 49, footnote 1).

13. Quoted from Leviticus 18.5 (also see Ezek. 20:11, 13, 21; etc.).

14. Stern adds: "Most Christians … suppose that *erga nomou*, literally 'works of law,' a [phrase] which appears three times in [Gal. 2:16], must mean 'actions done in obedience to the Torah.' But this is wrong. One of the best-kept secrets of the New Testament is that when [Paul] writes *nomos* he frequently does not mean *law* [in the sense of the Torah], but *legalism*" (*Jewish New Testament Commentary*, p. 536; "Gal. 2:16"). Stern carefully notes Paul's overarching validation and defense of the Law, describing *legalism* as the perversion of the Torah into a mechanical set of rules (p. 537). While such a *legalistic* application of the Law was no doubt a problem in the early Church, Stern unfortunately stops short of applying the phrase "works of law" to Pharisaism.

15. Quoting God Himself, the prophet Ezekiel wrote: "[The one who has] walked in My statutes, and has kept My ordinances to deal truly, **he is righteous, he shall surely live**" (Ezek. 18:9). King David wrote: "My tongue shall speak of Your word, for **all Your commandments are righteousness**" (Psa. 119:172). As noted earlier, God declared through Moses: "And you shall keep My statutes and My judgments, which if a man does, he **shall [find life] in them**" (Lev. 18:5).

It must be understood, however, that obedience to God's laws and commandments cannot *earn* one salvation—for reconciliation and salvation are free gifts (Rom. 6:23; 11:5-6; Eph. 2:5, 8; etc.). Rather, obedience must be viewed as a *precondition*; God simply cannot grant salvation to one who is opposed to His way of life as *defined* by His Law—for only the *doers* of the Law shall be justified by God (Rom. 2:13).

16. A better rendering of Galatians 3:10 would be, "For as many as are **relying on [Pharisaic] works of law** are under a curse, because it is written, 'Cursed is everyone who does not continue in all things that have been written in the Book of the Law to do them.' "

17. Thus, Gentiles (the *elect*) are no longer "strangers from the covenants" (Eph. 2:12), but "fellow heirs" (Eph. 3:6) of the promises made to Abraham (Gal. 3:28-29).

18. Two additional passages are important in this regard:
"When all these things have come upon you—both the blessings and the curses which I have set before you, for you will remember My warnings once you are scattered among all the nations where I, the LORD your God, will have sent you—you, and your children, will return to Me with all your heart and with all your soul and obey all that I have commanded you today in the Law. Then I, the LORD your God, will turn away your captivity; I will have compassion on you and gather you from all the nations where you have been scattered. Even if you have been carried into the outermost parts of the heavens, I will gather you from there. And I, the LORD your God, will bring you into the land which your fathers possessed, and you shall possess it. And I will bless you and multiply and prosper you even above that which your fathers enjoyed. And I, the LORD your God, **will circumcise your hearts and the hearts of your children**—so that you will love Me with all your heart and with all your soul, *that you may live*" (Deut. 30:1-8; author's paraphrase). Also:
"Thus says the LORD your God, 'I will gather you from among the people and assemble you out of the nations where you have been scattered. And I will give you the land of Israel…. **I will give you a single heart**, and **I will put a new spirit within you**. And I will remove your stony heart of disbelief and give you a heart of flesh, so that you may live according to My laws and commandments. And you shall be My people, and I will be your God" (Ezek. 11:17-20; author's paraphrase).

19. According to Ariel, modern Jewish views of the Messiah and the Kingdom of God are terribly watered down—even to the point of denying the reality of a true messianic age. "Reform Judaism [has] rejected traditional Jewish messianism. Its liturgical changes include the **removal from the prayer book of all references to the Messiah** and to an eventual return to the Land of Israel. The idea of the [literal] personal Messiah [has been] reinterpreted as the longing for the universal brotherhood within the context of ethical monotheism. More recently, the Reform concept of **messianism has come to mean the result of human effort on behalf of creating the perfect world**.... This is **a messianic age without a Messiah**—the fulfillment of the particular destiny of the Jewish people in a modern, universalistic mode" (*What Do Jews Believe?*, p. 245; emphasis added).

The Orthodox view is no better. "Conservative Judaism understands the body of rabbinic ideas on messianism as elaborate *metaphors* generated by deep-seated human and communal needs." Thus, the prophet Daniel's "stone cut out without hands" is only an elaborate *metaphor*; the elect will inherit a *symbolic* kingdom; and eternal life is but a *myth*. Rather than being taken literally, as was once the case, ideas of a messianic age now "express the longing for a time of universal peace and social justice and for the ingathering of all Jews to Israel" (p. 245).

In Conservative Judaism, the idea of a new Temple to which the Messiah might come has become largely outdated. God's "final judgment" on the nations is no longer taken literally, but is now seen as the "idea of God's justice." Ultimately, on the question of the Messiah, the Conservative credo is agnostic: "We do not know when the Messiah will come, nor whether He will be a charismatic human figure or [merely] a symbol of the redemption of humankind from the evils of the world. Through the doctrine of a messianic figure, Judaism teaches us that every individual human being must live as if he or she, individually, has the responsibility to bring about the messianic age" (p. 246).

Judaism's lackluster approach to a messianic age is perhaps summed up in this final note from Ariel: "Despite centuries of active messianic hope, Judaism is [today] more comfortable with deferred than attainable messianism.... The broadest definition of [modern] Jewish messianism is hope for a better future for humanity" (p. 246).

20. As Zechariah notes, the Jews will come to understand that Jesus is the one "they" had killed. Paul wrote that the Jews were the ones "who killed both the Lord Jesus and their own prophets" (I Thess. 2:15). Yet, it must be understood that these are indictments against the Jewish *leaders*—not the people as a whole. In one of His encounters with the scribes and Pharisees, Jesus said that *they* fully shared in the guilt of their fathers—the ones who had killed the prophets—because they were of the *same* mind and spirit (Matt. 23:29-39). The emphasis was on the *leaders*, not the people.

Did the People of the Land actually consent to Jesus' murder? Recall the words of the Jews' ancestors: "His blood be on us and on our children" (Matt. 27:25). The mob that uttered these profound words was, however, *not representative* of the People of the Land—**let alone every succeeding generation of Jews**. As Galen Peterson notes, this mob was "raised up by the leaders who opposed [Jesus]. In fact, on [just] the previous day, the [Jewish] leaders were **concerned that the many followers of Jesus would cause an uproar if He were to be arrested publicly** (Matt. 26:5)" (*The Everlasting Tradition*, pp. 100-101; emphasis added). Matthew 27:20 confirms that "the chief priests and the elders persuaded the multitudes to demand [the release of] Barabbas, and [that the Romans were] to destroy Jesus."

Note also that just five days before His crucifixion the people gave Jesus a very enthusiastic welcome to Jerusalem. "And the multitudes, those who were going before and those who were following behind, were shouting, saying, 'Hosanna to the Son of David! Blessed is He Who comes in the name of the Lord. Hosanna in the highest!' Now when He entered Jerusalem, the entire city was moved, saying, 'Who is this?' And the multitudes said, 'This is Jesus the prophet, the one Who is from Nazareth of Galilee' " (Matt. 21:8-11). Clearly, the Common People supported Jesus.

Obviously, the Romans killed Jesus—but they did so at the behest of a corrupt Jewish leadership. However, Jesus stated that He *willingly* laid down His life for *all* mankind (John 10:18)—for we have *all* sinned and are *all* guilty in requiring Christ's death.

Nevertheless, the Jews' fateful cry—"His blood be on us and on our children"—has had profound consequences. As a people, the Jews have no doubt been greatly persecuted, suffering repeated periods of exile and enduring such horrors as the Holocaust. Some past Jewish authorities have, however, been willing to acknowledge that the Jews have suffered because of their *own* sins. For example, the following quotation from a Karaite Jew laments the fact that, after the destruction of the Temple in 70 AD, Jews were unable to keep the Passover in the land of Israel as required. Note the clear admission of sin: "Today … **by reason of our many sins**, we are scattered over the four corners of the earth; we are dispersed in the lands of the Gentiles; we are soiled with their ritual uncleanness and unable to reach the House of the Lord…. [Because we are in exile and no longer in the land of Israel, the] ordinance of the Passover sacrifice no longer applies to us, and the reason for this is **our fathers' exceeding disobedience to God and our own following in their sinful footsteps**" (Leon Nemoy, *Karaite Anthology*, p. 206; emphasis added).

But as Zechariah's prophecy wonderfully shows, the Jewish people *will bitterly repent*—not only for what their *fathers* have done, but for their *own* ongoing rejection of Jesus as the Messiah and for having elevated the Talmud above Scripture.

Appendices

The Development of the Talmud

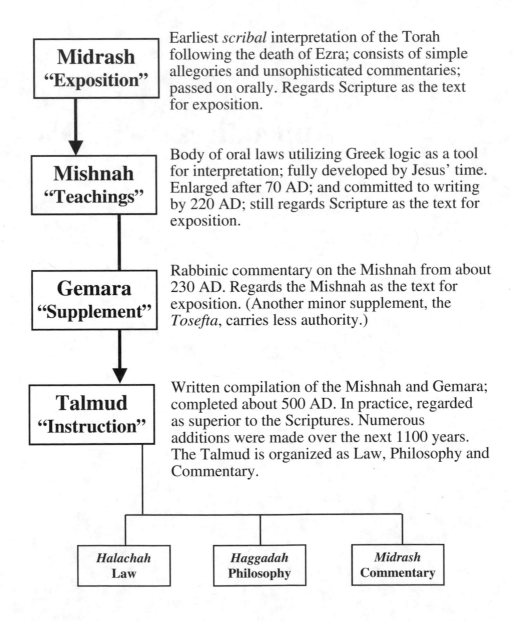

Midrash "Exposition"

Earliest *scribal* interpretation of the Torah following the death of Ezra; consists of simple allegories and unsophisticated commentaries; passed on orally. Regards Scripture as the text for exposition.

Mishnah "Teachings"

Body of oral laws utilizing Greek logic as a tool for interpretation; fully developed by Jesus' time. Enlarged after 70 AD; and committed to writing by 220 AD; still regards Scripture as the text for exposition.

Gemara "Supplement"

Rabbinic commentary on the Mishnah from about 230 AD. Regards the Mishnah as the text for exposition. (Another minor supplement, the *Tosefta*, carries less authority.)

Talmud "Instruction"

Written compilation of the Mishnah and Gemara; completed about 500 AD. In practice, regarded as superior to the Scriptures. Numerous additions were made over the next 1100 years. The Talmud is organized as Law, Philosophy and Commentary.

Halachah **Law**

Haggadah **Philosophy**

Midrash **Commentary**

APPENDIX TWO

The Jewish Code of Law

While the Talmud is clearly upheld as the principal text of Judaism, numerous rabbinic writings have over the centuries added to the mass of Jewish *halachah* (law or legislation), bringing controversy and confusion to the Judaic religion. In some ways, the Talmud was never really "closed" in 500 AD. In *The Jewish Book of Why*, author Alfred Kolatch explains that novel "rulings and interpretations" continued to develop among rabbis as Jewish communities were established farther and farther from the Judaic centers of learning in Babylon and Palestine. He writes: "Throughout the middle ages, scholars such as Rashi (1040-1105) in France wrote commentaries on the Scriptures and the Talmud. Questions of law (*halachah*) were addressed by scholars on issues where the Talmud did not offer direct guidance or was incomplete" (p. 5). The commentaries of Rashi (Rabbi Solomon Yitzchaki) are revered in Judaism as *divinely-inspired*. In fact, because it is the consensus of rabbis that the Pentateuch cannot be understood apart from the insight provided by Rashi, his writings are regarded as *equal to* or *greater than* the text of the written Torah—which God Himself gave to the nation of Israel by the hand of Moses. Following Rashi, another esteemed sage—Rabbi Moses Maimonides (1135-1204)—made his indelible mark on Judaism with his highly authoritative *Mishneh Torah*.

Kolatch notes that by the 12th century Jewish authorities were becoming concerned about the wide variety of opinion and interpretation that was developing. "An effort to create uniformity began.... The German rabbi Jacob Levi Mollin wrote an early Jewish code (published after his death in 1427) that established standards for synagogue practice and community conduct. His efforts were expanded a century later by Joseph Caro, a 16th-century Spanish scholar, with the *Shulchan Aruch* ('The Prepared Table'), or 'Code of Jewish Law' " (pp. 5-6). Caro's chief critic, Moses Isserles, subsequently added to the work, resulting in a version that is today regarded by Orthodox Jews as the authoritative legal code of Judaism (p. 6).

Still, Judaism continued to develop and revise its *halachah* as new attitudes and customs emerged with the spread of the religion around the world. In the middle part of the 19th century, a definitive Code of Jewish Law emerged—the *Kitzur Shulchan Aruch* by Rabbi Solomon Ganzfried (1804-1886). *Kitzur* means "abbreviated," as Ganzfried's 1864 version is actually a summary of the work produced by Caro.

According to the Internet site Wikipedia, the *Kitzur* (as it is typically called) was "written for God-fearing Jews who are not in a position to study and comprehend the [original and much more detailed] *Shulchan Aruch* [by Caro]." Composed in a Hebrew that can be easily understood, the *Kitzur*

151

"states what is permitted and what is forbidden without ambiguity." As Ganzfried was Hungarian, his work reflects the customs of the Jews of Hungary at that time (wikipedia.org/wiki/Shlomo_Ganzfried).

The *Encyclopedia Judaica* notes that Ganzfried's code "set forth the laws required to be known by every Jew, written in simple language and appropriately arranged.... The *Kitzur* was an immediate and extraordinary success.... In the century since [its initial publication], it has been reprinted more than any other Jewish work, with the exception of the Talmud..." (vol. 7, p. 314).

As previously noted, Avi ben Mordechai, a former observant Orthodox Jew, has personally experienced the *oppressive burden* of rabbinic codes of law. In his commentary on the book of Galatians, Mordechai writes, "[After many years,] **I realized that the [rabbis']** *halachah* **had no end in sight; that it was nothing short of a deep, black hole and an endless system of legal minutiae. It was always tiring for me to try to keep up with all the daily demands [of Judaic law]**. I did not have a difficult time agreeing with Rebbe Nachman of Breslov (1772-1810) who once said that his **daily religious obligations felt like a crushing burden** (*The Empty Chair*, p. 40)" (*Galatians—A Torah-Based Commentary in First-Century Hebraic Context*, p. 48; emphasis added).

The words of the renowned Rabbi Joseph Hertz also bear repeating: "Religion in the Talmud [and as thus expressed in the *Kitzur*] attempts to **penetrate the whole of human life** with the sense of law and right. Nothing human is in its eyes mean or trivial; **everything is regulated and sanctified by religion**. Religious precept and duty accompany man from his earliest years to the grave and beyond it. [The codes] guide his desires and actions at every moment" (Foreword to *The Babylonian Talmud*, Soncino Edition, pp. 25-26; emphasis added).

To give the reader a taste of Jewish *halachah*, we have reproduced portions from Ganzfried's *Kitzur* or "Code of Jewish Law" as translated by Hyman Goldin. The work was published in 1993 by the Hebrew Publishing Company, Rockaway Beach, New York. We have included the entire *Table of Contents*, as it gives a good summary of the kind of subjects covered by the *Kitzur*. Following the content listing are abridged "sample" portions representing a cross-section of the book; key phrases have been emphasized in bold type.

Keep in mind that the Code of Jewish Law is based directly on the precepts of the Talmud. Note the absolute *absurdity* of the entries as the *Kitzur* attempts to legislate daily life down to the most minute detail—as if followers of Rabbinic Judaism were utterly void of conscience or common sense.

Code of Jewish Law

KITZUR SHULHAN ARUKH

A COMPILATION OF JEWISH LAWS AND CUSTOMS

By
RABBI SOLOMON GANZFRIED

TRANSLATED BY
HYMAN E. GOLDIN, LL.B.

ANNOTATED REVISED EDITION

Hebrew Publishing Company

NEW YORK

1993

Appendix Two

CODE OF JEWISH LAW

CONTENTS

VOLUME 1

CHAPTER		PAGE
1	Rules for Conduct Upon Rising in the Morning	1
2	Hand Washing in the Morning	3
3	On Dressing and Deportment	5
4	Rules of Decency	7
5	Cleanness of Places Used for Holy Purposes	8
6	Laws Relating to Benedictions	12
7	The Morning Benedictions	16
8	What May not be Done from Dawn Until Praying Time	17
9	The Tzitzit (Fringes)	19
10	The Tefillin (Phylacteries)	26
11	The Mezuzah	34
12	Purity of Body, and Places for Holding Services	39
13	The Sanctity of the Synagogue and the House of Study	43
14	Pesuke Dezimerah (Special Verses of Psalms)	45
15	Kaddish, Barhu, Minyan, and Hazan	47
16	The Shema and its Benedictions	51
17	Laws Concerning the Reading of Shema	52
18	The Shemoneh Esreh (Silent Prayer)	55
19	Laws Concerning "Mashiv Haruah" and "Tal Umatar"	62
20	The Hazan's Repetition of the Shemoneh Esreh	65
21	The Making up of Omitted Prayers	68
22	The Tahanun (Petition for Grace)	70
23	The Reading of the Torah	72
24	Laws Concerning Errors and Defects in a Sefer Torah	78
25	Rules Concerning Ashre, Uva Letziyon, etc.	82
26	The Mourner's Kaddish	83
27	The Study of the Torah	87
28	The Scroll and Other Holy Books	89
29	Moral Laws	91
30	Talebearing, Slander, Vengeance, and Bearing a Grudge	97
31	All of Man's Intentions Must be for the Sake of Heaven	100
32	Rules Concerning Physical Wellbeing	101
33	Things Forbidden Because they are Dangerous	108
34	Laws Concerning Charity	110
35	The Separation of Hallah (First Portion of the Dough)	115
36	The Salting of Meat	116
37	The Immersion of Vessels	119

38	Laws Concerning Bread, Cooked Food, and Milk of a Non-Jew	121
39	Eating and Drinking Before the Regular Meals	124
40	Washing the Hands Before Meals	125
41	The Breaking of Bread and Hamotzi	130
42	Laws Concerning Meals	132
43	Benedictions Over Special Courses During Meals	135
44	Laws Concerning the Washing of Hands and the Saying of Grace After Meals	137
45	Formal Grace (of Three or More)	141
46	Forbidden Foods	146
47	Non-Jewish Wine and Making the Vessels Fit for Use	
	Notes to Volume I	I

VOLUME 2

CHAPTER		PAGE
48	Benedictions Over the Five Species of Grain	1
49	The Benediction Over Wine and "Hatov Vehametiv"	4
50	Benedictions Said Before Enjoying Food and Drink	6
51	The Concluding Benediction	10
52	The Benedictions, "Bore Peri Haetz," "Bore Peri Haadamah," and "Shehakol"	13
53	Benedictions Over Soup, Fruit and Vegetable Extracts	17
54	Principal and Accessory Foods	18
55	Order of Precedence Relating to Benedictions	20
56	Benedictions Pronounced Erroneously	21
57	Benediction Over Food Served more than Originally Intended	22
58	Benediction Over Fragrance	24
59	Benedictions Over Joy and Grief	26
60	Benedictions Over Sights in Nature	30
61	The Benediction "Haggomel"	33
62	Concerning Commerce	36
63	Wronging by Means of Words	39
64	Dealing in Forbidden Objects	40
65	Interest on Loans	41
66	Agreements to Trade in Business	48
67	Vows and Oaths	51
68	Prayers When Traveling	54
69	The Minhah (Afternoon) Service	57
70	The Maariv (Evening) Service	59
71	The Order of the Night	60
72	The Holiness of the Sabbath	63
73	Work Done by a Non-Jew on the Sabbath	68

74 Embarking on a Vessel on the Sabbath   70
75 The Sabbath Candles   71
76 Prayers on Sabbath and Festivals   75
77 The Kiddush and the Sabbath Meals   79
78 The Torah Reading on the Sabbath and Festivals   84
79 Laws Concerning Maftir   87
80 Some Labors Forbidden on the Sabbath   89
81 The Four Premises With Regard to Sabbath Laws   104
82 The Prohibition Against Removing Things from One
    Domain Into Another   105
83 The Enclosure of Spaces   108
84 Carrying Garments or Ornaments on the Sabbath   110
85 If a Fire Breaks Out on the Sabbath   113
86 Bathing on the Sabbath   114
87 The Resting of Cattle on the Sabbath   116
88 *Muktzeh*, Things Forbidden to Be Handled on the Sabbath   120
89 Concerning a Base for Things Forbidden   124
90 Doing Things that are Not Actual-Work by a Non-Jew   125
91 One in Pain, and One Not Critically Ill   130
92 One Who is Critically Ill—Forced to Transgress a Precept   133
93 Concerning Childbirth   135
94 Inter-Community of Court   136
95 Inter-Community of Boundaries   141
96 The Maariv Service and the Havdalah   145
97 Laws Concerning Rosh Hodesh (New Moon)   148
    Notes to Volume II   XIII

VOLUME 3

CHAPTER   PAGE

98   Laws Concerning Festivals   1
99   Things Forbidden to be Handled on Festivals   7
100 The Benediction of the Priests (Birkat Kohanim)   8
101 The Preparation of Foods on the First Day of a Festival
     for the Second Day   13
102 "Eruv Tavshilin" (Combination of Dishes)   14
103 Rejoicing on a Festival   16
104 Hol Hammoed (Intermediate Days of a Festival)   19
105 Things Forbidden Because they Require Exertion   21
106 Buying and Selling During Hol Hammoed   22
107 The Month of Nisan   23
108 The Wheat and Flour for the Matzah   23
109 The Water Used for Kneading Matzah   24
110 The Kneading and Baking of Matzah   26

111 The Search for Leaven   28
112 Leaven Which May and Which May Not be
     Retained on Pesah   31
113 The Day Before Pesah and the Baking of Matzot   32
114 The Selling of Hametz   34
115 If the Day Before Pesah Occurs on a Sabbath   39
116 The Ceremonial Purification of Vessels   40
117 Various Laws Concerning Pesah   43
118 The Seder (Program) for Pesah Nights   45
119 Pesah Night—Continued   48
120 Sefirah (Counting of the Omer)   52
121 Public Fast Days   54
122 The Interval Between the Seventeenth of Tammuz and
     the Ninth of Av   56
123 The Day Preceding the Ninth of Av   60
124 The Ninth of Av   60
125 When the Ninth of Av Occurs on Saturday or Sunday   65
126 Commemorating the Destruction of the Temple   66
127 Private Fast Days   67
128 The Month of Elul   70
129 Rosh Hashanah   74
130 The Ten Days of Penitence   80
131 The Day Before Yom Kippur   81
132 Yom Kippur Eve   86
133 Yom Kippur   87
134 The Sukkah (Tabernacle)   93
135 Dwelling in the Sukkah   96
136 The Lulav and the Other Species   101
137 The Taking of the Lulav and the Hakkafot (Procession)   103
138 Hoshana Rabbah; Shemini Atzeret; Simhat Torah   106
139 Hanukkah   108
140 The Four Parshiyot   114
141 The Reading of the Megillah   115
142 The Sending of Portions—Gifts to the Needy-Purim
     Seudah (Feast)   119
     Notes to Volume III   XVIII

VOLUME 4

CHAPTER   PAGE

143 Honoring Father and Mother   1
144 Honor Due the Teacher, Scholar, Aged and Priest   4
145 Laws Concerning Marriage   6
146 The Fast of the Bridegroom and Bride   9

147 The Nuptial Ceremony   10
148 The Privacy Following the Nuptial Ceremony   11
149 Grace at Weddings and Entertaining the Groom and
     the Bride   11
150 Laws of Chastity   13
151 The Sin of Discharging Semen in Vain   17
152 Prohibition Against Being Alone with Women   19
153 A Woman who is Menstrually Unclean   21
154 Regulations Concerning the Menses   24
155 Separation Before Menstrual Term   26
156 Perception of Blood as the Result of Cohabitation   30
157 Prenuptial Laws   31
158 Childbirth and Miscarriage   32
159 Putting on White Linen and Counting the Clean Days   33
160 How to Shampoo the Hair   35
161 What Constitutes Interposition   36
162 Immersion   40
163 The Law of Circumcision   43
164 The Redemption of the Firstborn   45
165 The Training of Children   47
166 Enchantment and Superstition   49
167 Laws Concerning Idolatry   51
168 Images that are Forbidden   53
169 Tattooing and Depilation   54
170 Shaving the Hair of the Temples and Beard   54
171 A Male May Not Put On a Woman's Garment
     and Vice Versa   55
172 Laws Concerning New Crops   55
173 The Law of Orlah (Fruits of the First Three Years)   56
174 The Grafting of Trees   57
175 The Interbreeding of Cattle   57
176 Laws Concerning Shatnez (Wool Mixed with Linen)   58
177 The Firstborn of Clean Animals   59
178 The Firstborn of an Ass   62
179 Laws Concerning Loans   63
180 Cancellation of Debts in the Sabbatical Year   64
181 Litigation and Testimony   67
182 Laws Concerning Theft and Robbery   71
183 Damages to Property   75
184 If One causes Physical Injury   76
185 Borrowing and Hiring   78
186 The Muzzling of Animals   80
187 Articles Lost and Found   80
188 Laws Concerning Bailments   81
189 Unloading and Loading   82

190 Protection of Life and Property — 83
191 Cruelty to Animals — 84
192 The Sick, the Physician, and the Remedies — 84
193 Visiting the Sick — 87
194 A Dying Person and Watching the Body — 89
195 The Rending of the Garments — 91
196 Laws Concerning an Onan — 94
197 The Purification, Shrouds, and Utilization of Anything Belonging to the Dead — 98
198 Removal of the Corpse, Funeral and Burial Service — 100
199 The Interment and the Cemetery — 103
200 Burial on a Festival — 106
201 The Suicide and the Wicked — 108
202 The Defilement of a Kohen — 109
203 Relatives for whom Mourning Must be Observed — 113
204 The Time When Mourning Begins — 114
205 The Meal of Condolence — 116
206 "Timely" and "Delayed" News — 117
207 Comforting the Mourners — 119
208 The Work a Mourner is Forbidden to Perform — 120
209 The Prohibition to Bathe, Anoint, Wear Shoes, and Cohabit — 122
210 The Study of the Torah and Exchange of Greetings by Mourners — 123
211 Other Things a Mourner May Not Do — 125
212 Things Forbidden as "Rejoicing" After the Seven Days — 127
213 The Marriage of a Mourner and of a Groom or a Bride Who Becomes a Mourner — 128
214 When a Mourner may Leave His House — 129
215 Excessive Grief is Forbidden — 129
216 Parts of the Seventh and Thirtieth Mourning Days — 130
217 If One Neglected to Observe Mourning — 131
218 Testimony Relating to Mourning — 131
219 Mourning on a Sabbath or Festival — 132
220 The Mourning Period Suspended by a Festival — 133
221 Fasting on the Day of Yahrzeit — 135
     Notes to Volume IV — XXVIII

CHAPTER 2

Hand Washing in the Morning

1. Since every man upon rising from his sleep in the morning is like a new-born creature, insofar as the worship of the Creator is concerned, he should prepare himself for worship by washing his hands out of a vessel, just as the priests used to wash their hands daily out of the wash-basin before performing their service in the Temple. This hand-washing is based on the biblical verse (Psalms 26:6-7): "I will wash my hands in innocency, and I will compass Thy altar, O Lord; that I may publish with a loud voice," etc. There is **another reason given by the Kabbalists** (*Zohar*, quoted in Beth Joseph) for this morning hand-washing: **when a man is asleep, the holy soul departs from his body, and an unclean spirit descends upon him. When rising from sleep, the unclean spirit departs from his entire body, except from his fingers, and does not depart until one spills water upon them three times alternately.** One is not allowed to walk four cubits (six feet) without having one's hands washed, except in cases of extreme necessity.

2. The first garment which a male must put on, is the *tallit katan* (the small four-fringed garment, commonly known as the *arba kanfoth, four cornered*), for one is **not allowed to walk even as much as four cubits without having a fringed garment on**. But as his hands are still unwashed, he may not say the benediction on putting it on.

3. The **ritual hand-washing** in the morning is performed as follows: Take a cup of water with the right hand and put it in the left; pour some water upon the right hand. Take the cup back in the right hand and pour some water on the left. This performance is repeated three times. It is best to pour the water over the hands as far as the wrists, but in case of emergency it suffices if the water covers the hands up to the joints of the fingers. One must also wash his face in honor of the Creator, as it is said (Genesis 9:6): "For in the image of God He hath made the man." One must also rinse the mouth, because we must pronounce the Great Name in purity and cleanliness.

4. The hands must be washed into a vessel only. The water thus used must not be utilized for any other purpose, **because an evil spirit rests on it** (contaminated, and injurious to health), and it must not be spilt in a place frequented by human beings.

5. Before the morning hand-washing, one should not touch either the mouth, the nose, the eyes, the ears, the lower orifice or any kind of food, or an open vein, because **the evil spirit that rests upon the hands** before washing will cause injury to these things.

6. It is best to perform the morning ablution with water poured from a vessel by human effort, just as it must be done when washing the hands before meals. But in case of emergency, and one wishes to pray, one may wash his hands in any manner, even when the water is not poured by human effort, and one may pronounce the benediction: *Al netilat yadayim* (concerning the washing of the hands). If there is a river or snow at hand, one should dip the hand in it three times. If, however, there is no water in any form available, one may wipe one's hands with some material, and say the benediction: "Blesses art ... for *cleansing* (not *washing*) the hands." Afterwards, upon finding water and the required vessel, one must wash the hands properly without pronouncing any benediction.

7. It is written (Psalms 103:1): "Bless the Lord, O my soul; and all that is within me, bless His holy name." Since it is a man's duty to bless the Holy Name with all that is in him, he is not allowed to begin worshiping God before he has **cleaned himself of bodily impurities**. As one ordinarily has to respond to the call of nature in the morning, therefore one shall not pronounce the benediction over washing the hands in the morning until one has eased one's self, then wash the hands again, pronounce the necessary benediction, and afterward proceed with the rest of the benedictions as given in the prayer-books.

8. If a person rises from his sleep while it is still night, and washes his hands as is required, and then stays awake until dawn; or if he falls asleep again while it is yet night; or if he sleeps sixty breaths (about one-half hour) in the daytime; or if he is awake the whole night—in all these cases it is doubtful whether or not hand-washing is necessary. He shall therefore wash his hands alternately three times, but without pronouncing the benediction.

9. Hands must be washed on the following occasions: On awakening from sleep, on leaving the lavatory or bath, after paring one's nails, after having one's hair cut, after taking *off* the shoes with bare hands, after having sexual intercourse, after touching a vermin or searching the clothes for vermin, after combing one's head, after touching parts of the body which are generally covered, after leaving a cemetery, after walking in a funeral procession or leaving a house where a corpse lay, and after blood-letting.

CHAPTER 3

On Dressing and Deportment

1. It is written (Micah 6:8): "And to walk humbly with thy God." Therefore it is the duty of every man to be modest in all his ways. **When putting on or removing his shirt or any other undergarment, he should be careful not to expose his body unduly. He should put it on or remove it while**

still lying covered in bed. He should never say to himself: "Lo, I am all alone in my inner chamber and in the dark, who can see me?" For the glory of the Holy One, blessed be He, fills the universe, and darkness and light are alike to Him, blessed be His name; and modesty and a **sense of shame** indicate humility before Him, blessed be His name.

CHAPTER 4

Rules of Decency

4. **While in the lavatory, it is forbidden to think of sacred matters**; it is, therefore, best to concentrate there upon one's business affairs and accounts, so that one may not be led to think either of holy matters or, God forbid, indulge in sinful thoughts. On the Sabbath, when it is forbidden to think of business, one should think of some interesting things that one has either seen or heard, or something similar to that.

CHAPTER 5

Cleanness of Places Used for Holy Purposes

2. It is forbidden even to think of anything holy in a place where there is excrement or urine, or anything that produces a bad odor, unless it is covered, as it is said (Deuteronomy 23:14): "And thou shalt cover what cometh from thee."

4. Whenever there exists any doubt concerning the existence of unclean matter, we must not utter a holy word, before we examine the place. It is forbidden to pray in a house in which there is foul matter in the [attic].

5. We must keep away, while praying, from the excrement and urine of an infant who is able to eat as much as the size of an olive, of any bread-stuff, even when cooked, in the space of time that an adult can eat a slice. It is better, however, to stay away from the excrement of an infant eight days old.

6. When praying, we must keep at a distance from the excrement of a human being, even if it has no bad odor, and from the excrement of a cat, marten, and Idumean cock. We are not bound to remove from the excrement of any other animal or bird, because it ordinarily produces no bad odor, but we must remove from it if it does.

8. How far must we keep away from excrement (in order to be allowed to utter holy words)? If the excrement is in the rear, one must remove a distance of no less than four cubits from the spot where the bad odor ceases; even if one is unable to smell, one must keep away the same distance.

However, if it does not have a foul odor, it suffices to remove a distance of four cubits from the place where it is found. If the unclean matter is in front of one, one must remove from it until it disappears from view.

11. If one had let wind, one is forbidden to utter anything holy until the bad odor had ceased; the same applies to a case where the bad odor had issued from his neighbor. But if one is engaged in the study of the Torah, one need not interrupt his study on account of a bad odor that had issued from his neighbor.

12. We must keep away from a lavatory (when praying), even though it is enclosed by partitions and does not contain any unclean matter.

14. It is **forbidden to speak or to think of any holy matter in the bath-house**. It is forbidden to utter any name by which the Holy One, blessed be He, is known, either in a bath-house or in a filthy alley…. It is forbidden to say *Shalom* (peace) to a friend in a bath-house, for *Shalom* is the name of the Holy One, blessed be He; as it is written (Judges 6:24): "And he called it, *Adonai-Shalom*." Some authorities are of the opinion that if a man's name is *Shalom*, he must not be addressed by his name in the places mentioned above. Others permit it, because there is no intention of saying anything pertaining to peace, but simply to call the man by his name. The general custom is to be lenient in this regard, but the God-fearing should follow the stricter opinion.

CHAPTER 8

What May not be Done from Dawn Until Praying Time

1. As soon as the day dawns, that is, when the first light of the sun is seen in the East—since this is the time when prayers may begin (if one had by chance prayed at that early hour, one had complied with his duty) we are not permitted to begin any kind of work, or transact business, or start a journey until one had prayed, as it is said (Psalms 85:13): "Righteousness shall go before him; and he shall make its footsteps a way to walk in." "Righteousness" means prayer, wherein we declare the righteousness of our Creator, and only afterward are we to direct our footsteps on the road of our material desires.

2. **One is not allowed to eat or drink before praying**, as it is said (Leviticus 19: 26): "Ye shall not eat with the blood," which means that you shall not eat before you pray for your lives. To one who first eats and drinks and then prays, the following Scriptural text applies (I Kings 14:9): "And hast cast Me behind thy back." Do not read *Geveha* (thy back), but read *Geeha* (thy pride); the Holy One, blessed be He, said: "After this man had

catered to his pride, he then vouchsafed to accept the yoke of the Kingdom of Heaven." Before praying, it is forbidden even to drink coffee or tea with sugar and milk. But if one is old or feeble and cannot wait for his food until the congregation leaves the synagogue, especially on Sabbaths and festivals, when the services are prolonged, one may pray the *Shaharit* (morning prayer) at home, then recite the *kiddush*, and partake of some food. Then he should go to the synagogue, listen attentively while the congregation prays the *Shaharit*, and afterwards pray with them the *Musaph* (additional prayers); but one should not drink coffee with sugar, or the like, without first accepting the yoke of the Kingdom of Heaven. However, if one is ill, this is not an act of pampering one's ego. If one cannot concentrate upon the prayers while hungry or thirsty, one may eat and drink before praying.

3. There are some authorities who hold that even if a man awakes at midnight, he is not allowed to taste any food before praying; and it is proper to follow this stricter opinion. But if he has a weak heart, he may partake of food and drink to fortify himself for the Divine Commands.

4. Water, tea or coffee without sugar or milk may be taken before praying, even after dawn, because there is no trace of egotistic indulgence in this.

5. Before praying in the morning, we are not allowed to go to a neighbor to meet him or to say "good morning" as it is said (Isaiah 2:22): "Withdraw yourselves from man, whose breath is still in his nostrils; because for what is he to be esteemed?" This means, what is his importance, that you have honored him before you have honored Me? But if we meet a neighbor casually, we are allowed to salute him. It is proper, however, to alter somewhat the usual form of salutation, so that we remember that we must not engage in other matters before praying.

CHAPTER 40

Washing the Hands Before Meals

1. Before eating bread over which the benediction Hamotzi (who bringeth forth) is said, one must [**ritually**] wash his hands first [**see Matthew 15:2**]. If the bread is no less than the size of an egg, he must say the benediction for washing hands; but if it is less than that, he need not say the benediction.

2. The water used for washing the hands must be poured out of a vessel that is perfect, having neither a hole nor a crack. It must also be even at the top without any indents or projecting parts. When using a vessel having a spout, we must not let the water run through the spout, because that part is not the vessel proper since it does not hold any liquid. We must, therefore, pour the water from the edge of the vessel which contains the liquid.

4. It is difficult to ascertain the exact quantity of water required for washing the hands. We should, therefore, pour water lavishly on our hands, for Rab Hisda said (Shabbat 62b): "I wash with handfuls of water and handfuls of goodness are given me." We first wash our right hand and then our left. The water must cover the entire hand up to the wrist. No part of the hands should be left unwashed; therefore, the fingers must be slightly parted and raised somewhat upward, in order that the water may run down the entire length of the fingers. It must also cover the finger tips and the full circumference of the fingers. The entire hand should be covered with one outpouring of water. We should, therefore, not wash the hands out of a vessel with a narrow opening through which the water cannot flow out freely. It is best to pour water twice on each hand.

5. After washing both hands, we rub them together and then raise them upward, as it is written (Psalms 134:2): "Lift up your hands," etc. Then, before drying them, we recite the benediction: "Blessed art Thou, O Lord our God, King of the universe, who **hath sanctified us by His commandments and hath commanded us [in the Talmud] concerning the washing of the hands**." He who is accustomed to pour water twice on each hand, should first pour once on each hand, rub them together, pronounce the benediction, and thereafter pour a second time. We must be careful to have our hands thoroughly dried, and **we should not dry them with our shirts, because it is harmful to the memory.**

6. If after pouring the water upon one hand, he touched it with the other hand, or someone else had touched it, the water on the hand becomes contaminated by the contact. The hand must, therefore, be dried and then washed a second time. But if that happens after he had pronounced the benediction, the benediction need not be repeated.

8. If the color of the water has changed, either because of the place or because something fell into it, it is unfit for the **ritual washing of the hands**; but if the change was due to natural causes, the water is fit.

9. If one touches water before washing the hands, the water does not become defiled by it. Therefore, upon leaving the lavatory, one may take handful of water out of the barrel to wash the hands with it; and the remainder may be used for washing the hands before meals. However, if we dip the hands in the water to clean them, even if we have dipped in it only our little finger for the purpose of cleaning it, all the water becomes **invalid for the ritual washing**, since some work has been done with it.

13. The water must come down upon the hands by manual power; if it comes down spontaneously, it is invalid for the **ritual washing**.

14. It is forbidden to eat without first washing the hands, even if they are wrapped in a cloth. If one is on a journey and has no water, but water can be obtained either within four miles ahead or within a mile in the rear, one must travel that distance in order to wash the hands before eating. But if no water can be obtained even within such distances … one may wrap the hands in a cloth or put on gloves and eat.

CHAPTER 44

Laws Concerning the Washing of Hands and the Saying of Grace After Meals

1. Many people are lenient regarding the **washing of hands after meals**, but the God-fearing should be careful to observe it scrupulously. We are required to wash only the first two joints of our fingers, holding our hands downward before drying them. He who leads in saying the Grace should wash his hands first.

2. **We must not pour this water on the ground where people walk, because an evil spirit rests upon it**. We must wash into a vessel or underneath the table. We dry our hands before reciting Grace, and we must not pause between the washing and the reciting of Grace.

4. It is customary either to remove the knives left on the table before reciting Grace, or else to cover them. For **the table is compared to an altar**, and concerning the altar, it is written (Deuteronomy 27:5): "Thou shalt not lift up any iron upon them." For iron shortens the life of man while the altar prolongs life, and it is improper that one which shortens life should be raised on one that prolongs it…. The custom prevails in many communities not to cover the knives on the Sabbath or on festivals; for on weekdays they represent the brutal might of Esau, but **on the Sabbath and festivals there is no Satan or evil** occurrence. **And a custom in Israel is as valid as Law**.

5. Even if we have eaten only a piece of bread no larger than the size of an olive, we must say the Grace thereafter.

6. Grace after meals should be recited neither standing nor walking, but sitting. If we have walked to and fro in the house while eating, or if we have been standing or reclining, we must sit when reciting the Grace, in order that we may recite it with devotion. While saying Grace, we should not recline on our seats, because it is indicative of pride, but we should sit erect, put on the coat and hat, in order that the fear of Heaven be upon us, and that our minds be concentrated upon saying the Grace with reverence and awe.

7. It is the custom to respond *Amen* to all the prayers beginning with *Harahaman* (the all-merciful) contained in the Grace, for it is stated in the

Midrash that when we hear someone pray for a certain thing or bless an Israelite, even not mentioning the Divine Name, we are bound to respond *Amen* to it.

18. If a non-Jew is present in the room when Grace is recited, we should add: "Us the sons of the Covenant, all of us together."

CHAPTER 46

Forbidden Foods

1. The blood found in eggs is forbidden. Occasionally, it is forbidden to eat the entire egg on account of blood-spots. Therefore, the egg should be examined before using it in the preparation of food.

2. The use of the blood of fish is permitted, but if it is collected into a vessel, its use is forbidden for the sake of appearance, because people might think that it is forbidden blood. If, however, it is evident that it is the blood of a fish, as when it contains scales, then its use is permissible.

3. If we bite off a piece of bread or any other food, and blood from our gums is upon it, we must cut off the tinted part and throw it away, The blood from the gums may be soaked up on a weekday, since it has not dis-charged itself, but not on a Sabbath.

4. Blood is sometimes found in milk, which comes out of the cow's udder together with the milk; when that occurs, **a rabbi should be consulted**.

5. Meat and dairy products may not be eaten or cooked together, nor is it permissible to derive any benefit from such mixed foods. If, therefore, meat and dairy products happen to become mixed together, **a rabbi should be consulted**, as in certain instances a benefit may be derived from it, while in others it may not.

6. Two Jewish acquaintances may not eat at one table, if one eats meat and the other dairy products, even though they are at odds, unless they make a noticeable mark between them, for instance, by having a separate cover laid for each, or by placing upon the table a certain article that generally does not belong there, between their respective food. They must be careful not to drink any liquid out of the same vessel, as the food clings to it.

8. It is customary to mark all utensils used for dairy foods, so that they might not be interchanged with those used for meat.

9. After eating meat or a dish prepared with meat, we should wait six hours before eating dairy food, and the one who masticates food for an infant is

also obliged to wait that length of time. If after waiting six hours, we find particles of meat between our teeth, we must remove it, but we need not wait thereafter. We should cleanse our mouth and rinse it, that is, we should eat a little bread to cleanse our mouth with it, and then rinse our mouth with water or any other liquid.

11. After eating cheese, we may eat meat immediately thereafter at another meal, but we must carefully examine our hands to make sure that no particles of cheese cling to them; we must also cleanse the teeth and rinse the mouth.

12. If we desire to eat meat after eating cheese, we must remove from the table the rest of the bread of which we ate with the cheese. Cheese should not be eaten upon the tablecloth on which we have eaten meat, and conversely, no meat should be eaten upon the tablecloth upon which we have eaten cheese; nor should we cut bread to eat with cheese, with a knife used for cutting meat, or vice versa, even if the knife is clean.

13. If we cut onions or some other pungent things with a knife used for cutting meat, and put it in food made of milk, or vice versa, **a rabbi should be consulted** as to the fitness of the food.

14. If we prepare a dish of meat with the extract of almonds, we must put whole almonds in it on account of its deceptive appearance (because it looks like milk, thus averting the suspicion of having transgressed the law, by having boiled meat and milk together).

17. If we give something in a sack to a non-Jew, either to be forwarded or to be stored, it is necessary that the stitches of the sack be on the inside and it must be tied and sealed.

18. If we happen to forward, through a non-Jew, a slaughtered beast or fowl or anything else without a seal, then we must **consult a rabbi** about it.

19. Cheese or other articles of food which are in the hands of a non-Jew, although they are sealed or stamped, stating that they are **ritually fit** for food, are, nevertheless, unfit for use as long as we do not know who has sealed them.

20. Care should be taken that a Jew and a non-Jew should not cook or fry together in uncovered pots or frying pans, one pot containing food which is **ritually fit**, and the other containing **ritually unfit** food.

22. Care must be taken not to leave culinary utensils in the house of a non-Jew, lest he make use of them.

25. We must not knead dough with milk, lest it be eaten with meat....

26. If bread has been baked and meat has been roasted in the same oven and the oven was closed while the meat was uncovered, it is forbidden to eat that bread with dairy foods. It is permitted, however, to eat the bread with milk if the roasted meat was covered....

27. If milk or grease overflows on the bottom of an oven, the oven must be cleansed by means of glowing heat in accordance with the law, that is to say, glowing coal should be spread upon the entire surface so that it is heated white.

CHAPTER 72

The Holiness of the Sabbath

1. The holy Sabbath is the great sign and covenant which the Holy One, blessed be He, has given us to bear witness that "In six days God made the heavens and the earth and all that is in them, and He rested on the seventh day." This belief, that God is the Creator of the universe, is the foundation of our faith.

2. He who violates the Sabbath publicly is regarded as an idolater in every respect; if he touches wine, it becomes unfit for use; the bread he bakes is like the bread of an idolater, so is his cooked food. "Publicly" in this regard is when ten Jews know of the desecration, even if they don't actually see it. **This is the law as deduced from the Talmud and the commentaries**.

4. It is preferable to make the purchases for the Sabbath on Friday rather than on Thursday. However, articles of food requiring preparation should be procured on Thursday. While making the purchases, we should say: "It is in honor of the Sabbath." In accordance with the ordinances of Ezra, the clothes for the Sabbath should be washed on Thursday, not on Friday, as on that day all attention is needed for the preparation of the Sabbath needs.

9. No regular work should be done on Friday from the *Minhah ketannah* (small *minhah;* 3:30 p.m.) on. But casual work is permissible. It is forbidden to make clothes for someone else. But when a person is poor and he desires to earn enough for the Sabbath meals, he may work all day Friday, just the same as on *Hol Hammoed* (Intermediate Days of the festivals). Giving a haircut to a Jew is permissible all day on Friday, even if one is a professional barber and he does it for pay, inasmuch as it is obvious that the hair cutting is for the sake of the Sabbath. It is customary to close shops an hour before the Sabbath sets in.

10. From the ninth hour (3:30 p.m.) on, we should abstain from having a regular meal ... so that we may eat the Sabbath meal with relish.

11. A Jew must read every week the entire weekly portion of the Torah; that is, he must read the Scriptural text twice, and the *Targum* once. The reading may begin on Sunday. However, it is best to do so Friday afternoon. One should read twice each *Parshah* (subdivision), whether it ends a chapter or not, or even when it ends in the middle of a verse, and then read the *Targum* once. After finishing the *Targum,* one must read one verse of the Torah, so as to conclude the *Parshah* with a Biblical verse....

12. On Friday, one must wash the face, hands, and feet in warm water, and if possible, one should bathe the whole body in warm water and then **immerse in a ritual pool**.

14. On Friday, one must wash his head, pare his nails, and cut his hair, if too long. Finger and toe nails should not be cut on the same day, nor should the nails and the hair be cut on *Rosh Hodesh* (New Moon) even when it occurs on a Friday. Some are careful not to cut the nails in consecutive order, but alternately, starting with the finger next to the thumb of the right hand.... On the left hand, one starts with the fourth finger.... Some are also careful not to cut the nails on Thursday. For they begin to grow on the third day, which is the Sabbath. One must burn the nails after they are cut.

15. On Friday, one should review his deeds of the past week, repent and make amends for all misdeeds, because the Sabbath eve embodies all the weekdays, just as the eve of *Rosh Hodesh* embodies the whole month.

16. One should try to wear fine clothes as well as a nice *tallit* on the Sabbath; for it is written (Isaiah 58:13): "And thou shalt honor it," which is explained by the Rabbis to mean that the garments worn on the Sabbath shall not be the same as those worn on weekdays. And even when one is on a journey, among non-Jews, one shall put on the Sabbath clothes, for the attire is not in honor of men but in deference to the Sabbath.

17. Cooked food must be removed from the burning coals before the Sabbath begins. In the event one forgot to do so, one may not remove the pot, for it might touch the coal and increase the fire. **It may, however, be removed by a non-Jew.**

20. The sealed door of the oven should **be opened on the Sabbath by a non-Jew**. If a non-Jew is not available, a minor should do it. But in the absence of either, it may be done by anyone, but in a manner which is not ordinarily done on weekdays.

21. If one puts a pot of coffee into a hole in the ground on Friday to be used on the Sabbath, and covers it with pillows or something similar so that it keep warm; if he hides it in sand, he is not permitted to cover the whole vessel with the sand. Even if only a part of the vessel is covered with the sand and the rest of it is covered with garments, so that the vessel is covered on all sides, it is likewise forbidden. To make it legal, one must cover only one-half or one-third of the pot with the sand, the rest of it should remain uncovered, and then he may put a board or an inverted vessel on the top of the hole, so that there is a vacant space between the top cover and the pot containing the coffee, then he may put pillows or garments on the top.

CHAPTER 73

Work Done by a Non-Jew on the Sabbath

1. A Jew is forbidden to allow a non-Jew to do work for him on the Sabbath. This law is based upon the Biblical verse (Exodus 12:16): "No manner of work shall be done," which implies even by a non-Jew. **However, if the work is delivered to the non-Jew on Friday, it is permissible even if he does it on the Sabbath**, but only on the following conditions: (a) The non-Jew should take the work before the Sabbath, but not on the Sabbath day.

2. (b) The amount of compensation should be stipulated in advance, then the non-Jew does the work for his own sake, in order to get paid. Therefore, one who employs a non-Jewish servant, is forbidden to allow the latter to do any work on the Sabbath, as the work is done solely for the benefit of the Jew. If a non-Jew travels to a certain place (before the Sabbath), and a Jew asks him to deliver a letter, which will have to be carried on the Sabbath, he should be given some reward. Then he does it for compensation and not gratis.

5. (e) The work should not be connected with the soil, such as building or farm work ... such as plowing or reaping, even if the non-Jew is hired at a stipulated price for the whole task. If, however, the non-Jew has a share in the crops, and it is customary in that region for a farm worker to receive a share in the crops, it is permissible. If the farm is far away, where there is no Jew in the vicinity within two thousand cubits (three thousand feet), it is permissible if the non-Jew performs the work at a stipulated sum, so long as he is not hired by the day.

6. If a non-Jew has illegally built a house for a Jew on the Sabbath, it is well to be scrupulous and not move into it. (There are many divergent opinions about this).

7. The owner of a farm or a mill may rent it to a non-Jew, although he will work there on the Sabbath. But it is forbidden to rent a bathing establishment

to a non-Jew. If the Jew does not own the bathing establishment, but only rented it from a non-Jew, he should **consult a rabbi on how to act**. The owner of a hotel, a glass factory, a brick factory, and the like, should also consult a rabbi how to act.

8. A Jew is forbidden, under any circumstances, to allow a non-Jew to do work at his house on the Sabbath. Even if a non-Jewish servant desires to do some work for himself on the Sabbath, he should be forbidden by the Jewish employer.

9. If a non-Jewish tailor made a garment for a Jew and brought it to him on the Sabbath, he is permitted to put it on. If, however, it is known that the tailor has completed it on the Sabbath, it should not be worn, unless in a case of extreme necessity.

CHAPTER 74

Embarking on a Vessel on the Sabbath

1. We must not board a sea-going vessel the three days preceding the Sabbath, that is, from Wednesday on. But if we are bound on a sacred mission, we may embark even on a Friday.

3. Boarding a ship on Friday is permissible only when one goes on board and remains there until nightfall. Even if one goes home and remains there overnight, one is still permitted to embark on the Sabbath, so long as the ship does not make the trip for Jews only. But since he *was* home on the Sabbath, he had established a residence for the Sabbath at the house. Therefore, if the ship has made a longer journey than two thousand cubits, and has reached land on the Sabbath, he is not permitted to walk there more than four cubits from the landing.

4. It is permissible to board a vessel on the Sabbath for the sake of praying with an assembly of ten, or for the sake of performing another religious duty, provided the vessel makes the trip also for others. It is, nevertheless, preferable that the Jew should go on board on Friday while it is yet daytime, and remain there till after nightfall, after which he may return home and come back again on the Sabbath, but it is not permitted if the vessel makes the trip for Jews only.

CHAPTER 75

The Sabbath Candles

1. Everyone must put all work aside and light the Sabbath candles at least one-half hour before the stars emerge. If *Mizemor shir leyom hasaabbat* (A Psalm, a song for the Sabbath) has already been recited at the synagogue, even if it is two hours before nightfall, the Sabbath laws become binding upon the minority from that time on, and any manner of work is forbidden.

2. It is meritorious to light as many candles as possible in honor of the Sabbath. Some light ten candles, others seven. In no event should less than two candles be lit....

3. The precept is best performed by using olive oil or almond oil which is generally used for this purpose. But there are certain oils which are ritually unfit. The wick too, should be of good quality, such as vine-fiber flax, or hemp, for some other materials are unfit for the purpose. The Sabbath candles may also be made of tallow, as is generally done in our regions. But it is forbidden to put some tallow in a vessel and place a wick in it. The one who lights the candles should see to it that he ignites most of the wick protruding from the candles. The same applies to tallow candles.

4. It is a well-established rule that the benediction for a precept must be said prior to its performance. This, however, cannot be practiced in the case of lighting the Sabbath candles, for by pronouncing the benediction the woman ushers in the Sabbath, after which no labor is to be performed. Therefore, the woman first lights the candles, shuts out the light by covering her face with her hands while pronouncing the benediction, then she removes her hands and looks at the light, which act makes it akin to saying the benediction before kindling the candles.

5. Men as well as women are obliged to light Sabbath candles. However, the fulfillment of this duty was left primarily to the woman, because she is always at home and attends to household duties. Another reason is that because **the woman caused the fall of Adam and thereby extinguished the light of the world** and darkened his soul which is called *light*, as it is written (Proverbs 20:27); "The soul of man is the light of God;" therefore, it is her duty to make amends by lighting the candles in honor of the Sabbath.

6. Happy are the women who make it a custom to wash themselves and to put on the Sabbath apparel before lighting the candles. However, they should first say the *Minhah* (afternoon) prayer, as by lighting the candles they usher in the Sabbath, and they would be unable to pray the weekday *Minhah* afterward. If a woman is delayed by her occupation, and reaches

home about one-half hour before the Sabbath sets in, and if she should wash and change, she would run the risk of profaning the Sabbath, it is better that she should light the candles as she is, rather than risk a probable profanation of the Sabbath. If the husband sees that she is tardy in coming, it is mandatory for him to light the candles, and disregard her resentment.

7. When a man lights the Sabbath candles, knowing that he will afterwards have to do some work, it is advisable that he make a spoken or mental reservation that he does not thereby assume the Sabbath. If he inadvertently omits to make such a reservation, he is nevertheless, permitted to do work thereafter, as a husband's lighting of the candles is not ordinarily an act of ushering in the Sabbath.

8. The candles should be lit in the room where the meals are served, in order to indicate that they are lit in honor of the Sabbath. They should not be lit in one place and then transferred to another, except in an emergency…. If one wishes to use for the Sabbath a candle that has been burning, it should be extinguished and then relit in order to make it clear that it is dedicated to the Sabbath.

9. It is necessary to light candles in every room that is being used. If one is at home with his wife, who lights candles in one room and pronounces a benediction, it is not required to pronounce a benediction over the candles lit in other rooms….

10. It is the custom that if many women light candles in the same house, each woman lights candles and pronounces a benediction, because the more light the more joy. However, two women should not put their candles in one candlestick; it may, however, be done in an emergency….

14. If a woman has once neglected to light the Sabbath candles, **she must light an extra candle every Friday as long as she lives**. If she has neglected to light candles several times, she must add an extra candle for each time. This is done to impress upon her to be careful in the future; therefore, if she was prevented from lighting the candles by an accident, she need not light additional candles.

CHAPTER 80

Some Labors Forbidden on the Sabbath

The principal works we are forbidden to perform on the Sabbath are already known to most of the children of Israel. The list given herein comprises works that are not generally known to be forbidden; they are common things performed in the course of our daily lives.

1. It is forbidden to do work that requires concentration before a lamp. The Rabbis have forbidden this, lest one forgets and tilts the lamp in order to bring the oil closer to the wick, and then **one will be guilty of "igniting."** It is, however, the prevailing custom to permit studying before the light of our modern candles, in which the tallow or the wax firmly sticks to the wick. But one must make a certain mark, so as to remember not to snuff off the wick. According to the view of Maimonides, the last named act is a violation of a Mosaic Law. It is impermissible to snuff off the wick, even through a non-Jew.

2. It is forbidden to open a door or a window opposite a burning candle, lest the flame be extinguished; but one may close the window or the door. It is forbidden to open or to close the door of an oven in which a fire is burning, for by so doing, one either increases or decreases the fire.

3. Pouring boiling gravy on pieces of bread or *matzah* is forbidden. One should first pour the gravy into a dish, let it cool off until it is fit to eat, and then put the bread or the *matzah* in it; but as long as the gravy is hot, even if it is already in the dish, it is forbidden to put either bread or *matzah* in it. It is likewise forbidden to put salt or spices into the gravy, even if it is already in the dish, and certainly not into the pot, as long as it is boiling hot, but we must wait until it cools off a little so that it is fit to eat. Some are more lenient with salt which has already been dissolved. However, a blessing upon the one who adheres to the stricter opinion regarding this. It is likewise forbidden to pour hot coffee or tea into a cup containing sugar. But we must pour the coffee or the tea into the cup and then put the sugar in it. In cases of necessity, one may be lenient about this.

4. It is forbidden to place fruit or water upon a hot stove, because the water might boil and the fruit might bake. Even if we intend only to warm it, nevertheless, since it is possible that on this spot it may boil or bake, it is forbidden to warm it there.

5. On the Sabbath, it is forbidden to store away victuals in any wrapping, even if it would not increase its warmth. Therefore, if we remove a pot containing victuals which have been cooked or heated in it, we are forbidden to wrap it or cover it with pillows, bolsters, or the like, in order to preserve its warmth.

6. Any article of food which cannot be eaten at all without being rinsed with water must not be rinsed on the Sabbath, even with cold water. It is allowed, however, to soak herring in cold water, since it is fit for food even before soaking.

10. If fruit spilled from a vessel, either in the house or in the courtyard, they may be gathered together on the Sabbath, if they are in one spot; but if they

are scattered, when it requires physical exertion to do so, they may not be gathered into a basket, but they may be picked up and eaten one by one.

11. It is permissible to remove peas or the like from their pods, if the pods are still green and can also be eaten, because this is like separating one piece of food from another; but if the pods have become dry and no longer suitable for eating, it is forbidden to remove the peas from them.

12. **It is forbidden to squeeze fruit to make a beverage, like squeezing lemons into water to make lemonade.** Some authorities even prohibit to suck juice out of fruit with the mouth. At any rate, in eating grapes, one should not suck out the juice and throw away the skins.

13. A woman is not allowed to squeeze milk from her breasts into a vessel and feed the child with it; but she is allowed to squeeze out a little milk, in order to induce the child to take hold of the breast and suck it.

14. It is forbidden to crush snow or hail with the hands in order to obtain water; but it is permissible to put it into a cup of wine or water to cool the liquid, letting it melt of itself.

15. When we separate food, we must take only what we need for immediate consumption, but not a quantity that will be enough also for later use…. We may not peel garlic or onions and put them away, because it constitutes the **violations known as "separation."** We are allowed to peel only what we need immediately. The upper shell which surrounds the whole garlic may not be removed even when needed for immediate consumption, because this constitutes a secondary act of "threshing."

17. It is forbidden to strain any kind of beverage, for concerning this, there are many conflicting opinions. One is, however, permitted to drink through a cloth, as the **law forbidding** "separation" applies only where the food or drink is prepared prior to eating or drinking it, but in this case, one is simply holding back the waste from entering into the mouth. Nevertheless, some authorities disapprove of drinking water through a cloth, because it constitutes "**washing**." The last law may be relaxed in cases of emergency where there is no pure water available. One, however, should not drink through the sleeve of one's shirt, because in this case it is feared that one will "**wring**" it.

19. If a fly has fallen into beverage or food, we must not remove the fly only, but should take some of the food or the beverage with it.

20. Pepper or salt, needed for seasoning food, may be crushed with the handle of a knife, or in any other convenient way, but may not be crushed in a mortar.

21. It is forbidden to cut onions or any other vegetables, except immediately before a meal, and even then they should not be cut into very thin slices.

22. It is forbidden to salt any substance which will be affected by the salt in such a way as to become soft or less pungent, because it constitutes the **violation known as "tanning."** Therefore, it is forbidden to salt raw cucumbers, radishes, or onions, even if the quantity is limited to that which is needed for an immediate meal. But one may dip each piece in salt before eating it.

23. It is forbidden to salt a large quantity of boiled beans or peas together, because it tends to make them softer. This is forbidden even if one intends to eat them immediately.

24. Salads made of lettuce, cucumbers or onions, may be salted immediately before the meal, because oil and vinegar are generally added immediately, which weaken the effect of the salt.

25. **The law forbidding "construction" applies also to edibles**, as for instance, making cheese, or arranging fruit in a certain orderly way. Therefore, when making a salad of sliced onions and eggs or the milt of herring, **one must be careful not to arrange them symmetrically, but put them on the plate at random**.

26. On washing the dishes, one should not pour hot water on them; but he should pour the water into a vessel and then put the dishes into that vessel. **We must not wash the dishes with a cloth, lest we wring it afterward**; but we may wash them with a cloth especially used for this purpose, which we are not careful to wring even on weekdays. We are not allowed to use a detergent of oats, or the like, in washing glasses. Only dishes needed for the Sabbath may be washed on the Sabbath.

27. **Whatever a Jew is forbidden to do on the Sabbath, is forbidden also to have it done through a non-Jew**. Nevertheless, in the wintertime, since **it is permissible to make a fire in the stove through a non-Jew for the purpose of heating the house**, the custom prevails that the non-Jew places the cold victuals on the stove before he makes the fire; since the intention in making the fire is not to warm the victuals but to heat the house. **But the victuals should not be placed on the stove after it was heated**. It is certain, however, that **if the intention in making the fire is not for the sake of heating the house, but for heating the victuals, it is forbidden**. Some authorities forbid it even when the intention is to heat the house. Although the custom is to depend on the authorities who allow it, a scrupulous person should refrain from such a practice when it is not too urgent.... Although the fire is made for the purpose of heating the house, and a non-Jew places the victuals thereon before the fire is made, the God-fearing avoid it.

28. One who spills liquid on the soil where anything is apt to grow, is guilty of **violating the law against "sowing**," because the liquid accelerates the growth. Therefore, one should be careful not to eat in a garden on the Sabbath, because it is impossible to be so careful as not to spill some liquid upon the soil; and, besides, **in a garden there is a law forbidding the moving of articles**.

29. It is forbidden to wipe anything with a sponge that has no handle.

30. It is forbidden to spit in a place where the wind will scatter the saliva.

31. A maiden is forbidden either to make braids or to take them apart on the Sabbath [**violates the law against tying knots**]. But she is allowed to fix her hair with her hands. The hair must not be combed with a brush made of bristle if it is very hard, because it is impossible not to pluck out some hair with it; but if it is not hard, the hair may be set with it, and especially so if it is made for that particular purpose.

32. One may wipe off dirt from a garment with a rag, but no water may be spilled on it, because it would be **equivalent to washing**. Therefore, if a child urinates on a garment, it is forbidden to spill water on it (but if he urinates on the ground or in a vessel made of wood or of leather, it is permissible to spill water on it). When one washes the hands, one should rub them briskly, one against the other to leave as little water on them as possible before using the towel (for when there is only moisture on them, the wiping does not constitute "**washing**").

34. If water spills on the table, it is forbidden to wipe it with a cloth which one values, for since it absorbs much water, **one might wring it out** [**which is a violation**]. Neither should one use a cloth in drying glasses or other vessels having a narrow opening, for the liquid might be squeezed out of the cloth.

35. If one is caught in the rain and his clothes get wet, he may go home and remove the clothes, but he is **not allowed to spread them out so that they may dry**; even if one's clothes are only moist with perspiration, he is not allowed to spread them out, certainly not in front of a fire. Even when one has the wet clothes on, he is not allowed to stand in front of a fire where it is very hot. One is likewise forbidden to shake off water from a garment. A costly garment, of which one takes special care, must not even be handled when taken off, **for fear that he might wring it**.

36. If one walks and reaches a brook, one may jump over it even if it is wide; jumping is better than the effort of walking round about it. One is not permitted to cross it by wading, **lest he will wring his clothes** after crossing. One must not walk along the sloping bank of a stream on the Sabbath, for he might slip, fall into the water, wet his clothes and then wring them.

38. Wet mud on a garment may be scraped off with a fingernail or with a knife, but not when it is dry, for it is then **equivalent to the act of "grinding."**

39. It is forbidden to shake off snow or dust from a black garment, but it is permissible to remove feathers from it with the hand. Some people refrain even from the latter.

40. It is allowed to remove mud from the feet or the shoes with something which may be handled on the Sabbath, or they may be wiped by rubbing them on a beam, but it is forbidden to wipe them on a wall or on the ground. In cases of emergency, as when there is excrement on the foot or on the shoe and there is nothing available which may be handled on the Sabbath, one may wipe it on a wall; and if there is no wall, he may wipe it on the ground. If there is water available, he may even wash the shoe with it, if the shoe is made of leather (because in the case of leather, the mere flushing of it does not constitute "washing," unless he rubs one side against the other, in the manner of launderers). But one is not allowed to scrape off excrement from a leather shoe with a knife….

42. On the Sabbath, it is forbidden to paint anything even with a dye that is not permanent. Therefore, a woman is not allowed to use rouge. When our hands are colored by fruit juice, we must not touch any garment because we thus dye it. We are likewise **forbidden to wipe a bleeding nose or wound with a cloth**.

44. It is forbidden to tear or to twine even two threads or two loose hairs on the Sabbath [**violates the law against weaving or tying knots**].

45. It is the practice when we wind a thread or a cord around an object, that we make two knots, one on the top of the other [a double knot]. On the Sabbath, **we are not allowed to make two knots**, even on an object which we generally loosen on the same day. When putting a kerchief around the neck on the Sabbath, we must not make two knots on it, and even on Friday, we must not make two knots on it, as we will not be allowed to untie it on the Sabbath, as stated herein below. It is forbidden to hold the two ends of a thread or a cord together, and make one knot on both, for in this case, even one knot will hold it fast. It is permissible to take the two ends, make first one knot, and on the top of it make a loop, if it is a thing which is generally untied the same day. If not, it is forbidden even if in this instance we intend to untie it the same day. It is permissible to make two or more loops, one on top of the other, even if it is intended to hold for many days.

46. It is forbidden to untie any knot which may not be tied on the Sabbath. **If a knot causes us pain, it may be loosened by a non-Jew**.

48. Garments that are made with a string or a strap in them for fastening, such as trousers, shoes, or undershirts, if the garment is new, it is not permitted to insert the string in them on the Sabbath, for it is akin to **perfecting a garment**. If the garment is old, and the aperture is not narrow, so that there is no trouble inserting it, it is permissible.

49. Sometimes when a seam becomes loose and the parts of a garment become separated, the thread is pulled and the loose parts tighten temporarily. **This act constitutes "sewing," and may not be done on the Sabbath**.

52. It is forbidden to catch any living thing on the Sabbath, even a flea; but if an insect stings a person, it may be removed and thrown off, but one is not allowed to kill it because it is forbidden to kill on the Sabbath anything that possesses life. It is, however, permissible to kill lice, since they are created only by perspiration (nevertheless, those found on clothes may not be killed, but should be thrown off; only those found in the head may be killed).

53. If we wish to close a chest or a vessel in which there are flies, we must let them fly out first, because by closing the chest on them we snare them. However, it is not necessary to examine the chest to see that no living thing is therein; we simply have to chase out those we see.

54. It is forbidden to draw blood on the Sabbath, even to suck the blood from the gums. It is likewise forbidden to put a plaster on a wound to draw out blood and pus. And it is certainly forbidden to squeeze blood or pus from a boil.

55. Shreds of skin which have become separated from the base of the fingernails should not be removed either by means of an instrument or by hand, or with the teeth. A nail, most of which has been torn off and causes pain, may be removed with the hand, but not with an instrument. But if less than half has become separated, it should not be removed even by hand.

57. If meat has not been salted for three days after the slaughter, and the third day occurs on the Sabbath, **a non-Jew may rinse such meat on the Sabbath**, so that it should not become forbidden food, but it may not be rinsed by a Jew.

58. It is forbidden to cover anything with a plaster, or wax, or tar. Therefore, it is forbidden to put wax or congealed oil into a hole in order to close it up, or to stick it onto something as a mark. It is, however, permissible to smear food, like butter, on bread.

59. It is forbidden to cut or break any object that is not food; but food, even for beasts, may be cut and broken. It is allowed to cut up straw with which to pick the teeth.

60. It is forbidden to make any use of a tree, whether it is green or dried up, even if we do not shake the tree thereby (as **shaking the tree is in itself a violation**, because it may not be moved on the Sabbath). We must not climb on it, nor suspend ourselves from it. It is also forbidden to place any article on it or remove anything from it, or to tie an animal to it. It is even forbidden to make use of the sides of the tree; hence, if a basket is suspended from the tree, it is forbidden to take anything out of the basket or to put anything in it, inasmuch as the basket is considered as the side of the tree.

61. **Flowers** or plants which are cultivated in a vessel, whether for their beauty or their fragrance, **are forbidden to be plucked**, just as it is forbidden to pluck them from a tree.

62. It is **forbidden to write or to draw a picture**, even with the finger in liquid spilled on the table, or on the rime [frost] of window panes, or anything similar to it, no matter how impermanent such writing is. It is even forbidden to make a mark upon any object with the fingernails.

63. Just as it is **forbidden to write on the Sabbath**, so is it **forbidden to erase any writing**. Nevertheless, it is permissible to break and to eat on the Sabbath tarts upon which letters or figures have been made; but if they have been made as a charm for children, one should avoid doing it.

64. Some authorities **forbid the opening or the closing of books, when words are written on the edges of the leaves**. Others permit it; and this is the prevailing practice. But since some authorities forbid it, it is best to avoid writing on the edges of pages.

72. It is forbidden to remove or to reset doors or windows on the Sabbath, even when they hang on iron hinges and are easily removed or reset; **one who resets them is guilty of construction**, and **one who removes them is guilty of demolition**.

73. It is forbidden to sweep the house, even if the floor is made of stone or of boards, **but it may be done by a non-Jew**. However, even a Jew is allowed to sweep if he is doing it in an entirely unusual manner, as when he sweeps it with goose feathers, or the like.

82. It is **forbidden to carry a covering** as a protection from the sun or from the rain, which is **commonly known as an umbrella**, because it is considered as making a tent.

87. On the Sabbath, **it is forbidden to make a musical sound**, either with an instrument or with the limbs of the body (except the mouth).

91. There are many divergent views regarding the folding of garments on the Sabbath, and it is best not to fold them.

CHAPTER 86

Bathing on the Sabbath

1. One is forbidden to wash his whole body, or even the greater part of the body, in warm water even if the water was warmed before the Sabbath. It is forbidden even if he washes the body a small part at a time. It is forbidden to enter a bathhouse for the purpose of perspiring there. It is, however, permissible to wash one's face and bathe one's feet with water made warm before the Sabbath.

2. It is permissible to wash the entire body with water which flows warm from its origin, such as the hot springs of Tiberias, if the water is on the ground and the place is not covered with a roof. However, if the water is in a receptacle or if the place is covered with a roof, it is forbidden.

3. It is permissible to immerse the whole body in cold water, but one must not thereafter stand in front of a hot oven to warm up, for that would make it like washing with warm water. Even if one has washed only the hands in cold water, one is not allowed to warm them by an oven while they are still wet, because it is equivalent to washing with water that has been warmed up [on the Sabbath].

4. A bather must be careful **not to squeeze the water from his hair**. He must likewise refrain from swimming, because swimming on the Sabbath and on festivals is forbidden. It is also **forbidden to make anything float**, such as chips of wood. One who bathes in a place from where it is **forbidden to carry anything out on the Sabbath**, must shake off all the water from his body and from his hair before leaving, so that he will carry no water out from one premise into another.

CHAPTER 90

Doing Things that are not Actual Work;
Work Through a Non-Jew

7. On the Sabbath, one may say to a workman: "Do you think you will be able to see me this evening?" Although the workman understands that he wants to see him in the evening in order to hire him to do some work, [there is no violation because] only a direct proposal is forbidden. One, however, should not say, "Be ready for me this evening," as that is like saying in plain words that one desires to hire him.

APPENDIX THREE

Who and What is a Jew?

Most people, including Christians, carelessly assume that Jews are the modern-day equivalent of the biblical nation of Israel. In fact, one of the most significant misrepresentations in Judaism is the fallacious claim that the Jews are the *sum total* of the people of Israel. Scripture, however, shows that authentic Jews are descendants of the distinct nation of *Judah*, which was composed of only *three* of the twelve tribes that originally made up the ancient Kingdom of Israel. As for the remaining tribes, Jewish and Christian scholars alike have relegated them to the pages of history, claiming that their assimilation into various Gentile nations has rendered them nonexistent. But is this so? Who were the Jews anciently? And by what criteria is a person considered Jewish today?

As can be easily shown from the Old Testament, the original nation of Israel was composed of twelve tribes. Following the death of Solomon, the nation was divided into two kingdoms. The southern kingdom, referred to as Judah, the "House of Judah," or by its capital, Jerusalem, was made up of three tribes—Judah, Benjamin and Levi—blended as if *one*. Hence, in II Kings 17:18, Judah is said to be the *only* remaining tribe after the northern kingdom was removed. In close proximity to Jerusalem, the tiny tribe of Benjamin was practically considered part of Judah. The Scriptures also show that the tribe of Levi, because of their association with the Temple, settled with Judah.

The northern kingdom, referred to as Israel, the "House of Israel," or by its capital, Samaria, was composed of the remaining tribes. The half-tribes of Ephraim and Manasseh were each counted separately, thus making a total of ten tribes. For their evil in God's eyes, the entire "house of Israel" was taken into captivity by the Assyrians in the 6th century BC and never allowed to return. In fact, pagan peoples were brought in to take their place as the tribes settled into the lands of their captors (II Kings 17:23-24). In Matthew 10:6, Jesus instructed His disciples to take the message of the Gospel to these "lost" sheep, which proves that both their identity and whereabouts were known to the early church. (The so-called "lost ten tribes" had by this time migrated into parts of northwestern Europe and the British Isles, forming well established communities; for more information on the identity and location of the modern-day tribes of Israel, please visit the Web site cbcg.org/books.htm#10Tribes.)

The nation of Judah—referred to as "the Jews" for the first time in II Kings 16:6, where they are actually at war with the northern kingdom—also went into captivity (II Kings 24:10, 14), only to return some 70 years later to rebuild Jerusalem and the Temple. Ezra refers to the returning exiles—those of "Judah and Benjamin, and the priests, and the Levites" (Ezra 1:5)—as *Jews of Judah* (Ezra 5:1). In the most literal sense, a Jew may be viewed as a direct descendant of the *tribe* of Judah (the term "Jew" is a derivative of the Hebrew "Judah"). In common biblical usage, however, *Jew* had come to refer collectively to those who were of the *nation* of Judah. In Esther 2:5, Mordecai is said to be a Jew of Benjamite lineage—showing that even in foreign lands the term was likewise used. In a similar case, the apostle Paul claimed to be a Jew (Acts 21:39), when he was actually of the *tribe* of Benjamin (Phil. 3:5). Thus, in first-century Palestine, the term "Jew" carried no particular religious connotation, but referred to one who was native to the area of Judea.

Today, a "pure" Jew—one who can actually trace his lineage to the ancient "House of Judah"—is a rarity. In *Judaism Discovered*, Michael Hoffman notes that "contemporary Jews are mostly … of mixed race. A substantial segment of [even] so-called Israeli Jews today are … genetically indistinguishable from their Arab neighbors" (p. 838). He adds that the overwhelming majority of Jews in America are actually descendants of East European tribes that *converted to Judaism* in the middle of the 8th century. In fact, Jewish scholars readily acknowledge that throughout history such conversion has "accounted for a substantial part of Jewish population growth" (wikipedia.org/wiki/Jews).

Indeed, as Hoffman suggests, it was with the *spread of Judaism* that the identity of a "Jew" has come to be associated with *religion* rather than genetics or nationality. On this point, he writes that, today, "the heirs of the Pharisees are discerned not by racial or ethnic criteria but by a supremacist ideology" (p. 838). Yet, while anyone can "convert" to Judaism and become a "Jew," the issue is a bit more complex. Unlike most ethnic groups, being Jewish can be a matter of race *or* religion.

Being Jewish—Race or Religion?

In Orthodox Judaism, Jewish identity has traditionally been based on strict matrilineal descent or genuine religious conversion. In modern, secular usage, Jews include 1) those born to a Jewish family regardless of religious practice; 2) those who have *some* Jewish ancestral background or lineage (even if not strictly matrilineal); and 3) those without any Jewish ancestral background who have *formally converted* to the practice of Judaism. Also, the term "ethnic Jew" is used to describe a person of Jewish parentage who does not practice Judaism but still identifies strongly with Jews culturally and fraternally (wikipedia.org/wiki/Jews).

It is important to note that a person born to non-Jewish parents who believes and observes every law and custom of Judaism is still considered a non-Jew until he has undergone the *formal process of conversion*. Once this process is completed, the individual is held to be as much a "Jew" as one born to Jewish parents. However, a person *born to a Jewish mother* who is an atheist and never practices the Jewish religion is *still* a Jew, even in the eyes of the ultra-Orthodox. Likewise, one who is born Jewish and practices Judaism can convert to *another religion* and still maintain their status as a Jew. In this regard, being a Jew is a matter of *race*, strictly based on lineage.

But when it comes to Judaism—a religion of *thought* and *culture*, and not of race or nationality—being a Jew centers on formal conversion. "Common ancestry is not required to be a Jew. Many Jews worldwide share common ancestry, as shown by genetic research; however, [one] can be a Jew without sharing this common ancestry, for example, by *converting*." This is how numerous African-Americans and Asians have become "Jews" (jewfaq.org/whoisjew.htm).

Branches of Modern Judaism

In modern Judaism, there are three main groups: Orthodox, Reform and Conservative. Several minor groups and subgroups also exist. On the "right" is **Orthodox Judaism**, which is purely rabbinical and Talmudic in nature. Only Orthodox Jews accept the absolute authority of the Talmud, and generally see themselves as practicing *normative Judaism* as opposed to being part of a particular movement. Subgroups include the ultra-Orthodox, the so-called "Modern" Orthodox, and various Hasidic movements.

On the "left" is **Reform Judaism**, a relatively modern movement in which the use of phylacteries has been abandoned, synagogue services have been shortened, and various prayers and rituals considered "useless" have been discarded. Sometimes referred to as Progressive Judaism, the movement originated in Germany as a backlash against Orthodoxy; its goals were to integrate Jews into society and encourage the *personal* interpretation of the Scriptures.

In the center is **Conservative Judaism**, which emerged in America as largely a mix of Orthodox and Reform ideals. In theory, the Conservative movement (which is hardly conservative) sought to liberalize elements of Orthodox theology (such as dietary laws) while restoring some of the more traditional practices abandoned by Reform Jews. As opposed to being a narrowly defined school of thought, Conservative Judaism is actually a *broad* religious movement with a wide range of beliefs and practices—many of which are more liberal than what is acceptable in Orthodoxy, yet more conservative than what is allowed in the Reform movement.

As noted, only Orthodoxy accepts the authority of the Talmud. In *Exploring the World of the Jew*, John Phillips writes that both the Reform and Conservative movements have "debunked the myth that the Talmud was inspired." According to Phillips, both movements were ultimately intended to allow Jews to practice a form of "Judaism" in which they could be comfortable in a Gentile world (p. 75). Similarly, *Karaite Jews* disregard both the Talmud and rabbinic opinion, maintaining that it is the responsibility of each Jew to study the Scriptures for themselves. Unlike other Jewish groups, Karaites determine Jewishness through the paternal line.

According to Hoffman, Judaism is the "religion of Orthodoxy" (p. 142). From their perspective, Orthodox Jews are the sole practitioners of authentic Judaism. Thus, Reform and Conservative Jews do not enjoy the same legal status as do Orthodox Jews in the State of Israel. Hoffman notes that "conversion to Judaism within the Israeli state is only recognized [by the state] if [the conversion rites are] performed by the Orthodox Rabbinate" (p. 141). Thus, conversion to Reform or Conservative Judaism presents an ongoing problem for those wanting to become "Jews" in the Jewish state.

In spite of the rifts caused by the Reform and Conservative movements, the Orthodox and ultra-Orthodox branches of Judaism are currently experiencing renewed growth. According to historian Yaakov Wise of the University of Manchester, Reform Judaism is *shrinking* in numbers while Orthodox and ultra-Orthodox Jews are increasing. "Ultra-Orthodox British and American Jews are set to outnumber their more secular counterparts by the second half of this century.... [Moreover,] European ultra-Orthodox Jewry is expanding more rapidly than at any time since World War Two. Almost three out of every four British Jewish births are ultra-Orthodox." If the current trends continue, says Dr. Wise, "profound cultural and political changes" will take place among British and American Jews. According to Wise, the ultra-Orthodox population in America is expected to double every 20 years.

The State of Israel is experiencing similar changes. Wise notes that "by the year 2020, the ultra-Orthodox population of Israel will double to one million, and make up 17 percent of the total population" (Hoffman, p. 142; from "Majority of Jews will be Ultra-Orthodox by 2050"; University of Manchester (England) press release, July 23, 2007).

The Apostle Paul's Perspective on Judaic "Works of Law"

First-century Pharisaism was a *works-based* religion that could only bring a *form* of "righteousness" to its followers (Rom. 10:3)—the "pseudo-righteousness" to which Jesus alluded in Matthew 5:20. Having lived much of his life as a Pharisee—the *strictest* sect of Jewish religion (Acts 26:5)—the apostle Paul was intimately familiar with Judaic "works of law." (The Greek word for *strict* means *rigorous* and *exacting*, hence Jesus' reference in Matthew 23:4 to Pharisaic "burdens.") Years after his conversion, Paul found himself having to confront various "Judaizers"—those with Pharisaic beliefs who were intent on pushing traditional "works of law" on newly-converted Christians.

The churches of Galatia faced just such an affront. Scholars have long recognized that Paul's epistle to the Galatians primarily addresses the issue of Judaizers who wanted the Galatian believers to adopt Jewish customs, become circumcised, and even follow the traditions of the Pharisees. However, by confusing Pharisaism with the "religion" of the Old Testament, such scholars have *assumed* that the Galatians were being pressured to adopt the "religion of Moses" as opposed to the so-called "enlightened" Gospel they had already learned from Paul. But such was not the case; the Judaizers were attempting to seduce the Galatians into practicing Pharisaic "works of law"—which, as this book has shown, have *nothing* to do with the true "religion" of Moses and the Old Testament.

Because of this erroneous association of Pharisaism with Moses, the phrase "works of law" (especially in Galatians) is quite misunderstood in mainstream Christianity—particularly considering the Protestant belief that the Law has been somehow nullified by Jesus' sacrifice. According to such skewed theology, on one side of the fence is Moses and the Torah—and, of course, the Pharisees, as representatives of that "Old Testament religion." On the other side is Jesus, Paul and grace. The poor Galatians were caught in the middle. Teaching a "gospel of liberation," Paul had supposedly *freed* the Galatians from the "yoke of bondage" to the Law, while the overzealous Pharisaic Judaizers were bent on bringing the converts squarely back "under the Law" of Moses.

But as we will see, the truth is far different. Paul had clearly taught the Galatians to carefully obey the laws and commandments of God—the true "religion" or *way of life* of the Old Testament—while living under the grace of God made possible by Jesus' sacrifice. Expressing dismay at how easily the Judaizers had led them astray, Paul asks, "O foolish Galatians, who has bewitched you?... Did you receive the Spirit of God by **works of**

law, or by the hearing of faith?" (Gal. 3:1-2). Clearly, such Judaizers were Pharisaic in origin and sought only to promote their brand of pseudo-righteousness based on *traditional*, ritual "works of law." Understanding Paul's use of the phrase "works of law" is the all-important *key*.

For example, in a vital passage generally misunderstood by mainstream Christians, Paul writes, "For as many as are **of the works of the law** are under the curse; for it is written, 'Cursed is everyone who does not continue in all things which are written in the Book of the Law, to do them' " (Gal. 3:10; *NKJV*). Most people misunderstand this verse to say that those who keep the Mosaic Law are cursed. After all, did not Jesus come to free man from that *harsh* Old Testament set of laws?

But is God's Law a curse? Stop and think. Could the same Law that David (a man after God's own *heart*) called "perfect" and "sure" in Psalm 19:7 be a curse? David pronounced a *blessing* on those who keep God's way: "*Blessed* are the undefiled in the way, **who walk in the Law [Torah] of the LORD**" (Psa. 119:1). Paul wrote that "the Law is indeed holy, and the commandment holy and righteous and good" (Rom. 7:12). The apostle James called the Law the "perfect Law of *liberty*"—because it liberates one *from* curses.

Read Galatians 3:10 again carefully. It quotes Deuteronomy 27:26, which says, "Cursed is he who does not **confirm all the words of this Law to do them**." The *curse* is on the one who *fails to obey* the Law—because obedience to God's way of life *brings life*. This is why Jesus told the rich young man, "if you desire to *enter into life*, keep the commandments" (Matt. 19:17). Most assuredly, the phrase "works of law" in this passage cannot be referring to obedience to God's laws and commandments—which clearly bring blessings, not curses. Thus, we must look for *another explanation* for Paul's use of the phrase.

As a Jew who once practiced Rabbinic Judaism, Avi ben Mordechai has done extensive research into Paul's use of such phrases as "works of law"—particularly in Galatians. In his book *Galatians—A Torah-Based Commentary in First-Century Hebraic Context*, he writes that the Gentile converts of Galatia were under considerable "internal pressure to submit to local Pharisaic decrees and traditions…" (p. 217). He argues that when the overall *context* of the book of Galatians is examined, the phrase *works of the law* "can be understood as a **false system of justification**, which was [based on] a **Pharisaic system of decrees and traditions**." He adds, "*Works of the law*, as it was understood in the first century, produced a torah of false 'righteousness' [based on the oral law] replete with its many reforms [ostensibly] developed by using the [written] Law of Moses as a source text. *Works of the law* had become another torah [the Pharisees' oral laws and traditions] added to the written Torah of Moses" (p. 216; emphasis added).

With this understanding, Paul's use of the phrase "works of law" in Galatians 3:10 becomes quite clear. Those trying to achieve "justification" or "righteousness" through adherence to Pharisaic codes of law—"works of law"—were *cursed* because they would, of necessity, be in violation of the written Law. God's Law and the Jews' oral law are completely incompatible; one *cannot observe both.* Adhering to the Pharisees' "works of law" meant the *rejection* of God's written Law; thus one becomes *cursed* as he fails to "confirm all the words of this Law **to do them.**" This is why Jesus reproved the Pharisees, saying, "Did not Moses give you the Law, and [yet] not one of you is [actually] practicing the Law?" (John 7:19). Christ also stated, "Full well do you *reject* the commandment of God so that you may *observe your own tradition*" (Mark 7:7-9)—and that such traditions had a *nullifying effect* on the Scriptures (Matt. 15:6).

Jewish author David Stern also sees the error of insisting that the phrase "works of law" must always apply to the Law of God. He writes: "Most Christians … suppose that *erga nomou,* literally 'works of law,' a [phrase] which appears three times [in Gal. 2:16], must mean 'actions done in obedience to the Torah.' But this is wrong. One of the best-kept secrets of the New Testament is that when [Paul] writes *nomos* he frequently does not mean *law* [in the sense of the Torah], but *legalism*" (*Jewish New Testament Commentary,* p. 536; "Gal. 2:16"). Stern describes *legalism* as the perversion of God's Law into a mechanical set of rules devoid of their spiritual intent (p. 537), but declines to directly implicate Pharisaic "works of law." Nevertheless, the principle is the same, as no humanly-devised "code of law" can bring justification or true righteousness.

Contrary to popular myth, Jesus did not come to annul God's Law, but to *expand* and *magnify* it by emphasizing its original spiritual intent (Matt. 5-6). At the same time, Jesus fully discredited the Pharisees' system of "works of law" that served only to corrupt the plain teachings of the Scriptures. Clearly, the Pharisees' traditional "works of law" were incongruous with the true "religion" of Moses and the Old Testament.

It was within this framework that Paul had prefaced his corrective epistle to the Galatians by stating that "a man is **not justified by works of law**"—not justified by adherence to Pharisaic codes of law. He adds that even "we [converted Jews] also have believed in Christ Jesus in order that we might be justified by the faith of Christ, and not by works of law; because **by works of law shall no flesh be justified**" (Gal. 2:16). He thus concludes, "I do not nullify the grace of God; for if righteousness [and justification] is through [Pharisaic] **works of law**, then Christ died in vain" (verse 21). Mordechai puts it like this: "If the Pharisaic system of law and tradition was able to impart life (which only the written commandments can do), then the death of Yeshua was for nothing" (p. 227).

Mordechai concludes that the "foundation of Paul's polemic was this: No amount of submission to the established traditions of men was (or is) able to justify (establish as righteous) one who wants to be joined to the 'saved' Torah community of Israel"—for "**submitting to the Pharisaic oral law … was to essentially nullify the teaching and work of [Jesus]**" (p. 218; emphasis added).

Mordechai notes that one of the reasons people often misunderstand Paul is that they approach his writings concerning the Law as if they were the "primary authority" of the entire body of Scripture. He argues that "most Christians are [taught] to establish doctrine *first* from Paul's words…" (p. 8). According to Mordechai, they use an upside-down methodology with the following (or a similar) structure (pp. 8-9):

Paul's Epistles
Gospel Narratives
Apostolic Writings
Old Testament
Mosaic Law

Using this approach, all of Scripture is viewed through the "lens" of Paul's writings. On the other hand, Mordechai contends that all of Scripture should be viewed ultimately through the written Torah. "From a Hebraic perspective, there is no body of law or philosophy among men that is greater than the divine revelation of teachings that were given to Moses at Mount Sinai" (p. 9). Paul's writings—because they *are* somewhat complex and subject to being misunderstood or even deliberately distorted (II Peter 3:16) —should be considered only within the framework of the Law and the Prophets. A sound, right-side-up methodology would be:

Pentateuch (Torah)
Old Testament Prophets
Writings ("Wisdom Literature")
Gospel Teachings of Jesus
Epistles of James, Peter, John, Jude
Epistles of Paul

This approach is based on the premise that God's righteous laws and commandments are *eternal*—as seen in such basic passages as Deuteronomy 5:29: "Oh, that there were such a heart in them that they would fear Me and **keep all My commandments always**, so that it might be well with them and with their children **forever**!" In Matthew 5:18, Jesus plainly stated that as long as the heaven and earth remain (which will be *forever*), no part of God's spiritual Law would ever be "done away with." Thus, Paul's writings must never be viewed as an attempt to alter, circumvent or annul God's eternal Law; rather, Paul must be seen as an expert expositor of the Law, one who is uniquely capable of revealing its finer points.

Mordechai also explains that a key reason Paul's writings are difficult to understand is that he typically employs an established scholarly style of writing based on the use of *ellipsis*—a sort of intellectual shorthand marked by the deliberate omission of words or phrases which requires the reader to make interpretive assumptions (*Galatians*, p. 49, footnote 1). This use of *ellipsis* can be found particularly in Romans chapters 10 and 14 as well as in Galatians chapters 2 and 3.

Mordechai's research validates the conclusions of Fred R. Coulter, who has also extensively studied Paul's use of the phrase "works of law." Coulter's research shows that in a few Pauline passages the phrase can refer to a basically *legalistic* approach to God's Law; in other places the phrase can point to sacrificial or Temple ritual laws. Moreover, like Mordechai, Coulter has concluded that the "works of law" passages in Galatians (as well as in several other places) can *only* refer to Pharisaic works.

In *Understanding Paul's Difficult Scriptures*, Coulter counters the popular misconception that Paul taught that God's Law has been rendered obsolete by Jesus' sacrifice. Coulter covers such topics as the "curse of the law," "works versus grace," "justification by faith," and more—proving unequivocally that the laws and commandments of God are fully in force today. He thoroughly examines the issue of "works of law"—delving even into the Greek subtleties that affect the understanding of the phrase.

In order to give clarity to the overall subject of Paul, the Law of God and Pharisaic "works-righteousness," Coulter's work is reproduced below in its entirety.

Understanding Paul's Difficult Scriptures
Concerning the Law and Commandments of God

by Fred R. Coulter

Because of a lack of knowledge concerning the first-century religion of the Pharisees (which would become Judaism), an erroneous foundational doctrine has developed in Evangelical Protestantism in which "born again" Christians are not required to keep the Law of God—especially the Sabbath and holy days as found in both the Old and New Testaments. Citing numerous "difficult-to-understand" passages from his epistles, they claim that the apostle Paul received a "superior revelation" that supersedes even the teachings of Jesus—and which gave him the authority to annul the requirement that a Christian is to keep the laws and commandments of God (which in some cases even extends to repentance and baptism).

How can that be?

In his book, *Sunday Fact & Sabbath Fiction*, Dr. Russell Tardo boldly declares, "Every bit of the law was nailed to Calvary's cross, having been completed and fulfilled in the person and life of Jesus Christ" (p. 43). Sadly, this broad assertion is widely believed by the majority of Protestants today. Pointing to Colossians 2:14-16 and similar passages, they attempt to use Scripture to justify their belief that *all* Old Testament laws were nailed to the cross—especially the Sabbath and annual festivals, and the laws of clean and unclean meats.

Because of false, convoluted misinterpretations, coupled with poor or inadequate translations of the original Greek texts of the apostle Paul's "hard-to-understand" writings—primarily those in Romans, Galatians and Colossians—Protestants typically believe that the laws and commandments of God are a curse, and unnecessary for salvation. It is claimed, therefore, that such laws were abolished by Jesus Christ—through His life, crucifixion and resurrection. But is that true? What are the correct explanations and correct translations of such difficult biblical passages?

Admittedly, some of Paul's writings are complicated and difficult to understand. Peter himself said as much. But as we will see, the problem is *not* with Paul's writings at all; the difficulty arises because some handle the Scriptures deceitfully (II Cor. 4:2), thus wrongly "dividing" the Word of God (II Tim. 2:15). Notice what Peter wrote: "And bear in mind that the longsuffering of our Lord *is* salvation, exactly as our beloved brother Paul, according to the wisdom given to him, has also written to you; as *he has* also in all *his* epistles, speaking in them concerning these things; in which are **some things** *that are* **difficult to understand, which the ignorant and unstable are twisting** *and distorting***, as** *they* **also** *twist and distort* **the rest of the Scriptures, to their own destruction**" (II Pet. 3:15-16).

Unfortunately, millions choose to believe the numerous "holier than thou" experts who twist and distort Paul's writings. Thus, they fulfill Isaiah's prophecy: "Woe unto them that are wise in their own eyes, and prudent in their own sight!... Who justify the wicked for a bribe, and take away the righteousness of the righteous from him!" (Isa. 5:21, 23).

Does this not describe the state of government and religion today? God warns that judgment will come as a result of casting aside the Law of God and replacing it with false interpretations and beliefs. Isaiah further proclaims: "Woe to those who call evil good and good evil; who put darkness for light and light for darkness; who put bitter for sweet and sweet for bitter!... Therefore as the fire devours the stubble, and the flame burns up the chaff, their root shall be like rottenness, and their blossoms shall go up like dust **because they have cast away the law of the LORD of hosts, and despised the Word of the Holy One of Israel**" (Isa. 5:20, 24).

Peter further warned that such teachers would deliberately blaspheme God and cast away the Law of the Lord through their false teachings: "But there were also false prophets among the people [of Israel], as indeed **there will be false teachers among you, who will stealthily introduce destructive heresies**, personally denying *the* Lord who bought them, and bringing swift destruction upon themselves. And **many people will follow** *as authoritative* **their destructive ways;** *and* **because of them, the way of the truth will be blasphemed**. Also, through insatiable greed they will with enticing messages exploit you for gain; for whom the judgment of old is in *full* force, and their destruction is *ever* watching" (II Pet. 2:1-3).

Is the Law of God a Curse?

This devious approach, described by Isaiah, causes most Protestants to completely misunderstand such critical passages as Galatians 3:13:

"**Christ has redeemed us from the curse of the law**, having become a curse for us [to save us from our sins] (for it is written, 'Cursed *is* everyone who hangs on a tree')." Typically, they violate this verse, **misreading** it as if it meant, "Christ has redeemed us from the law which is a curse." **Such an absurd reading is completely incorrect and without foundation—because THE LAW OF GOD IS NOT A CURSE!**

The truth is that **the perfect law of God is a wonderful blessing—not a curse!** Sin is the curse! Obedience to the laws and commandments of God results in numerous blessings (Deut. 28:1-14; Lev. 26:1-13). Sin—the transgression of the law (I John 3:4)—**results** in curses (Deut. 28:15-68; Lev. 26:13-45). Christ has not redeemed us from the law itself, but from the *curse of breaking the law*—the very curse we brought on ourselves because of our sins. He provides forgiveness and redemption through His perfect sacrifice and shed blood—redeeming us from the *death penalty*, which is the *curse* of breaking the Law. **He has not redeemed us from *keeping* the Law of God**—as if one no longer has an obligation to keep the laws and commandments of God.

The Purpose of God's Laws and Commandments: Before we can grasp what Paul actually wrote, we need to understand God's view of His own law and why He gave it to Israel and mankind. After wandering in the wilderness for forty years—because of Israel's lack of faith and their sins against God—Moses was inspired by God to write this concerning His Law: "And now, O Israel, hearken to the statutes and to the judgments which I teach you, in order to **do them, so that you may live** and go in and possess the land which the Lord God of your fathers gives to you. **You shall not add to the word which I command you; neither shall you take away from it, so that you may keep the commandments of the LORD your God which I command you**" (Deut. 4:1-2).

The children of Israel were to keep the commandments of God so that they might *live* with God's blessings. Thus, God's laws are obviously not a curse. How can Protestants possibly believe that Jesus abolished the entire Law—"nailing it to the cross"—when God commanded the children of Israel not to *add* to it or *diminish* anything from it? (Also see Deuteronomy 12:32 and similar references.)

God is a God of love. He gave His laws and commandments to be a *blessing* for Israel and a *benefit* to all mankind. "Therefore, know this day and fix it in your heart that the LORD is God in heaven above and on the earth beneath. There is none other. Therefore, you shall keep His statutes and His commandments which I command you this day, so **that it may go well with you** and with your children after you, and so **that you may prolong your days upon the earth**, which the LORD your God gives you forever.... And you shall be **careful** to do as the LORD your God has commanded you. You shall not turn aside to the right hand or to the left. You shall walk in all the ways which the LORD your God has commanded you **so that you may live** and that **it may be well with you**, and **you may prolong your days** in the land which you shall possess.

"Now these are the commandments, the statutes, and the judgments which the LORD our God commanded to teach you so that you might do them in the land where you go to possess it, that you might fear the LORD your God, to **keep all His statutes and His commandments** which I command you, you, and your son, and your son's son, **all the days of your life**, and **so that your days may be prolonged. Hear therefore, O Israel, and be diligent to observe it, so that it may be well with you**, and that you may greatly multiply, as the LORD God of our fathers has promised you, in the land that flows with milk and honey" (Deut. 4:39-40; 5:32-33; 6:1-3).

With these Scriptures in mind, we need to ask: What is a converted person's attitude toward the laws and commandments of God? Does the Lawgiver reject, despise, ridicule and abrogate His own laws? Absolutely not! Since truly converted people have the laws and commandments written in their hearts and minds (Heb. 10:16), they will love God's laws, think on them and live by them in the spirit of the Law (Rom. 7:6), as did King David. Notice his attitude toward the laws and commandments of God which he exalted and praised as perfect: "**The law of the LORD is perfect**, restoring the soul; the testimony of the LORD is sure, making wise the simple. The precepts of the LORD are right, rejoicing the heart: **the commandments of the LORD are pure**, enlightening the eyes. The fear of the LORD is clean, enduring forever; the judgments of the LORD are true and righteous altogether, more to be desired than gold, yea, much fine gold; sweeter also than honey and the honeycomb.

"**Moreover, by them Your servant is warned; in keeping them there is great reward**. Who can understand his errors? Oh, cleanse me from my secret faults; and keep back Your servant also from presumptuous sins; do not let them rule over me; then I shall be blameless, and I shall be innocent of great transgression" (Psa. 19:7-13).

David never once called the Law a curse! He fully understood that God gave His laws to mankind to **define** righteousness and sin. If we obey, the Law is not a curse, but a blessing. If we disobey, we bring the curse of the Law upon ourselves because of our own disobedience.

We also find much spiritual understanding about God's laws and commandments in Psalm 119. Notice the following key verses:

Psa. 119:142   "Your righteousness is an everlasting righteousness, and **Your law is the truth**."

Psa. 119:151   "**All Your commandments are truth**."

Psa. 119:160   "**Your word is true** from the beginning."

Psa. 119:172   "**All Your commandments are righteousness**."

Psa. 119:97   "**O how love I Your law**! It is my meditation all the day."

Psa. 119:113   "I hate those who are double-minded, but **Your law do I love**."

Psa. 119:119   "You destroy all the wicked of the earth like dross; therefore **I love Your testimonies**.

Psa. 119:127 "Therefore **I love Your commandments above gold**—yea, above fine gold.

Psa. 119:140 "**Your word is very pure; therefore Your servant loves it**."

Psa. 119:159 "Consider how **I love Your precepts**; O Lord, according to Your lovingkindness give me life."

Psa. 119:163 "I hate and despise lying, **but I love Your law**."

Psa. 119:167 "My soul has kept Your testimonies, and **I love them exceedingly**."

David's solemn, converted attitude of love toward God and His laws—as evidenced throughout Psalm 119—is undoubtedly prophetic of Jesus Christ's attitude and **love** of God's laws and commandments which He had during His ministry in the flesh when He "magnified the law and made it glorious" (see Isaiah 42:21) revealing its spiritual intent and purpose. An in-depth study of the entirety of Psalm 119 should be undertaken by the reader for a more comprehensive understanding of the laws and commandments of God.

Quoting Scripture, Jesus expounded on the greatest commandment of all: " 'You shall love *the* Lord your God with all your heart, and with all your soul, and with all your mind.' **This is *the* first and greatest commandment**; and *the* second *one is* like it: 'You shall love your neighbor as yourself.' **On these two commandments hang all the Law and the Prophets**" (Matt. 22:37-40). Reflecting on what Jesus said, the apostle John wrote that love and commandment-keeping go together like a hand and glove: "By this *standard* we know that we love the children of God: when we love God and keep His commandments. For this is the love of God: that we keep His commandments; and His commandments are not burdensome" (I John 5:2-3).

Jesus Christ Did Not Abolish the Law

Why do so many people—especially religious leaders—have so much defiant contempt for the laws and commandments of God? Paul gives the answer: "Because the carnal mind *is* enmity against God, for it is not subject to the law of God; neither indeed can it *be*" (Rom. 8:7). Lawless minds do not like to be constricted or constrained by "law." It "cramps" their style of living, exactly as Proverbs says: "All the ways of a man are clean in his own eyes.... **There is a way that seems right to a man, but the end thereof is the way of death**" (Prov. 16:2, 25). Satan desires that "his children" be "happy" in their rebellious behavior—hence, lawless generations.

On the other hand, when we understand these Scriptures and the fact that "all the Law and the Prophets" are under-girded by the love of God, how can anyone possibly believe that Jesus came to abolish the Law? What did

Jesus Himself proclaim concerning "the Law and the Prophets"? He emphatically declared, "**Do not think that I have come to abolish the Law or the Prophets**; I did not come to abolish, but to fulfill. For truly I say to you, **until the heaven and the earth shall pass away, one jot or one tittle shall in no way pass from the Law** until everything has been fulfilled" (Matt. 5:17-18).

As Jesus said, we are not even to think, or suppose—let alone teach in His name—that He came to abolish the Law or the Prophets! Furthermore, He established the heavens and earth as perpetual witnesses that the laws of God will not pass away—not even one seemingly insignificant *jot* or *tittle*! **Therefore, since heaven and earth still exist, Jesus has not abolished the Law or the Prophets**! Perfection is timeless.

Before Jesus came in the flesh, born of the virgin Mary, He was the Lord God of the Old Testament. He was the One Who spoke the Ten Commandments to Israel. Jesus is the Lawgiver in both the Old and New Testaments.

Indeed, when Jesus defeated Satan the devil during His temptation in the wilderness, He clearly stated, "It is written [in the Law], 'Man shall not live by bread alone, but **by every word** that proceeds out of *the* mouth of God' " (Matt. 4:4; Luke 4:4; Deut. 8:3).

Compare those words of Jesus to this ignorant statement: "The law is a unit of 613 commandments and all of it has been invalidated…. It has ceased to function as an authority over individuals" (*Sunday fact & Sabbath Fiction*, Dr. Russell Tardo, p. 31).

If the law was abolished, there would be no sin, because as Paul wrote, "[W]here no law is, *there is* no transgression" (Rom. 4:15). Likewise, if there is no transgression, the penalty for sin or the need for forgiveness vanishes. Consequently, there would be no need for a Savior, and Jesus would have died in vain. Ultimately, such anti-law reasoning leads to the conclusion that man is completely sufficient unto himself, which is nothing less than satanic humanism—the end result of *lawless* grace.

Notice what Jesus said about those who teach others to break even the "least" of God's commandments: "Therefore, whoever shall break one of these least commandments, **and shall teach men so**, shall be called least in the kingdom of heaven; but whoever shall practice and teach *them*, this one shall be called great in the kingdom of heaven" (Matt. 5:19).

Christ continued: "For I say to you, unless your righteousness shall exceed *the righteousness* of the scribes and Pharisees, there is no way *that* you shall enter into the kingdom of heaven" (Matt. 5:20). Jesus' statement here is enigmatic to say the least, since the scribes and Pharisees were *well known* for their "righteousness." Yet, the Pharisees' "righteousness" was derived not from the laws and commandments of God, but from their *own* traditions and laws as found in the codes of Jewish law. Jesus denounced the scribes and Pharisees for keeping their *own* laws and commandments— which were actually *contrary* to the laws and commandments of God: "Well did Isaiah prophesy concerning you hypocrites, as it is written, 'This people honors Me with their lips, but their hearts are far away from Me. **But in vain do they worship Me, teaching *for* doctrine the commandments of men.' For leaving the commandment of God, you hold fast the tradition of men**, *such as* the washing of pots and cups; and you practice many other things like *this*." Then He said to them, "**Full well do you reject the commandment of God, so that you may observe your *own* tradition**.... **[Thus you are guilty of] nullifying the authority of the Word of God by your tradition which you have passed down; and you practice many *traditions* such as this**" (Mark 7:6-8, 9, 13).

Here, Jesus is making it clear that we are not to follow in the footsteps of the Jewish religious leaders, but to walk in God's way as taught by Jesus Christ Himself. Indeed, this is how one's righteousness can *exceed* that of the scribes and Pharisees.

The key is understanding how Jesus "fulfilled" the Law (Matt. 5:17). To "fulfill" means "to fill to the full" or "to make complete." That is quite the *opposite* of abolishing the Law. **Indeed, Jesus "fulfilled" the Law by revealing its spiritual meaning and application in human behavior**—in how humans relate to one another and to God the Father and Jesus Christ. The scribes and Pharisees thought they were quite adept at keeping the letter of the Law—but in their corrupt hypocrisy they completely missed the spirit and intent of the Law.

The Gospels reveal that Jesus focused on the spirit of the law throughout His ministry. As evidenced in Matthew 5-7, Jesus specifically established this new spiritual standard of the application of the spirit of the Law for New Testament Christians, as compared to the letter of the Law required under the Old Testament.

Two examples are sufficient to show how Jesus "fulfilled" the Law by revealing its deep spiritual meaning: "You have heard that it was said to those *in* ancient *times*, 'You shall not commit murder; but whoever commits murder shall be subject to judgment.' But I say to you, everyone who is angry with his brother without cause shall be subject to judgment. Now *you have heard it said*, 'Whoever shall say to his brother, "Raca," shall be subject to *the judgment of* the council.' But *I say to you*, whoever shall say, '*You* fool,' shall be subject to the fire of Gehenna" (Matt. 5:21-22).

"You have heard that it was said to those *in* ancient *times*, 'You shall not commit adultery.' But I say to you, everyone who looks upon a woman to lust after her has already committed adultery with her in his heart" (Matt. 5:27-28).

These examples clearly illustrate the spiritual application of the laws and commandments of God as taught by Jesus Christ and found throughout the New Testament.

Over ten years after Jesus' death and resurrection, the apostle James, the "brother of the Lord," defined the true Christian approach to the Law of God, which he calls the "**Royal Law**." Notice how his writings agree exactly with Jesus' teachings in Matthew 5-7: "If you are truly keeping *the*

Royal Law according to the scripture, 'You shall love your neighbor as yourself,' you are doing well. But if you have respect of persons, you are practicing sin, being convicted by the law as transgressors; **for *if* anyone keeps the whole law, but sins in one *aspect*, he becomes guilty of all**.

"For He Who said, 'You shall not commit adultery,' also said, 'You shall not commit murder.' Now if you do not commit adultery, but you commit murder, you have become a transgressor of *the* law. In this manner speak and in this manner behave: as those who are about to be judged by *the* law of freedom" (James 2:8-12).

Finally, notice how God praised Abraham's faithful obedience when He passed the covenant promises on to Isaac: "And I will multiply your seed as the stars of the heavens and will give to your seed all these lands. And in your seed shall all the nations of the earth be blessed, because **Abraham obeyed My voice and kept My charge, My commandments, My statutes, and My laws**" (Gen. 26:4-5). Abraham is not only the father of Isaac and Jacob and the children of Israel in the Old Testament, He is also called the father of the New Testament faithful: "And if you *are* Christ's, then you are Abraham's seed, and heirs according to *the* promise" (Gal. 3:29). This means that if we are truly Christ's, then we will do as Abraham did. We will obey the voice of God, keep His charge, His commandments, His statutes and His laws. We will never believe that Jesus did away with the Law—or called the Law a curse.

Paul's Easy-to-Understand Scriptures

Before going on to examine Paul's more difficult writings, it is prudent that we first look at his easy-to-understand Scriptures—which unmistakably demonstrate Paul's attitude toward the Law of God. For example, he wrote the following to the Corinthians: "*For* circumcision is nothing, and uncircumcision is nothing; rather, **the keeping of God's commandments *is essential*"** (I Cor. 7:19). He further explained how he reached out to everyone, Jew and Gentile alike, in preaching the gospel. **But never at any time did he proclaim that the laws and commandments of God were no longer in effect for himself or the believer**: "Now to the Jews I became as a Jew, that I might gain *the* Jews; to those who are under law, as under law, that I might gain those who are under law; to those who are without law, as without law (**not being without law to God, but within law to Christ**), that I might gain those who are without law" (I Cor. 9:20-21).

Later, after Paul was brought from Jerusalem to Caesarea to stand trial, he stood and defended himself before the Jewish authorities and Felix the governor emphatically declaring that as an apostle of Jesus Christ he believed *all things* written in the Law and the Prophets: "Neither can they prove *the things* of which they now accuse me [abolishing the laws and commandments of God]. But I confess to you that according to the way which they call heresy [his teachings that Jesus was the Messiah, the Savior of mankind], **so serve I the God of my fathers, believing all things that are written in the Law and the Prophets**" (Acts 24:13-14). Paul also declared, "Therefore, the law *is* indeed holy, and the commandment holy and righteous and good" (Rom. 7:12).

Because a true believer is indeed justified by faith, Paul also answered those who believed in a "lawless grace" and claimed that justification through Christ's sacrifice eliminated the need to keep the laws and commandments of God. Notice what Paul wrote: "Since *it is* indeed one God Who will justify *the* circumcision by faith, and *the* uncircumcision through faith. Are we, then, abolishing law through faith? MAY IT NEVER BE! Rather, **we are establishing law**" (Rom. 3:30-31).

Far from having received some "greater revelation" that supersedes Christ's teachings, Paul's statement here is in full harmony with what Jesus taught: "**Do not think that I have come to abolish the Law or the Prophets.**" Under the New Covenant, true believers will lovingly obey Jesus Christ and God the Father from the heart. Notice Jesus' teachings concerning commandment-keeping—teachings which Evangelical Protestantism conveniently ignores: "**If you love Me, keep the commandments**— namely, My commandments.... The one who has My commandments and **is keeping them**, that is the one who loves Me; and the one who loves Me shall be loved by My Father, and I will love him and will manifest Myself to him.... If anyone loves Me, he will **keep My word**; and My Father will love him, and We will come to him and make Our abode with him. **The one who does not love Me does not keep My words; and the word that you hear is not Mine, but the Father's, Who sent Me**" (John 14:15, 21, 23-24). Notice that Jesus does not say that commandment-keeping is for the Jews only—but that it is required of everyone.

Through the Holy Spirit of God—which God gives to those who obey Him (Acts 5:32)—the Law is not abolished, but *established* by love and grace so that the laws and commandments can be written into one's heart and mind. The New Covenant is not for Israel and Judah alone, but is for all converts: " 'This *is* the covenant that I will establish with them after those days,' says *the* Lord: 'I will give My laws into their hearts, and I will inscribe them in their minds; and their sins and lawlessness I will not remember ever again.' Now where remission of these *is*, *it is* no longer *necessary to offer* [animal] sacrifices [at the Temple] for [the justification of] sin" (Heb. 10:16-18). As we will see, at the heart of the controversy over the Law is this: **Does justification come by rituals and works, or by faith through grace**?

Christ was raised from the dead so that we may be justified by faith through grace and put into **right standing** with God the Father. Paul shows that faith *and* belief are required for God to impute righteousness to us: "And he [Abraham] was fully persuaded that what He had promised, He is also able to do. As a result, **it was also imputed to him for righteousness**. But it was not written for his sake alone, that it was imputed to him; rather, *it was* also *written* for our sake, to whom it shall be imputed—**to those who believe in Him Who raised Jesus our Lord from the dead, Who was delivered for our offenses, and WAS RAISED FOR OUR JUSTIFICATION**" (Rom. 4:21-25).

Once we have been justified to God the Father—through the death and resurrection of Christ, having our sins forgiven by faith in Jesus—we are under the grace of God. Let us understand the true meaning of "grace."

Grace as defined in the New Testament comes from the Greek word *charis*, which means "favor, grace, gracious help or care, goodwill, the gracious intention of God or gift; the practical application of goodwill, a favor, gracious deed or benefaction, a store of grace, a state of grace, a deed of grace and a work of grace; to be grateful, gratitude or thanks." Moreover, grace denotes **the state of the relationship** between God and the believer through Jesus Christ. When Paul uses the word "grace" as part of an opening greeting or closing salutation, it is used to confer "divine grace" upon the one who is reading the Epistle.

Grace is the free and undeserved gift of God the Father through Jesus Christ. The grace of God is the greatest expression of God the Father's love and all-encompassing mercy. Grace is more than the forgiveness of sins. To be "**under grace**" means to *continually* be receiving God's divine love, favor, blessing, gracious care, help, goodwill, benefits, gifts and goodness. God the Father is the source from which grace comes to the believer. Furthermore, the ONLY MEANS by which grace is granted to the believer is through the birth, life, death and resurrection of Jesus Christ as the perfect sacrifice of God the Father. The believer enters into the grace of God through faith in the sacrifice of Jesus Christ for the forgiveness of his or her sins. God the Father grants His grace to each believer upon repentance of sins and baptism by immersion, which is our "covenant death" into Christ's death and is the outward manifestation of our repentance. Through grace, the believer's sins are forgiven and the righteousness of Jesus Christ is imputed to him or her.

Grace establishes a **new spiritual relationship** between the believer and God the Father and Jesus Christ. Through the unearned and unmerited gift of grace, the believer is not only called, chosen, forgiven and accepted by God the Father through His Beloved, but is also begotten with the Holy Spirit, making him or her a child of God and an heir of eternal life. From this point forward, the spiritually begotten believer begins a new life under grace. As the Scriptures reveal, living under grace requires the believer to **live by every Word of God** with complete love and devotion to God the Father and Jesus Christ. **Grace does not grant one license to practice sin by ignoring or rejecting the commandments of God**. Only those who keep His commandments can abide in His love and remain under His grace. Every believer who receives the grace of God has a personal obligation to God the Father and Jesus Christ to forsake his or her old, sinful thoughts and practices and to **live a new life, daily growing in the grace and knowledge**

of Jesus Christ. For every believer who lives under grace, Jesus Christ acts as Redeemer, High Priest and Advocate. If a Christian commits a sin, then Jesus—upon the believer's repentance—intercedes before the Father to obtain His mercy and grace, thus becoming the propitiation for such sins.

Far from abolishing the laws and commandments of God, this personal relationship between God the Father, Jesus Christ and the true believer *establishes* the Law through love and obedience.

In summary, there are *five keys* to understanding how we are to obey the spiritual intent God's laws and commandments under the New Covenant as magnified by Jesus Christ and taught in the New Testament:

1. One must have the Holy Spirit. This comes by repentance, baptism by full immersion in water and the laying on of hands to receive the impregnation of the Holy Spirit from God the Father into the spirit of one's mind. This is called circumcision of the heart (Rom. 2:28-29).

2. Through the power of the Holy Spirit, God writes His laws into one's heart and mind: " 'This *is* the covenant that I will establish with them after those days,' says *the* Lord: 'I will give My laws into their hearts, and I will inscribe them in their minds' " (Heb. 10:16). This is what Paul meant when he wrote: **"Are we, then, abolishing law through faith? MAY IT NEVER BE! Rather, we are establishing law"** (Rom. 3:31).

3. Since it is through faith and the grace of God that we are establishing law—by having them written in our hearts and minds by the power of the Holy Spirit—we are to no longer live in sin. Sin is the transgression of the Law (I John 3:4). Paul made this perfectly clear. "What then shall we say? Shall we continue in sin, so that grace may abound? MAY IT NEVER BE! We who died to sin, how shall we live any longer therein? Or are you ignorant that we, as many as were baptized into Christ Jesus, were baptized into His death?" (Rom. 6:1-3).

4. This means one will obey in the *spirit* of the Law and not in the letter of the law only, as Paul wrote, "so that we might serve in the newness of the spirit and not in *the* oldness of *the* letter" (Rom. 7:6).

5. Under the New Covenant, obedience to the laws and commandments of God is part of the operation of the *grace* of God that leads to eternal salvation.

With this background we can now begin to understand the true meaning of Paul's difficult Scriptures. We will first examine the seventh-day Sabbath question, because it is at the heart and core of the dilemma of understanding Paul's difficult passages. Our study will begin by looking at Paul's teaching concerning Sabbath-keeping in Hebrews 4:9.

The True Meaning of *Sabbatismos* in Hebrews 4:9

"There remaineth therefore a **rest** to the people of God" (Heb. 4:9, *King James Version*). As we will see, this is an incorrect translation, rooted in Orthodox bias against the holy Sabbath day of God.

Because of this erroneous translation—due largely to Protestant hostility against the seventh-day Sabbath and their preference for Sunday—this verse is almost universally misinterpreted and misunderstood. In fact, the true meaning of Hebrews 4:9 is the *very opposite* of the false interpretation assumed and taught by many churches, ministers and theologians.

Today, mainstream "Christianity" teaches that Christians are no longer required to observe the seventh-day Sabbath. They misconstrue Hebrews 4:9 to mean that Christ has given them "rest" (or, as some say, a "release") from commandment-keeping. This false claim feeds the premise that Jesus has "fulfilled the law" *for* them. As a result, people are told, the Christian has entered into a "spiritual rest" from sin, and that Jesus Himself is their "spiritual Sabbath," because Jesus kept the Sabbath in their stead.

Such absurd reasoning is completely contrary to the Word of God. Jesus Himself said that He did not come to abolish or "do away with" the laws and commandments of God (Matt. 5:17-18). Nor did He fulfill any commandment in order to release Christians from their obligation to keep God's laws. Indeed, He set the perfect example for us to *free us* from committing sin, which is the transgression of the Law (I Pet. 2:21-22; I John 3:4). Jesus did not come to keep the commandments *in our stead*. Years into his ministry, the apostle Paul said that he was still *zealous* for the laws of God (Acts 22:3)—which would certainly include the Sabbath commandment.

When we understand and absorb the full meaning of the Greek text of Hebrews 4:9, there is no question that the New Testament upholds the authority of the Fourth Commandment. The Greek word used here for "rest" is *sabbatismos*, which means "Sabbath rest, Sabbath observance" (Arndt and Gingrich, *A Greek-English Lexicon of the New Testament*).

This definition is confirmed by other historical works: "The words 'sabbath rest' are from the [Greek] noun *sabbatismos*, [which is] a unique word in the NT. This term appears also in Plutarch (*Superset. 3 [Moralia 166a]*) for sabbath observance, and in four post-canonical Christian writings which are not dependent on Heb. 4:9" (*The Anchor Bible Dictionary*, Vol. 5, p. 856). This is historical evidence that *true* Christians continued observing the seventh-day Sabbath long after Emperor Constantine declared in 325 AD that Sunday was the "Christian" day of worship.

While *sabbatismos* is a noun, the verb form of the word is *sabbatizo*, which means, "to keep the Sabbath" (*A Greek-English Lexicon of the New Testament*). This definition of *sabbatizo* is confirmed by its use in the Septuagint, a Greek translation of the Old Testament dating from the third century BC. Jews used the Septuagint in synagogues throughout the Roman Empire; Greek-speaking Jewish and Gentile converts to Christianity used this translation throughout the early New Testament period. This is why the apostle Paul quotes extensively from the Septuagint in his epistle to the Hebrews, which went to all the true churches of God—Jew and Gentile.

When Paul used *sabbatismos* in Hebrews 4:9, he did so knowing that its meaning was **well known** to the Greek-speaking believers of that day. After all, its verb form (*sabbatizo*) is widely employed in the Septuagint—which, as a translation, was as familiar to the Greek-speaking Jews and Gentiles of the early Church as the King James Bible is to Christians today.

For example, the use of the verb *sabbatizo* in Leviticus 23:32 in the Septuagint substantiates its meaning. *The Greek English Lexicon of the Septuagint* defines *sabbatizo* as "to keep [a] sabbath, to rest" (Lust, Eynikel, Hauspie). The English translation of this verse in the Septuagint reads: "It [the Day of Atonement] shall be a holy sabbath [literally, a Sabbath of Sabbaths] to you; and ye shall humble your souls, from the ninth day of the month: from evening to evening **shall ye keep your sabbaths**" (*The Septuagint With the Apocrypha*, Brenton).

The phrase "shall ye keep your sabbaths" is translated from the Greek, *sabbatieite ta sabbata*—which literally means, "you shall. **sabbathize** the Sabbaths." The form of the Greek verb *sabbatizo* is the second person plural *sabbatieite*, which means, "you **all** shall keep"—meaning *everyone* is to keep the Sabbath. Throughout the entire Septuagint, the verb *sabbatizo* is never used except in relation to Sabbath-keeping. Understanding this definition, the *KJV* translators translated *sabbatieite* as "shall ye celebrate your sabbath." However, they deliberately did not likewise translate *sabbatismos* in Hebrews 4:9—because of their Sunday-keeping bias in following the lead of the Roman Catholic Church.

There is no question that the Greek verb *sabbatizo* in Leviticus 23:32 is specifically referring to Sabbath observance. This meaning equally applies to the noun form *sabbatismos* as used by Paul. Thus, the continuity of the Septuagint's use of *sabbatizo* and the use of *sabbatismos* in Hebrews 4:9 confirms that Paul was upholding the observance of the seventh-day Sabbath for all true Christians.

The use of *sabbatismos* in Hebrews 4:9 directly contradicts any false teaching that the Fourth Commandment has been abolished. As the context of Hebrews 4 demonstrates, the observance of the seventh-day Sabbath as a day of rest and worship is as literally binding for the people of God today as it was since creation, or in the days of King David, or for Israel of old.

It becomes clear that Hebrews 4:9 does not mean that Christians have entered into some sort of "spiritual rest" which exempts them from their obligation to keep the Sabbath, or any other commandment of God. Rather, this verse must be taken as *instructive*—that Christians are indeed commanded to keep the Sabbath day. Consequently—in accordance with the original Greek—this verse should be translated: "**There remains,**

therefore, Sabbath-keeping for the people of God"—Jew and Gentile alike.

The *true* meaning of Hebrews 4:9 is diametrically *opposite* the false misinterpretation of Orthodox Christendom. Paul is emphatically declaring that Sabbath-keeping—and this means the annual holy day Sabbaths as well—is *required* for true Christians. He is not "spiritualizing away" or eliminating the weekly Sabbath or the annual Sabbaths of God.

The True Meaning of Galatians 4:8-10—
Did the Apostle Paul Abolish the Sabbath and Holy Days?

Orthodox Christianity views God's weekly Sabbath, annual feasts and holy days with considerable disdain. In their determination to retain their "Christianized" pagan Sunday and occult holiday worship, religious leaders and theologians have blindly and deliberately misinterpreted the writings of the apostle Paul to suit their own agendas, rather than seeking the "truth of God's Word." These misleading interpretations are designed to give the impression that Paul had taught Gentile Christians to abandon the biblical Sabbath and holy days of God—to reject anything "Jewish." To such religious leaders and theologians, "Jewish" means the *entire* Old Testament, viewed as the embodiment of Judaism. According to their way of thinking, the Old Testament is to be fully rejected or dismissed as though it had been entirely fulfilled or abolished. As a result, millions of professing "Christians" assume that in Galatians 4:8-10 Paul denounced any observance of God's Sabbath and holy days as "heretical"!

There is no question that Paul taught both Jews and Gentiles to observe the weekly Sabbath, as evidenced by the correct translation of Hebrews 4:9: "There remains, therefore, Sabbath-keeping for the people of God." Furthermore, when we examine Paul's ministry to the Gentiles, we find that **he taught them on the Sabbath day**, not on Sunday. At the beginning of his first evangelistic tour, Paul and Barnabas began preaching to the Jews and the Gentile proselytes **on the Sabbath day** in a synagogue in Antioch of Pisidia, in Asia Minor. After preaching the Gospel of Jesus Christ, His resurrection and the forgiveness of sins, Paul warned his listeners not to reject the words of God: " 'Therefore, be it known to you, men *and* brethren, that through this man *the* **remission of sins** is preached to you. And in Him everyone who believes is justified from all things, from which you could not be justified by the Law of Moses.

" 'Take heed, therefore, lest that which is spoken in the Prophets come upon you: "Behold, you despisers, and wonder and perish; for I work a work in your days, a work that you will in no way believe, *even* if one declares it to you." ' **And when the Jews had gone out of the synagogue, the Gentiles entreated *him* that these words might be spoken to them on the next Sabbath**. Now after the synagogue had been dismissed, many of the Jews and the [Gentile] proselytes who worshiped *there* followed Paul and Barnabas, who, speaking to them, **persuaded them to continue in the grace of God. And on the coming Sabbath, almost the whole city was**

gathered together to hear the Word of God" (Acts 13:38-44).

From this account we learn several fundamental truths about Paul's teaching of the Gospel of Jesus Christ.

1) If Paul's fundamental purpose was to teach Gentiles that they no longer needed to keep the laws and commandments of God—especially the Sabbath and holy days—why did he not simply encourage them to assemble on the next day, Sunday? Rather, **they assembled on the next Sabbath** to hear Paul and Barnabas preach the wonderful words of God.

2) Paul told them to "continue in the grace of God," which is not a repudiation of the laws and commandments of God. Grace is the operation of God to forgive sins, and put one in right standing—justified—through the blood of Jesus Christ from **past** sins. On the other hand, sin is the transgression of the Law (I John 3:4). Once forgiven and justified, one is to cease living in sin (John 5:14; 8:11; Rom. 6:1).

3) Faith in Jesus Christ and forgiveness of sin does not abolish the law. Paul wrote to the Romans, a Gentile church, "Are we, then, abolishing law through faith? MAY IT NEVER BE! Rather, **we are establishing law**" (Rom. 3:31; see Matt, 5:17). This is accomplished as true Christians have the laws and commandments written into their hearts and minds (Heb. 10:16-17). Paul also taught, "What then shall we say? Shall we continue in sin, so that grace may abound? MAY IT NEVER BE! **We who died to sin, how shall we live any longer therein**?" (Rom. 6:1-2).

4) This is a perfect example of how Sabbath-keeping and the grace of God go hand-in-hand. They are not opposed to one another. The Gentiles continued in the grace of God and met on the next Sabbath.

The Gospel of Paul and Galatians: The Gospel of Jesus Christ that Paul taught to the Galatians included keeping the laws and commandments of God. Following Jesus' example and teachings, Paul never sanctioned or endorsed the religions or laws and commandments of men—Jewish or Gentile (Mark 7:1-13; Acts 17:22-31). Neither did he teach a lawless grace. Rather, he taught that *all* had to forsake their ways, repent of their sins and keep the laws and commandments of God, and worship Him in spirit and in truth (Acts 17:30; Rom. 7:6; John 4:23-24).

In combating those who were teaching a different gospel, Paul proclaimed in the opening of his epistle to the Galatians that He preached the *true* Gospel of Jesus Christ—the same one that Jesus taught! Because of such false teachers, Paul emphatically wrote, "I am astonished that you are so quickly being turned away from Him Who called you into *the* grace of Christ, to a different gospel, which *in reality* is not another *gospel*; but there are some **who are troubling you** and are desiring to pervert the Gospel of Christ. But if we, or even an angel from heaven, should preach a gospel to you that is contrary to what we have preached, LET HIM BE ACCURSED! As we have said before, I also now say again. If anyone is preaching a gospel contrary to what you have received, LET HIM BE ACCURSED!

"Now then, am I striving to please men, or God? Or am I motivated to please men? For if I am yet pleasing men, I would not be a servant of Christ. But I certify to you, brethren, that the gospel that was preached by me is not according to man; because neither did I receive it from man, nor was I taught *it by man*; rather, *it was* by *the* revelation of Jesus Christ" (Gal. 1:6-12). If Paul had preached a gospel as distorted by theologians, past and present, he would have indeed been teaching *another* gospel.

In fact, the book of Galatians is one of the most universally misinterpreted and misconstrued books of the New Testament. While it is beyond the scope of this article to give a complete commentary on Paul's epistle to the Galatians, there are four pressing problems in Galatians Two and Three which should be addressed:

First, the Jews had imposed specific circumcision requirements—before the advent of Christianity—upon Gentile proselytes in order for them to attend a synagogue. Jesus, however, revealed that *true* circumcision was spiritual, accomplished through conversion and the receiving of the Holy Spirit. This circumcision "of the heart" superseded the requirement for physical circumcision (Acts 15; Rom. 2:25-29). Therefore, physical circumcision was no longer a requirement imposed upon Gentile converts to Christianity.

Second, Paul's rebuke of Peter, Barnabas, and the circumcision party from Jerusalem centered around *traditional* laws of Judaism which forbade Jews from keeping company with or eating with Gentiles. This instance was not a question concerning God's laws and commandments, because the Old Testament never commanded such separation of Jews and Gentiles.

Third—in reference to "the law" in Galatians Three—Paul was comparing God's covenant with Abraham and New Covenant justification by faith through grace *to* the "works of law" required under Judaism and its Temple rituals.

Fourth, in Galatians Three, most Protestants completely misunderstand verse 13, which reads, "**Christ has redeemed us from the curse of the law**, having become a curse for us [to save us from our sins] (for it is written, 'Cursed *is* everyone who hangs on a tree')." They *misread* it as follows: "**Christ has redeemed us from the law which is a curse**." **Such a reading is totally absurd and completely incorrect because THE LAW OF GOD IS NOT A CURSE!**

Without a thorough grounding in the Scriptures—Old and New Testament—the true laws and commandments of God, a knowledge of the oral traditional laws of Judaism, God's covenant with Abraham, God's covenant with Israel, and, finally, the New Covenant of the New Testament, it is not feasible to properly interpret Paul's epistle to the Galatians. This is why it is undoubtedly the most difficult book of the New Testament to comprehend.

As we have seen, the truth of the matter is that **the Law of God is perfect—not a curse!** *Sin* is a curse! Obedience to the laws and commandments of God results in blessings! (Deut. 28:1-14; Lev. 26:1-13). Sin—the transgression of the Law (I John 3:4)—*results* in curses (Deut. 28:15-68; Lev. 26:13-45).

How can a law that is perfect and righteous—given by a perfect, righteous God—be a curse? The point needs to be considered that *if* the Law is a curse, and the Law has been abolished, then it would mean that God Himself is a curse and has abolished Himself. But such is not the case, because God is love, Lawgiver and Sustainer, and Jesus Christ is upholding the entirety of the universe through *Law*—by the Word of His power (Heb. 1:1-3). Indeed, such religious interpretations and fantasies have produced a lawless grace that pervades Evangelical Christianity today.

Finally, notice that God praised Abraham's faithful obedience when He passed the covenant promises on to Isaac: "And I will multiply your seed as the stars of the heavens and will give to your seed all these lands. And in your seed shall all the nations of the earth be blessed, **because Abraham obeyed My voice and kept My charge, My commandments, My statutes, and My laws**" (Gen. 26:4-5). Abraham is the father of the New Testament faithful as well: "And if you *are* Christ's, then you are Abraham's seed, and heirs according to *the* promise" (Gal. 3:29). This means that if we are truly Christ's, then we will obey the voice of God, keep His charge, His commandments, His statutes and His laws, as Abraham did. We will never believe that Jesus did away with the Law, nor call the Law a curse.

Galatians 4:8-10—The Background

In order to determine the correct meaning of Galatians 4:8-10, we need to realize first that the churches of Galatia were composed mainly of Gentile converts who, as former pagans, had served Greek and Asian gods and goddesses. They were not Jews, and had never followed the traditional practices of Judaism or the Old Testament Scriptures.

Moreover, Galatians Four must be considered in the overall context of *all* of Paul's teachings in *all* of his fourteen epistles. Without a doubt, Paul taught all Gentile converts in every church he established to observe the same things (I Cor. 7:17). As we carefully examine what he wrote, it will become clear that Paul did not condemn the Galatians for observing the Sabbath and holy days of God as most theologians and Sunday churchgoers casually assume.

In Paul's epistle to the Corinthians, he made it crystal clear that the things he wrote to them were the commandments of the Lord: "WHAT? Did the Word of God originate with you? Or did it come only to you *and no one else*? **If anyone thinks that he is a prophet or spiritual, let him acknowledge that the things I write to you are commandments of the Lord**. But if anyone *chooses* to be ignorant, let him be ignorant" (I Cor. 14:36-38).

What did Paul command them to observe? Was it Sunday and other pagan, occult holidays—or was it the Sabbath and God's Passover and feasts? This is profoundly important because what Paul wrote were "the commandments of the Lord" for the New Testament Church—Jews and Gentiles. While Paul condemned their sins, he commanded the Corinthians—and thus the entire Church—to **keep the Passover and the Feast of Unleavened Bread** in the right spirit and attitude: "Your glorying [in sin] *is* not good. Don't you know that a little leaven [a type of sin] leavens the whole lump? Therefore, purge out the old leaven [the old sinful ways], so that you may become a new lump [truly converted in Christ], *even* as you are unleavened [in your homes]. **For Christ our Passover was sacrificed for us. For this reason, LET US KEEP THE FEAST**, not with old leaven, nor with *the* leaven of malice and wickedness, but with *the* unleavened *bread* of sincerity and truth" (I Cor. 5:6-8).

The church in Corinth was also mostly Gentile. Paul would never have commanded them to observe Passover and Unleavened Bread and then condemn the churches of Galatia for observing God's Sabbath and feasts! That would only be construed as hypocrisy and create confusion. God is not hypercritical, nor is He the author of confusion (I Cor. 14:33).

Those who accept the false premise that Paul taught *against* the Sabbath and holy days of God—and that he instead taught the churches to observe Christianized pagan Sunday and occult holidays in their place—fail to realize that before any of the Galatian Gentiles were converted, **they worshiped pagan gods and observed occult holidays** ("days, months, times and years"). However, **upon conversion, they repented of their sins and forsook all their pagan occult religious practices** (Acts 19:8-27).

Interwoven throughout the Scriptures, God condemns all pagan, occult practices. Notice particularly God's warnings in Deuteronomy: "**Be careful to observe and obey all these words which I command you, so that it may go well with you** and with your children after you forever when you do *that which is* good and right in the sight of the LORD your God. When the LORD your God shall cut off the nations before you, where you go to possess them, and you take their place and dwell in their land, **take heed to yourself that you do not become ensnared by following them, after they are destroyed from before you, and that you do not ask about their gods, saying, 'How did these nations serve their gods that I may also do likewise?' You shall not do so to the LORD your God, for every abomination to the LORD, which He hates, they have done to their gods; even their sons and their daughters they have burned in the fire to their gods. Whatsoever thing that I command you, be careful to do it. You shall not add to it, nor take away from it**" (Deut. 12:28-32).

God also commanded the children of Israel not to follow demonic, occult practices or observe pagan religious times: "[Y]ou shall not learn to do according to the abominations of those nations. There shall not be found among you anyone who makes his son or his daughter to pass through the fire, or that uses **divination**, or an **observer of times**, or a **fortuneteller**, or a **witch**, or a **charmer**, or a **consulter with familiar spirits**, or a **wizard**, or **one who seeks oracles** from the dead. For all that do these things *are* an abomination to the LORD. And because of these abominations, the LORD your God drives them out from before you. You shall be blameless before the LORD your God. For these nations whom you shall possess hearkened to observers of times and to diviners; but **as for you, the LORD your God has not allowed you to do so**" (Deut. 18:9-14). Since Paul believed all things in the Law and the Prophets, we can be sure that he would never allow the Galatians to observe such pagan customs and holidays.

Galatians 4:8-10 Correctly Explained

Interestingly, the question of Sabbath and holy day observance was not the real issue in Galatians Four. After their conversion, the Spirit of God led the Galatians to worship God in spirit and in truth—which included keeping the Sabbath and holy days. Paul wrote that they had become the children of God: "And because you are sons, God has sent forth the Spirit of His Son into your hearts, crying, 'Abba, Father.' So then, you are no longer a servant, but a son. And if a son, *you are* also an heir of God through Christ" (Gal. 4:6-7).

Next, Paul reminds them of their pagan past and their former occult worship of demons. Notice the comparison: "Now on the one hand, **when you did not know God, you were in bondage to those who are not gods by nature** [the pagan deities and demons]" (Gal. 4:8). Their former pagan worship had nothing to do with the biblical Sabbath and holy days—or any other commandment or law of God!

In a severe admonition Paul warns them that they were in dire spiritual danger, because instead of obeying God, they were reverting back to their former pagan ways and blending their former pagan observances with their newly learned Christian way of life. In so doing, they were beginning to turn their backs on God the Father and Jesus Christ. Paul strongly rebukes them: "But on the other hand, after having known God—rather, after having been known by God—how *is it that* **you are turning again to the weak and impotent elements** [demon spirits of pagan religion], to which you again desire to be in bondage [to Satan the devil as in the past]? **You are *of* your own selves observing days, and months, and times and years**. I am afraid for you, lest somehow I have labored among you in vain" (verses 9-11). It is readily apparent that the problem was *not* that the Galatians were forsaking Sunday and holiday-keeping and reverting back to keeping the Sabbath and holy days, as Orthodox theologians and ministers claim. In fact, quite the opposite was happening, as we will see in the following analysis.

An Analysis of What Paul Wrote in Galatians 4:8-10

1) Paul speaks of the time *before* the Galatians were converted: "**Now on the one hand, when you did not know God, you were in**

bondage to those who are not gods by nature [the pagan deities and demons]" (verse 8). Before they were converted they knew nothing about the true God—the Father and Jesus Christ. Therefore, we can conclude that before they were converted, they did not observe God's Sabbath, feasts or holy days—**only after their conversion**.

2) Next, Paul speaks of their conversion and having come to know God: "…**after having known God—rather, after having been known by God**…" (Gal. 4:9). After they were converted, Paul taught them God's way of life in the grace of God, including the keeping of the Sabbath, feasts and holy days. Paul taught the observance of God's Sabbaths in *all* the churches.

3) Later—because they were beginning to accept a false gospel—the Galatians began leaving the true Christ and the true Gospel, and were returning to their former pagan religious practices and demon worship: "**How** *is it that* **you are turning again to the weak and impotent elements** [demon spirits of pagan religion]…" (verse 9).

4) In so doing, they were returning to the spiritual bondage of false, pagan gods and the accompanying religious days of worship: "…**to which YOU AGAIN DESIRE TO BE IN BONDAGE** [to Satan the devil as in the past]?" (verse 9).

5) Paul notes that rather than following the teachings of Jesus Christ, what they were doing was of their own choice and determination: "**You are** *of* **your own selves**…." Paul uses a special middle voice verb, *paratereithe*, which shows that they were acting of their *own* volition in making such decisions—and were not doing so because of Paul's teachings.

6) What were they reverting to? They were going *back* to "**observing** [for themselves] **days, and months, and times and years**" (verse 10). Again, before conversion they knew *nothing* of God, Jesus Christ or Christianity—or of the laws and commandments of God. Therefore it is not possible to take this phrase to mean that they were returning to the observance of God's Sabbath, feasts and holy days—or that they were following traditional Judaism. The phrase can **only refer to pagan days, months, times and years**, which they had formerly observed before they were converted.

Notice carefully that Paul did not use the words Sabbath, feasts or holy days in describing how the Galatians were reverting back to their former ways. If Paul was actually writing to them about the Sabbath, feasts or holy days of God, he would have used *those terms* instead of "days, months, times and years." Therefore, there is no real question that such "days, months, times and years" can *only* refer to pagan times of worship, not to the biblically commanded days of worship. This is why Paul finished his admonition to the Galatians with this warning: "I am afraid for you, lest somehow I have labored among you in vain" (Gal. 4:11).

As we have seen, Orthodox Christendom's interpretation and explanation of this complicated passage is entirely incorrect, and is only founded on bias against the Sabbath, feasts and holy days of God. Orthodoxy rejects the truth of God so that they may continue in their observance of a "Christianized" Sunday and the various occult holidays of this world.

Romans 14:1-6—Esteeming "One Day Above Another"

In the *KJV*, Romans 14:1-6 is poorly translated. The key passages universally misunderstood are verses five and six, which read: "**One man esteemeth one day above another: another esteemeth every day alike. Let every man be fully persuaded in his own mind. He that regardeth the day, regardeth it unto the Lord; and he that regardeth not the day, to the Lord he doth not regard it.**"

Unfortunately, for hundreds of years these verses have been used as justification for traditional Sunday-keeping and the rejection of the Sabbath and holy days of God. Protestantism boasts that these verses grant authority to observe Sunday. However, with a more accurate translation beginning with verse one, the context will show that the discussion is not about which day to keep as a day of religious observance. Rather, it has to do with vegetarianism versus eating meat, as well as the eating of meat on certain days.

Romans 14:1-6 reads: "Receive the one who is weak in the faith, but not for divisive arguments. Now on the one hand, one believes he may eat all things *that are lawful*; but on the other hand, another one, who is weak, eats only vegetables. The one who eats *meat* should not despise the one who does not eat *it*. And the one who does not eat *meat* should not condemn the one who eats *it*, for God has received him. Who are you to be judging another man's servant? To his own master he stands or falls. And he shall be made to stand because God is able to make him stand.

"Again, on the one hand, someone may prefer one day above another day *for eating meat*; but on the other hand, another may hold every day *to be alike*. Let each one be fully convinced in his own mind. The one who regards the day *in his eating* is regarding *it* to *the* Lord; and the one who does not regard the day is not regarding *it* to *the* Lord. The one who eats *meat* is eating to *the* Lord because he gives thanks to God; and the one who does not eat *meat* is abstaining to *the* Lord, and is giving thanks to God."

To further substantiate that the problem was vegetarianism versus eating meat, Paul continued to explain: "But if, **because of meat**, your brother is offended, you are no longer walking according to love. **With your meat**, do not destroy the one for whom Christ died.... For the kingdom of God is not a *matter of* eating and drinking; rather, *it is* righteousness and peace and joy in the Holy Spirit, because the one who serves Christ in these things *is* well pleasing to God and acceptable among men....

"**Do not destroy the work of God for the sake of meat**. All things *that are lawful are* indeed pure; but *it is* an evil thing for someone to cause an occasion of stumbling through his eating. *It is* **better not to eat meat, or drink wine, or** *anything else* **by which your brother stumbles, or is offended, or is made weak**. Do you have faith? Have *it* to yourself before God. Blessed *is* the one who does not condemn himself in what he approves" (verses 15, 17-18, 20-22).

Romans 14:1-6 Divided Into an A and B Pattern: Paul wrote these verses in an "A and B" pattern. When analyzed, this pattern shows that Paul did not give people license to pretentiously choose any day of the week as a holy day of worship. That is God's prerogative alone—not man's. Rather, Paul is writing about those who eat meat and those who are vegetarians.

A. "Receive the one who is weak in the faith, but not for divisive arguments. Now on the one hand, one believes he may eat all things *that are lawful*;
B. "...but on the other hand, another one, who is weak, eats only vegetables.

A. "The one who eats *meat* should not despise the one who does not eat *it*.
B. "And the one who does not eat *meat* should not condemn the one who eats *it*, for God has received him.

"Who are you to be judging another man's servant? To his own master he stands or falls. And he shall be made to stand because God is able to make him stand.

A. "Again, on the one hand, someone may prefer one day above another day *for eating meat*;
B. "...but on the other hand, another may hold every day *to be alike*.

"Let each one be fully convinced in his own mind.

A. "...the one who regards the day *in his eating* is regarding *it* to *the* Lord;
B. "...and the one who does not regard the day is not regarding *it* to *the* Lord.

A. "The one who eats *meat* is eating to *the* Lord because he gives thanks to God;
B. "...and the one who does not eat *meat* is abstaining to *the* Lord, and is giving thanks to God" (Rom. 14:1-6).

There is not one word in these verses that can be used to justify Sunday-keeping, or any other day, as a day of worship. Throughout the Bible,

God has always commanded and upheld the seventh-day Sabbath as the weekly day of worship, and His holy days as annual days of worship. Paul is simply writing about the problems between vegetarians and meat eaters—and the day on which some meat eaters chose to eat meat.

Colossians Two: Were the Ten Commandments Really Nailed to the Cross When Jesus Was Crucified?

Another example of misinterpreting Paul's writings is found in Colossians 2:14, 16-17, and stems from an extremely poor translation of the Greek text. Unfortunately, this particular misunderstanding has led millions to believe that all the laws and commandments were nailed to the cross when Jesus was crucified. As in the case of Galatians Four, we will notice that the Protestants' false interpretation is exactly the *opposite* of what Paul actually wrote and meant.

First, we will examine the *KJV* translation of each of these key passages, beginning with verse 14: "Blotting out the handwriting of ordinances that was against us, which was contrary to us, and took it out of the way, nailing it to his cross."

From this obscure translation, people presume that the phrase "handwriting of ordinances" constitutes the laws and commandments of God. Therefore, they conclude incorrectly that the Ten Commandments were nailed to the cross.

In the Greek, "handwriting of ordinances" is *chriographon tois dogmasin*—which literally means "handwriting in decrees or dogmas." In the New Testament, *dogma* always refers to "decrees" written by men (Luke 2:1; Acts 16:4; 17:7; Eph. 2:15). Nowhere in the entirety of the Bible does *dogma*, "decrees," refer to any part of the Law of God. Therefore, this phrase in Col. 2:14 has nothing to do with biblical Law.

But what does the expression "handwriting of ordinances" actually mean? As we will see, the phrase refers to a *written account* of one's sins, called "a note of debt." In his epical book *The Two Babylons*, Alexander Hislop writes concerning this pagan, Greek religious practice, which the converts in Colosse had undoubtedly formerly practiced (the practice was also found in ancient Chinese religion): "A work of some note on morals, called *Merits and Demerits Examined*, [describes how] a man is directed to keep a [written] debtor and creditor account with himself of the acts of each day, and at the end of the year to wind it up [in summary]. If the balance is in his favor, it serves as the foundation of a stock of merits for the ensuing year; and if against him, it must be liquidated by future good deeds [justification by works]. Various lists and comparative tables are given of both good and bad actions in the several relations of life; and benevolence is strongly inculcated in regard first to man, and, secondly, to the brute creation. To cause another's death is reckoned at one hundred on the side of demerit; while a single act of charitable relief counts as one on the other side" (page 147).

Thus, the phrase in Colossians 2:14 should be translated as "note of debt against us *with* the decrees *of our sins*"—or a symbolic listing of our sins against God. Our sins and the *debt* of our sins were nailed to the cross when Jesus Christ was crucified and died. Upon true repentance of sins to God the Father, Jesus Christ blots out the "note of debt" through the remission of our sins. Jesus Christ, Who knew no sin, was made sin for us. He was nailed to the cross as a sin offering for the sins of the whole world. **The "note of debt" of our sins was symbolically nailed to the cross, NOT the commandments of God which stand forever**.

When Col. 2:13 is included with the correct translation of verse 14, the true meaning of what Paul wrote becomes clear: "For you, who were *once* dead in *your* sins and in the uncircumcision of your flesh, He has *now* made alive with Him, having forgiven all your trespasses. He has **blotted out the note of debt against us *with* the decrees *of our sins***, which was contrary to us; and He has taken it away, having nailed it to the cross." Therefore, the actual meaning of these verses has nothing to do with nailing the Law to the cross, as falsely believed by millions of professing Christians.

The True Meaning of Colossians 2:16-17

The erroneous distortion of these two verses has caused Protestantism to denounce the observance of the biblical Sabbath, holy days and clean and unclean meats more than any other passage in the New Testament. Consequently, it has caused ministers and laymen alike to "rummage" through the New Testament in search of other Scriptures to substantiate this misinterpretation—resulting in a myriad of additional false interpretations and beliefs that appear to bolster their practices of Sunday-keeping and observing occult holidays. When one *casually* reads these verses, it does give the *appearance* that such an interpretation may be correct—but such is not the case.

In the *KJV*, Colossians 2:16 reads: "Let no man therefore judge you in meat, or in drink, or in respect of an holy day, or of the new moon, or of the sabbath *days*"—verse 17—"which are a shadow of things to come; but the body *is* of Christ."

To add further confusion to this doctrinal puzzle, the *New International Version* savaged verse 17 with the following deliberate mistranslation: "These are a shadow of things that **were to come**." In so doing, they reinforced the false idea that, since Christ has already come, the things that were "to come" have been fulfilled. Thus, they cling tenaciously to their mistaken belief that indeed "the life, death and resurrection terminated all these laws and commandments of God."

However, the Greek preposition the *NIV* translators mistranslated as the English past tense phrase "were to come" is actually a **present tense**, articular active plural participle, *toon mellontoon*, which is impossible to translate as a past tense completed action. An honest translation can only reflect the present tense, continuous, ongoing meaning of "the things to come," or "the coming things"—which can only mean the continuous unfolding of prophecy and the plan of God.

Importantly, we know the Colossian church was composed entirely of Gentile converts. Paul preached "the mystery among the Gentiles" (Col. 1:27), and refers to their spiritual circumcision of the heart through Jesus Christ—their conversion—in contrast to their physical condition of "uncircumcision" of the flesh (Col. 2:13).

As we find in Acts 19, Gentile converts forsook their pagan religion and worship of Greek gods and goddesses, when they were met with resistance and ridicule. And in the case of Paul, he was threatened with death because he gave up Judaism. Likewise, when the Colossians were converted, their lives were completely changed. They abandoned their past pagan religious practices, forsook the idol temples, and ceased to participate in pagan religious festivals and days of worship. Instead, they observed the seventh-day weekly Sabbath; and as Paul taught in all the churches, they were faithful to the holy days and festivals of the true God.

This caused those *outside* the church to make judgments against the Colossian brethren for having abandoned their former religious philosophy and worship of angels. When we understand the circumstances with which Paul was dealing when he wrote Colossians 2:16-17, then the true meaning of the passage becomes clear.

An Analysis of Colossians 2:16-17

Here is an accurate translation from the original Greek of Col. 2:16-17: "Therefore, do not allow anyone to judge you in eating or in drinking, or with regard to a festival, or new moon, or *the* Sabbaths"—verse 17—"which are a foreshadow of the things that are coming, but the body of Christ."

> **1)** The first phrase—"**Therefore, do not allow anyone to judge you**…"—means that because they were now converted and had changed their lives to believe and obey the Gospel, and were now keeping the laws and commandments of God instead of their former pagan ways, **therefore**, they were not to let anyone *outside* the Church judge them because of their new way of life.

> **2)** "…**in eating, or in drinking**…" When they were pagans they ate all meats—clean and unclean. After conversion they no longer ate unclean meats (I Tim. 4:1-5). Likewise, they no longer engaged in drunkenness as in the past, which was also part of their pagan religious practices. Now, because they had changed their ways, they were to ignore the judgments and criticisms of those outside the Church.

3) "…with regard to a festival, or new moon, or *the* Sabbaths…" Rather than showing that the Colossians were being judged for rejecting the festivals and Sabbaths of God, this phrase means the exact opposite. As in the case of the Galatians, as former pagans they had never observed any of the biblical festivals and Sabbaths before their conversion. Therefore, those outside the Church were not judging the Colossians because they were no longer keeping these things, rather they were judging them because after their conversion they were, indeed, keeping them. A word about "new moon." Since this is in the singular, it refers to the calculated Hebrew Calendar, and must be referring to the Feast of Trumpets, a holy day, because the first day of the seventh month (a new moon) is the beginning date for the calculations of the Hebrew Calendar.

4) "…which are a foreshadow of the things that are coming…" This important phrase shows that true Christians—those obeying God's way of life—will have an understanding of coming events in prophecy as the plan of God unfolds.

5) "…but the body of Christ." This phrase can reflect two meanings. First, since the Colossian brethren were being judged by those *outside* the church for their new, converted conduct, any judging concerning these matters should only be done in and by the Church, which is "the body of Christ." Second, this phrase can also mean that the *reality* of observing God's Sabbath and holy days can be found only in the "body of Christ"—the Church—not from *outside* the Church. In other words, the true knowledge and meaning of such days can be found only in the churches of God. As Jesus said, "Because it has been given to you to know the mysteries of the kingdom of heaven, but to them [outside the body of Christ—outside the true Church of God] it has not been given…. But blessed *are* your eyes, because they see; and your ears, because they hear. For truly I say to you, many prophets and righteous *men* have desired to see what you see, and have not seen; and to hear what you hear, and have not heard" (Matt. 13:11, 16-17).

The entire chapter of Colossians Two is a contrast between the way of God through Jesus Christ and the way of pagans with their religious philosophies and worship of fallen angels. When the verses of this chapter are divided into these two contrasting elements, the true meaning and full intent of what Paul wrote becomes clear. Below, the verses of Colossians Two are divided into: **A.** Things relating to Christ and God the Father and the Christian way of life; and **B.** Warnings against paganism, religious philosophy and the worship of fallen angels.

Colossians Two Divided into Elements A and B

A. "Now I want you to understand what great concern I have for you, and *for* those in Laodicea, and as many as have not seen my face in *the* flesh; that their hearts may be encouraged, being knit together in love unto all riches of **the full assurance of understanding**, unto *the* **knowledge of the mystery of God**, and of *the* Father, and of Christ; **in Whom are hid all the treasures of wisdom and knowledge**" (verses 1-3).
B. "Now I say this so that **no one may deceive you by persuasive speech**" (verse 4).

A. "For though I am indeed absent in the flesh, yet I am with you in spirit, rejoicing and beholding your order, and the steadfastness of your faith in Christ. Therefore, **as you have received Christ Jesus the Lord, be walking in Him; being rooted and built up in Him, and being confirmed in the faith, exactly as you were taught**, abounding in it with thanksgiving" (verses 4-7).
B. "Beware lest anyone takes you captive **through philosophy and vain deceit**, according to **the traditions of men**, according to the **elements of the world**, and not according to Christ" (verse 8).

A. "For in Him dwells all the fullness of the Godhead bodily; and **you are complete in Him**, Who is the Head of all principality and power; in Whom you have also been circumcised with *the* circumcision not made by hands, in putting off the body of the sins of the flesh by the circumcision of Christ; having been buried with Him in baptism, by which you have also been raised with *Him* through the inner working of God, Who raised Him from the dead. For you, who were *once* dead in *your* sins and in the uncircumcision of your flesh, He has *now* made alive with Him, **having forgiven all your trespasses. He has blotted out the note of debt against us *with* the decrees *of our sins***, which was contrary to us; and He has taken it away, having nailed it to the cross. After stripping the principalities and the powers, He made a public spectacle of them, *and* has triumphed over them in it [through His crucifixion and resurrection]" (verses 9-15).
B. "Therefore, **do not allow anyone to judge you** in eating or in drinking, or with regard to a festival, or new moon, or *the* Sabbaths, which are a foreshadow of the things that are coming, but the body of Christ. **Do not allow anyone to defraud you of the prize *by* doing *his* will in self-abasement and *the* worship of angels, intruding into things that he has not seen, vainly puffed up by his own carnal mind and not holding fast to the Head…**" (verses 16-19).

A. "[T]he Head from Whom all the body, being supplied and knit together by the joints and bands, is increasing *with* the increase of God. Therefore, **if you have died together** *with Christ* **from the elements** [see Gal. 4:8-10] **of the world…**" (verses 19-20).

B. "**…why are you subjecting yourselves to** *the* **decrees** *of men* **as if you were living in** *the* **world**? *They say*, 'You may not handle! You may not taste! You may not touch!' **The use of all such things leads to corruption.** *It is* **according to the commandments and doctrines of men**, which indeed have an outward appearance of wisdom **in voluntary worship** *of angels*, **and self-abasement, and unsparing treatment of** *the* **body**, not in any respect to the satisfying *of the needs* of the flesh" (verses 20-23).

When the chapter is taken as a whole—and one examines Paul's contrasting admonitions—it becomes obvious that Paul did not abolish the dietary laws of clean and unclean meats, the annual festivals or the weekly Sabbath, or adopt a pagan calendar system. Moreover, none of God's laws were nailed to the cross. Rather, Paul is clearly affirming that the Gentiles in Colosse were to continue to observe God's laws and commandments as they had been taught. Paul was instructing the Colossians to disregard the criticisms and harsh judgments of those *outside* the Church, because the observance of God's Sabbath and holy days are a continuous foreshadowing of events yet to occur in God's plan. By being faithful and keeping these commandments of God, they would always be worshiping the true God, be built up in Jesus Christ and never lose the understanding of God's plan. By true obedience to God the Father and Jesus Christ, they would never again be deceived by vain philosophies and decrees of men, nor would they be seduced into the worship of fallen angels—Satan and his demons. This is the *true* meaning of Colossians Two!

Ephesians 2:15-16:
Did Jesus Abolish the Commandments?

Now that we have a clear understanding of Colossians Two, it will not be difficult to realize what Paul wrote in Ephesians 2:15-16. In these verses the *KJV* reads: "Having abolished in his flesh the enmity, *even* the law of commandments *contained* in ordinances; for to make in himself of twain one new man, *so* making peace; and that he might reconcile both unto God in one body by the cross, having slain the enmity thereby."

The key phrase in this *inaccurate* translation—which has caused a great deal of confusion—is "abolished in his flesh the enmity, *even* the law of commandments *contained* in ordinances." What is the "law of commandments contained in ordinances"? Are these actually the commandments of God contained in the Old Testament, as most assume?

The word translated "ordinances" comes from the Greek *dogma* (Col. 2:14, 20), which always refers to "decrees, ordinances, decisions and commands of men" (Arndt and Gingrich). Paul is not referring here to the commandments of God contained in the Law of God. Moreover, not once in the New Testament is *dogma* used in reference to the laws and commandments of God.

To what decrees or dogmas of men is Paul referring? Notice, the context clearly reveals that he was writing about the *traditional* dogmas, decrees or commands of Judaism. The harsh traditional laws of Judaism created great hostility and enmity between Jews and Gentiles—as well as among the Jews themselves. Of these Jesus said, "For they bind heavy burdens and hard to bear, and lay *them* on the shoulders of men; but they will not move them with *one of* their own fingers" (Matt. 23:4).

In Mark Seven, Jesus Christ strongly rebuked the Jewish religious leaders for adhering to their traditional laws and rejecting the commandments of God: "[T]he Pharisees and the scribes questioned Him, *saying,* 'Why don't Your disciples walk according to the tradition of the elders, but eat bread with unwashed hands?' And He answered *and* said to them, 'Well did Isaiah prophesy concerning you hypocrites, as it is written, "This people honors Me with their lips, but their hearts are far away from Me. **But in vain do they worship Me, teaching** *for* **doctrine the commandments of men**." For leaving the commandment of God, **you hold fast the tradition of men**, *such as* the washing of pots and cups; and you practice many other things like *this*.' Then He said to them, '**Full well do you reject the commandment of God, so that you may observe your** *own* **tradition**. For Moses said, "Honor your father and your mother"; and, "The one who speaks evil of father or mother, let him be put to death." But you say, "If a man shall say to *his* father or mother, 'Whatever benefit you might receive from me *is* corban (that is, *set aside as* a gift to God),' he is not obligated to help his parents." And you excuse him from doing anything for his father or his mother, **nullifying the authority of the Word of God by your tradition which you have passed down**; and you practice many *traditions* such as this' " (Mark 7:5-13; also see Matt. 23).

Not only were the traditional decrees of Judaism contrary to the laws and commandments of God, they were so strange and harsh that they bred hostility and enmity among the Jewish people. Such traditions especially caused Jews to look down on Gentiles with contempt and disdain. In Ephesians 2:11-16, Paul describes this hostile relationship that existed between Jews and Gentiles before the coming of Christ and the preaching of the Gospel of peace. He emphasizes that the enmity was primarily the result of the Jews' nonsensical traditions.

For example, a major "thorn in the flesh" between the two groups was the Jews' tradition—from their added oral law—that Jews were not to keep company with Gentiles, or even eat with them. This was most certainly not a Law of God. In order to prevent this Jewish bias against Gentiles from becoming rooted in the Church, God revealed to the apostle Peter early on that such traditions of Judaism were totally unacceptable—and that He was fully annulling those laws and decrees.

When God first began to call Gentiles, Peter was sent through a special vision from God to the house of Cornelius in Caesarea. Cornelius was a Roman Army Centurion who feared the true God and prayed to Him. Notice what Peter said to Cornelius: "**You know that it is unlawful for a man who is a Jew** [who practiced Jewish traditional law] **to associate with or come near to anyone of another race**…" (Acts 10:28).

Peter explained to Cornelius and those gathered in his house that God had moved him through a vision to proclaim that such hateful Jewish decrees had been made null and void by God as contrary to His laws and commandments. Peter said, "But God has shown me *that* **no man should be called common or unclean**…. Of a truth I perceive that **God is not a respecter of persons, but in every nation the one who fears Him and works righteousness is acceptable to Him**" (Acts 10:28, 34-35).

In order to demonstrate to Peter, and hence all the apostles, that God was calling the Gentiles to the same salvation that began with the Jews and Israelites at the temple on the day of Pentecost in 30 AD, He supernaturally poured out the Holy Spirit upon the uncircumcised Gentiles gathered in Cornelius' house *before* they were baptized. Peter continued, " 'And He [Jesus] commanded us to preach to the people, and to fully testify that it is He Who has been appointed by God *to be* Judge of *the* living and *the* dead. To Him all the prophets bear witness, *that* everyone who believes in Him receives remission of sins through His name.' **While Peter was still speaking these words, the Holy Spirit came upon all those who were listening to the message. And the believers from the circumcision were astonished**, as many as had come with Peter, **that upon the Gentiles also the gift of the Holy Spirit had been poured out**; for they heard them speak in *other* languages and magnify God. Then Peter responded *by saying*, '**Can anyone forbid water, that these should not be baptized, who have also received the Holy Spirit as we** *did*?' And he commanded them to be baptized in the name of the Lord. Then they besought him to remain *for* a number of days" (Acts 10:42-48).

With this background—and an accurate translation of Ephesians 2:11-16—the true meaning of this difficult passage is crystal clear. We see that Paul was in no way abolishing the commandments of God—for no man can abolish the commandments of God any more than a man can destroy the heavens and earth (Deut. 30:16-20; Matt. 5:17-18; Mark 13:31).

Rather, God annulled the ridiculous, hateful, traditional laws of Judaism that were against Gentiles, as they had no place in the Church of God. Notice what Paul wrote: "Therefore, remember that you were once Gentiles in *the* flesh, who are called uncircumcision by those who are called circumcision in *the* flesh made by hands; *and* that you were without Christ at that time, alienated from the commonwealth of Israel, and strangers from the covenants of promise, having no hope, and without God in the world. But now in Christ Jesus, you who were once far off are made near by the blood of Christ. For He is our peace, Who has made both one, and has broken down the middle wall of partition [created by Jewish traditional laws and decrees], **having annulled in His flesh the enmity, the law of command-ments contained in** *the* **decrees** *of men*, **so that in Himself He might cre-ate both into one new man, making peace** [between Jews and Gentiles in the Church]; and *that* He might reconcile both to God in one body through the cross, **having slain the enmity** by it" (Eph. 2:11-16).

Romans 7:1-6—Are Christians "Released from the Law"?

An improper interpretation of this passage gives the appearance that Christians have been "released" from any obligation whatsoever to keep the laws and commandments of God. However, such teachings are, in reality, rooted in carnal-minded lawlessness and enmity against the laws of God (Rom. 8:7; I John 3:4). Those who believe and promote such blatant misrepresentations are lacking in scriptural knowledge and are unskilled in dividing the Word of truth—and thus make Jesus Christ and the apostle Paul lawless ministers of sin!

"Are you ignorant, brethren (for I am speaking to those who know law), that the law rules over a man for as long a time as he may live? **For the woman who is married is bound by law to the husband as long as he is living; but if the husband should die, she is released from the law** *that bound her* **to the husband**.

"So then, if she should marry another man as long as the husband is living, she shall be called an adulteress; **but if the husband should die, she is free from the law** *that bound her to the husband*, so that she is no longer an adulteress if she is married to another man. In the same way, my breth-ren, you also were made dead to the *marriage* law *of the Old Covenant* by the body of Christ in order for you to be married to another, Who was raised from *the* dead, that we should bring forth fruit to God. For as long as we were in the flesh, the passions of sins, which were through the law, were working within our own members to bring forth fruit unto death. **But now we have been released from the law because we have died** *to that* **in which we were held so that we might serve in newness of** *the* **spirit, and not in** *the* **oldness of** *the* **letter**" (Rom. 7:1-6).

Clearly, the context of this passage is the *marriage law* which binds a husband and wife together—until death terminates their marriage cove-nant. Based on this law, Paul makes a comparison—because the covenant between God and the children of Israel was a *marriage* covenant. The Lord God was likened to the husband and Israel was likened to His wife. God confirmed this marital covenant relationship when He inspired Isaiah to write, "**For your Maker** *is* **your husband**; the LORD of hosts is His name; and your Redeemer *is* the Holy One of Israel; the God of the whole earth shall He be called" (Isa. 54:5).

This marriage covenant between God and ancient Israel was based on physical promises of territory, long life, abundant material blessings, na-tional wealth and greatness, and God's protection in exchange for Israel's obedience in the letter of His laws and commandments. Yet Israel was an almost completely unfaithful wife.

Since marriage is binding by law until the death of either the husband or the wife, how could God terminate His marriage with Israel—apart from destroying every Israelite from all twelve tribes? Remember, God keeps His own laws, as they are a reflection of His inherent spiritual righteousness. Indeed, He was bound to Israel by His own immutable law.

However, the Lord God of the Old Covenant was the One Who became the Lord of the New Covenant—Jesus Christ. Therefore, the Lord God Who became Jesus Christ in the flesh was able to terminate the marriage covenant with Israel through His death on the cross. He could not enter into a *new* espousal covenant relationship with the Church until He had died. This was one of the key reasons He became God manifested in the flesh, so He could release Israel and Himself through His own death from their Old Covenant marriage.

After Jesus' death and resurrection, true Christians could then be espoused as chaste virgins to Jesus Christ as their future husband (II Cor. 11:2; Eph. 5:22-33). The marriage of the Lamb, the Husband, and the Church, the wife, will take place shortly after the first resurrection (Rev. 19:7-9).

Consequently, the phrase "released from the law" means that through Jesus' death (and the believer's symbolic death by water baptism), Jewish Christians have been *released* from their marriage agreement that bound them to the Old Covenant. It does *not* mean that New Covenant Christians are released from the obligation to keep the commandments and laws of God (Matt. 5:17-20). Rather, they are to obey the laws and commandments of God in the **newness of the spirit** of the Law, and not just in the letter of the Law (verse 6).

"Justification by Faith"—
Is the Righteousness of God Without Law?

In order to determine the actual meaning of the apostle Paul's difficult passages concerning "law/the law" and "righteousness," we need to first understand how Paul used these particular terms.

Paul's Use of the Term "Law": The English word "law" is translated from the Greek word νομος, *nomos*, "law." Without the article it means "law" in general; an individual "law"; or the general principle of "law" or "a law." When Paul uses the word "law" *with* the definite article—ο νομος, *ho nomos*—it means in the strictest sense the Pentateuch. In some cases it may refer to God's covenant with Israel or to the Ten Commandments. In the book of Hebrews, "the law" can refer to ritual laws of the temple system. "The law," *ho nomos*, can also refer to a *specific* law other than "the law/s of God." For example:

> Romans 7:23—"the law of my mind" and "the law of sin"
> Romans 8:2—"the law of the Spirit of life" and "the law of sin and death"
> Galatians 6:2—"the law of Christ"

"Law" Without the Definite Article: In more than half of the passages where Paul discusses "law," he uses the term *without* the definite article—a fact critical to understanding his writings. This is especially true where Paul refers to laws of Judaism and decrees of men. Numerous problems in interpreting and understanding Paul's Epistles have resulted due to the *KJV* and other English translators *adding* the definite article "the" to nearly all of Paul's Scriptures where he uses "law" (*nomos*) *without* the definite article. Moreover, the translators failed to indicate their insertions by italicizing the added definite article—i.e., *"the."* Thus, Orthodox Christendom has developed many false doctrines based upon misunderstandings caused by these additions.

However, in *The Holy Bible In Its Original Order—A Faithful Version*, when the definite article is *added* to the English translation of *nomos*, it is always noted by italicizing the article—as in, *"the* law." Thus, it is distinguished from *ho nomos*, where the definite article (*ho*) is actually translated from the Greek. In such cases the article is *not* italicized—"**the** law." Those who desire to undertake a more thorough study of this matter will find a Greek New Testament or a Greek-English Interlinear Bible quite helpful.

Below is a listing of the passages where Paul uses "law" and "the law" in his epistles.

1) There is *no* definite article in the Greek in these passages—simply *nomos*. If a definite article is *added*, it should be italicized—*"the* law." Rom. 2:12, 14, 23, 25, 27; 3:20, 21, 27, 28, 31; 4:14; 5:13, 20; 6: 14, 15. In Rom. 7:1-6, all uses of "law/the law" are referring to the principle of "law" and the "law" of marriage as it pertains to God's covenant with Israel. Rom. 7:7, 8, 9, 25; 9:31, 32; 10:4; 13:10; I Cor. 9:20; Gal. 2:16, 19, 21; 3:2, 5, 10, 11, 18, 21, 23; 4:4, 5, 21; 5:4, 18, 23; 6:13; Phil. 3:5, 6, 9; I Tim. 1:9; Heb. 7:12, 16; 8:10—plural; 9:19; 10:16—plural

2) These passages already *include* the definite article as part of the original Greek—*ho nomos*. Thus they appear as "**the** law." Rom. 2:13, 14, 15, 17, 18, 20, 23, 26, 27; 3:19, 21; 4:16; 7:7, 12, 14, 16, 22, 23; 8:2, 3, 4, 7; 10:5; I Cor. 9:8, 9; 14:21, 34; 15:56; Gal. 3:10, 12, 13, 17, 19, 21, 24; 4:21; 5:3, 14; 6:2; I Tim. 1:8; Heb. 7:5, 19, 28; 8:4; 9:22; 10:1, 8

Paul's Use of the Word "Righteousness": In addition to Paul's use of "law/the law," we need to understand the meaning of the word "righteousness" and how he used it. In the New Testament, "righteousness" is translated from the Greek word *dikaisune* (δικαιοσυνη), which is used to bring out *nine* different aspects of "righteousness."

1) The **righteousness of the law** is obedience in the letter of the law (Deut. 4:1-8; Luke 1:6; Rom. 2:27; Phil. 3:6, 9).

2) The **righteousness of law** refers to receiving **justification** of one's sins through Old Covenant sacrifices, rituals, oblations and washings at the temple (Lev. 1-7; 12-15).

3) The **righteousness of law** refers to a work of law in obedience to the traditional laws of Judaism—including any law of another religion (Mark 7:1-13; Acts 10:28; 11:3; Gal. 2:11-16; Rom. 9:32; Gal. 2:16).

4) The **righteousness of God** means the personal righteousness of God the Father and Christ—the pure, holy, spiritual conduct of God.

5) The **righteousness of God** also refers to God's **justification** of a repentant sinner's past sins—which is a unilateral action of God through His grace that is separate from the Law and the Prophets (Rom. 2:21-24).

6) The **righteousness of faith** is faithful obedience to the laws and commandments of God in their spiritual intent and meaning (Rom. 2:27; I Cor. 7:19; Phil. 1:11; 2:12-13; 3:9; I John 2:3-6; 5:2-3; II John 2-6; Heb. 10:16; Rev. 22:14).

7) The **righteousness of faith** also means God's **justification** of one's past sins through **faith** and **belief** in the sacrifice of Jesus Christ and His shed blood for the forgiveness of sins by grace (Rom. 2:14; 3:21-31; 4:2; 3:31; 5:1; Gal. 3:8-10; 5:4-5; Eph. 2:4-10).

8) The **imputed righteousness of God** means the righteousness that God imputes to a believer when he or she believes God and acts upon what He commands with a willing heart (Gen. 15:6; 26:5; Rom. 4:3-5; James 2:14-26).

9) The **imputed righteousness of God** also refers to righteousness imputed by God upon repentance—because the believer's sins have been forgiven and removed through belief in the sacrifice of Jesus Christ and His shed blood. This imputed righteousness does not mean that Jesus has kept the commandments *for* a person. Neither does it remove one's obligation to keep the commandments of God (Rom. 4:6, 11, 22-23). Indeed, it demands that one keep the commandments and laws of God in their full spiritual intent (Rom. 7:6).

In order to understand what Paul wrote in Romans 3:20-31, we will focus on the "righteousness of God"—meaning God's justification of a repentant sinner's past sins.

The *KJV* Translators' Great Errors in Romans

In the book of Romans, the *KJV* translators *added* the definite article "the"—though it was not in the original text—when translating the Greek phrase *ergon nomou* into "**the** works of **the** law." Also, they did not make the word "the" *italic* when writing "the works" or "the law" to show that it was their own addition. The correct translation, a "work of law," is vastly different in meaning from "the works of the law." Many religions require "good works" in order for one to achieve salvation. These are a "work of law." On the other hand, "the work of the law" is commandment-keeping (Rom. 2:14). Usually, Paul talks about a "work of law"—which is far broader than commandment-keeping, and included the traditional laws of Judaism which Christ condemned.

In order to fully understand what Paul is saying in this critical passage in Romans Three, we need to examine the context in which it was written. In so doing, we will come to realize that Paul is talking about how one receives justification by *faith*, as opposed to justification by a *work of a law*—whether by temple ritual or justification through a traditional law of Judaism. He is not proclaiming the elimination of the laws and commandments of God as millions claim and believe.

Romans 3:20-31 Examined

Citing these verses, Evangelical Protestants make the claim that it is not necessary for a person to keep the commandments of God—especially the Sabbath and holy days—in order to have salvation. Moreover, they assert that if one keeps the Sabbath and holy days of God, they are attempting to be *justified* by commandment-keeping rather than by the grace of God through the sacrifice of Jesus Christ. Are such claims true? Why should Sunday-keeping—a man-made tradition contrary to the Word of God—not be justification by works as well?

We need to ask, What did Paul actually mean in Romans 3:20-31? Did he really advocate the elimination of the laws and commandments of God?

In the *KJV*, Romans 3:20-21 reads: "Therefore **by the deeds** [works] **of the law there shall no flesh be justified in his sight**: for by the law *is* the knowledge of sin. But now **the righteousness of God WITHOUT THE LAW is manifested**, being witnessed by the law and the prophets."

This translation *seems* to indicate that there is no need to keep the laws of God, and that one can obtain righteousness "without the law"—that is, in the complete absence of law-keeping. But how can one who is "living in sin" also be righteous? Is that not a complete impossibility?

Furthermore, how can one be righteous *without* Law when the Bible specifically declares, "All Your commandments are righteousness"? (Psa. 119:172). Complicating matters even more, Romans 2:13 says, "The hearers of the law *are* not just before God, but the **doers of the law shall be justified**." What does Paul mean by this?

Romans 3:20-31 is indeed one of the most difficult-to-understand passages that Paul wrote. Did Paul actually mean that one could be righteous *without* commandment-keeping? How is it possible that "by the deeds of the law no one is justified," yet, "the doers of the law shall be justified"? What are the answers to these perplexing questions?

The Works of the Law: This phrase, "**the** works of **the** law" (*KJV*), is perhaps one of the most misunderstood phrases in the epistles of Paul. The confusion originates from an inaccurate translation of the Greek *ergon nomou* (εργων νομου), which literally means "works of law." It does not mean "**the** works of **the** law." In the *KJV*, as well as in other versions, translators have inserted two definite articles into this phrase that are not found in the Greek text. One definite article, "the," has been inserted before the word "works" and the other before the word "law," making it incorrectly read "**the** works of **the** law." The definite articles were added to help clarify the meaning because translators thought that *ergon nomou* referred exclusively to the laws and commandments of God. Consequently, it has been assumed that keeping the commandments of God is not required for salvation because "**the** works of **the** law" cannot justify anyone with God. While it is true that "works of law" can refer to the laws of God, Paul undoubtedly intended a far broader application of the phrase *ergon nomou*.

If the apostle Paul had intended the phrase to read "**the** works of **the** law," he most certainly would have written it that way in Greek. In fact, there is one verse, and one verse only, where Paul actually did write the entire phrase "**the** work of **the** law": "For when *the* Gentiles, which do not have *the* law, **practice by nature the things contained in the law**, these who do not have *the* law are a law unto themselves, who show **the work of the law** written in their own hearts, their consciences bearing witness, and their reasonings also, as they accuse or defend one another" (Rom. 2:14-15).

The Greek phrase in verse 15 is ***to ergon tou nomou*** (το εργον του νομου) which, when translated into English, reads "**the** work of **the** law." Here it is quite evident that Paul was indeed talking about the laws of God.

In all places where *ergon nomou* appears, it should be translated as "works of law" rather than "**the** works of **the** law." Paul used *ergon nomou*—without the definite articles—in seven places, which should all be translated "works of law":

> **1)** Rom. 9:31-32: "But Israel, although they followed after a law of righteousness, did not attain to a law of righteousness. Why? Because *they did* not *seek it* by faith, but by **works of law**; for they stumbled at the Stone of stumbling."
>
> **2-4)** Gal. 2:14-16: "But when I saw that they did not walk uprightly according to the truth of the gospel, I said to Peter in the presence of them all, 'If you, being a Jew, are living like the Gentiles, and not according to Judaism, why do you compel the Gentiles to judaize? We who are Jews by nature—and not sinners of *the* Gentiles—

knowing that a man is not justified by **works of law**, but through *the* faith of Jesus Christ, we also have believed in Christ Jesus in order that we might be justified by *the* faith of Christ, and not by **works of law**; because by **works of law** shall no flesh be justified.' "

5) Gal. 3:2: "This only I desire to learn from you: did you receive the Spirit of God by **works of law**, or by *the* hearing of faith?"

6) Gal. 3:5: "Therefore *consider this*: He Who is supplying the Spirit to you, and Who is working deeds of power among you, *is He doing it* by **works of law** or by *the* hearing of faith?"

7) Gal. 3:10: "For as many as are *relying* on **works of law** are under a curse, because it is written, 'Cursed *is* everyone who does not continue in all things that have been written in the book of the law to do them.' "

The True Meaning of "Works of Law": It is evident in these passages that Paul is including the traditional laws of Judaism in the phrase "works of law." In Galatians Two, Peter and the others were not following a law of God in eating separately from Gentiles, but were observing a traditional law of Judaism. Peter knew the Jews' traditions because fifteen years earlier he said to Cornelius, "You know that **it is unlawful for a man who is a Jew to associate with or come near to anyone of another race**…" (Acts 10:28). Peter was referring to a **man-made** traditional law of Judaism. Therefore, Paul's use of the phrase "works of law" includes all humanly-devised religious decrees, traditional laws of Judaism (Mark 7:1-13), as well as the ritual and sacrificial laws followed by Gentiles in worshipping their gods (Acts 14:8-18).

In addition, the phrase "works of law" can include all the rituals and sacrifices under the Old Covenant. Paul wrote that it was impossible for those rituals and sacrifices to atone for sin before God the Father in heaven: "For the law, having *only* a shadow of the good things that are coming, *and* not the image of those things, with the same sacrifices which they offer continually year by year, is never able to make perfect those who come *to worship*. Otherwise, would they not have ceased to be offered? For once those who worship had been purified, *they would* no longer be conscious of sin. On the contrary, in *offering* these *sacrifices* year by year, *there is* a remembrance of sins; because *it is* impossible *for the* blood of bulls and goats to take away sins" (Heb. 10:1-4).

In summary, "works of law" refers to the works of *any* law—the laws of God, the laws of Judaism, and the laws of pagan religions. Clearly, Paul used "works of law" in the broadest sense—which included *all* religious works of law.

Concerning keeping the laws of God in the spirit, Paul wrote to the Romans that they "might serve in newness of *the* spirit, and not in *the* oldness of *the* letter…. [For] the law *is* indeed holy, and the commandment holy and righteous and good…. For we know that the law is spiritual…" (Rom. 7:6, 12, 14). In these verses, Paul is referring to the spiritual intent of the commandments of God, known as "the spirit of the law." True Christians will obey the laws and commandments of God in newness of the spirit. Not only will their obedience come from their hearts, it will be manifest outwardly in their actions.

After a person has been converted, he or she is to walk in *newness* of life and do the "good works" of loving God and keeping His commandments. Commandment-keeping in the spirit of the law keeps a person from sinning, because "by the law is the knowledge of sin."

Justification by Faith: When a person is living in a state of sin, he or she is cut off from God. Thus, the sinner is in a completely helpless condition—because no work of any kind or of any law can forgive sin and remove sin from his or her life. No one can justify himself from sin. It is impossible, even as the proverb declares, **"Who can say, 'I have made my heart clean; I am pure from my sin'?"** (Prov. 20:9).

Only God, Who is the Heart-knowing God and Lawgiver, can—through His mercy and steadfast love—forgive sins and transgressions of His laws and commandments. No man, minister, rabbi, priest or pope, or any other religious potentate, or any law or work of law can forgive sin, because all sin is against God. Therefore, only God Himself personally can forgive sin: "Bless the LORD, O my soul, and forget not all His benefits; **Who forgives all your iniquities, Who heals all your diseases**…. For as the heavens are high above the earth, so is His mercy toward those who fear Him. **As far as the east is from the west, so far has He removed our transgressions from us**" (Psa. 103:2-3, 11-12).

God grants forgiveness only upon the sinner's genuine repentance toward God, which is accomplished privately through heartfelt prayer, and is evidenced by a broken heart and a contrite spirit. Notice King David's ancient prayer of repentance after He had grievously sinned: "Have mercy upon me, O God, according to Your lovingkindness; according to the multitude of Your tender mercies, **blot out my transgressions. Wash me thoroughly from my iniquity, and cleanse me from my sin, for I acknowledge my transgressions, and my sin is ever before me**. Against You, You only, have I sinned, and done evil in Your sight, that You might be justified when You speak and be clear when You judge…. Behold, **You desire truth in the inward parts**; and in the hidden part You shall make me to know wisdom. Purge me with hyssop, and I shall be clean; wash me, and I shall be whiter than snow. Make me to hear joy and gladness, that the bones which You have broken may rejoice. Hide Your face from my sins, and blot out all my iniquities. **Create in me a clean heart, O God, and renew a steadfast spirit within me**" (Psa. 51:1-4, 6-10).

In order to be made right with God and have sins forgiven and removed, the sinner must repent to God the Father and accept the sacrifice of the blood of Jesus Christ as full payment for his or her sins. Notice how Paul expressed it: "[We, as called, true Christians, are] to *the* praise of *the* glory of His grace, wherein He has made us objects of *His* grace in the Beloved *Son*; **in Whom we have redemption through His blood,** *even* **the remission of sins, according to the riches of His grace**" (Eph. 1:6-7).

Again, in writing to the Colossians, Paul shows God's operation of justification through the sacrifice of Jesus Christ and His shed blood. It is God the Father "Who has personally rescued us from the power of darkness and has transferred *us* unto the kingdom of the Son of His love; **in Whom we have redemption through His own blood,** *even* **the remission of sins**.... And, having made peace through the blood of His cross, by Him to reconcile all things to Himself; by Him, whether the things on the earth, or the things in heaven. **For you** *were* **once alienated and enemies in** *your* **minds by wicked works; but now He has reconciled** *you* **in the body of His flesh through death**, to present you holy and unblamable and unimpeachable before Him; if indeed you continue in the faith grounded and steadfast, and are not moved away from the hope of the gospel, which you have heard, *and* which was proclaimed in all the creation that is under heaven" (Col. 1:13-14, 20-23).

The apostle John writes: "If we confess our own sins, He is faithful and righteous, to forgive us our sins, and to cleanse us from all unrighteousness" (I John 1:9).

This is how God the Father justifies the repentant sinner *separate from* commandment-keeping. No one can be justified in the sight of God by *any* work of *any* law. Rather, justification is graciously granted to the believer based on repentance and faith in the sacrifice and shed blood of Jesus Christ. This *state* of justification is called the "gift of righteousness," or the "gift of justification," which God the Father freely imputes to the repentant believer (Rom. 5:17).

The function of the laws and commandments of God is to show men *how* to live, as well as to show them *what* sin is. No law can forgive sin. No law can give eternal life. That is not the function of law. Only God the Father can justify a person from sin through Jesus Christ's sacrifice and blood, which is *separate from* works of law and commandment-keeping. Finally, justification of past sins does *not* do away with the law or the good works that God requires of true believers. This is what Paul meant when he wrote: "The hearers of the law *are* not just before God, but **the doers of the law shall be justified**" (Rom. 2:13).

The Righteousness of God: The righteousness of God is shown by His grace in forgiving sin through the blood and sacrifice of Jesus. This righteousness places the forgiven sinner in right standing with God. Paul wrote: "For all have sinned, and come short of the glory of God; *but* are **being justified freely by His grace** through the redemption that *is* in Christ Jesus; Whom God has openly manifested *to be* a propitiation through **faith in His blood**, in order to demonstrate **His righteousness**, in respect to the remission of the sins that are past, through the forbearance of God; *yes*, to publicly declare **His righteousness** in the present time, that He might be just, and the one Who justifies the one who *is* of *the* faith of Jesus" (Rom. 3:23-26). The righteousness of God that Paul wrote of is the expression of God's love, mercy, forgiveness and justification through Jesus Christ. In a sense, in this context, the word "justification" could be freely substituted for the word "righteousness" because the righteousness of God means the justification that He freely gives to the repentant sinner.

"Without the Law": The phrase "without the law" in the *King James Version* (Rom. 3:21) is also misunderstood because "without" gives the impression that there is no law at all. In English, "without" conveys "the absence of." Shamefully, too many believe that Christians can disregard the laws and commandments of God. However, in Romans 3:21, "without" is an incorrect translation of the Greek *choris* (χωρις), which means "separately, apart from, by itself, without" (Bauer, Arndt and Gingrich, *Greek English Lexicon of the New Testament*, 1974). The correct translation of *choris* is "**separate from**"—thus the phrase should read, "separate from law." Since the laws and commandments of God have not ceased to exist, the phrase "separate from law" is more precise because it shows that the function of the law is **separate from** the function of justification by faith—which is accomplished through repentance and belief in the sacrifice of Jesus Christ.

The entire operation of justification is separate from and in addition to law and commandment-keeping. **Forgiveness and justification of one's past sins can *only* come through the life, crucifixion, death and resurrection of Jesus Christ. NO LAW-KEEPING OF ANY KIND OR ANY ACTION INITIATED BY ANYONE CAN ACCOMPLISH THAT!** *This* is what Paul is writing about—he is not writing about the abolition of God's Law!

Here is the full, correct translation of Romans 3:20-31. It shows that "the righteousness of God" is actually the *justification* of God through the operation of the forgiveness of a person's sins:

"Therefore, by works of law there shall no flesh be justified before Him; for through *the* law *is the* knowledge of sin. But now, *the* **righteousness of God** *that is* **separate from law has been revealed, being witnessed by the Law and the Prophets; even** *the* **righteousness of God** *that is* **through** *the* **faith of Jesus Christ**, toward all and upon all those who believe; for there is no difference. For all have sinned, and come short of the glory of God; *but* are being justified freely by His grace through the redemption that *is* in Christ Jesus; Whom God has openly manifested *to be* a propitiation through faith in His blood, in order to demonstrate **His righteousness** [justification], **in respect to the remission of sins that are past**, through the forbearance of God; *yes*, to publicly declare His righteousness in the present time, that He might be just, and the one Who justifies the one who *is* of *the* faith of Jesus.

"Therefore, where *is* boasting? It is excluded. Through what law? *The law* of works? By no means! Rather, *it is* through a law of faith. Consequently, **we reckon that a man is justified by faith, separate from works of law**. *Is He* the God of the Jews only? *Is He* not also *the God* of *the* Gentiles? YES! *He* *is* also God of *the* Gentiles, since *it is* indeed one God **Who will justify *the* circumcision by faith, and *the* uncircumcision through faith**.

"Are we, then, abolishing law through faith? MAY IT NEVER BE! Rather, we are establishing law [or making it to stand]."

Once a person has been justified of past sins through the righteousness of God as described by Paul—and one has received the Holy Spirit—then God begins to write His laws and commandments into his or her mind and heart, **thereby truly establishing the law**, not abolishing it. "For by one offering He has obtained eternal perfection *for* those who are sanctified. And the Holy Spirit also bears witness to us; for after He had previously said, 'This *is* the covenant that I will establish with them after those days,' says *the* Lord: '**I will give My laws into their hearts, and I will inscribe them in their minds; and their sins and lawlessness I will not remember ever again**' " (Heb. 10:14-17).

Romans 6:14—The True Meaning of the Phrase, "Not Under Law, But Under Grace"

This single verse, Romans 6:14—because it is typically taken out of context—has caused a great deal of confusion among nominal "Christians." Read in isolation, it gives the *appearance* that Christians are no longer required to keep the laws and commandments of God: "For sin shall not rule over you because you are not under law, but under grace."

But Romans 6:14 cannot be understood in isolation; the entire context of Romans Six must be examined if we are to understand Paul's intent. In fact, the key is actually given in the first two verses of the chapter. Paul asks and answers the question: "What then shall we say? Shall we continue in sin, so that grace may abound? MAY IT NEVER BE! We who died to sin, how shall we live any longer therein?" (verses 1-2).

Remember that *sin* is the transgression of the Law (I John 3:4). Obviously, then, if Christians are *not* to continue living in sin, they must be keeping the commandments and laws of God. However, God's laws are now kept in the spirit—under the grace of God!

Paul goes on in Romans Six to explain that the operation of baptism pictures the "death and burial" of the old sinful man—which justifies one to God the Father and brings forgiveness of past sins. He explains it this way: "Or are you ignorant that we, as many as were baptized into Christ Jesus, were baptized into His death [since Jesus died for our sins]? Therefore, we were buried with Him though the baptism into the death; so that, just as Christ was raised from *the* dead by the glory of the Father, in the same way, we also should walk in newness of life [now with the Holy Spirit of God—in spiritual obedience].

"For if we have been conjoined together in the likeness of His death, so also shall we be *in the likeness* of *His* resurrection. Knowing this, that our old man was co-crucified with *Him* **in order that the body of sin might be destroyed, so that we might no longer be enslaved to sin; because the**

one who has died *to sin* [through repentance and water baptism] **has been justified from sin** [through the blood of Jesus Christ].

"Now if we died together with Christ, we believe that we shall also live with Him, knowing that Christ, having been raised from *the* dead, dies no more; death no longer has any dominion over Him. For when He died, He died unto sin once for all; but in that He lives, He lives unto God. In the same way also, you should indeed **reckon yourselves to be dead to sin, but alive to God through Christ Jesus our Lord**.

"Therefore, **do not let sin rule in your mortal body by obeying it in the lusts thereof**. Likewise, do not yield your members as instruments of unrighteousness to sin; rather, yield yourselves to God as those who are alive from *the* dead, and your members *as* instruments of righteousness to God.

"For sin shall not rule over you because **you are not under law** [for forgiveness and justification], **but under grace** [for forgiveness and justification]. What then? Shall we sin because we are not under law [for forgiveness and justification], but under grace [for forgiveness and justification]? MAY IT NEVER BE! Don't you realize that to whom you yield yourselves *as* servants to obey, you are servants of the one you obey, whether *it is* of sin unto death, or of obedience unto righteousness? But thanks *be* to God, that you were *the* servants of sin, but you have obeyed from *the* heart that form of doctrine which was delivered to you" (verses 3-17).

Keep in mind that from Romans 3:20 to 6:23, Paul's entire explanation of justification of past sins by *grace* through the sacrifice and blood of Jesus Christ is contrasted with the absolute inability of any *law* to bring true spiritual justification to the sinner. That is the context in which Romans 6:14 was written. When Paul writes that Christians are "not under law, but under grace," he means that we are not trying to achieve justification through law—which is in fact impossible—but through God's grace. This, then, is the true, scriptural meaning of Romans 6:14.

The apostle John further explains the *continuous* justification and forgiveness of sins that believers have through faith in the sacrifice and blood of Jesus Christ: "If we proclaim that we have fellowship with Him, but we are walking in the darkness [living in sin], we are lying to ourselves, and we are not practicing the Truth ['Your Word is the Truth,' (John 17:17)]. However, if we walk in the light [of God's Word, in love and obedience], as He is in the light, *then* we have fellowship with one another, and **the blood of Jesus Christ, His own Son, cleanses us from all sin**.

"If we say that we do not have sin, we are deceiving ourselves, and the truth is not in us. **If we confess our own sins, He is faithful and righteous, to forgive us our sins, and to cleanse us from all unrighteousness**. If we say that we have not sinned, we make Him a liar, and His Word is not in us.

"My little children, I am writing these things to you so that you may not sin. And *yet*, **if anyone does sin, we have an Advocate with the Father; Jesus Christ** *the* **Righteous**; and He is *the* propitiation [continual source of mercy and forgiveness] for our sins; and not for our sins only, but also for *the sins* of the whole world" (I John 1:6-10; 2:1-2).

John then follows his explanation of forgiveness of our sins through the blood of Jesus Christ with the admonition that we are likewise required to keep God's commandments. This again substantiates that God's merciful grace does not allow anyone to continue to *live* in sin. Notice: "And by this *standard* we know that we know Him: if we keep His commandments. The one who says, 'I know Him,' and does not keep His commandments, is a liar, and the truth is not in him. On the other hand, **if anyone is keeping His Word, truly in this one the love of God is being perfected. By this *means* we know that we are in Him**. Anyone who claims to dwell in Him is obligating himself also to walk even as He Himself walked" (I John 2:3-6). **This is the full, true meaning of living in the grace of God**.

Romans 10:4—How is Jesus Christ "the End of the Law"?

In the *KJV*, Romans 10:4 reads: "For Christ is the end of the law for righteousness to every one that believeth." If this verse is read in isolation—without considering the context and historical background, or the underlying Greek—it does indeed give the impression that Christ brought the law to an end. But is that what it really means? If so, *which* law did Jesus end?

Because of this one verse, numerous people assume that all the laws and commandments of God have come to an end. But is this true? Is it possible for a man to *end* any law of God? Try ending the law of gravity. It can't be done. All things are subject to law and all men are subject to God's Law. Would Christ, Who is the Lawgiver, actually end all of God's law, so that people may freely sin without consequence? Absolutely not! But that's what millions of Protestants embrace from reading this one verse.

Rather than read this verse in isolation, let us examine the context in which Paul wrote the passage. Remember, men divided the Bible into chapters and verses. The context of Romans 10:4 actually begins not with verse one, but with Romans 9:30. Paul wrote: "What then shall we say? That *the* Gentiles, who did not follow after righteousness, have attained righteousness, even *the* righteousness [justification] that *is* by faith" (Rom. 9:30).

After one has been justified from past sins, they are to keep the commandments of God in the "spirit of the law." Paul wrote, "Since *it is* indeed one God Who will justify *the* circumcision by faith, and *the* uncircumcision through faith. **Are we, then, abolishing law through faith? MAY IT NEVER BE! Rather, we are establishing law**" (Rom. 3:30-31). And again, "So that even as sin has reigned unto death, so also might **the grace *of God* reign through righteousness** [justification] unto eternal life through Jesus Christ our Lord. What then shall we say? **Shall we continue in sin, so that grace may abound? MAY IT NEVER BE! We who died to sin, how shall we live any longer therein?**" (Rom. 5:20-21; 6:1-2).

Additionally, the Jews who rejected Jesus Christ and continued with their temple rituals and observation of the traditional laws of Judaism did

233

not attain to the justification of God by their works of law. **True** spiritual justification can only come through the grace of God and the sacrifice of Jesus Christ for the forgiveness of sins: "**But Israel, although they followed after a law** [In the Greek text there is *no* definite article "the" before "law"] **of righteousness** [justification], **did not attain to a law of righteousness** [justification]. **Why? Because** *they did* not *seek it* **by faith, but BY WORKS OF LAW** [In the Greek text there is *no* definite article "the" before "works" or "law"]; for they stumbled at the Stone of stumbling, exactly as it is written: 'Behold, I place in Sion a Stone of stumbling and a Rock of offense, but everyone who believes in Him shall not be ashamed' " (Rom. 9:31-33).

It is important to note that in the above passage there is no definite article before "law" or "works of law." Therefore, Paul is not referring to the Ten Commandments. Paul is actually writing about a "justification by works of law"—that is, through the operation of temple rituals and/or traditional laws of Judaism. Anyone who rejects Jesus Christ can **never** obtain justification of past sins through rituals or Jewish traditional laws, or laws of any other religion. This is why Paul said the Jews stumbled; Jesus was that "Rock of offense"—Whom they rejected. While the Jews attempted to obtain justification of sins through temple rituals and other laws, true spiritual justification of past sins can only come from God the Father through the sacrifice of Christ. This is only obtainable through repentance of sins and water baptism with true faith and belief in Jesus' shed blood—all through the operation of God's grace. This spiritual justification by faith—or "the righteousness of faith"—cannot be obtained by any "work of law."

Notice how Paul explains this in Chapter Ten: "Brethren, the earnest desire of my heart and my supplication to God for Israel is for salvation. For I testify of them that **they have a zeal for God, but not according to knowledge**. For they, being ignorant of the righteousness [justification] *that* comes from God, and seeking to establish their own righteousness [justification], have not submitted to the righteousness [justification] of God. **For Christ** *is the* **end** *of works* **of law for righteousness** [justification] **to everyone who believes**" (Rom. 10:1-4). In other words, *for those who believe*, true justification comes through Christ—thus putting an **end** to futile attempts at justification through ritual works.

So the actual meaning of Romans 10:4 is that Jesus Christ, through His sacrifice for sin, once for all time, ended the temple ritual laws and the traditional laws of Judaism for justification. By writing this, Paul did not unilaterally terminate all the laws of God as millions want to assume. He was emphasizing that true spiritual justification from God the Father is uniquely received through faith in the sacrifice and blood of Jesus Christ, which is the operation of faith and grace combined, and cannot be procured by any work of any law.

Paul's Teachings on Justification by Faith vs. Works of Law in the Book of Galatians

As we delve into the apostle Paul's writings in Galatians involving "justification by faith" and "works of law," keep these key background points in mind:

1) Paul instructed Christians in Rome that once we have been justified from past sins, we cannot continue to live in sin as a *way of life*—because sin is the "transgression" of God's Law (I John 3:4, *KJV*). He wrote: "What then shall we say? **Shall we continue in sin, so that grace may abound? MAY IT NEVER BE! We who died to sin, how shall we live any longer therein?**" (Rom. 6:1-2).

2) As Jesus Himself taught, it is *sin* to observe *any* humanly-devised, traditional religious law—be it Jewish, Catholic, Protestant, or of any other religion—in place of God's laws and commandments (see Mark 7:1-13).

3) Before Paul's conversion, he was, as Saul, one of Judaism's leading Pharisees. At the behest of the high priest, Saul executed orders to persecute, arrest, imprison and even martyr true Christians (Acts 8:1; 9:1-2; 22:3-5).

In his opening remarks to the Galatians, Paul enumerated how he was "advancing" in Judaism: "For you heard of my former conduct when I was in Judaism, how I was excessively **persecuting the church of God** and was destroying it; and I was **advancing in Judaism** *far* beyond many of *my* contemporaries in my *own* nation, **being more abundantly zealous for** *the* **traditions of my fathers**" (Gal. 1:13-14).

Galatians Two: Paul wrote that he was forced to rebuke Peter, Barnabas and other Jews publicly for their hypocrisy in reverting back to a traditional law of Judaism that forbade Jews from eating with Gentiles. Peter knew better, as God first used him to preach the Gospel and repentance to Gentiles, beginning with Cornelius and his household (Acts 10).

As will be seen, the account in Galatians Chapter Two does not involve any law or commandment of God—only traditional laws of Judaism, *which are sin*. Observing such traditional Jewish laws can never bring justification—or put one in "right standing" with God the Father. Let us scrutinize the entire account verse by verse:

"But when Peter came to Antioch, I withstood him to *his* face because he was to be condemned; for before certain *ones* came from James, he was eating with the Gentiles. However, when they came, he drew back and separated himself *from the Gentiles*, being afraid of those of *the* circumcision *party*. And the rest of *the* Jews joined him in *this* hypocritical act, insomuch that even Barnabas was carried away with their hypocrisy.

"But when I saw that they did not walk uprightly according to the truth of the gospel, I said to Peter in the presence of them all, '**If you, being a Jew, are living like the Gentiles, and not according to Judaism, why do you compel the Gentiles to Judaize?** [That is, to eat separately as do unconverted Jews.] We who are Jews by nature—and not sinners of *the* Gentiles—knowing that **a man is not justified by works of law, but**

through *the* faith of Jesus Christ, we also have believed in Christ Jesus in order that we might be justified by *the* faith of Christ, and not by works of law; because **by works of law shall no flesh be justified** [before God from past sins].

" 'Now then, if we are seeking to be justified in Christ, *and* we ourselves are found to be sinners, *is* Christ then *the* minister of sin? MAY IT NEVER BE! For if I build again those things that I destroyed [the adherence to the laws of Judaism], I am making myself a transgressor. For I through law [since the wages of sin is death] died [in the operation of baptism] to law [that is, to Judaism's traditional laws], in order that I may live to God [in love and obedience]. I have been crucified with Christ [by baptism], yet I live. *Indeed*, it is no longer I; but Christ lives in me. For *the life* that I am now living in *the* flesh, I live by faith—that *very faith* of the Son of God, Who loved me and gave Himself for me. I do not nullify the grace of God; for if righteousness [justification] *is* through *works of* law, then Christ died in vain' " (Gal. 2:11-21).

The whole purpose of repentance, baptism and justification by faith in the sacrifice and shed blood of Jesus Christ is to receive the Holy Spirit of God, which is our begettal from God the Father and the "earnest" (pledge or down payment) of our salvation (I John 3:9; Eph. 1:13-14). Paul wrote nothing in this passage that can be construed to mean he was abolishing the laws and commandments of God—for NO MAN CAN DO SO!

Galatians Three: Paul continues in Chapter Three, making it clear that any work of any law is not able to bring about justification for past sins. While God requires Christians to keep His laws and commandments in their full spiritual intent, no law has the power to forgive sin, justify a person to God spiritually, impart the Holy Spirit, or bestow eternal life. The function of God's laws and commandments is to *define sin*: "O foolish Galatians, who has bewitched you *into* not obeying the truth, before whose eyes Jesus Christ, crucified, was set forth in a written public proclamation? This only I desire to learn from you: **did you receive the Spirit of God by works of law, or by *the* hearing of faith?** Are you so foolish? Having begun in *the* Spirit, are you now being perfected in *the* flesh [through obedience to carnal laws of Judaism]?... Therefore, *consider this*: He Who is supplying the Spirit to you, and Who is working deeds of power among you, *is He doing it* **by works of law** or by *the* **hearing of faith**?" (Gal. 3:1-5).

Concerning the laws and commandments of God, Paul demonstrates that they are **not contrary** to God's promises of eternal life—which can only come through loving obedience and faith in Jesus Christ. "*Is* the law then contrary to the promises of God? MAY IT NEVER BE! **For if a law had been given that had the power to give life**, *then* righteousness [justification] would indeed have been by law. But the Scriptures have shut up all things under sin, so that by *the* faith of Jesus Christ the promise [of eternal life] might be given to those who believe. Now before faith came, we were guarded under law, having been shut up unto the faith that was yet to be revealed [at Christ's first coming]. In this way, the law was our tutor *to* *lead us* to Christ that we might be justified by faith. But since faith has come, we are no longer under a tutor" (Gal. 3:21-25).

After repentance, baptism and the laying of hands, God gives the Holy Spirit—which unites with the spirit of man within the believer (I John 3:9) bringing conversion (John 14:17). God, then begins to write His laws and commandments in the mind of the new believer (Heb. 10:16). Instead of the *external* tutoring of the law, the believer now begins to develop the mind of Christ by the Holy Spirit through faith (Phil. 2:5). This is the *internal* working of the Holy Spirit to lead the believer in all righteousness (Rom. 8:14).

Galatians Five: Judaism required that Gentile proselytes be circumcised in the flesh before they could enter the synagogue. They were then required to keep the whole law—meaning all of God's laws, as well as all the traditional laws of Judaism. False teachers were causing converts in Galatia to revert back to those teachings, which were mixed with pagan gnosticism derived from Hellenistic Judaism. This was the "yoke of bondage" of which Paul wrote. On the other hand, the laws and commandments of God were *never* a "yoke of bondage"—even when kept in the letter of the Law, as required under the Old Covenant (Deut. 4:1-8, 39-40; 5:1-21, 32-33; 6:1-25).

This is the reason Paul admonished the Galatians to remain unyielding in the *true* faith, warning them not to revert back to "works of law" of Judaism for justification: "Therefore, stand fast in the liberty wherewith Christ has made us free, and do not be held again in a yoke of bondage. Behold, I, Paul, tell you that if you become circumcised [in the flesh, rather than in the heart by the Spirit (Rom. 2:25-29; Col. 2:13)], Christ shall profit you nothing! Again, I am personally testifying to every man who is being [physically] circumcised that he is a debtor to do the whole law [all the Old Testament laws and the traditional laws of Judaism, thereby eliminating repentance, faith and baptism].

"You who are attempting to be justified by *works of* law, you are being deprived of any *spiritual* effect from Christ. You have fallen from grace! For we through *the* Spirit are waiting for *the* hope of righteousness by faith" (Gal. 5:1-5). This is also the meaning of Galatians 5:18. "But if you are led by *the* Spirit, you are not under [*works of*] law.

I Timothy 4:1-5—
Did Paul Teach That All Meat Is Good for Food?

There is no question that the apostle Paul believed—and thus taught—"all things that are written in the Law and the Prophets" (Acts 24:14). This certainly included God's commands concerning clean and unclean meats (as found in Leviticus 11 and Deuteronomy 14). But mainstream Christianity insists that Paul relaxed the biblical injunction against unclean meats. They often site I Timothy 4:1-5, which is misleading in the *KJV*: "Now the Spirit speaketh expressly, that in the latter times some shall depart from the faith, giving heed to seducing spirits, and doctrines of devils; speaking lies in hypocrisy; having their conscience seared with a hot iron; forbidding to marry, and *commanding* to abstain from meats, which God hath created to be received with thanksgiving of them which believe and know the truth. **For every creature of God *is* good, and nothing to be refused, if it be received with thanksgiving: for it is sanctified by the word of God and prayer**."

Here, Paul warns Timothy of an apostasy to occur in the end times—which would involve various "doctrines of demons." One such "doctrine" commands abstinence from certain meats—which Paul counters by *apparently* saying that *all* meat is good for food, that nothing is to be refused if it is received with thanksgiving. But is this really what Paul is saying? Is Paul upending centuries of Jewish adherence to Old Testament food laws?

Note first that this particular "doctrine" refers specifically to abstaining from meat that was "created to be received." Conversely, this substantiates that there are *other* meats which were *not* "created to be received." Indeed, God created meats which were never designed to be food—thus they are termed *unclean*. But *clean* meats were created to be received as food with thanksgiving. Thus, the passage is not dealing with meat in general, but only with *clean* meats—those "created to be received with thanksgiving."

Next, note that the meat being discussed has been "*sanctified* by the word of God." Where in the Bible is meat particularly sanctified—*set apart*—for human consumption? Why, obviously, Leviticus 11 and Deuteronomy 14, which lists meats to be avoided and those to be eaten. Thus, Paul did not say that *every* kind of meat was created by God for food—but that every *clean* meat was created by God for food.

Without question, Paul upheld the laws of clean and unclean meats as a requirement for Christians. He described the meats that Christians are permitted to eat as those which God has "created to be received with thanksgiving." Paul was actually condemning a false doctrine that prohibited the eating of *clean* meats. The correct translation helps resolve the matter:

"Now the Spirit tells *us* explicitly that in *the* latter times some shall apostatize from the faith, *and* shall follow deceiving spirits and doctrines of demons; speaking lies in hypocrisy, their consciences having been cauterized *with a hot iron*; forbidding to marry; *and* **commanding to abstain from meats, which God created to be received** with thanksgiving by the faithful, even *by* those who know the truth. For every creature of God *designated for human consumption* is good, and nothing to be refused, *if* it is received with thanksgiving, because it is [already] sanctified [set apart] by the Word of God [in Leviticus 11 and Deuteronomy 14] and prayer." (Please note how *The Holy Bible In Its Original Order—A Faithful Version* incorporates **inserted words and phrases** in *italic type* in the appropriate places to make the intended meaning clear. All such insertions are based fully on the contextual meaning of the passage.)

Paul adds that clean meats are also set apart by *prayer*. Indeed, we have Christ's own example of asking for God's blessing on our food (Luke 9:16; 24:30; etc.). This further sets the food apart as approved and even enhanced by God—but in no way can prayer make unclean meat clean.

Mark 7:1-5—Did Jesus Declare All Meats Clean?

It is a widely held conception of modern "Christianity" that Jesus set aside the laws and commandments of God—including those which prohibit certain meats as "unclean." An incident recorded in Mark Chapter Seven is often used as a proof-text for such a view. In this case, Jesus' disciples were criticized by the Jewish leadership for eating without first washing their hands. This dispute had nothing to do with clean and unclean meats. Rather, it revolved around Jewish tradition of ritual purity, such as ceremonial hand washing.

"Then the Pharisees and some of the scribes from Jerusalem came together to Him. And when they saw some of His disciples **eating with defiled hands (that is, unwashed** *hands*), they found fault. For the Pharisees and all the Jews, **holding fast to the tradition of the elders**, do not eat unless they wash their hands thoroughly. Even *when coming* from the market, they do not eat unless they *first* wash themselves. And there are many other **things that they have received to observe**, *such as the* washing of cups and pots and brass utensils and tables. For this reason, the Pharisees and the scribes questioned Him, *saying*, 'Why don't Your disciples walk according to the **tradition of the elders**, but eat bread with unwashed hands?' " (Mark 7:1-5).

Drawing a sharp distinction between the Jews' traditions and the commandments of God, Jesus accused the scribes and Pharisees of invalidating the Word of God by their traditions.

"And He answered *and* said to them, 'Well did Isaiah prophesy concerning you hypocrites, as it is written, "This people honors Me with their lips, but their hearts are far away from Me. But in vain do they worship Me, **teaching** *for* **doctrine the commandments of men**." For **leaving the commandment of God, you hold fast the tradition of men**, *such as* the washing of pots and cups [and ritual hand washing]; and you practice many other things like *this*.' Then He said to them, 'Full well do **you reject the commandment of God**, so that **you may observe your** *own* **tradition**' " (verses 6-9). Jesus sternly rebuked the Jews for "nullifying" the authority of the Word of God by their countless and restrictive traditions (verse 13).

Notice that Jesus' primary response was to defend and *fully support* the laws and commandments of God. In no way have God's laws been abrogated. Having made that point, He went on to deal with the question of eating with "unwashed hands." Addressing the multitude, He said, "Hear Me, all of you, and understand. There is nothing that enters into a man from outside which is able to defile him; but the things that come out from *within* him, those are the things which defile a man. If anyone has ears to hear, let him hear" (verses 14-16).

Obviously, unwashed hands will not particularly defile a person. But Jesus said there was "nothing that enters into a man from outside which is able to defile him." Does that mean unclean meats were no longer prohibited by God's law—that literally *nothing* can defile a person? What did Jesus mean?

It is important to realize that the dietary laws of Leviticus 11 and Deuteronomy 14 deal with health and cleanliness—not with spiritual holiness. Eating unclean meats can harm one physically, but they will not defile one spiritually. (However, a careless attitude toward any of God's laws can defile one spiritually.) Jesus is referring to one being spiritually *defiled*—not by anything eaten but by the thoughts and attitudes a person accepts into one's heart and mind.

Knowing that His disciples did not understand, Jesus said, "Don't you perceive that anything [food, germs] that enters into a man from outside is not able to [spiritually] defile him? **For it does not enter into his heart**, but into the belly, and *then* passes out into the sewer, purging all food." Food is simply processed, purged from the body. Jesus was talking *spiritually*, making the point that even the dirt on one's unwashed hands cannot defile the heart or make a person unholy.

The defilement of which Jesus spoke comes from *within*: "That which springs forth **from *within* a man, that defiles the man**. For from within, **out of the hearts of men**, go forth evil thoughts, adulteries, fornications, murders, thefts, covetousness, wickednesses, guile, licentiousness, an evil eye, blasphemy, pride, foolishness; all these evils go forth from within, and *these* defile a man" (verses 20-23).

The disputed phrase, "purging all meats" (verse 19, *KJV*), simply means that all foods are ultimately purged from the body. **Clean and unclean meats are nowhere discussed in this passage**. The *New International Version* and a few other translations spuriously add to verse 19, "In saying this, Jesus declared all foods 'clean' " (*NIV*, 1984). This is a deliberate, exaggerated disparity reflecting the translators' anti-law bias, **as no such phrase** exists in the original Greek texts.

What *if* Jesus had actually meant to abrogate the laws of clean and unclean meats? Such a position would have easily created one of the biggest controversies of His ministry. Imagine how the Pharisees would have pounced upon such a reversal had Jesus said that swine's flesh was good for food. But there is not so much as a *hint* in the account that the Jews took Jesus to be nullifying the Old Testament food laws. Quite the contrary. And Jesus' point was not at all missed by the Jewish leadership: Ritual washings are ineffective and unnecessary in preventing spiritual defilement; rather, true spiritual purity is a matter of the heart and mind.

Acts 10—Was Peter Shown that Unclean Meats are Clean?

Obviously, too many assume that the apostle Peter's vision in Acts 10 represents a reversal of God's laws prohibiting unclean *meats*. However, nowhere in the passage is it ever suggested that God had cleansed unclean meats. Rather, this is something "read into" the section by those with a predisposition against God's laws. When the passage is read properly, it becomes obvious that Peter's vision in no way authorized a change in the laws of clean and unclean meats. In fact, Peter's vision had nothing at all to do with clean and unclean meats.

While staying in Joppa, Peter went up on the housetop about noon to pray. In a vision from God, he saw heaven open and what appeared to be a great sheet descending toward him full of unclean wild beasts, creeping things and unclean birds. A voice came to Peter, saying "Rise, Peter, kill and eat" (verse 13).

Peter did not automatically assume that it was suddenly okay to eat unclean meats. He *knew* that Christian's were to continue living according to God's Law. His response shows that he obviously did not consider the laws concerning clean and unclean foods to be obsolete.

"In no way, Lord," he replied, "for I have never eaten anything *that is* common or unclean." The voice from heaven added, "What God has cleansed, you are not to call common" (verses 14-15).

The sheet of unclean animals went up and down *three* times. Again, Peter never indicated that he believed it was now permissible to eat unclean meat. Finally, he awoke, wondering what the vision actually meant. But without question, he knew what the vision did *not* mean—that it in no way reflected a change in the laws concerning unclean foods.

Subsequently, Peter was led by God to the home of Cornelius, a Gentile. Peter understood that he was to preach the gospel to Cornelius and to his household—and that they would be baptized and receive the Holy Spirit. Peter began to realize that God was opening the door of salvation to Gentiles. Suddenly, the meaning of the vision became clear. Talking to Cornelius, Peter said, "You know that it is unlawful for a man who is a Jew to associate with or come near to anyone of another race. **But God has shown me** [in the earlier vision] *that* **no man should be called common or unclean**" (verse 28).

Jewish tradition—based on a perversion of God's laws regarding what is clean and unclean—forbade Pharisaic Jews to have a close association with Gentiles. Jews considered Gentiles to be unclean, unsuitable for physical contact. Peter was quite familiar with these traditions of Judaism.

God was showing Peter and the New Testament Church that Gentiles were being offered salvation—that they could become *spiritually* circumcised. Thus, the subject matter of Acts Ten has nothing to do with clean and unclean meats. God simply used the vision of unclean animals to emphasize a point to Peter—that when God has spiritually cleansed a Gentile, he is not to be deemed common or unclean.

Ultimately, Peter understood that "God is not a respecter of persons, **but in every nation the one** [Jew or Gentile] **who fears Him and works righteousness is acceptable to Him**" (verses 34-35).

Kabbalah—Judaism's Dark Side

Within Orthodox Judaism, the highly philosophical discipline known as *Kabbalism* (from a Hebrew word meaning *received*) attempts to explain the "mystical relationship" between an infinite, eternal God and the universe (wikipedia.org/wiki/Kabbalah). Kabbalism features cryptic teachings on the nature of God, heaven, creation, the destiny of man, the soul, an afterlife, reincarnation, etc., and inclines heavily toward *gemantra*, a method by which the numerical value of each letter of the Hebrew alphabet is used to uncover alleged secrets hidden in the written Torah. As Jewish mysticism, Kabbalah is an "exotic blend of superstition, false hermeneutics, astrology and spiritism"—the "black arts" of Judaism (John Phillips, *Exploring the World of the Jew*, p. 71). While Kabbalistic doctrines are accepted by Orthodox Jews in varying degrees, other Jews—mainly from among the Conservative and Reform movements—have rejected them as heretical and adversative to Judaism. In spite of this overall rejection by the more liberal side of the religion, Kabbalistic themes can be found throughout Judaism. Today, many Jews accept the *academic* study of Kabbalah, but do not actually hold its views to be truth.

Origin and Background

According to one Jewish tradition, Kabbalism dates from the Garden of Eden as an esoteric revelation belonging to and preserved by privileged *tzaddikim* (righteous ones). As "received wisdom," Kabbalistic knowledge is more generally believed to be an integral part of the Jews' so-called "oral law" allegedly given by God to Moses on Mount Sinai. Like the oral law, Kabbalistic teachings were only to be passed on orally.

In early Rabbinical Judaism, Kabbalistic teachings were at times held in suspicion, considered dangerous, and even banned. By the Middle Ages, numerous Kabbalist brotherhoods existed throughout Europe—yet they were truly esoteric, remaining largely anonymous. In *Kabbalah—The Way of the Jewish Mystic*, Perle Epstein writes: "From the earliest times, the practice of Jewish mysticism has been secret. In 11th-century Spain, a philosopher named Ibn Gabirol labeled these secret oral teachings 'Kabbalah,' or [received] tradition…. Fearful of persecution from within and without the Jewish community, [Kabbalists] buried an already esoteric tradition even deeper…. True followers of the mystical tradition practiced in secret, until, in the 18th century, they emerged as European *Hasidim*" (pp. 13-14).

Historians generally date the start of Kabbalism as a major influence in Jewish thought with the 13th-century publication of the *Zohar* ("Book of Splendor"), considered to be the foundational text for Kabbalistic exegesis. The *Zohar* is attributed to Rabbi Shimon Yohai, but was greatly enlarged over centuries by various rabbis. As a guide written for the "enlightened ones," the *Zohar* was said to offer an ecstatic spiritual experience. Phillips writes: "Its teachings could not be grasped with the mind; they had to be perceived intuitively with the heart. **Those initiated into its mysteries moved further and further away from the real world and into a world of the imagination**" (p. 71; emphasis added).

The *Hasidic* movement of 18th-century Europe breathed new life into Kabbalism. Credited as having been established by Israel ben Eliezer (1698-1760)—known also as Baal shem Tov—*Hasidism* (from the Hebrew *hasid*, "pious") began as a Jewish "revivalist movement" that swept through parts of Eastern Europe, mostly Poland and Russia. Eliezer's teachings "simplifying the Kabbalah for the common man" as he developed numerous "schools of Hasidic Judaism" (wikipedia.org/wiki/Kabbalah).

It was Rabbi Eliezer's universal application of Kabbalism that made Hasidism so attractive. In *Hasidic Tales*, Andrew Harvey writes that Eliezer promoted the holiness of the common man through teachings that centered on a "heartfelt yearning" for God as opposed to the "intellectual mastery" of the written Torah as was featured in Rabbinical Judaism. Eliezer's emphasis was on "union with God" as opposed to the rabbis' focus on "scholarship and study" (p. 18). Harvey defines Hasidism as a "highly sophisticated understanding of Judaism" led by "scholar-mystics" who teach their students how to "deepen one's spiritual life" as they search for the "path to divine love." The Hasidim, he adds, are "those who become drunk ... with awe, humility [and] reverence for the presence of God in everything" (pp. 12, 18).

Kabbalistic Hasidism developed around charismatic mystics called *rebbes*, or "masters." While Eliezer taught that any devoted Hasidic disciple could achieve "union with God," later rebbes taught that only chosen mystics, the *tzaddikim*, could achieve such union. Hasidic disciples could, however, "come close [to union with God] by drawing close to their rebbe." Consequently, "focus shifted from God to the rebbe.... **Over time, the rebbe's role grew from mentor to intermediary**" (Harvey, p. 29; emphasis added). (Christians can readily see the danger in such teachings, as there is one Mediator between God and men, Jesus the Christ—I Timothy 2:5.)

Similarly, Epstein notes that "the difference between other spiritual masters [regular rabbis] and the Hasidic *tzaddikim* [enlightened righteous ones] is seen perfectly by the change in [the latter's] title: *Rav* [master], the [standard and] respectful form of address, was transformed by [the] Hasidim into *Rebbe*, a diminutive, personal, and untranslatable version of the word that denotes affection and, in later years of the movement, **the disciple's complete surrender to his teacher**" (p. 111; emphasis added). Epstein adds that Hasidic Jews "continue to **display a penchant for teacher worship that is still apparent today**" (p. 14; emphasis added). This is particularly noticeable in the Chabad-Lubavitch movement which began in the 1940s in Russia and Eastern Europe (see Chapter Seven under the section heading, The "Divine" Status of Rabbis.)

Kabbalistic Teachings

For centuries, Kabbalism was Judaism's dirty little secret. As the movement "crept down the back alleys of Judaism," its teachings, like the rabbis' oral law, accumulated with the passage of time. Kabbalism "fed on pseudo-prophecy, superstition, myth, numerology and assorted odds and ends of heresy" (Phillips, p. 71).

Jews who did not "fit in with Rabbinic Judaism" sought refuge in Kabbalah, believing that "its mysticism and occultism would open the door of knowledge and help them understand their strange destiny in the world." According to Phillips, the *Zohar* taught "ten spheres of divine manifestation" through which God was believed to "emerge from His vast, secret, unknowable immensity.... Initiates into the *Zohar* dealt in **covert allusions**, in **magic formulas**, in **theosophy**, and in **mystical speculation**" (Phillips, p. 71; emphasis added).

Likewise, Epstein writes that mystics move through ten "gates" or levels of "graduated mystical experience" (p. 5). Via the eighth gate—"examination of the soul"—the mystic "attempts to purify himself to the point where he will see without eyes, hear without ears, speak without tongue, perceive without the sense of perception, and deduce without reason." This is accomplished through *intense meditation* (p. 8). Once he has learned the lessons of the gates, the mystic "leaves the realm of Awe for the more deeply personal realm of Love" (p. 9). "With his soul sufficiently cleansed by the ethical and spiritual practice centered on Awe, the mystic … is prepared to reflect a vision of the Absolute [i.e., God]" (p. 34).

Oneness with God is the ultimate goal of the Kabbalist. "As the [mystic's] senses are … refined, he will become conversant with the ethereal world of angelic beings, pure color and sound, until finally he reaches the un-manifest level of awareness called *devekuth*, 'cleaving to God,' the highest state attainable by human consciousness" (Epstein, p. 4). Hinting at Kabbalism's *pantheistic* leanings, Harvey writes that "union with God is not something to be achieved but a given to be realized," as one is to experience "an awareness of God's [presence] *in*, *with*, and *as* all things" (p. 31).

Epstein adds that the mystic becomes "united with Divine Essence" through "exalted levels of consciousness" that include meditation, trance-like states and "visionary experiences which could not be performed by the mind alone" (p. 39). There is no doubt that such "visionary experiences" involve demonic influences. In reality, Kabbalism is **repackaged Eastern religion** and **ancient Babylonian occultism**, complete with magic, spiritism, astrology, superstition, emotionalism, and the worship of the creation—all of which is condemned in Scripture as both false and dangerous.

According to Kabbalists, the words and letters of the written Torah are seen as "divine emanations" that constitute the manifestation of God's will in the universe. "Supernatural powers were supposed to reside in the letters of the Hebrew alphabet. A mystical significance lurked in the very forms of the letters themselves, in the sounds that resulted when they were spoken, in their numerical value [each letter of the alphabet has a numerical value], and in their position when written on the page. Kabbalists would juggle the letters of the Hebrew alphabet for hours on end ... in the hope that they might stumble upon the ultimate secret of God" (Phillips, p. 71).

As with Eastern religion, Kabbalists look to the *self* as the ultimate source of spirituality. Accordingly, every human being has within his or her heart the "spark of the divine"—which can be realized via the creation. In *What Do Jews Believe?*, David Ariel writes: "[Kabbalist] Jews believe that all of human life can be understood as the spiritual process of experiencing God within the world. To experience the divine within the world is to realize God's presence. Ultimately, to know yourself is to know God" (p. 51). He adds: "Hasidism ... is founded on the premise that **true spirituality arises out of the heart of the individual**.... Genuine spirituality is to be found not in the prescribed formulas of institutional religion, but in the 'heart-knowledge' each individual possesses and in the human desire to achieve *devekuth*, communion with God." In short, the Kabbalist "believed that there was a deeper spiritual realm [which could be accessed by] listening to the world as the song of God" (pp. 81-82; emphasis added).

Such nonsensical, ethereal-like statements that focus on the *self* are typical of Kabbalism. Scripture, however, warns of trusting in the *human* heart. The prophet Jeremiah wrote that the *unconverted* heart is "deceitful above all things, and desperately wicked" (Jer. 17:9). Jesus had this to say about what typically comes from within the human heart: "That which springs forth from within a man, that defiles the man. For from within, **out of the hearts of men**, go forth evil thoughts, adulteries, fornications, murders, thefts, covetousness, wickedness, guile, licentiousness, an evil eye, blasphemy, pride, foolishness; **all these evils go forth from within**, and these defile a man" (Mark 7:20-23). Indeed, "there are ways that *appear* and *feel* right in the minds of men, but such ways only lead to death" (Prov. 14:12; author's paraphrase).

Kabbalism in Modern Judaism

As a subset of Jewish religion, Kabbalism remains the domain of the ultra-Orthodox movement. Still, Kabbalistic influences have pervaded all of Judaism, perhaps to a greater extent than most realize. On this point, Epstein writes that Kabbalism is "so incorporated into the everyday life of the Jews that it has gone unnoticed.... Kabbalah is not an intellectual discipline, nor is it—like the Talmud—a rational exegesis of Jewish laws. It is first and foremost a mystical practice, but one that is **fully dependent on**, **and integrated with**, **Judaism as a whole**" (pp. 15-16; emphasis added).

How popular is Kabbalism today? Epstein notes that Jewish "mysticism once again appears to be enjoying a popular resurgence" (p. 16). Ariel writes that "Hasidism conveys some of the most significant modern Jewish spiritual teachings about human destiny. Hasidism ... continues today as a religious revival movement among ultra-Orthodox Jews" (p. 81).

Likewise, Harvey writes that there is currently a revival of Hasidic and Kabbalistic thought among American ultra-Orthodox Jews (p. 12).

Without question, the foremost advocate of modern-day Kabbalism is the Chabad-Lubavitch faction, a staunchly Hasidic movement with roots in Eastern Europe. "No group [today] emphasizes in-depth Kabbalistic study … to the extent of the Chabad-Lubavitch movement, whose Rebbes [have] delivered tens of thousands of discourses, and whose students study these texts for three hours daily" (wikipedia.org/wiki/Kabbalah). According to the Chabad-Lubavitch Web site, chabad.org, the movement considers itself to be the most "dynamic force" in Jewish life today.

Kabbalism is a complex, multifaceted Jewish discipline. While this overview has only covered the highlights, it is clear that Kabbalism—as the "dark side" of Orthodox Judaism—is altogether contrary to the clear teachings of the Scriptures.

The Judeo-Christian Myth

One of the greatest contradictions in modern Christianity is the belief in a so-called "Judeo-Christian" tradition. America is proudly touted as a nation founded on Judeo-Christian principles; evangelical prophecy buffs weave complex eschatological scenarios around an imagined "Christian-Zionist" brotherhood; and, well-intentioned Christian pastors present their congregations with an apologetic view of their "Jewish brothers" that utterly misrepresents the stark differences between Judaism and Christianity. Is it any wonder that Christians typically look at Jews as spiritual "first cousins"? After all, Jews are only one step away from becoming Christian—if they would only accept Jesus as the Messiah. So goes the theory.

But is Rabbinical Judaism really compatible with Christianity? Most Christians naively think so. In *Judaism Discovered*, Michael Hoffman notes that the term *Judeo-Christianity* is "an oxymoron found on the lips of many Christians" (p. 139). Indeed, when one really understands the true nature of Judaism, it becomes obvious that the two religions are utterly incompatible—and quite at odds on numerous key issues. As the apostle Paul asks, *What fellowship has light with darkness?* (II Cor. 6:14). What connection is there between Jesus Christ and those who promote the Talmud?

Two misguided beliefs are behind the Judeo-Christian concept. First, there is the idea that both Judaism and Christianity are genuinely based on the Old Testament. However, in *practice* (which, after all, is what religion is all about), the Old Testament plays only a minor role in Judaism. As this book has shown, Judaism only *appears* to be based on the Scriptures while it is actually subservient to Talmudic law. Faring just as poorly, nominal Christianity largely rejects the Old Testament as "obsolete" while it attempts to build a liberalized theology almost exclusively on misapplied Pauline teachings. Second, there is the popular mainstream teaching that Christianity was derived *from* Judaism—that Christianity is somehow the final development of what was started under Judaism.

Was Judaism the Precursor to Christianity?

In scholarly circles, Christianity is generally held to be a messianic *sect* of Judaism. Many see Christianity as the logical progression of and *heir* to Judaism—insisting that Christianity exists only as a religion built upon Judaism. For example, conservative Presbyterian theologian Douglas Jones writes: "One of the best ways of beginning to think about the nature of Christianity is to think of it in the light of Judaism. Today, we so often think of Judaism and Christianity as two distinct religions.... But early Christianity never saw itself in that way. The earliest Christians saw themselves as faithful Jews simply **following Jewish teachings**.... **Christianity self-consciously saw itself as the continuing outgrowth, the fulfillment, of Judaism**" (*Why and What: A Brief Introduction to Christianity*; quoted by Hoffman, p. 180; emphasis added). Some Jewish scholars also believe that Judaism was the precursor to Christianity. For instance, in *What is a Jew?*, Rabbi Morris Kertzer writes, "Christianity grew out of Judaism and defined itself with reference to those Jewish beliefs and practices that it accepted and those it did not. Judaism spawned Christianity..." (p. 269).

But both Jones and Kertzer (and hundreds of scholars like them) err because they carelessly assume that Judaism equals the "religion" of the Old Testament—that first-century Jewish religion was the continuation of the "religion" of Moses and the prophets. Genuine apostolic Christianity (before it became corrupted into a Babylonian-styled Romish religion) is indeed based on the Old Testament (John 5:39; II Tim. 3:15-16; Eph. 2:20; etc.), but the "religion" of the Old Testament was *not* Judaism.

As this book has demonstrated, it is a grave error to ascribe the term *Judaism* to the ancient "religion" delivered to the nation of Israel by Moses. As Hoffman notes, the "erroneous assignment of the name 'Judaism' to the Old Testament religion" only creates confusion and misunderstanding. "The reader is given the distinct impression that modern Judaism bears within it the seeds of the religion of the Old Testament, that [Judaism] is [in effect] the Old Testament religion *without Christ*. Nothing could be further from the truth" (p. 181).

The Jewish religion of Jesus' day—Pharisaism, which evolved into Judaism—was based on traditions of men, *not* the Scriptures. Contrary to Jones, etc., the earliest Christians did not see themselves as Jews "following Jewish teachings." Rather, they were faithful followers of the *written* Torah of Moses as exemplified in the teachings of Jesus and the apostles. How can it be claimed that the "Jews' religion"—a religion that persecuted early Christians (Gal. 1:13-14) and was notably based on human traditions (Mark 7:7-9)—formed the foundation of Christianity? The idea is oxymoronic. On this point Hoffman writes, "Judaism was not viewed [by the early church] as the repository of the spiritual truths or knowledge of the Old testament, but as a post-biblical, Babylonian cult totally at variance with [genuine] biblical Christianity" (p. 144).

Jesus said, "I will build My church" (Matt. 16:18)—*not* upon the groundwork laid by the religionists of His day, but upon the sure foundation of the "apostles and prophets" with Himself as the very "corner stone" the scribes, Pharisees and priests had rejected (Eph. 2:20; Matt. 21:42). In fact, Jesus made it clear that the corrupt Jewish leadership—and, by extension, Judaism itself—was fully *disqualified* from having any meaningful role in the establishment of the Kingdom of God. "The kingdom of God shall be taken from you, and given to a nation [the Church] bringing forth the [required] fruits thereof" (Matt. 21:43). This is proof positive that the church did not "grow out of Judaism," but was formed deliberately and separately while unambiguously rejecting the "Jews' religion."

Ultimately, Christianity's roots are *Abrahamic*, but they are decidedly not *Judaic*.

The Politics of the Judeo-Christian Tradition

The so-called "Judeo-Christian tradition" is in reality a *myth* created purely for political and social reasons. In fact, the concept has more to do with post-1945 "anti-Semitic public relations" than it does with historical or religious reality. Apparently, the catch-phrase began to be used in the 1920s by the National Conference of Christians and Jews in an effort to combat anti-Semitism and to balance the then-dominant rhetoric that America was a "Christian-Protestant" nation. Essentially, the term "Judeo–Christian" was coined in an attempt to create a cross-denominational religious consensus that, by including Judaism, avoided the appearance of anti-Semitism. The Internet site Wikipedia notes: "Promoting the concept of America as a Judeo-Christian nation became a political program in the 1920s in response to the growth of anti-Semitism in America.... [Ultimately, the] phrase 'Judeo-Christian' entered the contemporary lexicon as the standard liberal term for the idea that Western values rest on a religious consensus that included Jews" (wikipedia.org/wiki/Judeo-Christian).

By the early 1950s, President Dwight Eisenhower was using the term to refer to the religious faith upon which the country was founded. In the politics of the 1990s, the idea of "Judeo-Christian values" was widely used to further the agenda of the "conservative right" movement.

Today, the term "Judeo-Christian" is used to refer to values and ideals that are thought to be common to both Judaism and Christianity. And granted, the two religions do share certain common values and ideals—but so do Christianity and Buddhism, or Judaism and Hinduism. However, the term Judeo-Christian implies a singular, common heritage or tradition upon which the two religions are founded—an idea that is contrary to both secular and religious history.

If America was founded on so-called Judeo-Christian values, then why did our founding fathers fail to recognize it as such? Many of them wrote extensively of their religious heritage and faith—but not one of them makes use of such a term. If the Judeo-Christian tradition is so fundamental to America's history, why did it take until the 20th century for writers and theologians to recognize its importance?

The Jewish View of the Judeo-Christian Tradition

While Christians may be blissfully ignorant of the huge incongruity between their religion and Judaism, Jews are not. In his book, *Jews and Christians: The Myth of a Common Tradition*, Rabbi Jacob Neusner contends that "there is not now, and there never has been, a dialogue between the religions of Judaism and Christianity" (back cover). Neusner, one of the world's foremost authorities on Judaism, writes that "Judaism and Christianity do not form a common tradition, the 'Judeo-Christian tradition.' They are not compatible. This is because the Christian Bible and the Judaic [oral] Torah [the Talmud] are not the same thing.... Each is possessed of its own integrity and autonomy, and if one is right, the other must be wrong.... [At] no point do Judaism, defined by the [oral] Torah, and Christianity, defined by the Bible, intersect. The [oral] Torah and the Bible form two utterly distinct statements of the knowledge of God" (Introduction, p. xi).

Neusner's frank assessment represents the overall Orthodox Jewish mindset. Following suit are a number of rabbis and Jewish scholars. Chief among them is Jewish theologian-novelist Arthur A. Cohen. In his widely read book, *The Myth of the Judeo-Christian Tradition*, Cohen questions the theological validity of the term and suggests that it was essentially an invention of American politics. He contends that the Judeo-Christian concept does not accurately reflect the religious realities of the two religions, and points to unbridgeable differences that make such a tradition impossible. "The Jews expected a redeemer to come out of Zion; Christianity affirmed that a redeemer had come out of Zion, but that He had come ... for *all* mankind. Judaism denied that claim" (p. xi). Here, Cohen strikes at the heart of why Christianity and Judaism can never be reconciled: Judaism relentlessly rejects the very Messiah that makes Christianity possible.

Addressing the question of why Jews cannot accept Jesus as the Messiah, Neusner writes, "Christians want to know *why not*. To me as a rabbi, the answer to that question is simple: Judaism and Christianity are completely different religions, not different versions of one religion (that of the 'Old Testament' or 'the written Torah'). The two faiths stand for different people talking about different things to different people.... If we go back to the beginnings of Christianity in the early centuries of the Christian era, we see this picture very clearly. Each [religion] addressed its own agenda, spoke to its own issues, and employed a language distinctive to is adherents. Neither exhibited understanding of what was important to the other" (p. 28).

While Christians ponder the reasons for the Jews' rejection of Jesus as the Messiah, the whole Judeo-Christian concept has proven to be a source of consternation for Jews. Of primary importance to Jews is the fact that the concept has tended to gloss over the distinctions between the two religions. Years before Neusner and Cohen penned their books, other Jewish writers were attempting to stress the differences between Judaism and Christianity. For example, Abba Hillel Silver's *Where Judaism Differs* and Leo Baeck's *Judaism and Christianity* were both motivated by a perceived need to clarify Judaism's distinctiveness "in a world where the term Judeo-Christian had obscured critical differences between the two faiths" (Jonathan Sarna, *American Judaism*, p. 266; quoted at wikipedia.org/wiki/Judeo-Christian).

Taking a defensive posture, Rabbi Gershon Winckler writes that the Judeo–Christian concept "is purely a Christian myth.... The term 'Judeo-Christian tradition' and 'Judeo-Christian morality' are wrong and misleading. They are a slap in the face for all the great [Jewish] teachers throughout history, whose responses to today's moral questions would in no way resemble those of the Vatican or the Christian Right…" (*The Way of the Boundary Crosser: An Introduction to Jewish Flexidoxy*, p. 221; quoted at wikipedia.org/wiki/Judeo-Christian).

Jewish law professor Stephen Feldman points out what he considers the dangerous element of "supersessionism" extant in the Judeo-Christian tradition. In his book, *Please Don't Wish Me a Merry Christmas: A Critical History of the Separation of Church and State*, he writes: "Once one recognizes that Christianity has historically engendered anti-Semitism, then this so-called [Judeo-Christian] tradition appears as dangerous Christian dogma (at least from a Jewish perspective). For Christians, the concept of a Judeo-Christian tradition comfortably suggests that Judaism progresses into Christianity—that Judaism is somehow completed in Christianity. The concept of a Judeo-Christian tradition flows from the Christian theology of *supersession*, whereby the Christian covenant (or Testament) with God supersedes the Jewish one. Christianity, according to this myth, reforms and replaces Judaism. The myth therefore implies, first, that Judaism needs reformation and replacement, and second, that modern Judaism remains merely as a 'relic.' Most importantly, the myth of the Judeo-Christian tradition insidiously *obscures* the real and significant differences between Judaism and Christianity" (quoted at wikipedia.org/wiki/Judeo-Christian).

In contrast, Reform and Conservative Jews typically embrace the Judeo-Christian concept as part of their ongoing alliance with conservative Christians. Messianic Jewish groups are also quite comfortable with the idea of a Judeo-Christian tradition.

Ultimately, the Judeo-Christian tradition is but a *myth* kept alive by misguided Christians who imagine significant agreement between the two religions. But as Hoffman quips, "Christ and His gospel are betrayed by those who declare an alleged Judeo-Christian tradition" (p. 145).

Bibliography

Ariel, David. *What Do Jews Believe?* New York: Schocken Books, 1995

Blech, Rabbi Benjamin. *Understanding Judaism.* New York: Alpha Books, 2003

Boyarin, Daniel. *Border Lines: The Partition of Judeo-Christianity.* Philadelphia: University of Pennsylvania Press, 2004

Cohen, Arthur. *The Myth of the Judeo-Christian Tradition.* New York: Harper & Row, 1970

Dilling, Elizabeth. *The Jewish Religion—Its Influence Today.* Torrance, Calif.: Noontide Press, 1983

Donin, Rabbi Hayim. *To Be A Jew—A Guide to Jewish Observance in Contemporary Life.* New York: Basic Books, 1972

Epstein, Perle. *Kabbalah—The Way of the Jewish Mystic.* Boston: Shambhala Publications, 2001

Finkelstein, Rabbi Louis. *The Pharisees.* Philadelphia: Jewish Publication Society, 1946

_____. *The Jews: Their History, Culture and Religion.* Philadelphia: Jewish Publication Society, 1949

Goldman, Ari. *Being Jewish.* New York: Simon & Schuster, 2000

Grayzel, Solomon. *A History of the Jews.* Philadelphia: Jewish Publication Society, 1968

Harvey, Andrew. *Hasidic Tales—The Legendary Tales of the Impassioned Hasidic Rabbis.* Woodstock, Vt.: Skylight Paths, 2005

Hislop, Alexander. *The Two Babylons.* Neptune, NJ: Loizeaux Brothers, 1959

Hoffman, Michael. *Judaism Discovered.* Coeur d'Alene, Idaho: Independent History & Research, 2008

Jeremias, Joachim. *Jerusalem in the Time of Jesus.* Philadelphia: Fortress Press, 1969

Johnson, Paul. *A History of the Jews.* New York: Harper & Row, 1987

Kertzer, Rabbi Morris. *What is a Jew?* New York: Simon & Schuster, 1996

Kolatch, Alfred. *The Jewish Book of Why.* New York: Penguin Group, 2000

Landman, Solomon, with Benjamin Efron. *Story Without End—An Informal History of the Jewish People.* New York: Holt, 1949

Martin, Ernest. *Is Judaism the Religion of Moses?* Originally published serially in *The Good News* magazine from 1960 to 1961 by Ambassador College Publications, Pasadena, Calif. Available as an e-Book through numerous Church of God Web sites; the version used can be found at www.cbcg.org.

_____. "Between The Testaments," from *Tomorrow's World* magazine. Pasadena, Calif.: Ambassador College Publications, Sept. 1971

Neusner, Rabbi Jacob. *Jews and Christians: The Myth of a Common Tradition.* New York: Global Publications, 2001

Parry, Rabbi Aaron. *The Talmud.* New York: Alpha Books/Penguin Group, 2004

Peterson, Galen. *The Everlasting Tradition.* Grand Rapids, Mich.: Kregel Publications, 1995

Pfeiffer, Charles. *Old Testament History.* Grand Rapids, Mich.: Baker Book House, 1973

Phillips, John. *Exploring the World of the Jew.* Neptune, NJ: Loizeaux Brothers, 1993

Robinson, George. *Essential Judaism—A Complete Guide to Beliefs, Customs and Rituals.* New York: Simon & Schuster, 2000

Rusk, Roger. *The Other End of the World.* Knoxville, Tenn.: Plantation House, 1988

Shulvass, Moses. *History of the Jewish People.* Chicago: Regnery Gateway, 1982

Tardo, Dr. Russell. *Sunday Facts and Sabbath Fiction.* Arabi, La.: Faithful Word Publications, 1992

Bible Translations, Reference Works, Biblical Helps

Babylonian Talmud, The. London: Soncino Press, 1934

Barnes, Albert. *Barnes' Commentary.* Commentaries and Topical Studies of the Online Bible, 2007

Bauer, Walter, with William Arndt and Wilbur Gingrich. *A Greek-English Lexicon of the New Testament.* Chicago: University of Chicago Press, 1952

Bibliography

Coulter, Fred R. *The Holy Bible In Its Original Order—A Faithful Version With Commentary.* Hollister, Calif.: York Publishing, 2008

Douglas, J. D. *New Bible Dictionary.* Carol Stream, Ill.: Tyndale House, 1982

_____. *Zondervan Pictorial Bible Encyclopedia.* Grand Rapids, Mich.: Zondervan, 1988

Encyclopedia Judaica. Jerusalem: Keter Publishing House, 1971

Encyclopedia of the Jewish Religion. New York: Adama Books, 1996

Freedman, David. *Anchor Bible Dictionary.* New York: Doubleday, 1992

Ganzfried, Rabbi Solomon. *Code of Jewish Law.* Rockaway Beach, NY: Hebrew Publishing Company, 1993

Gill, John. *Gill's Commentary.* Found at www.biblestudytools.com/commentaries.

Jewish Encyclopedia. New York: Funk and Wagnalls, 1905. Available online at www.jewishencyclopedia.com.

Josephus, Flavius. *Complete Works of Josephus.* Grand Rapids, Mich.: Kregel Publications, 1981

Karaite Anthology. Edited and translated by Leon Nemoy. New Haven, Conn.: Yale University Press, 1952. Recorded by Samuel Al-Magribi in 1484.

King James Version. Cambridge: Cambridge University Press, 1769

Maccabees, II. From *The Jerusalem Bible*, Garden City, NY: Doubleday, 1968

McClintock, John, with James Strong. *Cyclopedia of Biblical, Theological and Ecclesiastical Literature.* Grand Rapids, Mich.: Baker Book House, 1981

McGarvey, J. W. *McGarvey's Commentary.* Commentaries and Topical Studies of the Online Bible, 2007

Mordechai, Avi ben. *Galatians—A Torah-Based Commentary in First-Century Hebraic Context.* Jerusalem: Millennium 7000 Communications, 2005

New American Standard Bible. La Habra, Calif.: Lockman Foundation, 1988

New International Version. Grand Rapids, Mich.: Zondervan, 1984

New King James Version. Nashville: Thomas Nelson, 1982

Smith, William. *Smith's Bible Dictionary.* Iowa Falls, Iowa: Riverside Book and Bible House, 1979

Stern, David. *Complete Jewish Bible.* Clarksville, Md.: Jewish New Testament Publications, 1998

_____. *Jewish New Testament Commentary.* Clarksville, Md.: Jewish New Testament Publications, 1999

Unger, Merrill. *Unger's Bible Dictionary.* Chicago: Moody Press, 1988

Universal Jewish Encyclopedia. New York: Universal Jewish Encyclopedia, Inc., 1943

Wikipedia. Online general encyclopedia; www.wikipedia.org.

Internet Sites

www.bible-history.com
www.chabad.org
www.earlyjewishwritings.com
www.hebrew4christians.com
www.jewfaq.org
www.karaite-korner.org
www.myjewishlearning.com